Communications Policy in Transition

Published in association with the Telecommunications Policy
Research Conference:

*The Internet Upheaval: Raising Questions, Seeking Answers in
Communications Policy*
edited by Ingo Vogelsang and Benjamin M. Compaine, 2000

Communications Policy in Transition: The Internet and Beyond
edited by Benjamin M. Compaine and Shane Greenstein, 2001

Communications Policy in Transition
The Internet and Beyond

edited by
Benjamin M. Compaine and Shane Greenstein

The MIT Press
Cambridge, Massachusetts
London, England

This book was set in Sabon by Asco Typesetters, Hong Kong, and printed and bound in the United States of America.

Library of Congress Cataloging-in-Publication Data

Communications policy in transition: the Internet and beyond / edited by Benjamin M. Compaine and Shane Greenstein.
    p. cm.
 Papers from the 28th Telecommunications Policy Research Conference held in Alexandria, Va. in the Fall of 2000.
 Includes bibliographical references and index.
 ISBN 0-262-03292-9 (hc.: alk. paper)
 1. Communication policy—United States—Congresses. 2. Internet—United States—Congresses. 3. Telecommunication policy—United States—Congresses. I. Compaine, Benjamin M. II. Greenstein, Shane M. III. Telecommunications Policy Research Conference (28th: 2000: Alexandria, Va.)
P95.82.U6 C66   2001
302.2—dc21   2001032622

Contents

Preface

Since 1973 there has been an annual conference on communications policy in the greater Washington, D.C. area. This conference has been known as the Telecommunications Policy Research Conference, or TPRC for short. Its primary purpose is to promote a dialogue among policy makers, industry participants, and academics. This dialogue acquaints industry participants and policy makers with the best of recent research and familiarizes researchers with the needs of policy makers. When these conferences first began the gatherings were small. In the most recent decade the number of participants has grown to well over 300 people. This book presents fifteen papers from the 28th gathering of this conference in Alexandria, Virginia, in the fall of 2000. I write this preface as a longtime participant and as the chair of the Program Committee for that meeting.

This volume draws from over 80 papers presented, which, in turn, were selected from over 200 submitted. Reflecting the conference itself, this book mixes both ephemeral issues and perennial questions, comparing heterogeneous policy perspectives. As with the conference, this book aspires not only to teach others and continue a dialogue, but also to bring positive change. Hence, not only should the book be enjoyed for its contributions to this dialogue, but the book's most important contribution also may be intangible, manifest later in more informed policy decisions or path-breaking research.

For this meeting the Board for TPRC proposed a new title for the conference, "TPRC presents the 28th Annual Research Conference on Information, Communications, and Internet Policy." The new title aptly summarizes the historical stature of the conference and the transitional state of its subject. The conference is one of the longest-running policy conferences on communications policy in the United States. At the same time, its focus has changed to reflect the currents of its time. It is no longer just about *telecommunications* policy research, a label appropriate for a far narrower range of issues than the conference truly covers.

It is normal practice for the TPRC Board to remove itself from the operations of the Program Committee, providing the committee with wide latitude in determining the shape of the sessions and presenters. This places extraordinary duties with the committee, requiring hard work over many months. For the 2000 conference the Program Committee consisted of Phil Agre, University of California, Los Angeles; Jean Camp, Harvard University; Robert Cannon, Federal Communications Commission; Julie Cohen, Georgetown University; Lorrie Faith Cranor, AT&T Labs–Research; Neil Gandal, Tel Aviv University; Shane Greenstein, Northwestern University; Lee McKnight, Tufts University; Michael Neibel, European Commission; and Martin Taschdjian, The National Cable Television Center. They deserve thanks and recognition.

TPRC Inc. is a nonprofit organization governed by a Board of Directors. In 2000 the Board was chaired by Jorge Schement of Pennsylvania State University and consisted of Walter Baer of the Rand Corporation; Robert Blau of Bell South; Benjamin Compaine of the Massachusetts Institute of Technology; Charles Firestone of the Aspen Institute; Heather Hudson of the University of San Francisco; Jeff MacKie-Mason of the University of Michigan; Lloyd Morrisett of the Children's Television Workshop; Michael Nelson of IBM; and Richard Taylor of Pennsylvania State University. Much of their work is unseen directly; yet it is essential to keeping the Conference vibrant, well-funded, and tightly administered. They too deserve thanks and recognition.

For many years TPRC contracted with Economists, Inc., to provide administrative support for the conference. The 2000 conference was the final year of this highly successful arrangement. Since 1989 the support has been provided primarily by Dawn Higgins, assisted by Lori Rodriguez. Once again, as in the past, they handled these operations with extraordinary competence, calm efficiency, and grace. We thank them for making this Conference operate with ineffable seamlessness.

In closing I am grateful that the TPRC Board gave me the opportunity to organize the Program Committee in 2000. I am also grateful that the TPRC Board appointed Ben Compaine and me co-editors of this book, giving us the opportunity to make accessible some of the valuable papers from the 2000 conference. To be sure, I took satisfaction from both activities for their inherent joys. Yet, that would be too narrow a construction of my true motive for doing them. To be frank, I agreed to do both these activities with the hope that they will contribute to the future in a positive manner. In that spirit Ben and I request that you, the reader, put this book's contents to good use, one that justifies our efforts.

Shane Greenstein

Introduction

Ben Compaine and Shane Greenstein

Twenty years ago, telecommunications policy and regulation was in a considerable state of confusion. The Federal Communications Commission (FCC) was still grappling with sphinx-like riddles of what should be considered basic telecommunications services and what should be viewed as enhanced—or intelligent—services. What should be regulated and by whom? The newspaper industry was on the policy warpath with the hint that the all-powerful AT&T monopoly considered electronic classified ads as being part of its business. The new competitors for interexchange phone connections—MCI and Sprint among them—were still struggling with terms of access and connection.

Then, in one bold move, there seemed to be a solution: AT&T agreed to settle a major antitrust suit against it by the U.S. Justice Department. AT&T became nine separate corporate entities: equipment manufacturing, long-distance carriage, and seven regional, local operating companies. Suddenly the outline for future policy and regulation seemed clear to many stakeholders. Local service, it was widely held, was a natural monopoly and would continued to be regulated as in the past by the states. Equipment manufacturing was clearly a competitive arena and, without the baggage of possible cross subsidization, could now be totally unregulated. Long-distance (interexchange) service had all the characteristics of being reasonably competitive, although with about 90% of the market AT&T would have to continue to be regulated at the federal level until its small competitors could stand on their own.

During the 1980s, as the fallout of the January 1, 1984 breakup of AT&T worked itself out, many of these expectations were borne out, though not as cleanly as many prognosticators had hoped. Wireless services, in the form of cellular, brought in a new set of players along with new divisions of the traditional players. The cable industry continued to grow, now and then making noises about expanding into telephony, while some of the regional Bells made feints at sending television signals over their networks. But ultimately it was the explosion of the Internet in the mid-1990s that complicated the mix. The Internet introduced a packet-switched architecture in competition with the circuit-switched model, but it also interconnected many parts of the new network with the old. The convergence of voice, video and text bits—predicted as early as the 1970s by a some farsighted analysts but pooh-poohed by most operators—became a reality. Legislation, capped by the Telecommunications Act of 1996, tried to update the regulatory regime to prepare for the 21st century. But it did this by creating "standards" such as "fair" and "reasonable" for the FCC and courts to apply, leading to continuing litigation and occasional gridlock.[1]

This book addresses several of the many arenas in which public policy makers, corporate strategists and social activists must reach accommodation, if not answers. Business models for current and new players may hinge on cost, availability, and capabilities of the underlying telecommunications infrastructure. Regulatory decisions and legislation grow not only from which players complain or plead the loudest but who can present the most compelling data and analysis. The following chapters are typical of the type of solid data-based policy analyses that may aid all levels of decision makers in understanding the threats and opportunities they face, the various business or policy options, and the possible outcomes of implementing possible decisions.

Regulatory Treatment of Access

In the United States three different regulatory regimes govern three modes of providing access to communications facilities. A long history of common carrier regulation, both at the state and federal level, governs the provision of the lines associated with the delivery of voice telephony. A different regulatory tradition governs the provision of lines associated with cable television. And a third tradition, associated with regulatory forbearance, governs the provision of some competitive information services, such as Internet service provision. All three of these regimes underwent change after the 1996 Act.

What determines the boundary between the regulated and unregulated part of the voice network? This question is essential to understanding telephone company behavior in nonregulated markets and to understanding the behavior of firms that compete in these markets. Yet even for experts these rules are confusing, arising from multiple FCC hearings, revisions and court-ordered interpretations. In chapter 1 Robert Cannon reviews the historical origins of these boundaries and their present state under the 1996 Act. This article distills these rules into accessible guidelines. That is, he explains their features to those not trained in legal language and those who have not followed their piecemeal development over the years. The goal here is to explain and distill rather than assess and critique, a task of importance since these rules increasingly touch on the livelihoods of many more players than just the *cognoscenti* of FCC decision making.

The regulatory treatment of broadband access is particularly important for its diffusion. Shawn O'Donnell, in chapter 2, examines the details of broadband architectures and ISP service profiles, with particular reference to the implementation of ISP service at many cable providers. The analysis distills these services into their component activities in light of the debate over "open access" of Internet-based services. He examines the engineering architecture underneath typical broadband deployment and goes into the organizational arrangements associated with delivering service in practice. He uses this analysis to address how a regulator might implement open-access rules by mandating unbundled services, arguing that present facility owners have incentive to build the next generation of networks in a manner hostile to many forms of unbundled service. This analysis also reconsiders the boundaries between the delivery of Internet-based services and the development of content for delivery.

In the following chapter Joshua Mindel and Marvin Sirbu address this topic by examining the consequence of changing one dimension of the present asymmetric treatment of different access modes. What would happen if the FCC reclassified IP transport as a telecommunication service while continuing to treat most applications as information services? They have particular interest in understanding this scenario because it is one common proposal for reducing asymmetric treatment of different access modes. Their analysis highlights the consequences for ISPs access to right-of-ways, for ISP obligations to meet reporting requirements, and for ISP duties as traditional communications carriers. The authors also identify key provisions in the 1996 Act that give the FCC authority to waive specific obligations in the event that a reclassification take place. Rather than settling all open questions associated with this proposal, which is far too ambitious a research task for a short analysis, the analysis instead identifies a number of issues such a move would raise in state commissions; it also challenges readers to consider the full array of obligations triggered by the reclassification of IP transport.

Internet Architecture in a Commercial Era

The commercialization of the Internet has, of course, altered the landscape of many policy issues in communications. What factors shape the design of that new network? The design of the Internet follows a set of engineering and architectural principles that are collectively known as "end-to-end." These govern application development in the system, specifying, among other things, the functional location for general purpose and specific applications—in others words, how specific applications should and should not interact with other levels of the system, placing most of the intelligence for the system at its end instead of its core. These principles have certain advantages for development of complex networks and have served it well for two decades. However, these principles were developed when the Internet was a research network. As it increasingly becomes a commercial network, will new factors reshape the design of the architecture?

In chapter 4 Marjory Blumenthal and David Clark argue that end-to-end principles come under stress from commercial motives and provide a taxonomy of the range of commercial motives coming into conflict with end-to-end principles. They highlight the incentives to develop secure applications, more complex applications, specialization and broadening of product lines, government mandates to regulate commerce, and the incentive for some actors to adapt or customize applications to non-technical users. This analysis sets the stage for provocative thinking about how the architecture might evolve as it expands into a greater range of commercial applications. The analysis provides both a blueprint for understanding tensions between commercial firms and public agencies, and a forecast about where policy tensions will likely arise in the future.

In a related argument, Hans Kruse, William Yurcik, and Lawrence Lessig in chapter 5 investigate the factors threatening the end-to-end architectural design of the Internet. Their paper frames the changes in the network as a trade-off between transparent interactions of multiple applications and the ability of the network to meet desirable performance criteria. That is, some desirable features require a violation of transparency, which raises the likelihood of unexpected interactions between protocols. The paper identifies distinct types of conflicts between protocol interactions, particularly in the context of the development of the next generation of Internet protocol, IPv6. The authors argue for the presumption towards preserving end-to-end principles in the next generation of design, outlining a number of interoperability issues where those trade-offs will be most salient.

Along with changes in its architecture, there have been changes in the operation of the commercial Internet. In this light, in chapter 6 Rob Frieden analyzes peering and payment policies of ISPs, which have increasingly become hierarchical, involving commercial transactions between ISPs at different "tiers." The author analyzes the commercial logic behind these transactions and identifies the areas in which potential conflict arises between bargaining partners. He provides an extensive taxonomy of the debates over these transactions, framing these in terms of potential antitrust conflicts or behavior that might constitute abuse of ownership of bottleneck facilities. The paper considers whether these disputes should fall under the purview of international dispute-resolution institutions, such as the WTO or the ITU. There are many plausible future scenarios in which strong regulatory intervention may or may not be necessary to insure the conduct of healthy commercial transactions. Frieden tends to take a cautiously optimistic outlook, concluding that strong intervention may be needed, but is not likely.

Emily Moto Murase concludes this section as she examines the design of the Internet in a comparative international context. She compares the emerging Internet infrastructures in Japan and the United States, which differ in their propensity to use wireless and wireline access modes, respectively. The author argues that these differences do not arise from cultural factors such as different keyboards, languages, or habits associated with different home use of computing resources. Instead, she argues that government policies gave rise to substantial price declines in wireless access in Japan, especially in comparison to wireline access. These policies also shaped the rapid development of ubiquitous wireless facilities. In contrast, U.S. policies associated with unmeasured local telephone service reinforced a PC-based wireline mode for Internet access. Hence, the paper emphasizes the comparative commercial determinants of network design. It shows how the adoption of access by users responds to commercial motives, which, in turn, respond to government policies. The paper ends with discussion about which of these factors will persist or decline over time.

Communications Infrastructure Development

Who will build the next generation of communications infrastructure? The U.S. telephone system is in transition, especially at the local level, balancing different public and private objectives. In some localities, the existing telephony network is making a rapid transition into one that accommodates competitive supply of many local communications services. In others, public actors take actions to meet goals that the private network does not address.

Local and state governments have discretion under the 1996 Act to initiate private–public projects that foster advanced infrastructure as a strategic investment. Sharon Strover and Lon Berquist devote chapter 8 to scrutinizing recent public initiatives at the boundaries between public and privately funded infrastructure, a boundary that is defined differently in various localities. The paper develops a framework for understanding the variety of initiatives undertaken by local and state authorities, providing analysis of different types of roles municipalities and regulators can play. These initiatives are necessarily controversial. Their supporters argue that they enhance the public good. Their detractors argue that they distort normal marketplace operations. This framework helps understand the circumstances surrounding such investment, the economic factors shaping investment, and their interaction with universal service policies.

What types of stresses does the presence of, and the transition to, competitive local provision put on the incumbent public switch network? On public goals related to its use, such as universal service? In chapter 9 Gregory Rosston and Bradley Wimmer analyze a unique combination of data about incumbent costs and revenues in local telephony, shedding light on telephone rate rebalancing and its consequences for competitive entry of competitive local exchange companies. The authors quantify the size of the implicit subsidies at different locations in the current setting, examining departures of revenues and costs. This allows them to develop three lines of analysis. First, they show how much rebalancing would be necessary to achieve efficient and competitive (though not necessarily politically feasible) local rates. Second, they test the effectiveness of alternative universal service funding arrangements. Third, they make predictions about where competition is likely to arise and compare these against data on actual entry in Bell Atlantic wire centers, verifying the central tenets behind their analysis.

The End of the Digital Divide?

One of the more lively policy issues since the birth of the Information Age has been the unknown impact of uneven availability of information across society. This has been referred to over the decades as "universal service," "information haves and have-nots," the "computer gap," and, most recently, the "digital divide." Although information disparity was likely much greater in the centuries before writing and before mass literacy, the value of information was generally lower in an agrarian or even industrial economy than in one that runs on data and knowledge.

The issue of differences in information access and capabilities has numerous dimensions. The three chapters in part IV, "The End of the Digital Divide?" look at three pieces of the elephant. In chapter 10, Christian Sandvig focuses in on how children use the Internet, based on empirical observations. The flip side of making sure that school-age children have access to the wealth of information available over the Internet is the fear that they may be using it for the "wrong" type of uses, e.g., chat, game playing and other entertainment activities, even seeking out sites with indecent content. Funding of computers in schools and libraries has been given a high national priority, but Sandvig asks whether we are willing to accept the full range of activities kids will engage in online when given unsupervised access. He argues that many present policies have central tenets and concerns that do not align with actual computer use. Sandvig's paper, by the way, won the top prize in

TPRC's competition for student papers and shone in a very crowded field of first-rate research by young scholars.

In chapter 11, David Gabel and Florence Kwan tackle a different piece of the beast: access to broadband telecommunications services. While the vast majority of the population has access to free or low-cost dial-up access, the next policy battlefield seems to be access to faster and continuous connectivity through cable, high-speed telephone, or even satellite services. There are actually two questions involved here. First, is it reasonable to push the debate of universal access to the Internet beyond basic access? In 2001 basic access is still dial-up service with a modem. Is there an "entitlement" to high-speed access? Is this different from an analogy of providing basic dial tone on a universal basis to creating subsidies to provide call waiting, call ID, and voice mail on a universal basis as well? And if broadband data service is a social goal, is there reason to expect market forces to make it happen or will there be a need for government intervention? Gable and Kwan look in particular at the final question, using unique data to show where commercial markets have made progress in diffusing broadband access to households.

Finally, in chapter 12, Benjamin Compaine asks whether there is really an issue here at all. Taking an historical perspective, he shows that television, VCRs, personal computers, and now the Internet, among other information technology-driven services, have followed similar patterns. In each case various gaps quickly disappeared as the costs of hardware moved quickly downward, ease of use lowered the skill level needed, and access became more widespread. Compaine concludes that new and expensive technologies have to start that application somewhere, and that tends to be with one or two groups: those who find it of great value, such as commercial entities and/or those consumers who can best afford it. Then, bolstered by declining unit costs, greater simplicity, growing acculturation and improved availability, adoption widens to all or most of society. It is a repeated and organic process that he recommends should inform pubic policy-makers who are considering their actions.

Information Policy and Commercial Behavior

Although much of this volume is concerned with policies affecting the telecommunications infrastructure, all of that is really the means to providing content for end users. Whether used for e-mail, to get news, or to make a purchase, the overall telecommunications networks and the Internet overlay are a means to an end: some form of content. The final section of the book deal with some of those issues.

Neil Gandal addresses a critical feature of the World Wide Web: the evolving search engines that try to provide some order and guidance. Starting with the manual indexing service that grew into the Yahoo portal, search engines have had several iterations in their brief period of existence. With the search engines constantly among the top 25 most visited Web sites, they are among the most frequently used destinations. Gandal asks whether the early entrants have held any long-term advantages in this highly competitive arena. He employs two models to reach his conclusion that ultimately performance matters more than brand name.

Another contentious content issue that has exploded along with the Internet relates to intellectual property. One Internet mantra— "information wants to be free"—flies in the face of long-standing and, in the U.S., constitutional guarantees of commercial protection for the creators of intellectual property. Often these issues are hammered out in dense legal briefs by attorneys immersed in copyright law. In chapter 14 one such specialist, Seth Greenstein, examines how the traditional approach to copyright applies in the particular case of distributed applications. These applications are specifically designed to take advantage of the cost and structure of the Internet to allow users to share content, without regard to whether a particular use is free from copyright infringement (such as typical postings on a Listserv) or has potential for violating accepted copyright liability, such as the original model of the music distribution system created by Napster.

The book ends with another information policy issue that has its roots in decades-old policies that govern the retransmission content of broadcast television programming by cable operators. In its current iteration, the issue has become whether the compulsory retransmission license that applies between broadcasters and cable operators should be applied to retransmission of such programming via the Internet. This was not an urgent issue when most Internet connections were dial-up, which greatly limited the potential for viewing television-like programming. But as broadband connectivity spreads, traditional broadcasters have recognized higher stakes. Michael Wirth and Larry Collette articulate the issue and the stakes, review the history of compulsory licensing for cable and satellite DBS providers, and introduce the arguments both for and against Congress extending similar regulation to Internet service providers. They provide their own recommendations and rationale.

The State of Communications Policy at the Start of the 21st Century

It is difficult to summarize the state of communications policy at the turn of the millennium. It is, perhaps, most useful to highlight the transitions that arose due to unprecedented events, many of them associated with the diffusion and commercialization of the Internet and the passage of the 1996 Act.

Until recently, the pace of technical change in most communications services was presumed to be easily monitored from centralized administrative agencies at the state and federal level. This presumption was obviously outdated prior to the commercialization of the Internet and it only became more so after its commercialization. Today, market actors regularly address a variety of commercial and structural challenges with little government interference but at the boundaries of government regulation, and under considerable technical and commercial uncertainty. Many legacy regulatory rules either facilitate or hinder these commercial activities, specifying how commercial firms transact with the regulated public switch network.

It remains to be seen whether these and related legacy institutions are still appropriate for the basic staples of communications policies. In such an era, there are an endless set of issues to discuss, distill, and analyze. In the following chapters we have showcased several areas where frontier research continues to take place.

Note

1. See, for example, W. Russell Neuman, Lee McKnight, and Richard Jay Solomon, *The Gordian Knot: Political Gridlock on the Information Highway* (Cambridge, MA: The MIT Press, 1997).

Contributors

Following are the affiliations of the editors and chapter authors at the time their papers were presented.

Editors

Benjamin M. Compaine, senior research affiliate, Internet & Telecoms Convergence Consortium, Massachusetts Institute of Technology

Shane Greenstein, Associate Professor in the Management and Strategy Department of the Kellogg Graduate School of Management at Northwestern University

Authors

Lon Berquist, Department of Radio, Television and Film, University of Texas

Marjory S. Blumenthal, Computer Science & Telecommunications Board, National Academy of Sciences

Robert Cannon, Senior Counsel, Office of Plans and Policy, Federal Communications Commission

David D. Clark, Laboratory for Computer Science, Massachusetts Institute of Technology

Larry Collette, Department of Mass Communications and Journalism Studies, University of Denver

Rob Frieden, College of Communications, Pennsylvania State University

David Gabel, Queens College, City University of New York

Neil Gandal, Tel Aviv University and University of California, Berkeley

Seth D. Greenstein, Partner, McDermott, Will & Emery

Hans Kruse, J. Warren McClure School of Communication Systems Management, Ohio University

Florence Kwan, Graduate School and University Center, City University of New York

Lawrence Lessig, Professor of Law, Stanford Law School, Stanford University

Joshua L. Mindel, Engineering and Public Policy Department, Carnegie Mellon University

Emily Moto Murase, Department of Communication, Stanford University

Shawn O'Donnell, Annenberg Public Policy Center, University of Pennsylvania and MIT Research Program on Communications Policy

Gregory L. Rosston, Stanford Institute for Economic Policy Research, Stanford University

Christian Sandvig, Department of Communication, Stanford University

Marvin A. Sirbu, Engineering and Public Policy Department, Carnegie Mellon University

Sharon Strover, Department of Radio, Television and Film, University of Texas

Bradley S. Wimmer, University of Nevada, Las Vegas

Michael Wirth, University of Denver, Department of Mass Communications and Journalism Studies

William Yurcik, Department of Applied Computer Science, Illinois State University

I

Differing Regulatory Treatment of Access Modes

1

Where Internet Service Providers and Telephone Companies Compete: A Guide to the *Computer Inquiries*, Enhanced Service Providers, and Information Service Providers

Robert Cannon[1]

Introduction

ISPs[2] are both consumers of and competitors with telephone companies. The ISP market is competitive with approximately 7100 ISPs in North America[3] and a choice of seven or more ISPs for most Americans.[4] The telephone market, as the result of the Telecommunications Act of 1996, is experiencing transformation, moving from a market dominated by monopolies to a market with new entrants bringing new services, new choices, and new prices to consumers. Nevertheless, in many markets, the telephone companies retain strong market power in their regulated telephone service market that they could use to an unfair advantage in the nonregulated, competitive, and innovative Internet services market.

The FCC has historically been concerned with the playing field where ISPs and telephone companies compete. In 1966, before the first packet was transmitted on the ARPANET and before the Internet[5] itself,[6] the FCC was curious about the difference between computers that facilitate communications and computers with which people communicate. The Commission pondered the regulatory implications of this distinction and whether both of these types of computers should be regulated as basic phone service. In order to answer these questions, the Commission launched the first *Computer Inquiry*.[7]

The *Computer Inquiries* have now been active for over 30 years. They have involved several proceedings before the Commission, appeals to Federal Court, remands, and a trip to the Supreme Court. They have occurred during the Information Revolution and the passage of the Telecommunications Act of 1996. Some of the rules have been codified into the Code of Federal Regulations; some have not. Some rules are in effect, some have been vacated, and some are the subject of current regulatory proceedings.

The complexity of this proceeding presents a challenge for comprehending the current landscape. This Guide seeks to present a consolidated statement of the current rules for enhanced service providers.

This Guide does not seek to review the history of the *Computer Inquiries*. Many fine papers before this Guide have presented such reviews.[7] This paper does not address Competitive Local Exchange Carrier (CLEC) concerns (even though CLECs and ISPs have been working closely together). This Guide does not cover all of the regulations governing telecommunications carrier behavior that may affect ISPs. For example, a number of the merger proceedings have addressed Internet-related concerns. The focus of this Guide is the current rules that came out of the *Computer Inquiries*.

The Computer Inquiries

The *Computer I Inquiry* reviewed a new and growing area of communications, where people interacted with computers and the computers processed the commands and spit back new information. The Commission saw this competitive market as distinct from telephone service.

The Commission was also concerned with telephone monopolies entering this new competitive market.[8] Thus, one of the goals of the *Computer Inquiry* proceedings was to create a level playing field where telephone companies using their economic might could not unfairly enter the enhanced service provider market and destroy its competitive and innovative nature. The proceedings devised a set of rules to protect against improper cost allocation and discrimination by Bell Operating Companies (BOCs).[9]

The *Computer Inquiries* have resulted in two current regulatory schemes: *Computer II* (structural separation) and *Computer III* (non-structural separation). Note that *Computer III* supplemented but did not replace *Computer II*. A telephone company falling under these rules can elect to proceed under either regime.[10] A BOC must comply with one set of rules; if the BOC has not satisfied the requirements of *Computer II* or *Computer III*, the BOC is not authorized to provide enhanced services.

In order to determine which regulations apply to the behavior of the BOCs, one must determine whether the BOCs' Enhanced Service Provider (ESP) has successfully complied with *Computer II* or *Computer III*.

Enhanced Service Providers

The first issue for the Commission was to distinguish between computers that facilitate the transmission of communications and computers with which people interact. This exploration resulted in the "enhanced service" and "basic service" distinction.

Basic telecommunications service is defined as "the offering of a pure transmission capability over a communications path that is virtually transparent in terms of its interaction with customer supplied information."[11]

Enhanced service, essentially, is defined as everything else. This is the category of Internet Service Providers. In order to devise a bright-line test, the Commission determined that where a service is offered with any level of enhancement, it is generally considered an enhanced service:

> For the purpose of this subpart, the term 'enhanced service' shall refer to services, offered over common carrier transmission facilities used in interstate communications, which employ computer processing applications that act on the format, content, protocol or similar aspects of the subscriber's transmitted information; provide the subscriber additional, different, or restructured information; or involve subscriber interaction with stored information.[12]

Examples of enhanced services include Internet access service,[13] online service, computer bulletin boards, video dialtone,[14] voice mail,[15] electronic publishing, and others.[16] The mere fact that a network is packet-switched does not necessarily mean that it is an enhanced service.[17]

The implication of the distinction is that basic telecommunications service is regulated as common carriage under Title II of the Communications Act; enhanced services are not regulated under Title II.[18]

The Telecommunications Act of 1996 defined "Information Service" as "the offering of a capability for generating, acquiring, storing, transforming, processing, retrieving, utilizing, or making available information via telecommunications, and includes electronic publishing."[19] The Commission has determined that "information services consist of all services that the Commission previously considered to be enhanced services" (however, the Commission has also determined that while all enhanced services are information services, not all information services are enhanced services).[20]

Bell Operating Companies

The *Computer Inquiry* rules apply to enhanced service providers, Bell Operating Companies (BOCs), and GTE[21]; they do not necessarily apply to all telecommunications carriers. BOCs are the local telephone operating companies that were created during the breakup of AT&T. As a result of mergers, consolidations, and acquisitions, the list of BOCs has evolved into the following:[22]

RBOC[23]	Owner of the following BOCs[24]
Verizon	Bell Atlantic, GTE, The Chesapeake and Potomac Telephone Company, The Chesapeake and Potomac Telephone Company of Maryland, The Chesapeake and Potomac Telephone Company of Virginia, The Chesapeake and Potomac Telephone Company of West Virginia, NYNEX, The New York Telephone Company, The Bell Telephone Company of Pennsylvania, The Diamond State Telephone Company, New Jersey Bell Telephone Company, New England Telephone and Telegraph Company
SBC	Southwestern Bell, Ameritech, Pacific Bell, Nevada Bell, Illinois Bell, Indiana Bell, Michigan Bell, Ohio Bell, and Wisconsin Telephone
Bell South	South Central Bell, Southeastern Bell, and Southern Bell
Qwest	US West, Mountain Bell, Northwestern Bell, and Pacific Northwest Bell[25]

Although these companies are responsible for the vast majority of the local access lines,[26] there are approximately 1200 other local exchange carriers (LECs).[27] These others are not considered BOCs.

Access Charge Exemption

Although the Commission has recognized that enhanced service providers (ESPs), including ISPs, use interstate access services, since 1983 it has exempted ESPs from the payment of certain interstate access charges. Pursuant to this exemption, ESPs are treated as end users for purposes of assessing access charges. Thus,

ESPs generally pay local business rates and interstate subscriber line charges for their switched access connections to local exchange company central offices. They also pay the special access surcharge on their special access lines under the same conditions applicable to end users. In the *Access Charge Reform Order*, the Commission decided to maintain the existing pricing structure and continue to treat ESPs as end users for the purpose of applying access charges. The Commission stated that retaining the ESP exemption would avoid disrupting the still-evolving information services industry and advance the goals of the Telecommunications Act of 1996 to "preserve the vibrant and competitive free market that presently exists for the Internet and other interactive computer services."[28]

Computer II—Structural Separation

The first of the two regulatory regimes that a BOC can elect to follow in order to enter the enhanced service provider market is *Computer II*. In order to enter the ESP market, BOCs must set up a structurally separate ESP subsidiary.[29]

The requirements of *Computer II* can be found at 47 C.F.R. §64.702. These rules indicate that BOCs may enter the ESP market if

• It is done through a separate corporate entity that obtains all telecommunications facilities and services pursuant to tariff and may not own its own telecommunications facilities;

• The separate subsidiary operates independently in the furnishing of enhanced services and customer premise equipment;

• The separate subsidiary deals with any affiliated manufacturer on an arm's-length basis;

• Any joint research and development must be done on a compensatory basis; and

• All transactions between the separate subsidiary and the carrier or its affiliates must be reduced to writing.[30]

BOCs electing to provide enhanced services through a separate subsidiary must also comply with the following requirements:

• The BOC cannot engage in the sale or promotion of the enhanced services or customer premise equipment on behalf of the separate enhanced services subsidiary, (i.e., Bell cannot promote the services of the separate subsidiary Bell. net);

• The BOC cannot provide to its separate enhanced services subsidiary computer services that are used in any way for the provision of its common carrier services; and

• The BOC's capitalization plan for the separate corporation must be approved by the FCC.[31]

Computer III—Nonstructural Safeguards

Purpose

The second regulatory regime that BOCs can follow in order to enter the ESP/ISP market is the *Computer III* regime, which sets forth non-structural safeguards. The Commission had concluded that the separate subsidiary obligations under the *Computer II* regime were unnecessarily cumbersome. The Commission believed that it was possible to achieve the goals of the *Computer Trilogy* without requiring BOCs to create structurally separate subsidiaries.[32] Therefore, the Commission devised nonstructural safeguards known as "Comparably Efficient Interconnection (CEI)" and "Open Network Architecture (ONA)."

Status of Rulemaking

The *Computer III* rulemaking resulted in a series of appeals to the Court of Appeals for the 9th Circuit. In *California III*, the 9th Circuit reviewed the Commission's move from structural to nonstructural safeguards and

found that, in granting full structural relief based on the BOC ONA plans, the Commission had not adequately explained its apparent "retreat" from requiring "fundamental unbundling" of BOC networks as a component of ONA and a condition for lifting structural separation. The court was therefore concerned that ONA unbundling, as implemented, failed to prevent the BOCs from engaging in discrimination against competing ESPs in providing access to basic services.[33]

The Commission concluded that the Court in *California III* vacated only the Commission's ONA rules, not the CEI rules. Therefore, the Commission issued the *Interim Waiver Order* that permitted BOCs to provide enhanced services if they complied with the CEI rules.[34] In addition, BOCs must comply with procedures set forth in their ONA plans that they had already filed with and had approved by the Commission.[35] The Commission also released a Further Notice of Proposed Rulemaking in order to resolve the issues addressed in *California III*.[36] This rulemaking is still pending.[37]

In sum, currently under *Computer III*, CEI is an ongoing obligation where BOCs choose to provide enhanced services and the ONA plans that were filed remain binding.

Comparably Efficient Interconnection

Computer III has two phases. The first is Comparatively Efficient Interconnection (CEI). Where a BOC seeks to offer an enhanced service, it may do so on an "integrated basis" with its basic service provided that the BOC create a CEI Plan.[38] "In these CEI plans, the Commission require[s] the BOCs to demonstrate how they [will] provide competing enhanced service providers (ESPs) with 'equal access' to all basic underlying network services the BOCs [use] to provide their own enhanced services."[39] CEI was designed to prevent cross-subsidization and discrimination.[40]

Phase I was designed to be an interim phase until Phase II, Open Network Architecture, was implemented. The Ninth Circuit Court of Appeals, however, vacated the Commission's ONA rules. The Commission also released the *Interim Order* indicating that if BOCs wanted to deploy any new ESP services, they must create CEI plans.[41]

Where to Find CEI Plans

Previously, CEI plans had to be filed with the Commission for approval. In March of 1999, the Commission issued an order revising *Computer III* obligations, stating that BOCs need only post their CEI plans on their websites and file notice with the Commission concerning where those plans could be found.[42] In December of 1999, the Commission clarified that BOCs must post to their websites all existing and new CEI plans and amendments.[43] In other words, this provision is retroactive—a CEI plan must be posted to its webpage even if it was filed with the FCC prior to March 1999.

Nine Parameters

In a CEI plan, a BOC must describe how it intends to comply with the CEI "equal access" parameters for the specific enhanced service it intends to offer. The CEI equal access parameters, discussed in greater detail below, include: interface functionality; unbundling of basic services; resale; technical characteristics; installation, maintenance and repair; end user access; CEI availability; minimization of transport costs; and availability to all interested customers or ESPs.[44]

The Commission made clear that the CEI parameters could be satisfied in a flexible manner, consistent with the particular services at issue. The Commission "did not require absolute technical equality, but rather sought to provide fairness and efficiency for all competing enhanced service providers." Factors in evaluating whether this standard has been met include the absence of systematic differences between the basic services given to the carrier and to others, end-user perception of quality, and utility to other ESPs.[45]

Interface Functionality

The BOC must "make available standardized hardware and software interfaces that are able to support transmission, switching, and signaling functions identical to those utilized in the enhanced service provided by the carrier." This provision ensures that a competitive ISP will know what interfaces it must use to interconnect with the BOC's network.[46]

Unbundling of Basic Service

The BOC must unbundle, and associate with a specific rate in the tariff, the basic services and basic service functions that underlie the carrier's enhanced service offering. This provision ensures that a competitive ISP can purchase the underlying telecommunications services on which it bases its enhanced services. For example, an ISP might purchase tariffed transport services for its voicemail service.[47]

Nonproprietary information used by the carrier in providing the unbundled basic services must be made available as part of CEI. In addition, any options available to a carrier in the provision of such basic services or functions must be included in the unbundled offerings.[48]

Resale

The BOC's "enhanced service operations [must] take the basic services used in its enhanced services offerings at their unbundled tariffed rates as a means of preventing improper cost-shifting to regulated operations and anticompetitive pricing in unregulated markets." This provision ensures that both BOC and non-BOC ISPs pay the same amount for the underlying telecommunications services obtained from the BOC.[49]

Technical Characteristics

The BOC must provide basic services with technical characteristics that are equal to the technical characteristics the carrier uses for its own enhanced services. This provision ensures that a competitive ISP can base its enhanced offering on telecommunications services that are of equal quality to those which the BOC's customers receive.[50]

These characteristics include, but are not limited to: transmission parameters, such as bandwidth and bit rates; quality, such as bit error rate and delay distortions; and reliability, such as mean time between failures. The Phase I Reconsideration stated that the standard "does not demand impossible or grossly inefficient over-engineering of the network so that absolute equality is always achieved." We specifically recognized, for example, that the signal level of an analog data connection will decrease to some extent with the loop distance from the central office.[51]

Installation, Maintenance, and Repair

The BOC must provide the same time periods for installation, maintenance, and repair of the basic services and facilities included in a CEI offering as those the carrier provides to its own enhanced service operations. This provision ensures that a competitive ISP can offer its customers support services of equal quality to those which the BOC's customers receive.[52]

Carriers also must satisfy reporting and other requirements showing that they have met this requirement.[53]

End User Access

The BOC must provide to all end users the same abbreviated dialing and signaling capabilities that are needed to activate or obtain access to enhanced services that use the carrier's facilities, and provides to end users equal opportunities to obtain access to basic facilities through derived channels, whether they use the enhanced service offerings of the carrier or of a competitive provider. This provision ensures that a competitive ISP's customers will have the same access as the BOC's customers to special network functions offered in conjunction with information services.[54]

CEI Availability

The BOC must make its CEI offering available and fully operational on the date that it offers its corresponding enhanced service to the public, and provide a reasonable period of time when prospective users of the CEI offering can use the CEI facilities and services for purposes of testing their enhanced service offerings. This provision ensures that a non-BOC ISP is not put at a competitive disadvantage by a BOC initiating a service before the BOC makes interconnection with the BOC's network available to competitive ISPs, so that they are able to initiate a comparable service.[55]

Consequently, the Commission has required the BOCs to notify unaffiliated ESPs in advance about the impending deployment of new basic services.... In addition, the Commission has separately stated that a carrier's CEI plan should contain a description of the geographic areas in which it will offer the enhanced service, as well as the network locations within those areas through which it will provide such service.[56]

Minimization of Transport Costs

The BOC must provide competitors with interconnection facilities that minimize transport costs. This provision ensures that BOCs can not require competitive ISPs to purchase unnecessarily expensive methods of interconnection with the BOC's network.[57]

The Commission does not require LECs to provide physical collocation for ONA. The Commission has upheld the use of price parity by the BOCs to satisfy their obligation to minimize transmission costs, and specifically has found two miles to be a reasonable minimum distance for price parity associated with a distance-sensitive banded tariff.[58]

We clarified that multiplexing those connections to aggregate traffic is not the only acceptable cost-reduction technique. Instead, a BOC may satisfy this requirement by charging the same transmission rates to all enhanced service providers, including its own enhanced service operations and those of noncollocated competitors.[59]

Recipients of CEI

The BOC is prohibited from restricting the availability of the CEI offering to any particular class of customer or enhanced service competitor. This provision ensures that BOCs do not engage in anticompetitive teaming with one competitive ISP and against others.[60]

Open Network Architecture

The second phase of *Computer III* is Open Network Architecture (ONA).

During the second stage of *Computer III*, the BOCs developed and implemented Open Network Architecture (ONA) plans detailing the unbundling of basic network services; after the Commission approved these ONA plans and the BOCs filed tariffs for ONA services, they [would have been] permitted to provide integrated enhanced services without filing service-specific CEI plans.[61]

The ONA requirements apply to the BOCs and GTE.[62]

The ONA requirements apply to the BOCs regardless of whether they provide information services on an integrated or separated basis.[63]

In response to the Ninth Circuit Court of Appeals vacating the Commission's ONA rules, the Commission also released an Interim Order indicating that the BOCs are bound by any previously approved ONA plans, and that if BOCs wanted to deploy any new ESP services, they must create a CEI plan.[64]

How It Works

ONA is the overall design of a carrier's basic network services to permit all users of the basic network, including the information services operations of the carrier and its competitors, to interconnect to specific basic network functions and interfaces on an unbundled and equal-access basis. The BOCs and GTE[65] through ONA must unbundle key components, or elements, of their basic services and make them available under tariff, regardless of whether their information services operations utilize the unbundled components. Such unbundling ensures that competitors of the carrier's information services operations can develop information services that utilize the carrier's network on an economical and efficient basis.[66]

This serves to create a level playing field where the BOC-affiliated ESPs and non-affiliated ESPs have the opportunity to take based network services on the same tariffs, terms and conditions.

[T]he Commission declined to adopt any specific network architecture proposals or specific unbundling requirements, but instead set forth general standards for ONA. BOCs were required to file initial ONA plans presenting a set of "unbundled basic service functions that could be commonly used in the provision of enhanced services to the extent technologically feasible." The Commission stated that, by adopting general requirements rather than mandating a particular architecture for implementing ONA, it wished to encourage development of efficient interconnection arrangements. The Commission also noted that inefficiencies might result from "unnecessarily unbundled or splintered services."[67]

The Commission

required the BOCs to meet a defined set of unbundling criteria in order for structural separation to be lifted. In the *BOC ONA Order*, the Commission generally approved the "common ONA model" proposed by the BOCs. The common ONA model was based on the existing architecture of the BOC local exchange networks, and consisted of unbundled services categorized as basic service arrangements (BSAs), basic service elements (BSEs), complementary network services (CNSs), and ancillary network services (ANSs).[68]

The Commission required the BOCs, while preparing their ONA plans, to meet with ESPs in order to determine the needs of industry.[69]

Purpose of ONA

In devising ONA as a precondition to removal of structural separation for the enhanced service operations of the BOCs, we sought to establish a regulatory framework that would permit the BOCs to participate efficiently in the enhanced services market while preventing anticompetitive conduct based on BOC control of underlying, local communications networks. We found that while structural separation is one way to serve the goal of preventing anticompetitive conduct, it does so at significant cost by imposing inefficient restrictions on the ways the BOCs can develop, technically configure, and offer enhanced services to the public. We also concluded in *Computer III* that another major goal of ONA should be to increase opportunities for all enhanced service providers (ESPs) to use the BOCs' regulated networks in highly efficient ways so that they can both expand their markets for their present services and develop new offerings that can better serve the American public.[70]

Basic Service Element

Basic Service Elements (BSE) "are optional unbundled features (such as Calling Number Identification) that an ESP may require or find useful it configuring an enhanced service."[71] They have also been defined as "unbundled basic service 'building blocks.'"[72] The Commission concluded that these are basic services that ESPs need in order to provide service.[73]

The *ONA Order* required the BOCs to provide BSEs within the Commission's interstate access tariff framework. The Commission concluded that such unbundled BSEs should include all basic services that satisfy its three 'BSE selection' criteria—"expected market demand for such elements, their utility as perceived by enhanced service competitors, and the technical and costing feasibility of such unbundling."[74] Such services are referred to as "interstate BSEs." "Thus, if an ESP takes an interstate access arrangement (e.g., a feature group) for access to a BOC's network, any interstate BSEs that are technically compatible with that access arrangement must be unbundled in its federal tariff."[75] BOCs are required to "offer all interstate BSEs in the federal access tariffs to the degree technically possible."[76]

Basic Serving Arrangement

BOCs are also required to tariff Basic Serving Arrangements (BSAs).[77]

BSAs are the fundamental tariffed switching and transport services that allow an ESP to communicate with its customers through the BOC network. Under the common ONA model, an ESP and its customers must obtain some form of BSA in order to access the network functionalities that an ESP needs to offer its specific services. Examples of BSAs include line-side and trunk-side circuit-switched service, line-side and trunk-side packet-switched service, and various grades of local private line service.[78]

[B]oth BSAs and BSEs are essential basic service building blocks of a truly open network architecture and thus both are subject to our ONA rules.[79]

Complementary Network Service

CNSs are optional unbundled basic service features (such as stutter dial tone) that an end user may obtain from a carrier in order to access or to receive an enhanced service.[80]

CNSs have two principal characteristics. First, CNSs are associated with end users', rather than ESPs', access arrangements. Second, CNSs are locally tariffed, basic services that the BOCs will offer to end users whether or not such users are customers of ESPs—that is, such services give end users access to the network for a variety of applications, not merely enhanced service applications.[81]

Examples of CNSs include

'Custom Calling' services, such as call waiting and call forwarding; variations of such services, such as call forwarding on busy or no answer; and other optional features, such as hunting.[82]

The Commission did not direct the BOCs to create the CNS class of basic services under ONA. However, the Commission saw no reason to prohibit the use of the CNS category by BOCs as long as adequate safeguards exist to protect against potential discrimination in the delivery of CNSs to ESP customers. Indeed, the Commission concluded that it may be of some benefit to retain a category of services that organizes network capabilities for end users and provides them a measure of flexibility in choosing such capability with their enhanced services.[83]

The Commission emphasized that BOCs must "provide CNSs on a nondiscriminatory basis—that is, since the BOCs provide CNSs as basic services to end users, the BOCs cannot favor their own enhanced service customers in any way in the provision of CNSs."[84] At the time the Commission reviewed the BOC's ONA plans, it concluded that

[b]ecause the BOCs provide CNSs to all end users pursuant to tariff for purposes other than simply to facilitate provision of an enhanced service, the potential for any discriminatory behavior by the BOCs in offering such services is speculative. Moreover, the BOCs' standardized ordering and provisioning systems for providing basic services to end users provide still more assurance that the BOCs will not be able to discriminate against end users who purchase CNSs for use with a competing ESP's enhanced services.[85]

CNSs and BSEs are at times indistinguishable; different BOCs listed essentially the same services differently, one listing it as a CNS and the other as a BSE.[86] Nevertheless, the Commission concluded that

the BOCs' service classifications should not have different practical consequences for federal tariffing purposes. [W]e require the BOCs to provide BSEs within our interstate access tariff framework. We conclude here that such unbundled BSEs should include all basic services that satisfy our three "BSE selection" criteria regardless of whether the BOCs now classify such services as BSEs or CNSs. We refer to such services as "interstate BSEs." Thus, if an ESP takes an interstate access arrangement (e.g., a feature group) for access to a BOC's network, any interstate BSEs that are technically compatible with that access arrangement must be unbundled in its federal tariff. Accordingly, for federal tariffing purposes, there is no separate service category of CNSs (a result that is consistent with the definition of CNSs in the common model as state-tariffed services.)[87]

Ancillary Network Service

"ANSs are other services that the BOCs say fall outside of the ONA construct, but which may be useful to ESPs."[88] Examples of ANS include unregulated services such as billing services, collection, protocol processing.[89]

When the Commission reviewed the BOCs ONA plans, the Commission noted that the BOCs did include a number of regulated, basic services in this category. In order to avoid confusion, the Commission directed BOCs to amend their ONA plans, moving any regulated services from ANS to BSE, BSA, or CNS.[90] This was designed to leave only unregulated services in the ANS class.

The Commission concluded that

ANSs are competitive, deregulated services that are not subject to regulation under Title II. ESPs can obtain ANSs from sources other than the local exchange carriers. Thus, while the Commission has ancillary authority under Title I to require the provision of a particular ANS, there is no reason for us to exercise that authority here.[91]

Specifically, in terms of billing and collection services, the Commission found that these services had been deregulated, were incidental to communications, and need not be tariffed. Therefore, the Commission did not require BOCs to offer these services pursuant to the ONA requirements. However, BOCs were required "to describe any services they plan to offer that would provide ESPs with information that is useful for 'bill preparation such as the calling number, billing address or duration of a call.' "[92]

Discrimination

The BOCs and GTE are also required to establish procedures to ensure that they do not discriminate in their provision of ONA services, including the installation, maintenance, and quality of such services, to unaffiliated ISPs and their customers. For example, they must establish and publish standard intervals for routine installation orders based on type and quantity of services ordered, and follow these intervals in assigning due dates for installation, which are applicable to orders placed by competing service providers as well as orders placed by their own information services operations. In addition, they must standardize their maintenance procedures where possible, by assigning repair dates based on nondiscriminatory criteria (e.g., available work force and severity of problem), and handling trouble reports on a first-come, first-served basis.[93]

The Commission require[d] carriers to state explicitly in their ONA plans that they will offer their BSAs and BSEs in compliance with the *Computer III* nondiscrimination and equal access safeguards.[94]

Letters of Authorization

One particular issue arose with CNSs. Some BOCs were requiring ESPs to present a written letter of authorization prior to the BOCs initiating

CNS service. The Commission's primary concern in reviewing this situation was discrimination. If the BOC was making the same letter of authorization requirement of its own ESP as it was of non-affiliated ESPs, then there was no issue of discrimination. If, however, the BOC was not requiring a letter of authorization from its own ESPs, then this was a discriminatory practice and impermissible.[95]

Resale

Another issue that arose was resale restrictions placed on ESPs by the BOCs. Again, the Commission found that where resale restrictions applied equally to the general body of subscribers, then there was little anticompetitive danger. However, where resale restrictions apply only to unaffiliated ESPs, they have the potential to violate the antidiscrimination principles of ONA. The FCC emphasized its "strong federal policy against resale restrictions, which are a type of use restriction."[96]

Operations Support Systems

The Commission required BOCs to specify the Operations Support Systems (OSS) they would offer ESPs

and to discuss their ability to offer such services in the future. In the BOC ONA Recon. Order, the Commission determined that continuing development of OSS services is important to the kinds of services ESPs can provide, and defined certain OSS services as ONA services. The Commission recognized that permitting ESPs only indirect access to OSS functions, while allowing affiliates direct access, could result in an uneven playing field. To ensure comparably efficient access, the Commission required a BOC to provide the same access to OSS services to its affiliated enhanced service operations that the BOC provides to unaffiliated ESPs.[97]

Nondiscrimination Reporting

In order to demonstrate compliance with the nondiscrimination requirements outlined above [and ensuring BOCs provide the access promised in their CEI plans[98]], the BOCs and GTE must file quarterly nondiscrimination reports comparing the timeliness of their installation and maintenance of ONA services for their own information services operations versus the information services operations of their competitors. If a BOC or GTE demonstrates in its ONA plan that it lacks the ability to discriminate with respect to installation and maintenance services, and files an annual affidavit to that effect, it may modify its quarterly report to compare installation and maintenance services provided to its own information services operations with services provided to a sampling of all customers.[99] In their quarterly reports, the BOCs and GTE must include information on total orders, due dates missed, and average intervals for a set of service categories specified by the Commission,[100] following a format specified by the Commission.[101]

These reports are filed with the Secretary of the Commission and the Common Carrier Bureau's Policy Division, and are on the Electronic Comment Filing System under CC Docket No. 95-20.

Deployment

The BOCs in their ONA plans were required to give specific dates for deployment of their initial ONA services.[102] BOCs also have a continuing obligation pursuant to the Commission's Network Information Disclosure rules[103] to provide timely notice of service deployments and alterations.

New Services

The Commission's rules anticipated a continuously evolving network and created an ongoing obligation for BOCs both to be responsive to the needs of the ESPs and to provide appropriate information when the BOCs deploy new services.

Under the ONA rules, when a BOC seeks to deploy a new BSE or otherwise alter the services in its ONA plan, the BOC must amend its ONA plan at least ninety days prior to the deployment of that service, submitting it to the Commission for approval.[104]

ESPs may also request new ONA services from the BOCs.

[W]hen an ISP identifies a new network functionality that it wants to use to provide an information service, it can request the service directly from the BOC or GTE through a 120-day process specified in our rules, or it can request that the Network Interconnection Interoperability Forum (NIIF) sponsored by the Alliance for Telecommunications Industry Solutions (ATIS)[105] consider the technical feasibility of the service. Under the Commission's 120-day request process, an ISP that requests a new ONA basic service from the BOC or GTE must receive a response within 120 days regarding whether the BOC or GTE will provide the service. The BOC or GTE must give specific reasons if it will not offer the service. The BOC or GTE's evaluation of the ISP request is to be based on the ONA selection criteria set forth in the original *Phase I Order*: (1) market area demand; (2) utility to ISPs as perceived by the ISPs themselves; (3) feasibility of offering the service based on its cost; and (4) technical feasibility of offering the service. If an ISP objects to the BOC or GTE's response, it may seek redress from the Commission by filing a petition for declaratory ruling.[106]

Additionally, ISPs can ask the NIIF for technical assistance in developing and requesting new network services. Upon request, the NIIF will establish a task force composed of representatives from different industry sectors to evaluate the technical feasibility of the service, and through a consensus process, make recommendations on how the service can be implemented. ISPs can then take the information to a specific BOC or GTE and request the service under the 120-day process using the NIIF result to show that the request is technically feasible.[107]

Approved ONA Plans

During the period from 1988 to 1992, the Commission approved the BOCs' ONA plans, which described the basic services that the BOCs would provide to unaffiliated and affiliated ESPs and the terms on which these services would be provided. During the two-year period from 1992 to 1993, the Bureau approved the lifting of structural separation for individual BOCs upon their showing that their initial ONA plans complied with the requirements of the *BOC Safeguards Order*, and these decisions were later affirmed by the Commission.[108]

Annual Filing Requirements

The BOCs and GTE are required to file annual ONA reports that include information on:

1. annual projected deployment schedules for ONA service, by type of service (BSA, BSE, CNS), in terms of percentage of access lines served system-wide and by market area;

2. disposition of new ONA service requests from ISPs;

3. disposition of ONA service requests that have previously been designated for further evaluation;

4. disposition of ONA service requests that were previously deemed technically infeasible;

5. information on Signaling System 7 (SS7), Integrated Services Digital Network (ISDN), and Intelligent Network (IN) projected development in terms of percentage of access lines served system-wide and on a market area basis;

6. new ONA services available through SS7, ISDN, and IN;

7. progress in the IILC (now NIIF) on continuing activities implementing service-specific and long-term uniformity issues;

8. progress in providing billing information including Billing Name and Address (BNA), line-side Calling Number Identification (CNI), or possible CNI alternatives, and call detail services to ISPs;

9. progress in developing and implementing Operation Support Systems (OSS) services and ESP access to those services;

10. progress on the uniform provision of OSS services; and

11. a list of BSEs used in the provision of BOC/GTE's own enhanced services. In addition, the BOCs are required to report annually on the unbundling of new technologies arising from their own initiative, in response to requests by ISPs, or resulting from requirements imposed by the Commission.

In addition to the annual ONA reports discussed above, the BOCs and GTE are required to file semi-annual ONA reports. These semi-annual reports include:

1. a consolidated nationwide matrix of ONA services and state and federal ONA tariffs;

2. computer disks and printouts of data regarding state and federal tariffs;

3. a printed copy and a diskette copy of the *ONA Services User Guide*;

4. updated information on 118 categories of network capabilities requested by ISPs and how such requests were addressed, with details and matrices; and

5. updated information on BOC responses to the requests and matrices.[109]

Other Nonstructural Safeguards

In addition to CEI and ONA, there are certain other nonstructual safeguards with which a carrier must comply. While *Computer II & III* applies to BOCs, these rules can apply to all carriers.

Discrimination

Beyond the specific anti-discrimination provisions in *Computer III* that apply to BOCs, all carriers are subject to the anti-discrimination provisions in Section 202 of the Communications Act of 1934.[110] This is one of the essential characteristics of being a common carrier, that the carrier must provide services to all end users on the same terms and conditions and is not permitted to select who it will and will not provide service to. Specifically, the carrier cannot select to provide service to its affiliates but not to those not affiliated with the carrier.

Bundling

CPE

Promulgated as a part of *Computer II*, the Commission's bundling rules apply to all carriers all the time. These rules prohibit carriers from bundling customer premises equipment (i.e., modems) with the provision of telecommunications services.[111] Note that this rule restricts the conduct of a carrier, but not necessarily the conduct of an affiliated separate subsidiary (i.e., bell.net) of the carrier.[112]

Basic and Enhanced Services

All "carriers that own common carrier transmission facilities and provide enhanced services must unbundle basic from enhanced services and offer transmission capacity to other enhanced service providers under the same tariffed terms and conditions under which they provide such services to their own enhanced service operations."[113]

Customer Proprietary Network Information

A significant concern is the situation where non-affiliated ISPs order services from their telecommunications *supplier* BOC and, in the same act, provide sensitive proprietary customer information to their *competitor* BOC. The *Computer Inquiries* recognized the problem that BOCs can use information gathered as a supplier to unfairly compete with ESP competitors. Thus, the Commission created restrictions on the ability of the BOC to use that information. In *Computer III*, the Commission required BOCs and GTE to (1) make CPNI available, upon customer request, to unaffiliated enhanced service vendors, on the same terms and conditions that are available to their own enhanced services personnel; (2) limit their enhanced services personnel from obtaining access to a customer's CPNI if the customer so requests; and (3) notify multi-line business customers annually of their CPNI rights.[114]

In addition, the Commission prohibited BOCs and GTE from providing to its affiliated ESP "any customer proprietary information unless such information is available to any member of the public on the same terms and conditions."[115]

In 1996, Congress passed the new *Privacy of Customer Information* provision, codified as Section 222 of the Communications Act.[116] Section 222 contains the restrictions on the use of customer information by all carriers, not just BOCs. This includes Customer Proprietary Network Information and Carrier Information.

The FCC concluded that Section 222 replaced "the Computer III CPNI framework in all material respects."[117] However, the Order where the FCC made that conclusion was vacated by a federal appeals court.[118]

Section 222 defines Customer Proprietary Network Information (CPNI) as

(a) information that relates to the quantity, technical configuration, type, destination, and amount of use of a telecommunications service subscribed to by any customer of a telecommunications carrier, and that is made available to the carrier by the customer solely by virtue of the customer-carrier relationship; and (b) information contained in the bills pertaining to telephone exchange service or telephone toll service received by a customer of a carrier.

Except that such term does not include subscriber list information.[119]

Subscriber list information, essentially the information listed in a phone book, is defined as

Any information

(a) identifying the listed names of subscribers of a carrier and such subscribers' telephone numbers, addresses, or primary advertising classifications (as such classification are assigned at the time of the establishment of such service), or any combination of such listed names, numbers, addresses, or classifications; and
(b) that the carrier or an affiliate has published, caused to be published, or accepted for publication in any directory format.[120]

According to Section 222,

Except as required by law or with the approval of the customer, a telecommunications carrier that receives or obtains customer proprietary network information by virtue of its provision of a telecommunications service shall only use, disclose, or permit access to individually identifiable customer proprietary network information in its provision of (a) the telecommunications service from which such information is derived, or (b) services necessary to, or used in, the provision of such telecommunications service, including the publishing of directories.[121]

In other words, information gathered in order to provide telecommunications service can be used only for the provision of that service. A carrier could not use the information it has gathered from providing telephone service in order to market Internet services.[122] The key exception is whether the carrier has the approval of the customer to use that information for other purposes.

It is important to understand that these rules apply only where information is derived from the provision of telecommunications services; they do not apply where the LEC is providing non-telecommunications services such as Internet services.[123]

Many ISPs are also Competitive Local Exchange Carriers (CLECs). Another portion of Section 222 addresses customer information in the context of intercarrier relations. It states

A telecommunications carrier that receives or obtains proprietary information from another carrier for purposes of providing any telecommunications service shall use such information only for such purpose, and shall not use such information for its own marketing efforts.[124]

In 1998, the Commission promulgated rules implementing Section 222 of the Communication Act.[125] U.S. West filed an appeal concerning the FCC rules with the Tenth Circuit Court of Appeals, which vacated the FCC rules as violating the First Amendment.[126]

Where does this leave CPNI? The FCC rules implementing Section 222 have been vacated; Section 222 has not been vacated and remains binding. Furthermore, since the FCC's Section 222 rules were vacated, the previous FCC's *Computer III* CPNI rules remain in place.

Network Information Disclosure

Computer II and *Computer III* articulated requirements for the disclosure of network information by BOCs.[127] These requirements have been superseded by the Telecommunications Act of 1996.[128] The regulations implementing the new statutory requirements can be found at 47 C.F.R. §§51.325–335.

In sum, these rules require all incumbent local exchange carriers (ILECs[129]) to provide public notice regarding any network changes that affect a competing service provider's (including an information service provider[130]) performance or ability to provide service or will affect the ILEC's interoperability with other service providers.[131] Until the ILEC has disclosed this information publicly, it may not disclosure this information to anyone, particularly its own affiliates.[132] The rules set forth requirements for the content of the notice,[133] the methods of notice,[134] and the timing of notice.[135] Information about DSL readiness of the network would fall within the Network Information Disclosure rules.

Cross Subsidization

Pursuant to the Commission's "Allocation of Cost" rules, a carrier may not use services not subject to competition to subsidize services that are subject to competition. In other words, a carrier could not usenoncompetitive telephone revenues to subsidize its Internet access services.[136]

Accounting Safeguards

Carriers are subject to a series of accounting safeguards that can be found in Subpart I of Part 64 of Title 47, Code of Federal Regulations. The rules require that the carriers be subject to annual independent audits to ensure, for example, that they are not improperly cross subsidizing their services.[137] The final reports of these independent audits are publicly available and can be obtained by contacting the Accounting Safeguards Division of the FCC's Common Carrier Bureau.[138] Information about Common Carriers accounting can be found in the

Commission's ARMIS database,[139] publicly available on the FCC Web site. Pursuant to Section 64.903, the Commission has a cost allocation manual indicating how different common carrier costs should be allocated between regulated and unregulated services.[140]

Notes

Disclaimer   This Guide is a guide only; nothing in this Guide modifies Commission rules and regulations. Where this Guide diverges from FCC rules or regulations, those rules and regulations are authoritative. In addition, given the breadth of the regulatory history on this subject, this Guide could not possibly be exhaustive, covering every issue relevant to enhanced service providers. It is intended that this Guide provide the public with sufficient information to comprehend the topic and also provide clear references to FCC rules, regulations, and orders so that the public will know where to look for more in depth information.

It is the intention of this Guide to stay as true to the original language and requirements of the Commission orders as possible. Therefore, at times and where appropriate, language taken directly from Commission orders is presented without further modification.

The views expressed in this Guide are the author's alone. They do not necessarily represent those of the Commission, any FCC Commissioner, or the staff.

1. The Commission has defined ISPs as follows:

An ISP is an entity that provides its customers the ability to obtain on-line information through the Internet. ISPs purchase analog and digital lines from local exchange carriers to connect to their dial-in subscribers. Under one typical arrangement, an ISP customer dials a seven-digit number to reach the ISP server in the same local calling area. The ISP, in turn, combines "computer processing, information storage, protocol conversion, and routing with transmission to enable users to access Internet content and services." Under this arrangement, the end user generally pays the LEC a flat monthly fee for use of the local exchange network and generally pays the ISP a flat, monthly fee for Internet access. The ISP typically purchases business lines from a LEC, for which it pays a flat monthly fee that allows unlimited incoming calls.

In re Implementation of the Local Competition Provisions in the Telecommunications Act of 1996, Inter-Carrier Compensation for ISP-Bound Traffic, CC Docket No. 96-98, CC Docket No. 99-68, *Notice of Proposed Rulemaking and Declaratory Ruling*, 14 F.C.C.R. 3689, 14 FCC Rcd. 3689, par. 4 (February 26, 1999) (hereinafter *Inter-Carrier Compensation Order 1999*).

2. Bill McCarthy, Editor's Notes, *Boardwatch Magazine* (March 2000) ("As of February 1, there are 7,136 ISPs in North America").

3. Shane Greenstein, *Distribution of ISPs* (1998): ⟨http://www.kellogg.nwu.edu/faculty/greenstein/images/htm/Research/Maps/mapoct98.pdf⟩; Tom Downes and Shane Greenstein, *Universal Access and Local Commercial Internet Markets* at 38 (June 8, 1998), ⟨http://www.kellogg.nwu.edu/faculty/greenstein/images/htm/Research/isppap4.pdf⟩.

4. *See FNC Resolution: Definition of "Internet"* (October 24, 1995): ⟨http://www.fnc.gov/Internet_res.html⟩; 47 U.S.C. §231(e)(3).

5. *See* Barry M. Leiner, Vinton G. Cerf, David D. Clark, Robert E. Kahn, et al., *A Brief History of the Internet*: ⟨http://www.isoc.org/internet/history/brief.html⟩; Robert Hobbes Zakon, *Hobbes Internet Timeline* ⟨http://www.isoc.org/guest/zakon/Internet/History/HIT.html⟩; *PBS Life on the Internet: Net Timeline* ⟨http://www.pbs.org/internet/timeline/index.html⟩.

6. *In re* Regulatory & Policy Problems Presented by the Interdependence of Computer and Communication Services & Facilities, *Notice of Inquiry*, 7 FCC 2d 11, par. 25 (1966).

7. Jason Oxman, OPP Working Paper 31, *The FCC and the Unregulation of the Internet* (July 1999); Barbara Espin, OPP Working Paper 30, *Internet Over Cable: Defining the Future In Terms of the Past* (August 1998); Kevin Werbach, OPP Paper 29, *Digital Tornado: The Internet and Telecommunications Policy* (March 1997). OPP papers are available at ⟨http://www.fcc.gov/opp/workingp.html⟩.

8. *See, e.g., In re* Of Regulatory And Policy Problems Presented By The Interdependence Of Computer And Communication Services And Facilities, Docket No. 16979, *Final Decision and Order*, 28 F.C.C.2d 267, par. 9 (March 18, 1971) (hereinafter *Computer I*).

9. *In re* Computer III Remand Proceedings: Bell Operating Company Provision of Enhanced Services, CC Docket No. 95-20, CC Docket No. 98-10, *Report and Order*, par. 7 (March 10, 1999) (hereinafter *Computer III Order 1999*).

10. *Id.* par. 29.

11. *Computer and Communications Industry Association v. Federal Communications Commission*, 693 F.2d 198, 204, 224 U.S.APP.D.C. 83 (D.C. Cir. 1982). *See also* 47 U.S.C. §153(43).

12. 47 C.F.R. §64.702(a).

13. *See, e.g., In re* Bell Atlantic Telephone Companies Offer of Comparably Efficient Interconnection to Providers of Internet Access Services, CCBPol 96-09, *Order* (June 6, 1996).

14. *In re* Bell Atlantic Telephone Companies, Offer of Comparably Efficient Interconnection to Providers of Video Dialtone-Related Enhanced Services, DA 95-1283, *Order* (June 9, 1995) (hereinafter *Bell Atlantic's CEI Plan*).

15. *See, e.g., In re* Southwestern Bell CEI Plan for the Provision of Voice Messaging Services, DA 88-1469, *Memorandum Opinion and Order*, 3 FCC Rcd. 6912, 65 Rad. Reg. 2d (P&F) 527, par. 1 (September 29, 1988).

16. *See, e.g., In re* Ameritech's Comparably Efficient Interconnection Plan for Electronic Vaulting Service, CCBPol 97-03, *Order* (December 31, 1997) (hereinafter *Ameritech's CEI Plan*).

17. *See In re* Independent Data Communications Manufacturers Association, Inc., Petition for Declaratory Ruling That AT&T's InterSpan Frame Relay Service Is a Basic Service; DA 95-2190, *Memorandum Opinion and Order*, 10

F.C.C.R. 13,717, 10 FCC Rcd. 13,717, 1 Communications Reg. (P&F) 409, pars. 4 and 11 (October 18, 1995) (hereinafter *Frame Relay*) (concluding that frame relay and X.25 services are basic services).

18. 47 C.F.R. §64.702(a).

19. Telecommunications Act of 1996, Pub. L. 104–104, 110 Stat. 56 (codified in scattered sections of 47 U.S.C. §§151–170). This is essentially the same definition of Information Services that was used by the Federal Court in the Modified Final Judgment that broke up AT&T and devised how BOCs would be permitted to operate. See *United States v. AT&T*, 552 F.Supp. 131, 179 (D.D.C. 1982), *aff'd sub nom. Maryland v. United States*, 460 U.S. 1001 (1983), *vacated sub nom. United States v. Western Elec. Co.*, slip op. CA 82-0192 (D.D.C. Apr. 11, 1996) (defining "information services" as "the offering of a capability for generating, acquiring, storing, transforming, processing, retrieving, utilizing or making available information which may be conveyed via telecommunications...").

20. *In re* The Implementation of Sections 255 and 251(a) (2) of the Communications Act of 1934, as Enacted by the Telecommunications Act of 1996, WT Docket No. 96-198, *Report and Order And Further Notice Of Inquiry*, par. 74 (September 29, 1999); *In re* The Implementation of the Non-Accounting Safeguards of Sections 271 and 272 of the Communications Act of 1934, as Amended, *First Report and Order and Notice of Proposed Rulemaking*, Docket 96–149, 11 F.C.C.R. 21,905, 13 F.C.C.R. 11,230, 11 FCC Rcd. 21,905, 13 FCC Rcd. 11,230, 5 Communications Reg. (P&F) 696, par. 102 (December 24, 1996).

21. The FCC approved the merger of Bell Atlantic and GTE on June 16, 2000. FCC Press Release: Federal Communications Commission Approves Bell Atlantic–GTE Merger with Conditions (June 16, 2000).

22. *See also* Regional Bell Operating Companies ⟨http://www.bellatlantic.com/bellcom/index3.htm⟩ (accessed April 18, 2000) (listing Regional Bell Operating Companies).

23. "Regional Bell Operating Company (RBOC): One of the seven holding companies formed by divestiture by the American Telephone and Telegraph Company of its local Bell System operating companies, and to which one or more of the Bell System local telephone companies were assigned." Federal Standard 1037C (August 7, 1996), ⟨http://glossary.its.bldrdoc.gov/fs-1037/fs-1037c.htm⟩. There are only four RBOCs remaining as a result of mergers and acquisitions.

24. 47 USC §153(4). Note that Cincinnati Bell (Broadwing) and Southern New England Bell (SNET) are not BOCs.

25. US West has merged with Qwest, which is not a BOC. *In re* Qwest Communications International Inc. and US WEST, Inc. Applications for Transfer of Control of Domestic and International Sections 214 and 310 Authorizations and Application to Transfer Control of a Submarine Cable Landing License, *Memorandum Opinion and Order*, CC Docket No. 99-272, 15 FCC Rcd. 5376 (March 10, 2000).

26. *See* Y2K Communications Sector Report: Wireline Telecommunications Supplement (October 1999): ⟨http://www.fcc.gov/year2000/telephoneb.html⟩ (stating that the seven largest LECs, including SPRINT and GTE, comprise 92–94 percent of the local access lines in the country). *See also* FCC's Y2K Communications Sector Report at 31 (March 1999): ⟨http://www.fcc.gov/year2000/y2kcsr.html⟩.

27. "The term 'local exchange carrier' means any person that is engaged in the provision of telephone exchange service or exchange access. Such term does not include a person insofar as such person is engaged in the provision of a commercial mobile service under section 332(c) of this title, except to the extent that the Commission finds that such service should be included in the definition of such term." 47 U.S.C. §153(26).

28. *In re* GTE Telephone Operators GTOC Tariff No. 1 GTE Transmittal No. 1148, *Memorandum Opinion and Order*, CC Docket No. 98-79, 13 FCC Rcd. 22466, par. 7 (October 30, 1998), *recon. denied* (February 26, 1999).

29. *Computer III Order 1999*, 14 FCC Rcd. at 4294, par. 7; *In re* Bell Operating Companies Joint Petition for Waiver of Computer II Rules, DA 95-2264,10 FCC Rcd. 13758, *Order*, par. 3 (October 31, 1995) (hereinafter *BOCs Joint Petition*); *In re* Amendment of Section 64.702 of the Commission's Rules and Regulations (Second Computer Inquiry), *Final Decision*, 77 F.C.C.2d 384, par. 229 (1980).

30. 47 C.F.R. §64.702(c).

31. 47 C.F.R. §64.702(d). Some provisions of section 64.702(d) have been superseded by provisions of the Telecommunications Act of 1996. *See* Network Information Disclosure, page 47, and Customer Proprietary Network Information, page 43.

32. *Computer III Order 1999*, 14 FCC Rcd. at 4294, par. 7.

33. *In re* Computer III Further Remand Proceedings: Bell Operating Company Provision Of Enhanced Services, CC Docket No. 95-20, 1998 Biennial Regulatory Review—Review of Computer III and ONA Safeguards and Requirements, CC Docket No. 98-10, FCC 98-8, *Further Notice of Proposed Rulemaking*, 13 FCC Rcd. 6040, par. 15 (January 30, 1998) (hereinafter *Computer III FNPRM 1998*). *See California v. FCC*, 39 F.3d 919 (9th Cir. 1994), *cert. denied*, 115 S.Ct. 1427 (1995).

34. *See Computer III FNPRM 1998*, 13 FCC Rcd. at 6052, par. 16.

35. *Ameritech's CEI Plan*, 13 FCC Rcd. at 83, par. 6; *BOCs Joint Petition*, 10 FCC Rcd. at 13762, par. 22; *Bell Atlantic's CEI Plan*, 11 FCC Rcd. at 987, par. 4; *In re* Computer III Further Remand Proceedings: Bell Operating Company Provision Of Enhanced Services, CC Docket No. 95-20, *Notice of Proposed Rulemaking*, 10 FCC Rcd. 8360, pars. 9–12 (February 21, 1995) (hereinafter *Computer III Remand 1995*).

36. *Computer III Remand 1995*, 10 FCC Rcd. 8360. *See also Computer III FNPRM 1998*, 13 FCC Rcd. 6040; *Computer III Order 1999*, 14 FCC Rcd. at 4292, par. 4 (eliminating requirement that BOCs receive approval of CEI plans

from FCC. Permitting BOCs to simply post plans on websites and provide notice to FCC); *In re* Computer III Further Remand Proceedings; 1998 Biennial Regulatory Review—Review of Computer III and ONA Safeguards and Requirements, CC Docket Nos. 95-20, 98-10, *Order* (December 9, 1999) (hereinafter *Computer III Order on Reconsideration 1999*) (denying CIX's petition for reconsideration).

37. This Guide presents a summary of the *Computer III* rules as they currently are and does not address the issues raised in the current rulemaking.

38. *See, e.g., Computer III FNPRM 1998*, 13 FCC Rcd. at 6043, par. 2; *Ameritech's CEI Plan*, 13 FCC Rcd. at 87, par. 4; *Bell Atlantic's CEI Plan*, 11 FCC Rcd. at 987, par. 2.

39. *BOCs Joint Petition*, 10 FCC Rcd. at 13759, par. 3. *See also Ameritech's CEI Plan*, 13 FCC Rcd. at 87, par. 8 (stating "The CEI requirements are designed to give ESPs equal and efficient access to the basic services that the BOCs use to provide their own enhanced services.").

40. *Ameritech's CEI Plan*, 13 FCC Rcd. at 82, par. 3; *In re* Filing and Review of Open Network Architecture Plans, CC Docket No. 88-2, Phase I, *Memorandum Opinion and Order*, pars. 4, 17 (December 22, 1988) (hereinafter *ONA Review*).

41. *See* "Status of Rulemaking," p. 17, for important information on litigation concerning these rules and the status of an FCC proceeding that will revise these rules.

42. *Computer III Order 1999*, 14 FCC Rcd. at 4297, pars. 4, 11–12.

43. *Computer III Order on Reconsideration 1999*, 14 FCC Rcd. at 21630, par. 6.

44. *Joint Petition*, 10 FCC Rcd. at 13764, par. 35.

45. *In re* Application of Open Network Architecture and Nondiscrimination Safeguards to GTE Corporation, CC Docket No. 92-256, *Memorandum Opinion and Order*, 11 FCC Rcd. 1388, par. 41 (July 29, 1995) (hereinafter *GTE ONA*).

46. *Computer III Order 1999*, 14 FCC Rcd. at 4298, par. 13. *See, e.g., BOC's Joint Petition*, 10 FCC Rcd. at 13765, par. 37; *GTE ONA*, 11 FCC Rcd. at 1409, par. 42; *Bell Atlantic's CEI Plan*, 11 FCC Rcd. at 994, par. 17; *ONA Review*, 4 FCC Rcd. at 72, par. 137.

47. *Computer III* Order 1999, 14 FCC Rcd. at 4298, par. 13. *See, e.g., Ameritech's CEI Plan*, 13 FCC Rcd. at 88, par. 17; *GTE ONA*, 11 FCC Rcd. at 1410, par. 44; *Bell Atlantic's CEI Plan*, 11 FCC Rcd. at 991–992.

48. *Ameritech's CEI Plan*, 13 FCC Rcd. at 89, par. 17.

49. *Computer III Order 1999*, 14 FCC Rcd. at 4298, par. 13. *See, e.g., Ameritech's CEI Plan*, 13 FCC Rcd. at 90, par. 25; *BOC's Joint Petition*, 10 FCC Rcd. at 13765, par. 38; *GTE ONA*, 11 FCC Rcd. at 1411, par. 46; *Bell Atlantic's CEI Plan*, 11 FCC Rcd. at 995, par. 19.

50. *Computer III Order 1999*, 14 FCC Rcd. 4298, par. 13. *See, e.g., Ameritech's CEI Plan*, 13 FCC Rcd. at 91, par. 27; *BOC's Joint Petition*, 10

FCC Rcd. at 13765, par. 39; *GTE ONA*, 11 FCC Rcd. at 1411, par. 48; *Bell Atlantic's CEI Plan*, 11 FCC Rcd. at 995, par. 21; *ONA Review*, 4 FCC Rcd. at 75, par. 144.

51. *ONA Review*, 4 FCC Rcd. at 75, par. 144.

52. *Computer III Order 1999*, 14 FCC Rcd. at 4298, par. 13. *See, e.g., Ameritech's CEI Plan*, 13 FCC Rcd. at 92, par. 30; *BOC's Joint Petition*, 10 FCC Rcd. at 13765, par. 40; *GTE ONA*, 11 FCC Rcd. at 1412, par. 50; *Bell Atlantic's CEI Plan*, 11 FCC Rcd. at 995–96, par. 23.

53. *Ameritech's CEI Plan*, 13 FCC Rcd. at 92, par. 30.

54. *Computer III Order 1999*, 14 FCC Rcd. at 4298–99, par. 13. *See, e.g., Ameritech's CEI Plan*, 13 FCC Rcd. at 92–93, par. 32; *BOC's Joint Petition*, 10 FCC Rcd. at 13765, par. 41; *GTE ONA*, 11 FCC Rcd. at 1412, par. 51; *Bell Atlantic's CEI Plan*, 11 FCC Rcd. at 996, par. 25.

55. *Computer III Order 1999*, 14 FCC Rcd. at 4299, par. 13. *See, e.g., BOC's Joint Petition*, 10 FCC Rcd. 13765, par. 42; *GTE ONA*, 11 FCC Rcd. at 1412–13, par. 53; *Bell Atlantic's CEI Plan*, 11 FCC Rcd. at 997, par. 27.

56. *Ameritech's CEI Plan*, 13 FCC Rcd. at 93–94, par. 34.

57. *Computer III Order 1999*, 14 FCC Rcd. at 4299, par. 13. *See, e.g., Ameritech's CEI Plan*, 13 FCC Rcd. at 94, par. 36; *BOC's Joint Petition*, 10 FCC Rcd. at 13765, par. 43; *Bell Atlantic's CEI Plan*, 11 FCC Rcd. at 997, par. 29.

58. *GTE ONA*, 11 FCC Rcd. at 1414, pars. 55–57.

59. *ONA Review*, 4 FCC Rcd. at 19–20, par. 22. *See also ONA Review*, 4 FCC Rcd. at 78, pars. 150–51 (stating "The Phase I Order declined to require the BOCs to provide collocation opportunities to ESPs. Instead, we required BOCs to provide interstate facilities that minimize transmission costs. We stated that loop or trunk multiplexing is one technique for minimizing such costs and that collocation is another option, and required carriers to demonstrate what steps they would take to reduce transmission costs for competitors. The Phase II Reconsideration held that BOCs could satisfy our requirement to minimize transmission costs by offering price parity. We said that "carriers need only minimize transmission costs through some means or charge themselves the same rates that they charge others.").

60. *Computer III Order 1999*, 14 FCC Rcd. at 4299, par. 13. *See, e.g., Ameritech's CEI Plan*, 13 FCC Rcd. at 95, par. 38; *BOC's Joint Petition*, 10 FCC Rcd. at 13765, par. 44; *GTE ONA*, 10 FCC Rcd. at 1414, par. 58; *Bell Atlantic's CEI Plan*, 11 FCC Rcd. at 998, par. 31.

61. *BOC's Joint Petition*, 10 FCC Rcd. at 13759, par. 3.

62. *See ONA Review*, 4 FCC Rcd. at 18, par. 19 (stating that ONA requirements do not apply to AT&T).

63. *Ameritech's CEI Plan*, 13 FCC Rcd. at 85, par. 7 n. 18. *See also BOC's Joint Petition*, 10 FCC Rcd. at 13763, par. 26.

64. *See* Status of Rulemaking, page 17, for important information on litigation concerning these rules and the status of an FCC proceeding that will revise these rules.

65. *See also GTE ONA*, 11 FCC Rcd 1388, par. 2 (noting that ONA requirements were extended to GTE).

66. *Computer III Order 1999*, 14 FCC Rcd at 4298, par. 8 n. 15. *See also Computer III Remand 1995*, 10 FCC Rcd 8366, pars. 15–16.

67. *Computer III FNPRM 1998*, 13 FCC Rcd. at 6056–57, par. 25.

68. *Id.*, par. 26. See also *ONA Review*, 4 FCC Rcd. at 36, par. 56.

69. *ONA Review*, 4 FCC Rcd. at 18, par. 18.

70. *ONA Review*, 4 FCC Rcd. at 11, par. 2. *See also Computer III Remand 1995*, 10 FCC Rcd. at 8372, par. 17 ("ONA exists to promote a fair competitive marketplace for the provision of enhanced services."); *ONA Review*, 4 FCC Rcd. at 15, par. 14 ("Properly implemented, ONA will do more than prevent the BOCs from discriminating against their competitors in the provision of basic services that BOCs provide to their own ESP affiliates.").

71. *ONA Review*, 4 FCC Rcd. at 36, par. 57.

72. *Id.*, par. 30.

73. *Id.*, par. 75.

74. *Id.*, par. 112.

75. *Id.*, par. 86.

76. *Id.*, par. 10; *GTE ONA*, 10 FCC Rcd. at 7770–71, par. 14.

77. *GTE ONA*, 10 FCC Rcd. at 7770–71, par. 14.

78. *ONA Review*, 4 FCC Rcd. at 36, par. 56.

79. *Id.*, par. 77.

80. *Id.*, par. 57.

81. *Id.*, par. 83.

82. *Id.*, par. 280.

83. *Id.*, par. 84.

84. *Id.*, par. 85.

85. *Id.*, par. 85.

86. *Id.*, note 157.

87. *Id.*, par. 86.

88. *Id.*, par. 57.

89. *GTE ONA*, 11 FCC Rcd. at 1395–96, par. 12.

90. *ONA Review*, 4 FCC Rcd. at 58, par. 106.

91. *GTE ONA*, 11 FCC Rcd. at 1395–96, par. 12.

92. *Id.*, par. 91. *See ONA Review*, 4 FCC Rcd. at 1392–93, pars. 108–09.

93. *Computer III FNPRM 1998*, 13 FCC Rcd. at 6099–6100, par. 112.

94. *GTE ONA*, 11 FCC Rcd. at 1400, par. 25.

95. *GTE ONA*, 11 FCC Rcd. at 1399, par. 23; *In re* Filing and Review of ONA Plans, Phase 1, CC Docket No. 88-2, *Memorandum Opinion and Order*, 6 FCC

Rcd. 7646, 70 Rad. Reg. 2d (P&F) 90, 1991 WL 638511, par. 56 (Dec. 19, 1990); *In re* Filing and Review of ONA Plans, Phase 1, CC Docket 88–2, *Memorandum Opinion and Order*, 5 FCC Rcd. 3084, par. 23 (May 8, 1990). *See also ONA Review*, 4 FCC Rcd. at 50, par. 88 (declining to rule on issue at that time, but directing BOCs to supplement record).

96. *ONA Review*, 4 FCC Rcd. at 171, par. 325. *See also GTE ONA*, 11 FCC Rcd. at 1398, par. 16.

97. *GTE ONA*, 11 FCC Rcd. at 1427–28, par. 93. *See also ONA Review*, 4 FCC Rcd. at 59, par. 110.

98. *In re* The Bell Atlantic Telephone Companies' Offer Of Comparably Efficient Interconnection To Intranet Management Service Providers, CCBPol 98-01, DA 98-1655, *Order*, 13 FCC Rcd. 15617, par. 27 (CCB August 20, 1998); *Ameritech's CEI Plan*, 13 FCC Rcd. at 97, par. 45; *BOC's Joint Petition*, 13 FCC Rcd. at 13758–59, par. 3.

99. In addition, BOCs must file "an annual affidavit, signed by the officer principally responsible for installation procedures, attesting that the BOC had followed installation procedures described in the BOC's ONA plan, and that the BOC had not, in fact, discriminated in the quality of services it had provided." *Computer III FNPRM 1998*, 13 FCC Rcd. at 6100, note 263.

100. *Computer III FNPRM 1998*, 13 FCC Rcd. at 6100, note 264:

The specified service categories include: (1) Circuit Switched Line: Business Line, PBX, Centrex, WATS, Mobile, Feature Group A, Foreign Exchange; (2) Circuit Switched Trunk: Feature Group B, Feature Group D, DID (Line and Trunk); (3) Packet Switched Services (X.25 and X.75): Packet DDD Access Line, Packet Synchronous Access Line, Packet Asynchronous Access Line; (4) Dedicated Metallic: Protection Alarm, Protection Relaying, Control Circuit; (5) Dedicated Telegraph Grade: Telegraph Grade 75 Baud, Telegraph 150 Baud; (6) Dedicated Voice Grade: Voice Non-Switched Line, Voice Switched Line, Voice Switched Trunk, Voice and Tone-Radio Land Line, Data Low Speed, Basic Data and Voice, Voice and Data-PSN Access Tie Trunk, Voice and Data-SSN Access, Voice and Data-SSN-Intermachine Trunk, Data Extension-Voice Grade Data, Protection Relay Voice Grade, Telephoto and Facsimile; (7) Dedicated Program Audio: Program Audio 200–3500 HZ, Program Audio 100–5000 HZ, Program Audio 50–8000 HZ, Program Audio 50–15000 HZ; (8) Dedicated Video: TV Channel-One Way 15kHz Audio, TV Channel-One Way 5 kHz Audio; (9) Dedicated Digital: Digital Voice Circuit, Digital Data-2.4kb/s, Digital Data-4.8kb/s, Digital Data-9.6kb/s, Digital Data-56kb/s; (10) Dedicated High Capacity Digital: 1.544 MBPS BSA; (11) Dedicated High Capacity Digital (Greater than 1.544 MBPS): Dedicated Digital-3.152 MBPS, Dedicated Digital-6.312 MBPS, Dedicated Digital-44.736 MBPS, Dedicated Digital-45 MBPS or Higher; (12) Dedicated Alert Transport; (13) Dedicated Derived Channel; (14) Dedicated Network Access Link (DNAL).

101. *Computer III FNPRM 1998*, 13 FCC Rcd. at 6100, par. 113.

For installation reports, the Commission requires the BOCs and GTE to report separately for their own affiliated enhanced services operations and for all other customers, whether ISPs or other carriers, and to include information, for each specified service category, on: (1) total orders; (2) due dates missed; (3) percentage of due dates missed; and (4) average interval. The BOCs and GTE are also required to report maintenance activities separately for their own affiliated enhanced services operations and for all other customers. For maintenance activities with due dates, carriers are required to report: (1) total orders; (2) due dates missed; (3) percentage of due dates missed; and (4) average interval. For maintenance activities without due dates, carriers are required to report only total orders and average interval. *Id.* at 6100, para. 113, note 265.

102. *GTE ONA*, 11 FCC Rcd. at 1400, par. 27.

103. *See* p. 42 (discussing Network Information Disclosure rules).

104. *Computer III FNPRM 1998*, 13 FCC Rcd. at 6086, par. 81.

105. ATIS' Network Interconnection Interoperability Forum can be found online at ⟨http://www.atis.org/atis/clc/niif/niifhom.htm⟩.

106. *Computer III FNPRM 1998*, 13 FCC Rcd. at 6086–87, pars. 82–83. *See also GTE ONA*, 11 FCC Rcd. at 1402, par. 27; *Computer III Remand 1995*, 10 FCC Rcd. at 8374–5, pars. 20–22; *ONA Review*, 4 FCC Rcd. at 205, pars. 390, 396–97.

107. *Computer III FNPRM 1998*, 13 FCC Rcd. at 6087, par. 84.

108. *Id.*, par. 13.

109. *Id.*, pars. 103 & 108. See also *GTE ONA*, 11 FCC Rcd. at 1404, par. 32; *Computer III Remand 1999*, 10 FCC Rcd. at 8377–8, par. 27.

110. Sec. 202. Discriminations and preferences:

(a) Charges, services, etc. It shall be unlawful for any common carrier to make any unjust or unreasonable discrimination in charges, practices, classifications, regulations, facilities, or services for or in connection with like communication service, directly or indirectly, by any means or device, or to make or give any undue or unreasonable preference or advantage to any particular person, class of persons, or locality, or to subject any particular person, class of persons, or locality to any undue or unreasonable prejudice or disadvantage.
(b) Charges or services included. Charges or services, whenever referred to in this chapter, include charges for, or services in connection with, the use of common carrier lines of communication, whether derived from wire or radio facilities, in chain broadcasting or incidental to radio communication of any kind.
(c) Penalty. Any carrier who knowingly violates the provisions of this section shall forfeit to the United States the sum of $6,000 for each such offense and $300 for each and every day of the continuance of such offense.

47 U.S.C. §202.

111. 47 C.F.R. §64.702(e):

Except as otherwise ordered by the Commission, after March 1, 1982, the carrier provision of customer-premises equipment used in conjunction with the interstate telecommunications network shall be separate and distinct from provision of common carrier communications services and not offered on a tariffed basis.

112. Note that these rules are current the subject of an open proceeding before the FCC. *See In re* Review Of Customer Premises Equipment And Enhanced Services Unbundling Rules In the Interexchange, Exchange Access and Local Exchange Markets, CC Docket No. 98-183; CC Docket No. 96-61, *Notice of Proposed Rulemaking*, 13 FCC Rcd. 21531 (October 9, 1998) (hereinafter CPE Review).

113. *In re* Amendment of Section 64.702 of the Commission's Rules and Regulations (Second Computer Inquiry), Docket No. 20828, *Final Decision*, 77 FCC 2d 384, par. 231 (May 2, 1980); *Frame Relay*, 10 FCC Rcd. at 13719, par. 13. *See also CPE Review*, 13 FCC Rcd. at 21549, par. 33.

Note that this requirement is currently the subject of several open proceedings. The FCC has asked whether this unbundling obligation should be expanded from coverage of "enhanced services" to include all "information services." *Computer III FNPRM 1998*, 13 FCC Rcd. at 6070, par. 42. The FCC has also asked whether this obligation ought to be removed in the context of "interstate, domestic, interexchange services offered by nondominant interexchange carriers." *CPE Review*, 13 FCC Rcd. at 21550, par. 35.

114. *BOC's Joint Petition*, 10 FCC Rcd. at 13765, par. 46. *See also Ameritech's CEI Plan*, 13 FCC Rcd. at 95–6, par. 41; *GTE ONA*, 11 FCC Rcd. 1388; *Bell Atlantic's CEI Plan*, 13 FCC Rcd. at 83; *ONA Review*, 4 FCC Rcd. at 20, pars. 25, 398–447.

115. 47 C.F.R. §64.702(d)(3).

116. 47 U.S.C. §222.

117. *In re* Implementation of the Telecommunications Act of 1996; Telecommunications Carriers' Use of Customer Proprietary Network Information and Other Customer Information; CC Docket No. 96-115, CC Docket No. 96-149, *Second Report and Order and Further Notice Of Proposed Rulemaking*, 13 FCC Rcd. 8061, par. 180 (February 19, 1998) (hereinafter *CPNI*).

118. *US West v. FCC*, Docket 98-9518, 182 F.3d 1224 (10th Cir., Aug. 18, 1999), *cert. denied sub. nom. Competition Policy Institute v. U.S. West*, Docket 99-1427, 120 S. Ct. 2215 (June 2000).

119. 47 U.S.C. §222(f)(1).

120. 47 U.S.C. §222(f)(3).

121. 47 U.S.C. §222(c)(1).

122. *See CPNI*, 13 FCC Rcd. 8061; *In re* Implementation of the Telecommunications Act of 1996 Telecommunications Carriers' Use of Customer Proprietary Network Information and Other Customer Information; CC Docket No. 96-115, CC Docket No. 96-149, *Order on Recon and Petitions for Forebearance*, 14 FCC Rcd. 14409, pars. 46–47 (September 3, 1999) (hereinafter *CPNI Recon*) (concluding that the provision of Internet services is not necessary to the provision of telecommunications service).

123. *See CPNI Recon*, 14 FCC Rcd. at 14492–93, par. 159; *In re* Implementation of the Telecommunications Act of 1996: Telecommunications Carriers' Use of Customer Proprietary Network Information and Other Customer Information, CC Docket No. 96-115, *Order*, 13 FCC Rcd. 12390, par. 1 (CCB May 21, 1998).

124. 47 U.S.C. §222(b).

125. 47 C.F.R. §64.2005. *See CPNI*, 13 FCC Rcd. 8061.

126. *US West, Inc.*, 182 F.3d at 1240.

127. *See* 47 C.F.R. §64.702(d)(2) (network information disclosure requirements for BOCs providing enhanced services through separate subsidiaries); *Computer III Order 1999*, 14 FCC Rcd. at 4314–18, pars. 39–43; *Ameritech's CEI Plan*, 13 FCC Rcd. at 96–7, par. 43; *BOC's Joint Petition*, 10 FCC Rcd. 13758; *Bell*

Atlantic's CEI Plan, 11 FCC Rcd. 985; *ONA Review,* 4 FCC Rcd. at 252, par. 489.

128. *Computer III Order 1999,* 14 FCC Rcd. at 42929, par. 4. 47 USC §251(c)(5) states:

In addition to the duties contained in subsection (b), each incumbent local exchange carrier has the following duties ... (5) NOTICE OF CHANGES.—The duty to provide reasonable public notice of changes in the information necessary for the transmission and routing of services using that local exchange carrier's facilities or networks, as well as of any other changes that would affect the interoperability of those facilities and networks.

129. An ILEC is defined as follows:

For purposes of this section, the term "incumbent local exchange carrier" means, with respect to an area, the local exchange carrier that—

(a) on February 8, 1996, provided telephone exchange service in such area; and

(b) (i) on February 8, 1996, was deemed to be a member of the exchange carrier association pursuant to section 69.601(b) of the Commission's regulations (47 C.F.R. 69.601(b)); or

(ii) is a person or entity that, on or after February 8, 1996, became a successor or assign of a member described in clause (i).

47 U.S.C. 251(h) (1996).

130. 47 C.F.R. §51.325(d).

131. 47 C.F.R. §51.325(a).

132. 47 C.F.R. §51.325(c).

133. 47 C.F.R. §51.327.

134. 47 C.F.R. §51.329.

135. 47 C.F.R. §§51.331–33.

136. 47 C.F.R. §64.901(c):

A telecommunications carrier may not use services that are not competitive to subsidize services subject to competition. Services included in the definition of universal service shall bear no more than a reasonable share of the joint and common costs of facilities used to provide those services.

See also 47 U.S.C. §254(k) (articulating same restriction).

137. *See* 65 Fed. Reg. 16,328, 16,335 (Mar. 28, 2000) (to be codified at 47 C.F.R. §64.904).

138. The Accounting Safeguards Division can be found online at ⟨http://www.fcc.gov/ccb/asd/⟩. You may also wish to contact the ITS to obtain copies of these reports.

139. The ARMIS database contains "financial, operational, service quality, and network infrastructure data from the largest local exchange carriers" and can be found online at ⟨http://www.fcc.gov/ccb/armis/⟩.

140. *See* 65 Fed. Reg. at 16,335 (to be codified at 47 C.F.R. §64.903).

2

Broadband Architectures, ISP Business Plans, and Open Access

Shawn O'Donnell

Background

Something suspiciously resembling a double standard exists in U.S. regulation of broadband access carriers. Incumbent local exchange carriers—ILECs—are required to open their networks to competing service providers, while cable television companies are not. Where did Congress and the FCC get it right? In the telco case, where open access is required, and there is a nascent competitive market for telephony and DSL services, or in the case of cable data networks, where consumers usually have no choice but to buy their service from the cable company's affiliated ISP? Or is disparity the best policy?

ILECs are indignant at the double standard. They say, impose the same standards on both pipelines. Either place the same burden on our competitors, or, better yet, free us from open access requirements, too. Cable companies, for their part, deny that their behavior is anti-competitive. They feel they deserve to compete with the ILECs as best they can.

The FCC faces a dilemma. The Commission wants to promote investment, deployment, and market-driven outcomes. But any open access requirement will, to some degree, discourage investment in infrastructure. On the other hand, if the Commission sits on the sidelines while market concentration grows, it will become difficult to undo damage that could have been prevented by early intervention. The stakes are high. Should the broadband pipeline market succumb to concentration, the content and online commerce markets could follow. There are risks on either prong of the FCC's dilemma. FCC action or inaction could unwittingly undermine its goal of universal, competitive broadband local access.

For now, the FCC has chosen to sit back and watch. According to the FCC's Cable Services Bureau Chief Deborah Lathen,

The Commission has adopted a policy of vigilant restraint, refraining from mandating "open access" at this time, while closely monitoring for anticompetitive developments that may require intervention. Additionally, the Commission is also actively promoting the development of many broadband competitors—including wireless, satellite, cable, and telephone provider—by limiting regulatory burdens, by making more spectrum available, and by making spectrum use more flexible. Competition from multiple broadband providers is seen as the best way to prevent a monopoly by one provider.[1]

The FCC's ultimate hope is that multiple pipelines will make restrictions on any single pipeline unnecessary. In a market with two, or three, or perhaps more paths for broadband information into the home, facilities owners will presumably find it in their interest to provide non-discriminatory access to all content providers over their networks. At least that's the theory. But it assumes that *multiple* carriers will be in a position to compete for *each* customer's business. That may be the case in certain densely populated areas. But it may not be the case for most consumers.

The FCC is encouraged by the plans of AT&T and AOL/Time Warner to open their networks to alternate ISPs. The Commission takes these developments as a sign that intervention is not required. But they might also interpret the concessions as an effort to take the wind out of the sails of open access advocates. If not for the fear of Congress or the FCC imposing open access requirements, the industry would not have acted on its own.

Is there any cause for concern here? This paper reviews broadband architectures and ISP service profiles to show that open access is technically feasible and economically viable, even if implementation is not always trivial. The decisive factor is planning. If broadband networks are built with interconnection in mind, it will be easier to implement open access. Hence, I argue, the FCC should encourage the deployment of open-access-ready networks. Incentives that the FCC can offer at this stage to cable operators to design open access into their networks will have two benefits. First, they will lower the costs of implementing open access regulations should the FCC decide to act in the future. More significantly, if broadband network operators are encouraged to build open-access-ready networks, they will be better positioned to offer open access on their own, thereby eliminating the need for regulation.

Broadband Access Architectures

The problem of open access for broadband access networks depends in large part on where a subscriber's traffic first contends with other subscribers' traffic for network resources. There are three locations where contention can first occur:

1. at a carrier aggregation point remote from the subscriber's location (a telephone company central office or a cable company head-end,)
2. on the transmission medium, immediately upon leaving the subscriber's premises, or
3. at some point between the subscriber's location and the carrier's point of presence.

The point of first contention is critical to open access because contention means that the network operator must allocate network resources. Which users get what network resources, and when? The open access controversy revolves around this question: whose service provider is making the allocation of resources? Are both users the customers of the service provider making the resource allocation decision? Or is only one user a customer of the provider making the allocation decision, and one user a customer of an alternative ISP? Or are both users the customers of different, alternative ISPs? If all users are customers of the same affiliated service provider, then they can expect the provider to manage network resources in a manner consistent with the service offering. But if any of the users are customers of ISPs not affiliated with the network operator, the alternative ISPs and the network operator will have to negotiate terms—for quality of service and allocation of costs—that govern how much of the network's resources a competitive ISP's customers may use.

The first possible location of contention—at the operator's point-of-presence—is characteristic of DSL service, the second is typical of cable data services, and the third is associated with special cases in the provision of DSL. The following sections describe these three possibilities, outlining how each architecture relates to the provisioning of open access services over broadband networks. We begin with the simpler DSL options, then proceed to the cable data option.

DSL Architectures

The Standard DSL Architecture

Figure 2.1 illustrates a typical DSL architecture. If the DSL subscriber uses the ILEC's DSL service, the twisted pair enters the telco central office and passes through a line-splitter (if necessary) to isolate the voice and data slices of spectrum. Next, the signal enters the DSL Access Multiplexer (DSLAM). On the other side of the DSLAM, the customer's data passes through the telco's data network, continuing on to the Internet. A CLEC customer's data takes a similar path through the CLEC's DSLAM and data network. The only difference between the two cases is that the CLEC customer's wiring takes a detour from the central office to the CLEC's equipment, which may be located either in a separate cage in the central office or in a nearby building.

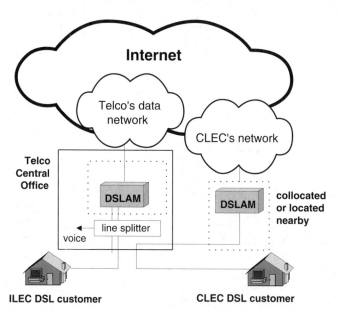

Figure 2.1
The standard DSL architecture.

It is easy to open DSL architectures to multiple ISPs. The twisted pair from the customer's premises to the DSLAM is dedicated to that customer. In this architecture, DSL providers maintain their own DSLAMs, and the Internet side of the DSLAM is connected to the ISP's own network.[2] Neither the ILEC or CLEC data networks carry traffic for customers of other ISPs. The independent wiring for each customer and the separate DSLAMs eliminate the fundamental open access problem: contention does not occur until customers' data is safely under the policy umbrella of their own ISPs.

Architecture for DSL over Digital Loop Carrier

In some areas, telephone companies economized on the use of copper in local loops by aggregating multiple subscriber lines near their subscribers and running a shared digital circuit to the central office. This technology is referred to as Digital Loop Carrier, or DLC, and illustrated in figure 2.2. Since there is no dedicated copper pair from the subscriber to the central office, the open access technology is now more difficult to implement.

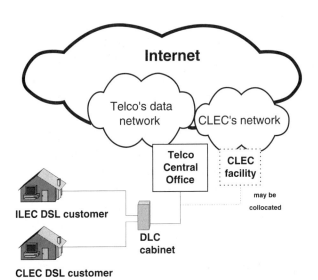

Figure 2.2
DSL with Digital Loop Carrier.

The problem is rather low-tech: DLC equipment is installed in small, curbside metal cabinets. Space inside the cabinets is limited. To provide DSL service over the DLC system, the box must accommodate both the DLC equipment and a small DSLAM. The conventional open-access DSL model requires separate DSLAMs for each ISP, but because of limited space in the roadside cabinets, this is not likely to be an option for subscribers on DLC. If the mini-DSLAMs installed in the cabinets are designed with open access in mind, however, they can be equipped with multiple network interfaces to accommodate multiple ISPs. Data destined for a CLEC could be multiplexed onto the ILEC's data feed, or a new dedicated line could be pulled from the cabinet to the CLEC's facility.

Cable Data Architecture

The options for implementing open access for cable data networks depend on the medium access control standards used in the network. In the United States, the cable industry's Data-Over-Cable System Interface Specification (DOCSIS) is the overwhelmingly dominant standard. An alternative standard for cable modems was in development by the IEEE's 802.14 committee until March, 2000. The 802.14 committee was working on an Asynchronous Transfer Mode (ATM)-like standard that would have afforded a straightforward method of implementing open access. (If subscriber's packets were encapsulated in cells and switched through an ATM network, each subscriber's traffic could be sent directly to a network access point maintained by the appropriate ISP.) The American cable industry felt that the IEEE group was not converging rapidly enough on a standard, so it decided to pursue its own IP-based standard through the DOCSIS forum. The IEEE group withdrew its charter and disbanded because of lack of support by the cable industry.[3]

Cable operators have a variety of options in network architecture. DOCSIS does not dictate the structure of the data network—it is principally a physical and MAC layer specification. Two classes of cable data network architecture have been common: bridged and routed architectures. In a bridged architecture, the entire cable system is connected together via bridges (roughly speaking, dumb routers that broadcast all incoming information on all output interfaces). Simple bridged architectures were more common in the earliest deployments of cable data systems, but their limited scalability has led later system architects to opt for routed architectures. (Bridged systems do not isolate one segment of the network from another. Bridged networks cannot expand beyond a certain size, therefore, and they are more susceptible to disruption by rogue users or defective equipment.) Since a large and increasing share of new upgraded systems being deployed use the routed architecture, this section details the routed network option only.

Figure 2.3 shows a simplified schematic of a routed cable data network. The cable modem in the subscriber's home sends information on the coax to a fiber node serving several hundred to several thousand homes. From the fiber node, a fiber optic cable carries information to the local cable head end. At the head end, a cable modem terminal server (CMTS) demodulates the upstream signals from users and forwards packets to a local router. From the router, the information passes through the cable operator's network and eventually on to the rest of the Internet. Figure

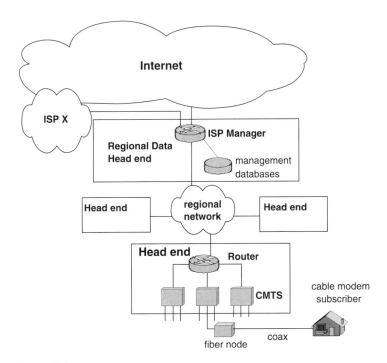

Figure 2.3
A cable broadband architecture.

2.3 illustrates that an alternate service provider, ISP X, connects to the cable operator's ISP Manager.

Conventional routing algorithms are based on assumptions about the character of the traffic passing through the network. Open access policies violate these assumptions. For example, it is normally possible to assume that any packet with a destination address that lies outside the administrative domain of a network should be shown the way to the nearest exit from the network. However, customers of alternate ISPs would possess IP addresses that lie outside of the range administered by the cable company. Thus the normal assumption about how to handle packets with "foreign" destination addresses would no longer be valid. The packet would be expelled from the cable network and directed (according to the usual rules) to the ISP, which would route it back to the cable operator. The loop would continue until the packet's time-to-live field expired, and no traffic would be delivered to the user.

To successfully direct packets to customers of other ISPs located on their networks, cable operators would have to increase the size of their routing tables. The larger routing tables would include entries for individual customers of other ISPs (and *only* those customers of the other ISPs) currently accessing the Internet via the cable operator's network. But keeping track of exactly which customers of other ISPs are located on a cable operator's network would be tedious work. It would require continuous updating of routing tables as computers went on- and off-line and changed their IP numbers. Such an approach would be impractical.

For outgoing packets, open access presents additional problems. In conventional routing schemes, packets are sent on a best path toward destination based solely on the destination address of the packet. Outgoing packets would be routed out of the cable network, regardless of which ISP's customers sent them. If alternate ISP customers are paying for premium handling of outgoing traffic, they will be unhappy that their traffic is being delivered as the cable company chooses. And the cable company might not be happy about forwarding traffic for other ISPs, unless it were being paid to do so.

There are several options for coaxing cable data networks to handle traffic for subscribers of other ISPs properly. The best choice will depend on the capabilities of the routers in the cable operator's data network. One set of options is available if the cable network's routers are capable of *policy routing* (or *policy-based routing*). Under policy routing, routing decisions can be based on any number of criteria, including the packet's source address, the type of data carried by the packet, the time of day, the level of congestion on the network, and so forth. A network that uses policy routing and specially maintained routing tables could accommodate multiple ISPs. Outgoing traffic could be routed based on the source and destination addresses, with packets from customers of other ISPs being routed to the ISPs network; similarly, incoming traffic could be directed to the appropriate subscribers, despite their "foreign" addresses.[4]

A much more manageable solution for implementing open access is *tunneling*. As the name implies, tunneling is an end-to-end operation. Depending on the type of tunneling used, the cable operator may not need to deploy any special equipment in the network. In tunneling, traffic for customers of alternate ISPs is encapsulated inside normal-looking packets and transmitted across the cable network. From the outside of the tunnel, there is nothing peculiar about the behavior of the network. The encapsulating packets are handled according to the usual shortest path, destination-address criteria.

Figure 2.4 shows a schematic of an IP tunnel for carrying traffic to the customer of an alternate ISP over a cable network. Inside the "tunnel," packets to and from the customer are encapsulated in packets with

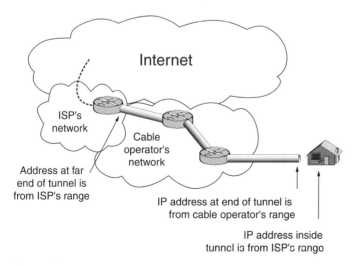

Figure 2.4
IP tunneling.

source and destination addresses of the ISP's gateway and the "outer" IP number of the user's computer. Inside the tunnel—in the encapsulated packet—are the real source and destination addresses and the payload data.

The options for managing tunnels include Generic Routing Encapsulation (GRE), Layer-2 Tunneling Protocol (L2TP), and Multiprotocol Label Switching (MPLS).

Generic Routing Encapsulation (GRE) is a tunneling protocol that can be used to forward a payload packet over an arbitrary delivery protocol. In the case of open access Internet service, both the payload and the delivery protocols are IP and the purpose of the tunneling is to override the standard routing protocols. GRE requires special software in the client machine and in the router at the far end of the tunnel.[5]

Layer-2 Tunneling Protocol provides a point-to-point connection over a public network. L2TP simulates a layer-2 (data link) connection between two points by encapsulating layer-2 data in a tunnel constructed at layer 3, the network level. L2TP requires implementations for the client and end-point router, only. Windows 2000 includes an L2TP implementation.[6]

Multiprotocol Label Switching[7] (MPLS) is a method for, among other things, extending routing functionality on networks. Since MPLS networks switch traffic based on labels rather than IP addresses, an arbitrary routing policy can be implemented in the rules for assigning and reacting to packet labels. For open access applications, the ability of MPLS to specify the handling of packets without regard to their IP destination or source addresses is a great advantage. MPLS would accomplish open access in much the same manner as IEEE 802.14 would have—by switching packets through the network to their destination, without relying solely on IP addresses.

A specially designed IP stack could implement tunneling over conventional IP networks. The special IP stack would effectively tunnel the "real" IP packets inside publicly visible IP packets. This solution is not as attractive as those that do not require replacing the standard IP stacks in client machines.

A Note on Costs

Most of the above methods of implementing open access require at most upgraded CMTS hardware and software upgrades for network infrastructure and client machines. A study of the capital cost of implementing open access by Tseng [2000] found that the incremental capital cost of implementing open access, under conservative assumptions, was no more than about $25 and perhaps less than $5.

Tseng emphasized that her model did not include the operational costs of managing a network with traffic for multiple ISPs. The more difficult aspect of open access will be not in hardware, but in network management. First-generation CMTSs were designed with basic functionality in mind. The marketing literature for next-generation CMTSs, such as those now being offered by RiverDelta, RedBack and Cisco, highlight the ability of the equipment to handle traffic for multiple ISPs. RiverDelta's offering, notably, is reportedly able to allocate bandwidth dynamically on the cable network to groups of customers of various ISPs. RiverDelta's product can also manage traffic by application. Such functionality makes it possible for a cable operator to offer access to other ISPs without sacrificing the ability to manage the amount of bandwidth available to different classes of users and applications.

It should be noted that the advanced traffic management tools incorporated in the next-generation equipment provide exactly the same functionality that cable operators will have to deploy to insure the quality of service on their own networks. As the number of subscribers to cable data service grows, together with the appetite of consumers for bandwidth, cable operators will have to exercise finer-grained control over the traffic of individual users, groups of users, and individual applications. Consequently, it might not be fair to attribute the entire cost of improved network management to open access.

Before moving on to examine ISP service profiles, we note two additional methods suggested for implementing open access: spectrum unbundling and network address translation. Neither of these methods, however, appears to be seriously considered for wide-scale application for open access.

Perhaps the most obvious solution for providing open access over cable networks is to set aside spectrum for each ISP wishing to serve customers on the network. Unfortunately, cable operators have not reserved enough spectrum for data services on their systems to make spectrum unbundling feasible. Spectrum unbundling has become something of a straw-man proposal for opponents of "forced access," since most open access advocates appear to recognize the inefficiencies of spectrum unbundling.

Before we brush off spectrum unbundling, however, we should note that it would be a simple solution for the problem, if only spectrum for data were not in such short supply on cable systems. In the future, when fiber optics push out to the home and ease the spectrum bottleneck, one can imagine optical spectrum or lambda-unbundling for competitive service providers.

Though it is currently impractical, spectrum unbundling has a major advantage over all other open access architectures: it isolates the traffic of each ISP and allows each to manage the traffic of its own customers. The alternatives discussed above all create complicated network management problems for facilities owners and alternate ISPs.

Network Address Translation (NAT) resolves open access addressing dilemmas by using different IP addresses for intra- and inter-network communications. To the outside world, a subscriber has a globally valid IP address belonging to the subscriber's ISP; but inside the local network, the subscriber's machine operates with a locally valid IP address. A gateway at the edge of the cable company's network performs the translation of addresses in IP headers from the globally valid address to the locally valid address and back again. Unlike the tunneling protocols, however, NAT does not work well with recently developed Virtual Private Network (VPN) protocols. Neither does NAT accommodate security schemes that include verification of the source and destination addresses of packets.

Broadband Services: What Does an ISP Do for You?

To be clear about just what is unbundled by broadband open access policies, it helps first to list the key "service profile" that ISPs perform for their customers.[8] The "Internet Service" that an ISP provides is actually a bundle of services. The following enumeration of ISP services may seem very fine-grained, but, as will be clear later, the details highlight the decisions that must be made when Internet access services are divided among facilities-based providers and non-facilities-based providers.

ISP services fall into three general categories: (1) fundamental networking and internetworking, (2) applications, and (3) customer relations.

Fundamental Networking and Internetworking

• *IP Number Assignment.*   All users of the Internet must be assigned an IP address by an ISP or an organization's network administrator. An IP address identifies the user's computer and gives remote systems information necessary to route data to the user's machine. Typically, a consumer would have a unique IP address for a single online session. Users on local area networks may share IP addresses (if they are located behind a firewall or use network address translation), or they may have IP addresses assigned on a long-term basis.

Consumers who connect to the Internet via a connection-oriented scheme, like PPP, are usually assigned an IP address upon establishing a connection. Customers who connect over a bridged or routed LAN typically obtain an IP address via the Dynamic Host Configuration Protocol (DHCP). In either case, the ISP must manage the IP numbers it administers as well as the mechanisms for assigning IP addresses to users.

• *Directory Services.*   The most commonly used directory service is the Domain Name Service (DNS), which translates human-readable (or nearly human-readable) addresses like www.tprc.org into 32-bit binary IP addresses used by computers, like 10001101110100111100101100010101 (the address corresponding to ⟨www.tprc.org⟩). In the future, consumers will require simplified access to directory services required for telephony, conferencing, and other higher-level services marketed by ISPs.

Also, if an ISP customer has registered a domain name, the ISP can perform the procedures necessary for maintaining information about the domain in the DNS hierarchy.

• *Outgoing Packet Routing and Connectivity.*   When a user transmits requests or data to a host computer, the ISP's network must direct the packet to the edge of its network and pass it to another provider that agrees to take traffic destined for the remote location. To forward packets to their destination optimally, the ISP must insure that its routers have up-to-date information about the best path to arbitrary points on the Internet.

An ISP purchases or negotiates for services from other carriers on behalf of its customers. Lower-tier ISPs purchase transit on behalf of their customers from higher-tier ISPs; higher-tier ISPs provide transit, peering, and interconnection services for their customers.

• *Incoming Packet Routing and Connectivity.*   Packets destined for a user from remote sites will be directed to the outside edge of the ISP's network. From there, the ISP is responsible for directing the packet to the user's computer.

• *Access.*   All broadband access companies provide equipment at their end of the connection. They may also provide the customer-premises equipment and the physical connection. Traditional dial-up ISPs and DSL providers using unbundled network elements supply only modem banks at the far end of the connection. Facilities-based providers, such as ILECs, cable companies, and wireless broadband companies, provide the physical medium.

• *Quality of Service and Network Management.* ISPs typically make good-faith though nebulous promises about the quality of service their customers can expect. ISPs monitor the loads on their networks and servers and try to provision additional capacity as their customers' needs grow.

Application Services

Application-level services offered by ISPs include the following:

• *Incoming Mail Services.* Email service is one of the most valued services delivered by an ISP. For individual consumers, incoming email services are typically provided by mail servers running the Post Office Protocol (POP) or the Internet Message Access Protocol (IMAP). For both these protocols, the ISP must maintain a server to store email until customers retrieve it. For business customers, ISPs typically forward mail directly to a mail server maintained by the client, though some companies outsource maintenance of a mail server to their ISP. For both individual consumers and businesses, ISP mail servers must accept connections from outside mail servers and accept traffic addressed to customers of the ISP.

• *Outgoing Mail Services.* To send email, customers of an ISP must be able to connect to outgoing email servers, typically running the Simple Mail Transfer Protocol (SMTP). The ISP's mail servers accept mail from the user's machine, then forward mail to the destination email host.

• *Mail List Services.* ISPs may offer customers mailing list services, including the ability to manage a mailing list.

• *Usenet News.* Most ISPs provide customers with access to news servers connected to Usenet news feeds using the Network News Transfer Protocol (NNTP). In addition to the news feed, the ISP maintains a server from which customers can retrieve recent postings or make postings to Usenet.

• *Caching.* Content caching by ISPs could be considered a fundamental network service, since the decision to stage content closer to users is ultimately an engineering decision. But currently caching is almost exclusively tied to one application: the Web. In the future, other forms of content may be pushed near the edge of the network to hit the optimum mixture of cost and performance. Frequently requested Web content that is cached locally at an ISPs minimizes traffic on the ISPs backbone connection and shortens the response time for web users. If managed properly, caching benefits both the ISP and the user.

• *Web Hosting.*   ISPs may provide Web hosting or virtual Web hosting services for customers.

Customer Relations

Finally, customer-relations-level services offered by ISPs include:

• *Tech Support.*   Customers expect their ISPs to provide help when they experience difficulty accessing online services.

• *Billing and Accounting.*   With the exception of advertiser-supported Internet access, vendors of Internet access monitor and bill for their subscribers' use of resources.

• *Security and Confidentiality.*   Technically, security can be implemented in the network infrastructure or by individual applications. ISPs maintain at least minimal levels of security, to prevent unauthorized users from accessing subscribers' email and hacking users' Web sites. ISPs may offer greater levels of security for customers engaged in e-commerce.

There are nearly countless possibilities for facilities- and non-facilities-based providers to divide the profile of services of interest to the ISP customer. Ultimately, service providers will choose a division of labor based on marketing decisions as well as details of the access network architecture.

Broadband Business Plans: Who does What?

If a cable company opens its network to competing ISPs, the ISP and the cable operator will be entering into a joint relationship with the ISP's customers. The ISP and the cable operator will be responsible for various elements of the service profile offered to subscribers. Exactly which services are to be performed by which party is for the ISP and the cable operator to determine. As illustrated in the following tables, there are dozens of decisions to be made about which company provides what services. (Table cells with more than one option indicate choices for providers and consumers to make.) Some of these decisions may be determined by technical constraints, but most are amenable to business analysis by the two parties, and should be resolved in favor of whoever can provide the most attractive solution.

First, consider the fundamental network and internetworking services (table 2.1). Next, the application services provided to subscribers (table 2.2). Finally, the customer relations services (table 2.3).

The only service listed in the tables that must be performed by the cable operator is basic access. The only services that must be performed by the ISP are the issuance of an IP number (even if done through the cable ops hardware) and incoming mail queueing. There are many opportunities here for the cable operator to appropriate pieces of the value added by alternative ISP. The cable operator could benefit both

Table 2.1
Fundamental networking and internetworking services

Fundamental networking and internet-working services	Who provides service: ISP or cable op?	Comments
IP number assignment	ISP ISP + cable	IP number must be from ISP's pool, but cable operator can issue number on behalf of ISP
Directory services	ISP cable	Either ISP or cable op can provide directory services, but value of managing directories is likely to grow with the variety of network apps.
Outgoing packet routing and connectivity	ISP + cable cable	Either both must manage outgoing routing, or the ISP can outsource outgoing traffic to cable op. Outgoing traffic would then be sent directly out from cable's network
Incoming packet routing and connectivity	ISP + cable	If the subscriber has an IP number from the ISP's pool, remote networks will forward packets to ISP. Both must be involved
Access	cable	Only the cable company manages the physical connection
Quality of service and network management	ISP + cable	Both the ISP and the cable op will be responsible for aspects of QoS

Table 2.2
Application services

Application services	Who provides service: ISP or cable op?	Comments
Incoming mail services	ISP	Mail to the domain of the ISP will be handled by the ISP
Outgoing mail services	ISP cable	Users may use outgoing mail servers of either ISP or cable op, if servers are configured appropriately
Mail list services	ISP third party	The ISP or a third party could offer mailing list services to subscribers
Usenet news	ISP third party	ISP could maintain news servers, or could outsource news services to cable operator or third party
Caching	ISP cable	ISPs could provide access to caches they maintain, or could outsource caching to cable op
Web hosting	ISP third party	ISP or third party could host web sites

Table 2.3
Customer relations

Customer relations	Who provides service: ISP or cable op?	Comments
Tech support	ISP + cable	Both the ISP and the cable op would have to be involved in solving subscribers' problems
Billing and accounting	ISP + cable	ISP would be responsible for billing; ISP and cable op would share responsibility for metering use and charges accrued by subscribers
Security and confidentiality	ISP + cable	Both the ISP and the cable op could expose subscribers to security threats or could divulge private information

politically and financially through these open access arrangements. The cable operator earns points from regulators for opening up its network and earns money from competitive ISPs for performing services on their behalf.

Indeed, one competitive cable operator has announced that it will offer open access in its overbuild systems because open access looks like a money-making proposition. Colorado-based WideOpenWest hopes soon to be awarded franchises for cable systems in Denver and Boulder, Colorado. WideOpenWest will be building new cable plant, so it will not be limited by old cable data equipment.[9] It will be building open access into its systems from the start.

Integrators, SLAs, and Verification

The simple who-does-what tables in the previous section included eight services that could be offered by more than one provider. At a minimum, consumers might have to choose among at least 256 combinations of services and service providers. Such a menu would be daunting to industry experts. It would be even more intimidating to the average Internet user. What can be done to help subscribers decide what choices to make in broadband access? Eli Noam's [1994] suggestion that *integrators* step in to make technically complicated decisions for consumers in highly competitive markets seems to make sense here. Consumers would hire integrators to serve as agents to contract for the best service at the best price and shield the consumer from the messy economic and technical details of how things get done.

In addition to finding the right product mix at the right price, integrators could also provide consumers with tools to assess the quality of the services they are receiving. For example, one of the dangers of concentration in the broadband ISP market cited by open access proponents is that cable operators would preferentially cache content from affiliated content providers. An integrator monitoring the performance its customers get would be in a position to say whether the facility owner was playing games with connectivity.

There is a need here for an honest broker to represent the interests of the consumer. Consumers are, on average, poorly equipped to challenge the service that they receive from their communications providers. It is difficult and costly for consumers to aggregate their modest interests. Cable operators and their content affiliates, on the other hand, have very high incentives to cooperate. Their small number simplifies negotiations.

Moreover, differential caching and routing need not be blatant to be effective in steering consumers to preferred content. The subtle manipulation of the technical performance of the network can condition users unconsciously to avoid certain "slower" web sites. A few extra milliseconds' delay strategically inserted here and there, for example, can effectively shepherd users from one website to another. Given how impatient e-commerce customers are with slow Web sites, it should not take much interference to effect a change in user behavior. The result would be the achievement in practice of a theoretical paradox first formulated by Yogi Berra: "Nobody goes to that site anymore. It's too crowded."

Since the strategic manipulation of network performance need not be flagrant to alter user behavior, it would be unwise to rely on human judgment to determine if some network administrators are favoring some content over other content on a network. Instead, an objective measure of the network performance is necessary. Monitoring the performance of the network would not only indicate if content discrimination is taking place, but it would also alert consumers when the performance of the network is below par. Depending on the specific problem, a monitor might also be able to identify the source of the problem.

Integrators could install monitoring software on customers' machines, measure the performance of the network, and aggregate the data across users to reveal any suspicious patterns. Consumers would not need to know—nor would they be interested in knowing—all the details measured by their integrators' network performance monitors. A simple thumbs-up or thumbs-down would indicate to the average consumer enough information about whether to get angry at the cable company, the ISP, or the kids down the street running Gnutella.

Conclusion

In ruling against the city of Portland's open access requirements, the US 9th Circuit Court of Appeals has decided that "the transmission of Internet service to subscribers over cable broadband facilities is a telecommunications service under the Communication Act."[10]

Maybe cable companies really do see the Internet as just another piece of programming they offer to their subscribers, like a movie or a Bonanza rerun. But it is not the cable company that offers customers the content on the Internet—it is the publishers of the content that make it available. The Internet is just a medium for getting information from one point to another. The 9th Circuit was correct to characterize what cable companies do as a "telecommunications service," though cable companies also provide "information services," like conventional dial-up ISPs. In the Court's opinion:

> To the extent @Home is a conventional ISP, its activities are one of an information service. However, to the extent that @Home provides its subscribers Internet transmission over its cable broadband facility, it is providing a telecommunications service as defined in the Communications Act.[11]

The survey of ISP service profiles in this paper suggests that it may be no easier for the law to separate broadband access telecommunications services from broadband information services, than it is to separate a browser from an operating system.

To sell unbundled broadband access, facilities owners and reseller ISPs must untangle the mix of services that ISPs offer and decide who is responsible for providing which services and at what quality. The mechanisms for managing and insuring the quality of unbundled services, however, are not a high priority in the design of broadband networks. The natural inclination of facilities owners could be to build networks so hostile to open access that it would be prohibitively expensive ever to open them.

What measures can regulators take to encourage facilities owners from foreclosing open access through an engineering fait accompli? The FCC and Congress can continue to breathe over the shoulders of the cable industry. The results thus far have been good for open access, with agreements and testbeds in the works. The FCC could also formulate incentives for cable operators who construct open-access-ready networks. If cable operators build open-access-friendly networks, they may be more willing to let competition have a try on their networks. They might find that building walled gardens around proprietary content is not the best way to expand the broadband access market.

Much of the temptation to exclude other information providers has to do with a fixation on content. The mania for content may be self-defeating, however. Industry players are acting as though content is the only profitable market. Cable operators are jealously guarding their ability to control all forms of content flowing through their networks. Pure DSL players are making deals with content providers to try and increase the value they can present to their subscribers. But carriers and technology companies have tried to move into content before, without much success. One sure way to improve chances in the content market is to exclude the competition from the pipeline, but that may not be a wise long-term corporate strategy. It is certainly not in the public interest.

Besides, what's wrong with being a carrier? It might not be so bad being a carrier in a commodity bandwidth market, so long as the growth in consumption of bandwidth is fast enough. If the price elasticity of demand for bandwidth is significantly greater than one, and if demand grows exponentially, then carrier revenues will grow steadily, despite dropping prices for bandwidth.[12] If that is the case, a wise posture for a broadband access carrier might be to open up the network to any and all content creators, maximize the volume of traffic flowing over the access pipeline, and watch the revenues flow in.

Finally, the numerous possibilities for combining services and service providers suggest that policy makers would benefit from a more complex analysis of broadband market structure. The economic and engineering linkages among the many services that make up broadband must be explored more thoroughly. Conclusions drawn by analyzing service markets in isolation will not resolve the larger policy issues driving the open access debate.

Notes

1. Lathen [1999, 15].

2. In this simplified architecture, we ignore the possibility that multiple ISPs share the same DSLAM. The Internet side of the DSLAM might be on a switched ATM network, which would make it simple to direct data from customers to their respective ISPs.

3. On architectures for cable modem systems, see Maxwell [1999], Abe [2000] Azzam & Ransom [2000], and Robert Russell, chair of 802.14, personal communications.

4. On routing and policy routing, see Huitema [2000].

5. See RFC1702, RFC 2784.

6. See RFC2662 and Shea [2000].

7. See RFC2547 and Davie and Rekhter [2000].

8. I use "service profile" in the sense described by Huston [1999].

9. Backover [2000].

10. AT&T et al. v. City of Portland, U.S. Court of Appeals, 9th Circuit, Appeal No. 99-35609, 6765.

11. Ibid. 6761.

12. See Lanning, O'Donnell and Neuman [2000] for an elaboration of this argument.

References

George Abe. 2000. *Residential Broadband*. 2nd edition. Indianapolis: Cisco Press.

AT&T et al. v. City of Portland, U.S. Court of Appeals, 9th Circuit, Appeal No. 99-35609. ⟨http://www.ce9.uscourts.gov⟩, June 22, 2000.

Albert Azzam and Neil Ransom. 1999. *Broadband Access Technologies*. New York: McGraw Hill.

Andrew Backover. 2000. "WideOpenWest lauds ISP open access." *Denver Post*, August 7. ⟨http://www.denverpost.com/business/biz0807c.htm⟩.

Randy Barrett and Carol Wilson. 2000. "DSL Deathknell," *InteractiveWeek*, March 29. ⟨http://www.zdnet.com/intweek/stories/news/0,4164,2486629,00. html⟩.

Bruce Davie and Yakov Rekhter. *MPLS: Technology and Applications*. San Francisco: Morgan Kaufmann Publishers.

John Fijoleck, Michelle Kuska, et al., eds. 1999. *Cable Modems: Current Technologies and Applications*. Piscataway: IEEE Press.

Geoff Huston. 1999. *ISP Survival Guide: Strategies for Running a Competitive ISP*. New York: John Wiley & Sons.

Christian Huitema. 2000. *Routing in the Internet*. 2nd edition. Upper Saddle River: Prentice Hall PTR.

Michelle Kuska. 1999. "MCNS/DOCSIS Strategy and Execution." in John Fijoleck, Michelle Kuska, et al., eds. *Cable Modems: Current Technologies and Applications*. Piscataway: IEEE Press.

Steven G. Lanning, Shawn O'Donnell, and W. Russell Neuman. 2000. "A Taxonomy of Communications Demand." In Ingo Vogelsang and Benjamin M. Compaine, eds. *The Internet Upheaval: Raising Questions, Seeking Answers in Communications Policy*. Cambridge: MIT Press. ⟨http://itel.mit.edu/itel/ publications.html⟩.

Deborah A. Lathen. 1999. "Broadband Today: A Staff Report to William E. Kennard, Chairman, Federal Communications Commission, On Industry Monitoring Sessions Convened By Cable Services Bureau", October. ⟨http://www.fcc.gov/Bureaus/Cable/Reports/broadbandtoday.pdf⟩.

Kim Maxwell. 1999. *Residential Broadband: An Insider's Guide to the Battle for the Last Mile.* New York: John Wiley & Sons.

Eli Noam. 1994. "Beyond Liberalization." *Telecommunications Policy* 18(4): 286–294.

Richard Shea. 2000. *L2TP: Implementation and Operation.* Reading: Addison-Wesley.

James Speta. 2000. "Handicapping the Race for the Last Mile?: A Critique of Open Access Rules for Broadband Platforms." *Yale Journal on Regulation* 17: 39–91.

Emy Tseng. 2000. "A Capital Cost Model for Open Access Cable Networks." MIT Internet & Telecoms Convergence Consortium report.

Enrique J. Hernandez Valencia. 1999. "Architectures for IP services over CATV Networks." In John Fijoleck, Michelle Kuska, et al., eds. *Cable Modems: Current Technologies and Applications.* Piscataway: IEEE Press.

3

Regulatory Treatment of IP Transport and Services

Joshua L. Mindel and Marvin A. Sirbu

Introduction

Current U.S. regulatory policy is incoherent in its treatment of packet-oriented data communications services. Services based on X.25, Frame Relay or ATM protocols are regulated as telecommunications services, while IP packet transport is lumped together with applications such as email and the World Wide Web—and treated as an unregulated information service. Uncertainty also reigns over the appropriate treatment of IP telephony. As IP transport becomes an ever more significant fraction of all telecommunications, public policy problems posed by this inconsistent treatment are likely to increase.

In this chapter, we undertake a thought experiment in which we consider the consequences that would ensue, under existing legislation, if the Federal Communications Commission were to reclassify IP transport as a telecommunications service, while continuing to treat most applications which run over IP as information services. We do not recommend that such a reclassification be taken, but rather seek to understand the obligations and benefits that such a reclassification might trigger.

We systematically examine the rights and obligations that apply to telecommunications service providers, particularly under Section 251 of the Telecommunications Act, identifying which obligations make sense for IP transport providers, and which might be waived under the Commission's forbearance authority as unnecessary given the intensely competitive nature of the IP transport market. Internet telephony is an application that rides on top of IP transport. We also examine those Section 251 rules that apply specifically to telephony and consider how they might be applied to IP telephony providers.

We conclude the following: (1) Reclassification of IP transport, and telephony services over IP transport, would have immediate benefits for some ISPs; (2) Some Section 251 obligations would be needed only if a dominant provider emerges; and (3) Many obligations could be waived under the Commission's authority to waive unnecessary regulations. We also raise concerns that such a reclassification may trigger new, potentially unnecessary obligations under state laws where Commission forbearance is not an option. Additional analyses, beyond the scope of this research, are needed to evaluate other obligations (e.g. Universal Service Funding) triggered by these potential reclassifications.

Background

Title I of the U.S. Telecommunications Act states its purpose as "regulating interstate and foreign commerce in communication by wire and radio so as to make available ... a rapid, efficient, Nation-wide, and world-wide wire and radio communication service with adequate facilities at reasonable charges...." [1] The legislation goes on to define a variety of activities that are to be subject to the Act, including *telecommunications, telecommunications service*, and *exchange access* as well as categories of companies such as *telecommunications carrier* and *local exchange carrier.*

As with any piece of legislation, the definitions of these terms are crucial, for they determine which firms and which services are to be regulated, and what obligations or prescriptions will be imposed. Since the early 1960s, the U.S. Federal Communications Commission, which enforces the Act, has wrestled with the question of the boundary between telecommunications services—which are to be regulated under the Act—and computer or information services, which fall outside the Act's regulatory jurisdiction.

The origins of the current telecommunications vs. information services boundary can be traced back to the 1956 Consent Decree, in which AT&T agreed to restrict itself to the business of "regulated communications" and, by implication, not to participate in the burgeoning computer industry. The Commission launched its first Computer Inquiry in 1966 to distinguish between regulated communications and computers connecting to telephone lines. The regulatory boundary started to take its current shape with Computer Inquiry II, which defined basic and enhanced services. *Basic service* was defined as a pure transmission service offered by a regulated telecommunications carrier over a communications path that is virtually transparent in terms of its interaction with customer supplied information. *Enhanced service* was defined as a service offered over common carrier transmission facilities that employed computer processing applications that modified the subscriber's transmitted information, or involved subscriber interaction with stored information. The Commission determined that while it held jurisdiction over both basic and enhanced services, it would not serve the public interest to regulate enhanced services since they were competitive.

These concepts were further refined in the Telecommunications Act of 1996, which defines both *telecommunications service* and *information services*. *Telecommunications* is defined in the Act as "the transmission, between or among points specified by the user, of information of the user's choosing, without change in the form or content of the information as sent and received." *Telecommunications service* means "the offering of telecommunications for a fee directly to the public...." In contrast, *information service* is defined as those services that do change the form or content, and that do not affect the management, control, or operation of a telecommunications system or the management of a telecommunications service [2].

On the face of it, *IP transport*—that is, the transport of Internet Protocol packets between points specified by the user and containing information of the user's choosing—would appear to meet the criteria for a *telecommunications service*. However, for historical reasons, the services provided on the Internet (e.g., e-mail, World Wide Web, Netnews) as well as simple IP transport have been classified as *information services* and thus remain outside the scope of telecommunications service regulations.

This result has increasingly been recognized as providing inconsistent treatment for very similar services. Thus, data communications services provided using the X.25, Asynchronous Transfer Mode (ATM), or Frame Relay protocols are classified as telecommunications services, whereas IP transport is not.

Figure 3.1 portrays a variety of services along a continuum, illustrating the boundary between unregulated services and telecommunications services whose providers have specific obligations and benefits.

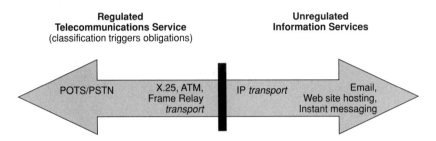

Figure 3.1
Telecommunications vs. information services regulatory boundary.

Communications via circuit-switched communications and via several packet-switched communications technologies (e.g., X.25, ATM, Frame Relay) are categorized as telecommunications services. Communications via IP packet-switched networks are categorized as information services. This inconsistent treatment of packet-switched technologies dilutes or blurs the meaningfulness of the regulatory boundary depicted in figure 3.1.

Over the past three years, the Federal Communications Commission (the *Commission*) has published two Working Papers, one Report to Congress, and numerous Orders and Notices that explicitly discuss these regulatory difficulties [3–6]. A few independently published papers directly address the issue as well [7].

Attention has been focused on this definitional incoherence, as it becomes apparent that IP transport will, over the next decade, become the predominant "service" provided over the nation's telecommunications networks. Data communication, and particularly data sent using IP, is rapidly eclipsing circuit-switched voice traffic in terms of the number of bits carried over telecommunications networks. Firms regulated as telecommunications service providers, or *telecommunications carriers*, carry obligations such as interconnection, non-discrimination, and contributions to the Universal Service Fund (USF). These obligations ensure that related public-policy goals are met. Firms classified as information service providers do not have these obligations. As unregulated IP transport providers displace existing telecommunications carriers, these public policy goals may be threatened.

At the same time, there are many in the Internet industry, Congress, and the Commission who have been very vocal in their insistence that the Internet should not be regulated in the same way as telecommunications carriers. Kende [8] argues that "any traditional telecommunications regulation of Internet backbone interconnection is made unnecessary by a competitive backbone market...." Some fear that government regulation will stifle the innovation and investment that characterize the industry today. Still others observe that government intervention, particularly investment in public goods such as R&D, has been extremely beneficial to the IP transport sector: e.g., ARPAnet,[1] NSFnet,[2] InterNIC,[3] NAPs,[4] and vBNS/Internet2.[5] Oxman [9] presents a summary of Commission rulings that have benefited IP-related services.

Regulation designed for a telecommunications industry characterized by franchise or *de facto* monopolies may not be appropriate for the vigorously competitive Internet industry. Indeed, the earliest regulation of telephony by the Interstate Commerce Commission (ICC) was designed to limit the power of telecommunications monopolies over pricing, interconnection, and entry. As parts of the industry—such as interexchange—became competitive, the Commission continued to closely regulate the behavior of *dominant* carriers. Much of the current regulatory debate is focused on how much to regulate the dominant incumbent local exchange carriers (ILECs) as we move towards competition in the local exchange. By contrast, no single ISP dominates the Internet to the extent that AT&T once dominated telephony.

Objective

Our chapter is motivated by the problem of blurred boundaries and inconsistent regulation of IP transport, as compared to other data communications services. Short of asking Congress to pass new legislation, can the Commission address the problem using the powers already granted to it under the 1996 Telecommunications Act?

One course of action the Commission might take is to redefine IP transport as a telecommunications service. Figure 3.2 portrays the shifted regulatory boundary that would result from this redefinition. Such a reclassification would trigger a range of obligations upon Internet Service Providers (ISPs) from which they have heretofore been exempt. It would also allow ISPs to benefit from the rights to which telecommunications service providers are entitled. As noted above, many of these obligations or restrictions were motivated by concerns over potential abuse of market power by telecommunications carriers. Under Section 10 of the Act [11],

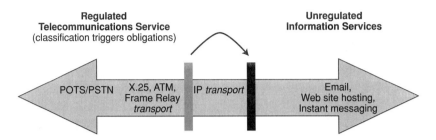

Figure 3.2
Regulatory boundary if IP transport is reclassified as a telecommunications service.

the Commission is authorized to waive many of the regulations required by the Act if a competitive marketplace is sufficient to protect consumers' interests.

Conceptually, therefore, we are interested in examining the following scenario. Suppose that the Commission defines IP transport as a new category of telecommunications service. Further, suppose that the Commission then chooses to use its forbearance authority to forbear from any unnecessary regulation that would be triggered by such a reclassification. What would be the implications of such a scenario? In particular, what would be the implications of such an action with respect to the issues of *interconnection* among IP transport providers and on *unbundling* of telecommunications services? Other rules triggered by the reclassification of IP transport, such as USF obligations, are beyond the scope of this paper.

Outline and Approach

The *IP Transport and Section 251* section of this paper contains the results of an analysis of how Section 251 (Interconnection) of the Act could be applied to IP transport. The *Telephony over IP Transport* section contains the results of a similar analysis that looked at IP telephony over IP transport. The interconnection rules that apply to all telecommunications carriers are of most interest. The unbundling rules for LECs, ILECs, and the Bell Operating Companies (BOCs) are based on limiting their exercise of monopoly power. These are less relevant to IP transport providers where there are no comparable dominant providers. LECs themselves can be viewed as the creation of an earlier unbundling decision.[6]

Table 3.1
Analysis templates

Phase 1	Why is this a policy concern for telecommunications carriers?
	How is this concern handled by telecommunications carriers?
Phase 2	What is the equivalent concern for IP transport providers?
	How is the equivalent concern handled by IP transport providers?
Phase 3	Under what circumstances might an obligation be mandated?
	What policies and actions might be useful for IP transport providers?

The analyses are technical, qualitative, and systematically applied to each of the interconnection and unbundling rules for telecommunications carriers. The first step is to clarify the underlying policy concern and review how this concern is addressed for telecommunications carriers. The next phase identifies the equivalent policy concern that exists for the provision of IP transport services, and reviews how this concern is currently handled by IP transport providers. The third phase is a thought experiment in which realistic situations are identified under which specific obligations might be mandated, or where the Commission should prefer to forbear. Table 3.1 shows the template used for the analysis.

Three tenets support this analysis: (1) IP transport services are distinct from applications that use IP transport services; (2) Interconnection and unbundling are motivated by different underlying economic forces and policy goals; and (3) History provides insight. Interconnection requirements are motivated by a desire to maximize positive network externalities, whereas unbundling requirements exist to restrict dominant firms from exercising market power through bundling.

The interconnection and unbundling rules in the amended Communications Act of 1934 (the *Act*) are organized into four hierarchically related sets, plus one additional rule set for the Commission itself. The first rule set applies to all telecommunications carriers. The first two rule sets apply to all LECs. The first three rule sets apply to all incumbent LECs. Finally, the first four rule sets apply to the BOCs. All of the rule sets are referred to as interconnection rules in the Act, though only the first and last sets are actually interconnection rules. The other rule sets focus on LEC unbundling. Table 3.2 lists the specific data sources in the Act.

Table 3.2
Analysis data sources

Section 251 (a)	Interconnection rules for all telecommunications carriers
Section 251 (b)	Unbundling rules for all local exchange carriers
Section 251 (c)	Unbundling rules for all incumbent local exchange carriers
Section 271 (c) (2)	Unbundling rules for all Bell Operating Companies
Section 251 (e)	Numbering administration authority and funding

IP Transport and Section 251

Only a few of the Act's requirements for interconnection among carriers have a reasonable interpretation when applied to IP transport providers. Where they do not, these requirements should be waived using the Commission's authority to forbear from regulation. Table 3.2 above identifies the sections in the Act that contain the interconnection and unbundling requirements. We discuss below several issues that deserve detailed consideration.

Interconnect with Facilities of Other Carriers

Each telecommunications carrier has the duty to interconnect directly or indirectly with the facilities ... of other telecommunications carriers. [13]

The duty to interconnect ensures that users can benefit from the positive externalities derived from a large interconnected pool of users. In the PSTN, LECs interconnect directly with IXCs via points-of-presence (POPs). Competitive Access Providers (CAPs) or Competitive Local Exchange Carriers (CLECs) may bypass a LEC and directly connect to an IXC, or may directly connect to an LEC at tandem switches or end offices. Through this web of connections, all PSTN carriers are interconnected either directly or indirectly.

Functionally, to interconnect in the PSTN implies both an exchange of content (voice, data, or fax) and an exchange of signaling information for call setup and takedown. This is made possible by a 64 Kbps digital circuit-switched network to carry voice/data/fax, and a separate packet-switched network to carry signaling information for call setup and routing.

In addition to the PSTN, there is a group of data services classified by the Commission as telecommunications services that appear subject to these interconnection obligations: X.25, ATM, and Frame Relay. Interestingly, though, the Commission has not explicitly addressed this requirement, despite the current paucity of Frame Relay and ATM network interconnection. While the Commission could address the lack of interconnection *sua sponte*, it generally prefers to wait until it receives a complaint or a petition for rulemaking. Despite the lack of interconnection, no such complaint has surfaced.

The policy concern for IP transport providers is essentially the same, except the network externalities are derived from the interconnection of both users and resources (e.g. online content). IP transport services interconnect via public (multilateral) and private (typically bilateral) traffic exchange points. Public traffic exchanges take place via NAPs, Metropolitan Area Exchanges (MAEs), and commercial Internet exchanges (CIX). To illustrate IP transport network interconnections, figure 3.3 depicts the multiple networks that might be traversed when a user browses a remote web site.

At the present time, all IP transport providers partake in interconnection agreements on a voluntary basis. For best-effort service networks, the interconnection arrangements are for peering or transit. Peering is an arrangement in which both service providers agree to: (1) Accept all traffic from the other; (2) Only forward traffic destined for the receiving network, or for downstream customers of that network; and (3) Exchange traffic without settlements.

In lieu of peering, a hierarchical arrangement called transit is available in which an upstream IP provider: (1) Accepts all traffic from the downstream provider, and agrees to forward it to its destination, whether or not that destination is on its network; and (2) Receives payment from the downstream provider. Technologically, peering and transit policies are implemented in the form of configuration information for the Border Gateway Protocol (BGP-4). BGP-4 is used to exchange routing information among ISPs [14].

Larger providers have incentives to withhold peering below certain thresholds of connectivity (e.g., multiple Network Access Points (NAPs), minimum traffic loads), and instead offer transit. Milgrom et al. [15] and

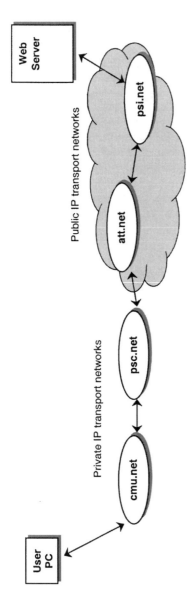

Figure 3.3
IP transport network interconnection.

others [16–18] discuss these incentives both quantitatively and qualitatively. The multiple-NAP requirement can be viewed as an *unbundling* of the smaller IP transport provider's network to help the larger network reduce free-riding by the smaller network. Smaller providers argue that larger providers discriminate by offering peering to some providers and not to others. The Commission has issued a Notice of Inquiry (NOI) that, among other issues, asks whether there was a perceived need for Commission regulation of peering [6].[7]

Within a few years, peering vs. transit issues will likely be overshadowed by the Service Level Agreements (SLAs) that will be required to interconnect QoS-capable networks [17]. An SLA will include a characterization of the treatment that the customer's traffic will be afforded (e.g., throughput, latency, packet loss rate), any traffic conditioning rules that must be adhered to by the customer in order to receive the specified treatment, measurement methods to verify compliance, and the price to be paid for the contracted level of service. SLAs will be negotiated by end users with ISPs, and by ISPs with each other in order to recursively provide end-to-end QoS for the end user's traffic as it crosses multiple ISPs.

The Internet Engineering Task Force and the Internet2 QBone Working Group are developing the DiffServ QoS architecture [19, 20]. The technologies are not yet mature enough for commercial deployment. With DiffServ, a bandwidth broker (BB) is an infrastructure component that coordinates provision of QoS IP transport service requests. User requests are sent to the BB and then to the appropriate router. BBs keep track of the current allocation of marked traffic and interpret new requests in light of policies (e.g., priorities) and current allocations. BBs will coordinate the setup and maintenance of bilateral service agreements for provision of QoS IP transport services across multiple providers.[8] Standardized information models are also being defined to ensure that policies and service definitions can be interpreted consistently across multiple provider networks [22, 23]. These standards are required to enable a subscriber to request an end-to-end QoS service that may (knowingly or unknowingly to the subscriber) be delivered via multiple providers' networks.

Policy Implications

To date, interconnection among IP transport providers has occurred entirely through voluntary agreements. The incentives for IP transport providers to cooperate and/or compete are far more complex, however, than they were in earlier phases of the Internet when fewer IP transport providers existed and user demand was weaker. There have been some complaints by smaller carriers that have been forced to purchase transit when they desired settlement-free peering.

In the absence of a single dominant ISP, all players have an economic incentive to interconnect in order to realize network externalities. To ensure that even dominant ISPs will voluntarily interconnect, the Commission could adopt a number of policies that are far short of the mandated pricing or Commission-as-arbitrator that characterizes regulation of interconnection among existing telecommunications carriers. For example, the Commission could:

• Require that ISPs establish publicly posted criteria for when another ISP is entitled to peering versus transit.[9]
• Require public disclosure of interconnection agreements.
• Require ISPs to offer other ISPs the same SLAs that they offer to end user customers. This is equivalent to allowing an ISP customer to resell the services implied by an SLA. In addition, an ISP may offer additional services to other ISPs that it does not offer to end user customers.
• Establish default technical standards if voluntary industry consensus processes are unable to reach agreement on interconnection standards.[10]

Resale

The duty not to prohibit, and not to impose unreasonable or discriminatory conditions or limitations on, the resale of its telecommunications services. [24]

The duty to provide *resale* is imposed on all *local exchange carriers*. A LEC is a carrier that provides *telephone exchange service* or *exchange access* service. The former, in turn, is defined as:

1. Service within a telephone exchange, or within a connected system of telephone exchanges within the same exchange area, operated to furnish to subscribers intercommunicating service of the character ordinarily furnished by a single exchange, and which is covered by the exchange service charge; or
2. Comparable service provided through a system of switches, transmission equipment, or other facilities (or combination thereof) by which a subscriber can originate and terminate a telecommunications service [2].

If IP transport is classified as a telecommunications service, then, within an exchange area, an ISP would appear to satisfy part 2 of the definition of an LEC. Such an IP transport provider would be subject to the requirements of Section 251b of the Act, which includes, among others, a requirement to allow other carriers to resell its services.

The Commission first began to mandate resale of telecommunications services in 1976 when it approved the application of Telenet Corporation to resell leased line service by the packet. AT&T had originally banned resale because it undermined flat-rate residential service. In the mid-'90s some ISPs attempted to ban resale for the same reason, but were forced to relent due to competition. More recently, cable modem service providers, such as Comcast, have banned resale as part of their tariffs.[11]

Mandatory resale has been viewed by regulators as a means to reduce opportunities for price discrimination by a dominant carrier by encouraging resale arbitrage of its services. It also provides competing carriers another avenue to achieve network ubiquity short of all new construction.

Reclassification of IP transport as a telecommunications service would require Internet local access providers, e.g., Comcast, to permit resale of their services by competing ISPs.

The response of AT&T to mandatory resale was to shift from flat-rate pricing schemes such as its WATS long-distance tariff to metered usage pricing. A similar response could be expected from IP access providers, through either packet counting (e.g., burstable service) or the introduction of multiple tiers of service offering different throughput levels.

Alternatively, the Commission could choose to waive this requirement on the grounds that, given the intense competition among Internet local access providers, price discrimination is not possible in the first place, so mandatory resale is unnecessary to discipline prices.

Reciprocal Compensation

The duty to establish reciprocal compensation arrangements for the transport and termination of telecommunications. [24]

ISPs that qualify as LECs would be obliged under this clause to provide reciprocal compensation when exchanging traffic with other ISPs at a local NAP. This would require detailed traffic accounting, which is not typically done today. It would also make it impossible for a local ISP to buy transit from a backbone ISP that was also a local competitor. Given the history in the Internet of interconnection without detailed accounting, it would make sense for the Commission to waive the reciprocal compensation obligation.

Numbering Administration

The Commission shall create or designate one or more impartial entities to administer telecommunications numbering. [25]

Numbering administration ensures that a consistent and nondiscriminatory method of telecommunications numbering is used that makes possible unique and routable telecommunications. The Act provides the Commission with responsibility for supervising numbering administration for telecommunications services [25]. In POTS, historically, there has been a single number (or name or address) space of the format xxx-yyy-zzzz.[12] In IP transport, there are three name spaces: domain names, IP addresses, and hardware addresses. Names and addresses are abstractions used to identify entities. As depicted in figure 3.4, names imply a higher level of abstraction than addresses.

The Act gives the Commission authority to designate an administrator of telecommunications numbers. For POTS, it is the North American Numbering Plan administrator. Currently, the highly controversial, private, non-profit Internet Corporation for Assigned Names and Numbers (ICANN) manages domain names and IP addresses along with the American Registry of Internet Numbers (ARIN) which assigns IP addresses. If IP transport is reclassified as a telecommunication service, ARIN, and perhaps ICANN, will come under the purview of the Commission.

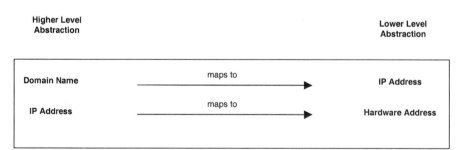

Figure 3.4
Hierarchical mappings between name spaces.

Number Portability

The term *number portability* means the ability of users of telecommunications services to retain, at the same location, existing telecommunications numbers without impairment of quality, reliability, or convenience when switching from one telecommunications carrier to another. [2]

Historically, telephone numbers have corresponded directly to a physical line card in a telephone switch at a LEC CO. There was a single name space. Number portability is achieved by establishing a new name space of logical telephone numbers and mapping each of them to a physical line card address space.[13] Separation of the physical line card number from a logical number is a form of unbundling. This unbundling makes it "less expensive and less disruptive for a customer to switch providers, thus freeing the customer to choose the local provider that offers the best value." [26] A user can change carrier and thus physical number while advertising the same logical phone number. Switching costs are primarily due to advertising to other telephone and fax users that a telephone number has changed.

A lack of number portability for IP transport networks also raises switching costs. As with the PSTN, higher-level names are more stable than lower-level names. Email addresses and web page links typically use domain names to refer to host computers. IP network nodes use IP addresses to communicate in an IP transport network. If a host's IP address changes, the mapping between the domain name and IP address is changed. Whether an IP address is defined dynamically or statically depends on the type of network node and how it is configured.

Since the early 1990s, when the number of Internet hosts and networks began to grow at a rapid rate, the Internet has implemented a hierarchical IP address space that reflects the overall Internet topology [27]. The hierarchy permits route aggregation (via Classless InterDomain Routing–CIDR) that limits the growth rate of the number of routes that are maintained in the routing tables of the core backbone networks [28].[14] The hierarchy also creates a dependency between upstream providers that allocate IP address blocks and downstream customers that use the IP address blocks.[15] This addressing scheme does not permit number portability for all IP transport providers because the IP address block is not portable. Service providers at the top of the IP address space hierarchy have portable IP address blocks.

When a downstream provider switches upstream providers, it incurs the switching cost of renumbering its IP addressable devices. These switching costs can constitute a *barrier to entry* for potential upstream providers [30]. These costs take the form of increased operational and coordination costs, rather than the advertising costs associated with a lack of number portability in the PSTN. A downstream provider will need to renumber its own equipment (e.g., routers, DNS servers), as well as coordinate with its downstream customers to renumber their equipment as well. Automated configuration protocols, such as the Dynamic Host Configuration Protocol (DHCP) in IPv4, and the auto configuration and neighbor discovery protocols in IPv6 reduce switching costs.

Figure 3.5 depicts an example of the renumbering that a customer will need to undergo when switching from one upstream provider to another.[16] In both cases the customer has an address block of 2048 IP addresses; with provider A they range from 190.10.80.0 to 190.10.87.255, and with provider B they range from 175.25.96.0 to 175.25.103.255. If a downstream customer is an end user that uses the domain name provided by the upstream provider, then switching costs include advertising as well. However, this is not a public-policy concern since portable domain names are easily available.

If IP transport is classified as a telecommunications service, the obligation for number portability will apply to IP transport providers. If this requirement is seen to apply to domain names, rather than to IP addresses, there is little difficulty in preserving a domain name while switching ISPs. A requirement that all *IP addresses* be portable would have a significant negative impact on ISP routing costs and is not currently in the public interest. One of the few actions the Commission could take would be to promote or mandate the rapid adoption of IPv6 to reduce (though not eliminate) switching costs.

Access to Rights-of-Way

The duty to afford access to the poles, ducts, conduits, and rights-of-way of such carrier to competing providers of telecommunications services on … terms … that are consistent with section 224. [24]

The term *pole attachment* means any attachment by a cable television system or provider of telecommunications service to a pole, duct, conduit, or right-of-way owned or controlled by a utility. [31]

a) Before switching providers

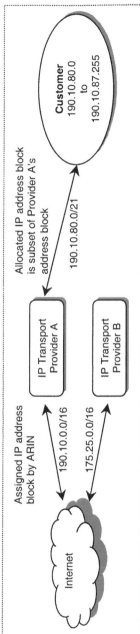

b) After switching providers

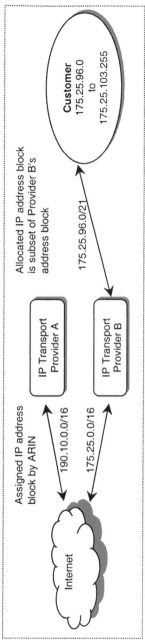

Figure 3.5
Example of renumbering caused by switching providers.

The term *utility* means any person who is a local exchange carrier or an electric, gas, water, steam, or other public utility, and who owns or controls poles, ducts, conduits, or rights-of-way used ... for any wire communications. Such term does not include any railroad. [31]

The unbundling of rights-of-way reduces the barriers to entry that competitors face in deploying transmission equipment for the provision of telecommunications services. By contrast, IP transport providers are not afforded the same nondiscriminatory access to rights-of-way.

Metricom, for example, is widely deploying small radios to provide wireless Internet access service. In a recent filing to the Commission, Metricom stated that some of the obstacles it faces in negotiating agreements with public utility companies (that own streetlights and power distribution poles located in the public right-of-way) exist because of its limited rights as an information service provider [32].

The simple act of reclassifying IP transport as a telecommunications service would solve Metricom's problem; as a telecommunications service provider it would automatically be entitled to benefit from the pole attachment and related provisions of the Act.

Telephony over IP Transport

Historically, the telecommunications industry grew up tightly coupled with telephone exchange services. Legislation for the telecommunications industry defined telecommunications in terms of the technology used to provide the services; e.g., telephone exchange service, call routing, etc. As computer communications grew in the 1960s, the associated legislation became more general, referring to telecommunications services, rather than to telephone services. In some places, the Communications Act refers to specific services and in others it doesn't. For example, as noted above, the definition of *telephone exchange service* starts out referring to *telephone service*, but as subsequently modified refers more generally to any *telecommunications service*. As a whole, the Communications Act has only partially graduated from the language of the telephone industry to the language of the telecommunications industry.

Today, we have IP telephony and multimedia calls that share some of the same characteristics as telephone exchange service (from a user's perspective), yet bear little resemblance from technological infrastructure or industrial organization perspectives. When services specifically identified in the Act, such as telephony, are provided over an IP transport provider's network, how should these services be treated from a regulatory perspective? Defining IP transport as a telecommunications service says nothing about the end-to-end services that might run over such a transport capability (see figure 3.6).

For example, Dialink corporation, using software and CPE from Netergy Networks, proposes to offer local exchange telephone service over any broadband local IP transport provider's network.[17] Voice packets will go directly from CPE to CPE over the IP transport infrastructure, while call setup is handled by communication between the CPE and a server managed by Dialink and running at the Exodus web hosting site. In this example, depicted in figure 3.7, who is providing the exchange? Is it the IP transport provider whose application-neutral transport enables CPE to communicate? Or is it Dialink that is providing crucial call setup functionality, but neither transmission nor switching?

It is useful to examine some of the rules designed to foster interconnection between incumbent LECs and emerging competitors, and explore what would be the equivalent when Voice-over IP (VoIP) is provided as described above.

Access to Directory Information

The duty to provide ... competing providers ... nondiscriminatory access to telephone numbers, ... directory assistance, and directory listing, with no unreasonable dialing delays. [24, 33]

White pages directory listings for customers of the other carrier's telephone exchange service. [33]

The unbundling of directory information reduces the barrier to entry that a competitor faces. Equivalent policy concerns will be raised for IP telephony when these services become viable substitutes (and competitors) for POTS.

IP transport applications use an Internet-wide, hierarchical, and distributed directory called the Domain Name System (DNS) to map between domain names and IP addresses. The draft ENUM standard, which will provide mappings between the ITU E.164 telephone numbers used in POTs and the IP-address-based telephony numbers, proposes a DNS-based architecture [34].

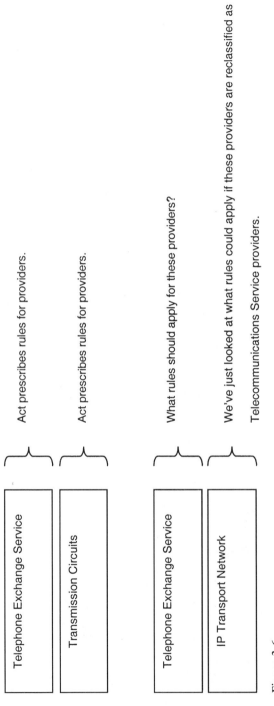

Figure 3.6
Telephone exchange service over multiple infrastructures.

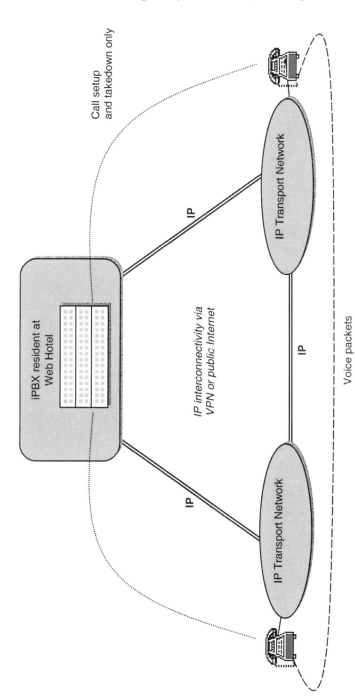

Figure 3.7
Who is providing telephone exchange service?

IP telephony providers will also need to be able to have their subscribers listed with Directory Assistance and appear in the White Pages.

Access to Signaling for Call Routing and Completion

Nondiscriminatory access to databases and associated signaling necessary for call routing and completion. [33]

The unbundling of call signaling in the PSTN is important to enable competitors to deploy telephony services without having to deploy the full cost of a redundant, out-of-band signaling system called Signaling System 7 (SS7)/Advanced Intelligent Network (AIN) [26]. Based on historical precedent, attention must be paid to which signaling elements are unbundled to ensure that competitors have access to all elements necessary for "peer" interconnection, rather than the more limited access afforded to customers that do not resell service.[18] The availability of unbundled signaling may influence the deployment of IP telephony services. Figure 3.8 depicts an example of unbundled signaling. A related issue with public policy overtones is the extent to which end users can manage and control telephony signaling [36, 37].

VoIP clearinghouses are emerging that lower the barriers to entry for IP telephony providers by enabling them to originate calls and hand them off to the clearinghouse for termination, as well as to receive calls to terminate from the clearinghouse [29].

Access to 911 and E911 Services

Nondiscriminatory access to 911 and E911 services. [33]

The unbundling of emergency services reduces the cost of providing a competing service. In the PSTN, the implementation of a 911 service requires that a mapping be available between the calling party's telephone number and a physical location (e.g., street address). Cellular PCS uses either a network-based solution (e.g., triangulation) or a handset-based solution (e.g., Global Positioning System (GPS)) to provide the E911/911 service center with the latitude and longitude of the caller's location. There will be an equivalent policy concern for IP telephony when it is considered a substitute for POTS. Implementation of a 911 service for IP telephony will require a mapping between the IP address of the device placing the call and the user's registered location. For mobile IP telephony, this implies a mapping that is frequently updated.

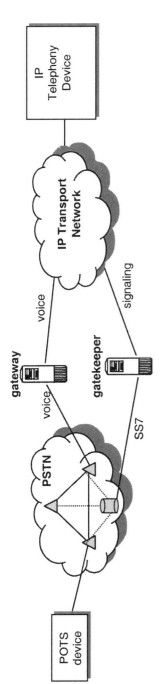

Figure 3.8
PSTN ↔ IP telephony signaling components.

Today, only certificated LECs are entitled/obliged to participate in E911 systems. In the future, it must be possible for ASPs like Dialink to participate as well. It does not appear to make sense to require Dialink to seek certification as an LEC. The Commission might also want to mandate that E911 centers be able to receive VoIP calls as IP without first going through a gateway to convert them to traditional circuit-switched calls. The Commission might also want to promote standards development for interconnecting IP telephone services to the E911 database.

Conclusions

At the beginning of this paper, we asked what would happen if IP transport was classified as a telecommunications service. We've looked at interconnection and unbundling obligations that might be applicable. We recall that the Commission has authority under Section 10 of the Act to waive unnecessary obligations. So, in looking at the policy implications of reclassifying IP transport as a telecommunications service, we looked at what benefits were realized and where the Commission would best waive requirements that are unnecessary.

We found that in the absence of a dominant IP transport provider with market power, many of the obligations and duties levied on traditional carriers could be waived for IP transport providers. In other cases, we found that mere reclassification of IP transport as a telecommunications service solved problems being experienced by some ISPs, such as access to right-of-way.

We should note that there are a number of significant reasons why the Commission might hesitate to pursue the scenario examined in this paper. Among other obligations that would be triggered by reclassifying IP transport as a telecommunications service, there are extensive reporting requirements, not all of which the Commission has the authority to waive.

Second, while Section 10 of the Act forbids State Commissions from enforcing any provisions of the Act from which the Commission has decided to forbear, the Act does not preclude State Commissions from applying their own provisions to telecommunications services. This implies that reclassifying IP transport services as telecommunications sevices exposes IP transport providers to state obligations unless state or new federal legislation allows these to be pre-empted [38].

Third, it is possible that a heightened concern for regulation will limit investment in the Internet and future innovation in services.

Finally, there is concern that, given the rapid rate of technological change, it will be impossible for the Commission to ensure that it has or maintains the correct degree of regulation and/or forbearance.

This analysis serves as a starting point for redefining the telecommunications vs. information services boundary. A case can be made for reclassifying IP transport as a new subcategory of telecommunications service while waiving unnecessary interconnection and unbundling obligations that would otherwise be triggered. Many obligations could be waived as unnecessary, given the competitive nature of the ISP industry. Additional analyses, beyond the scope of this paper, need to evaluate other obligations triggered by the reclassification of IP transport.

Notes

1. Advanced Research Projects Agency (ARPA) sent out the first Request for Proposals for ARPAnet in 1965, and ARPAnet was commissioned by the Department of Defense for research on networking in 1969 [9].

2. National Science Foundation (NSF) funded establishment of NSFnet in 1986 to provide universities with high-speed network connections [9].

3. NSF created InterNIC to provide directory and database services (via contract awarded to AT&T), registration services (via contract awarded to Network Solutions, Inc.), and information services (via CERFnet contract to General Atomics) [9].

4. Originally, four NAPs were created (in New York, Washington, D.C., Chicago, and San Francisco) and supported by NSF as part of the transition from the original U.S. government-financed Internet to a commercially operated Internet.

5. The very high performance Backbone Network Service (vBNS) and Internet2 are NSF-funded research networks that were initiated subsequent to the decommissioning of the original NSFnet in 1995.

6. In 1970, the Commission approved MCI's application to offer long-distance services as a common carrier. This required that AT&T's local exchange services be accessible to MCI's long-distance service so that callers (that connected to long distance services via local exchange services) could originate and terminate calls [12].

7. To date, the Commission has issued no rulings on this matter.

8. The Common Open Policy Service (COPS) protocol is one of several protocols that may be used for BB-to-BB communication [21].

9. Such a requirement was imposed on Worldcom as a condition for the Department of Justice's approval of its merger with MCI.

10. Cf. Section 256 of the Act.

11. See Comcast-@Home terms of service at ⟨http://www.comcastonline.com/ subscriber-v3-red.asp⟩.

12. As discussed in the following section, the requirement for number portability has created a second name space.

13. A system of regional number portability databases are to be managed by independent local number portability administrators. The costs of establishing number portability are to be borne by all telecommunications carriers [1].

14. Routes are aggregated to combine the characteristics of several routes so that a single route can be advertised, thereby reducing the number of routes that need to be maintained by core providers employing default-route-free routing tables. In October 1999, there were an estimated 70,000 routes in these routing tables, a fourfold increase over 1994 [29].

15. The American Registry for Internet Numbering (ARIN) has the authority to assign or allocate portable IP addresses, but increasingly relies upon large and established IP service providers to allocate hierarchical subsets of their IP address block to their downstream customers. The rationale for this policy is that more portable IP addresses cannot be aggregated and thus contribute to route growth. Prior to the early 1990s, ARIN assigned IP address blocks to organizations that requested them. Many of the large and established IP service providers were assigned IP address blocks during the reign of this policy. Under some circumstances, providers receive provider-independent (portable) addresses from ARIN.

16. 190.10.0.0/16 is the IPv4/CIDR address block advertised by the exterior gateway for Provider A. The "/16" implies that the first 16 bits of the 32-bit address correspond to the network portion of the address. Provider A allocates the 190.10.80.0/21 address block to the customer, providing the customer with 2^{11} or 2048 addresses; 32 bits minus 21 bits for the network portion leaves 11 bits for customer use.

17. ⟨http://www.netergynet.com/News-events/pr-archive/pr20000327a.html⟩.

18. In the 1980s, several Bell companies refused to provide unaffiliated wireless carriers with Type-2 interconnection. They were offered Type 1, which was more limited in terms of transmission quality, permissible billing arrangements, and efficient use of switching facilities [35].

References

[1] Congress, "Communications Act of 1934," 104th Congress of the United States, Washington, D.C., 1996.

[2] Congress, "Definitions," in Communications Act of 1934. Washington, D.C.: 104th Congress of the United States, 1996, Sec. 3.

[3] B. Esbin, "Internet over Cable: Defining the Future in Terms of the Past," Office of Plans & Policy, Federal Communications Commission, OPP Working Paper Series No. 30, August, 1998.

[4] K. Werbach, "Digital Tornado: The Internet and Telecommunications Policy," Office of Plans & Policy, Federal Communications Commission, Washington, D.C., OPP Working Paper Series No. 29, March, 1997.

[5] FCC, "In the Matter of Federal–State Joint Board on Universal Service, CC Docket No. 96-45, Report to Congress," Federal Communications Commission, Washington, D.C., FCC 98-67, April 10, 1998.

[6] FCC, "In the Matter of Inquiry Concerning the Deployment of Advanced Telecommunications Capability to All Americans in a Reasonable and Timely Fashion, and Possible Steps to Accelerate Such Deployment Pursuant to Section 706 of the Telecommunications Act of 1996, CC Docket No. 98-146, Notice of Inquiry," Federal Communications Commission, Washington, D.C., FCC 98-187, August 6, 1998.

[7] J. Weinberg, "The Internet and 'Telecommunications Services,' Access Charges, Universal Service Mechanisms and Other flotsam of the Regulatory System," presented at Telecommunications Policy Research Conference, Washington, D.C., 1998.

[8] M. Kende, "The Digital Handshake: Connecting Internet Backbones," Office of Plans & Policy, Federal Communications Commission, OPP Working Paper Series No. 32, September, 2000.

[9] R. Zakon, "Hobbes' Internet Timeline v5.0," ⟨http://www.isoc.org/zakon/Internet/History/HIT.html⟩, last accessed: December, 1999.

[10] J. Oxman, "The FCC and Unregulation of the Internet," Office of Plans & Policy, Federal Communications Commission, OPP Working Paper Series No. 31, July, 1999.

[11] Congress, "Competition in Provision of Telecommunications Service," in Communications Act of 1934. Washington, D.C.: 104th Congress of the United States, 1996, Sec 10.

[12] P. Huber, M. K. Kellogg, J. Thorne, and A. C. Schlick, "Long Distance Services," in Federal Telecommunications Law, 2nd ed. New York: Aspen Law and Business, 1999, pp. 739–740.

[13] Congress, "Interconnection: General Duty of Telecommunications Carriers," in Communications Act of 1934. Washington, D.C.: 104th Congress of the United States, 1996, Sec. 251(a).

[14] Y. Rekhter and P. Gross, "Application of the Border Gateway Protocol in the Internet," T.J. Research Center, IBM Corp., MCI, IETF RFC 1772, March, 1995.

[15] P. Milgrom, B. Mitchell, and P. Srinagesh, "Competitive Effects of Internet Peering Policies," presented at Telecommunications Policy Research Conference, Arlington, Virginia, 1999.

[16] S. Paltridge, "Internet Infrastructure Indicators," Working Party on Telecommunication and Information Service Policies, Directorate for Science, Technology, and Industry, Organisation for Economic Co-operation and Development (OECD), Paris, DSTI/ICCP/TISP(98)7/FINAL, October 28, 1998.

[17] G. C. Staple, "A Primer on Peering," in *TeleGeography 1999: Global Telecommunications Traffic Statistics and Commentary.* Washington, D.C.: TeleGeography, Inc., 1998, 128.

[18] R. Frieden, "When Internet Peers Become Customers: The Consequences of Settlement-based Interconnection," presented at Telecommunications Policy Research Conference, Arlington, VA, 1999.

[19] S. Blake, D. Black, M. Carlson, E. Davies, Z. Wang, and W. Weiss, "An Architecture for Differentiated Services," Network Working Group, Internet Engineering Task Force, Request for Comments (RFC) 2475, December, 1998.

[20] B. Teitelbaum, "QBone Architecture (v1.0)," Internet2 QoS Working Group, August, 1999.

[21] QoSForum, "Frequently Asked Questions about IP Quality of Service," Stardust Forums, Inc., ⟨http://www.qosforum.com/docs/faq/⟩, last accessed: December, 1999.

[22] E. Ellesson and J. Strassner, "Policy Framework Working Group," ⟨http://www.ietf.org/html.charters/policy-charter.html⟩, last accessed: December, 1999.

[23] DMTF, "Directory Enabled Network (DEN) FAQ," Distributed Management Task Force, Inc., ⟨http://www.dmtf.org/pres/rele/denfaq.html⟩, last accessed: December, 1999.

[24] Congress, "Interconnection: Obligations of All Local Exchange Carriers," in Communications Act of 1934. Washington, D.C.: 104th Congress of the United States, 1996, Sec. 251(b).

[25] Congress, "Numbering Administration," in Communications Act of 1934. Washington, D.C.: 104th Congress of the United States, 1996, Sec. 251(e).

[26] FCC, "In the Matter of Local Competition Provisions in the Telecommunications Act of 1996, CC Docket No. 96-98; Interconnection between Local Exchange Carriers and Commercial Mobile Radio Service Providers, CC Docket No. 95-185, First Report and Order," Federal Communications Commission, Washington, D.C., FCC 96-325, August 8, 1996.

[27] V. Fuller, T. Li, J. Yu, and K. Varadhan, "Classless Inter-Domain Routing (CIDR): An Address Assignment and Aggregation Strategy," BARRNet, Cisco Systems, MERIT, OARnet, IETF RFC 1519, September, 1993.

[28] Y. Rekhter and T. Li, "An Architecture for IP Address Allocation with CIDR," T.J. Watson Research Center, IBM Corp., Cisco Systems, IETF RFC 1518, September, 1993.

[29] J. Kowal, "TeleGeography 2000: Global Telecommunications Traffic Statistics & Commentary." Washington, D.C.: TeleGeography, Inc., 1999.

[30] C. Shapiro and H. R. Varian, "Recognizing Lock-In," in *Information Rules: A Strategic Guide to the Network Economy.* Boston: Harvard Business School Press, 1999, p. 109.

[31] Congress, "Regulation of Pole Attachments," in Communications Act of 1934. Washington, D.C.: 104th Congress of the United States, 1996, Sec. 224.

[32] Metricom, "In the Matter of Promotion of Competitive Networks in Local Telecommunications Markets, WT Docket No. 99-271, Comments of Metricom, Inc. Before the Federal Communications Commission," 1999.

[33] Congress, "Bell Operating Company Entry Into InterLata Services: Specific Interconnection Requirements," in Communications Act of 1934. Washington, D.C.: 104th Congress of the United States, 1996, Sec. 271(c)(2).

[34] A. Brown, "Telephone Number Mapping: ENUM Requirements," Internet Engineering Task Force, Internet Draft, November, 1999.

[35] P. Huber, M. K. Kellogg, J. Thorne, and C. S. Elwood, "Interconnecting Wireless Providers with Local Landline Networks," in *Federal Telecommunications Law*, 2nd ed. New York: Aspen Law and Business, 1999, pp. 941–942.

[36] D. D. Clark, "A Taxonomy of Internet Telephony Applications," presented at Telecommunications Policy Research Conference, Alexandria, VA, 1997.

[37] D. C. Sicker, "The Effect of Emerging Signaling Protocols on Future Telephony," *CCH Power and Telecom. Law*, vol. March/April, 1999.

[38] FCC, "Statutory Definitions," in In the Matter of Federal-State Joint Board on Universal Service, CC Docket No. 96-45, Report to Congress. Washington, D.C.: Federal Communications Commission, 1998, par. 48.

II

Internet Architecture Design in a Competitive Era

4

Rethinking The Design Of The Internet: The End-To-End Arguments Vs. The Brave New World

Marjory S. Blumenthal and David D. Clark

Introduction

The end-to-end arguments are a set of design principles that characterize (among other things) how the Internet has been designed. These principles were first articulated in the early 1980s,[1] and they have served as an architectural model in countless design debates for almost 20 years. The end-to-end arguments concern how application requirements should be met in a system. When a general-purpose system (for example, a network or an operating system) is built and specific applications are then built using this system (for example, e-mail or the World Wide Web over the Internet), there is a question of how these specific applications and their required supporting services should be designed. The end-to-end arguments suggest that specific application-level functions usually cannot, and preferably should not, be built into the lower levels of the system— the core of the network. The reason why was stated as follows in the original paper:

The function in question can completely and correctly be implemented only with the knowledge and help of the application standing at the endpoints of the communications system. Therefore, providing that questioned function as a feature of the communications systems itself is not possible.

In the original paper, the primary example of this end-to-end reasoning about application functions is the assurance of accurate and reliable transfer of information across the network. Even if any one lower-level subsystem, such as a network, tries hard to ensure reliability, data can be lost or corrupted after it leaves that subsystem. The ultimate check of correct execution has to be at the application level, at the endpoints of the transfer. There are many examples of this observation in practice.

Even if parts of an application-level function can potentially be implemented in the core of the network, the end-to-end arguments state that one should resist this approach if possible. There are a number of advantages of moving application-specific functions up out of the core of the network and providing only general-purpose system services there.

• The complexity of the core network is reduced, which reduces costs and facilitates future upgrades to the network.
• Generality in the network increases the chances that a new application can be added without having to change the core of the network.
• Applications do not have to depend on the successful implementation and operation of application-specific services in the network, which may increase their reliability.

Of course, the end-to-end arguments are not offered as an absolute. There are functions that can only be implemented in the core of the network, and issues of efficiency and performance may motivate core-located features. But the bias toward movement of function "up" from the core and "out" to the edge node has served very well as a central Internet design principle.

As a consequence of the end-to-end arguments, the Internet has evolved to have certain characteristics. The functions implemented "in" the Internet—by the routers that forward packets—have remained rather simple and general. The bulk of the functions that implement specific applications, such as e-mail, the World Wide Web, multi-player games, and so on, have been implemented in software on the computers attached to the "edge" of the Net. The edge orientation for applications and comparative simplicity within the Internet together have facilitated the creation of new applications, and they are part of the context for innovation on the Internet.

Moving Away from End-to-End

For its first 20 years, much of the Internet's design has been guided by the end-to-end arguments. To a large extent, the core of the network provides a very general data transfer service that is used by all the different applications running over it. The individual applications have been designed in different ways, but mostly in ways that are sensitive to the advantages of the end-to-end design approach. However, over the last few years, a number of new requirements have emerged for the Internet and its applications. To certain stakeholders, these various new requirements might best be met through the addition of new mechanism in the core of the network. This perspective has, in turn, raised concerns among those who wish to preserve the benefits of the original Internet design.

Here are some (interrelated) examples of emerging requirements for the Internet of today:

Operation in an Untrustworthy World
The examples in the original end-to-end paper assume that the endpoints are in willing cooperation to achieve their goals. Today, there is less and less reason to believe that we can trust other endpoints to behave as desired. The consequences of untrustworthy endpoints on the Net include attacks on the network as a whole, attacks on individual end-points, undesired forms of interactions such as spam e-mail, and annoyances such as Web pages that vanish due to end-node aberrations.[2] The situation is a predictable consequence of dramatic growth in the population of connected people and its diversification to include people with a wider range of motivations for using the Internet, leading to uses that some have deemed misuses or abuses. Making the network more trustworthy, while the endpoints cannot be trusted, seems to imply more mechanism in the center of the network to enforce "good" behavior.

Consider spam—unwanted bulk mail sent out for advertising or other purposes. Spam is not the most pernicious example of unwelcome end-node behavior—it usually annoys rather than disrupts. However, it provides a good example of how different approaches to control conform in different ways to the tenets of the end-to-end arguments. It is the person receiving spam, not the e-mail software, that desires to avoid receiving it. Staying within the end-to-end framework but applying the arguments at the ultimate endpoint (the human using the system) implies that the sender sends the spam, the software at the receiver receives it, and then the human receiver deletes it. The underlying protocols, including both the TCP layer and the higher SMTP mail-transfer layer, are just supporting mechanisms. However, because users resent the time (both personal and Internet-connection time) and sometimes money spent collecting and deleting the unwanted mail, some have proposed application-level functions elsewhere in the network, not just at the recipient's computer, to prevent spam from arriving at the edges.[3]

More Demanding Applications

The simple service model of the Internet (called "best-effort delivery") makes no guarantee about the throughput that any particular application will achieve at any moment. Applications such as file transfer, Web access, or e-mail are tolerant of fluctuations in rate—while a user may be frustrated by a slow delivery, the application still "works." Today, a new set of applications is emerging, typified by streaming audio and video, that appear to demand a more sophisticated Internet service that can assure each data stream a specified throughput, an assurance that the best-effort service cannot provide. Different approaches are possible, beginning with (re)design of applications to operate using only the current best-effort service, perhaps by dynamically adjusting the fidelity of the transmitted information as the network throughput varies.

At least some application designers reject this limitation on what they could design. Another approach would be to add new data transport services in the core of the network that provide predictable throughput and bounded delays, and there have been proposals along these lines.[4] However, the Internet Service Providers (see below) have not so far been willing to provide these new services. As a result, application builders have adopted the strategy of installing intermediate storage sites that position the streaming content close to the recipient, to increase the chance of successful delivery. Thus, unlike a simple end-to-end structure, the design of these new applications depends on a two-stage delivery via these intermediate servers.

ISP Service Differentiation

The deployment of enhanced delivery services for streaming media and other sorts of advanced Internet applications is shaped by the current business models of the larger Internet Service Providers. They (at least at present) seem to view enhanced data transport service as something to be provided within the bounds of the ISP as a competitive differentiator, sometimes tied to specific applications such as telephone service over the Internet, rather than a capability to be supported, end to end, across multiple providers' networks. If enhanced services are not provided end to end, then it is not possible to design applications needing these services using an endpoint implementation. Thus, as discussed above, there is an acceleration in the deployment of applications based on intermediate servers that can be positioned within each ISP; content is delivered to ISP customers within the island of enhanced service. This approach has an additional effect that has aroused concern among consumer activists: the differentiation of applications generated by parties that can afford to promote and utilize ISP-specific intermediate servers from those that depend on potentially lower-performance end-to-end transport.[5] The concern here, however, is that investment in closed islands of enhanced service, combined with investment in content servers within each island, decreases the motivation for investment in the alternative of open end-to-end services. Once started down one path of investment, the alternative may be harder to achieve.

The Rise of Third-Party Involvement

An increasingly visible issue is the demand by third parties to interpose themselves between communicating endpoints, irrespective of the desires of the ends.[6] Third parties may include officials of organizations (e.g., corporate network or ISP administrators implementing organizational policies or other oversight) or officials of governments, whose interests may range from taxation to law enforcement and public safety. Court-ordered wiretaps illustrate government interposition as a third party, whereas mandatory blocking of certain content may involve either government or organizational interposition.

Less Sophisticated Users

The Internet was designed, and used initially, by technologists. As the base of users broadens, the motivation grows to make the network easier to use. By implying that substantial software is present at the end-node, the end-to-end arguments are a source of complexity to the user: that software must be installed, configured, upgraded, and maintained. It is much more appealing to some to take advantage of software that is installed on a server somewhere else on the network.[7] The importance of ease of use will only grow with the changing nature of consumer computing. The computing world today includes more than PCs. It has embedded processors, portable user-interface devices such as computing appliances or personal digital assistants (PDAs, such as Palm devices), Web-enabled televisions and advanced set-top boxes, new kinds of cell phones, and so on. If the consumer is required to set up and configure separately each networked device he owns, what is the chance that at least one of them will be configured incorrectly? That risk would be lower with delegation of configuration, protection, and control to a common point that can act as an agent for a pool of devices.[8] This common point would become a part of the application execution context. With this approach, there would no longer be a single indivisible endpoint where the application runs.

While no one of these trends is by itself powerful enough to transform the Internet from an end-to-end network to a network with centralized function, the fact that they all might motivate a shift in the same direction could herald a significant overall change in the shape of the Net. Such change would alter the Internet's economic and social impacts. That recognition lies behind the politics of those changes and the rhetoric of parties for and against various directions that might be taken in developing and deploying mechanisms. That the end-to-end arguments have recently been invoked explicitly in political debates reflects the growth in the stakes and the intensification of the debates.[9] At issue is the conventional understanding of the "Internet philosophy": freedom of action, user empowerment, end-user responsibility for actions undertaken, and lack of controls "in" the Net that limit or regulate what users can do. The end-to-end arguments fostered that philosophy because they enabled the freedom to innovate, install new software at will, and run applications of the user's choice.

The end-to-end arguments presuppose to some extent certain kinds of relationships: between communicating parties at the ends, between parties at the ends and the providers of their network/Internet service, and of either end users or ISPs with a range of third parties that might have an interest in either of the first two types of relationship (and therefore the fact or content of communications). In cases where there is a tension among the interests of the parties, our thinking about the objectives (and about the merit of technical mechanisms we might or might not add to the network) is very much shaped by our values concerning the specifics of the case. If the communicating parties are described as "dissidents" and the third party trying to wiretap or block the conversation is a "repressive" government, most people raised in the context of free speech will align their interests with the end parties. Replace the word "dissident" with "terrorist" and the situation becomes less clear to many. Similarly, when are actions of an ISP responsible management of its facilities and service offerings, and when are they manipulative control of the nature and effective pricing of content and applications accessed through its facilities and services?

Perhaps the most contentious set of issues surrounds the increasing third-party involvement in communication between cooperating users. When communicating endpoints want to communicate but some third party demands to interpose itself into the path without their agreement, the end-to-end arguments do not provide an obvious framework to reason about this situation. We must abandon the end-to-end arguments, reject the demand of a third party because it does not "fit" our technical design principles, or find another design approach that preserves the power of the end-to-end arguments as much as possible.

Preservation of the end-to-end arguments would imply that if, in a given jurisdiction, there are political or managerial goals to be met, meeting them should be supported by technology and policies at higher levels of the system of network-based technology, not by mechanisms "in" the network. The new context of the Internet implies that decisions about where to place mechanisms will be more politicized and that more people may need more convincing about the merits of a pro-end-to-end decision than in the Internet's early days. It is time for a systematic examination of what it means to uphold or deviate from the end-to-end arguments as the Internet evolves.

The rest of this paper is organized as follows. We first catalog a number of new requirements for controls and protections in today's communications. We document the emerging calls for the Internet to address these new requirements. We then identify a range of possible solutions that might be used to meet these requirements. We look at technical options, but we emphasize that non-technical approaches (legal, social, economic) are important, valid, and often preferable. We then look at the implications for the rights and responsibilities of the various parties that comprise the Internet—the consumer as user, the commercial ISPs, the institutional network providers, governments, and so on. We describe the range of emerging players to emphasize the complexity of the space of stakeholders in this new world. We conclude with some observations and speculations on what the most fundamental changes are and what is most important to preserve from the past.

Examples of Requirements in Today's Communication

As the previous section suggested, many of the complexities in communication today reflect more diverse patterns of interaction among the different players. This section catalogs a number of requirements, to illustrate the breadth of the issues and to suggest the range of solutions that will be required.

Users Communicate but Don't Totally Trust Each Other

One important category of interaction occurs when two (or more) end-nodes want to communicate with each other but do not totally trust each other. There are many examples of this situation:

• Two parties want to negotiate a binding contract: they may need symmetric proof of signing, protection from repudiation of the contract, and so on.[10]
• One party needs external confirmation of who the other party in the communication is.
• At the other extreme, two parties want to communicate with each other but at least one of the parties wants to preserve its anonymity. This topic is of sufficient importance that we consider it in detail below.

Users Communicate but Desire Anonymity

There are a number of circumstances in which a desire for anonymity might arise, from anonymous political speech and whistle-blowers to preserving one's privacy while looking at a Web site. At least in the United States, the privilege of anonymous public political speech is seen as a protected right. In this context, the speakers will seek assurance that their anonymity cannot be penetrated, either at the time or afterwards. This concern is directed at third parties—not only individuals who might seek to uncover the speaker, but the government itself, which might want to repress certain expressions. Another example is on-line voting. Individual voters need some external assurance that their votes are anonymous. The voting system needs to ensure that only registered voters can vote and each votes at most once. The citizens, collectively, seek assurance that voting is not disrupted by some denial-of-service attack, the vote tally is accurate, and that there is no opportunity for voting fraud. A third example is the call for anonymous electronic cash on the Internet so as to complete an online purchase anonymously.[11]

The desire for anonymity is an example of a situation where the interests of the different end parties may not align. One end may wish to hide its identity, while the other end may need that identity or at least to confirm some attributes (e.g., status as an adult or citizenship) in order to authorize some action.

One's identity can be tracked on the network in a number of ways. For example, low-level identification such as e-mail addresses or the IP address of the user's computer can be used to correlate successive actions and build a user profile that can, in turn, be linked to higher-level identification that the user provides in specific circumstances.[12] The dynamic interplay of controls (e.g., attempts to identify) and their avoidance is an indication that the Internet is still flexible, the rules are still evolving, and the final form is not at all clear.[13]

End Parties Do Not Trust Their Own Software and Hardware

There is a growing perception that the hardware and software available to consumers today behave as a sort of double agent, releasing information about the consumer to other parties in support of marketing goals such as building profiles of individual consumers. For example, Web browsers today store "cookies" (small fragments of information sent over the network from a Web server) and send that data back to the same or different servers to provide a trail that links successive transactions, thereby providing a history of the user's behavior.[14] Processors may contain unique identifiers that can distinguish one computer from another, and various programs such as browsers could be modified to include that identifier in messages going out over the Internet, allowing those messages to be correlated.[15] Local network interfaces (e.g., Ethernet) contain unique identifiers, and there is fear that those identifiers might be used as a way to keep track of the behavior of individual people.[16] These various actions are being carried out by software (on the user's computer) that the user is more or less required to use (one of a small number of popular operating systems, Web browsers, and so on) as well as elective applications.[17]

The Ends vs. the Middle: Third Parties Assert Their Right to Be Included in Certain Sorts of Transactions

Another broad class of problem can be characterized as a third party asserting its right to interpose itself into a communication between end-nodes that fully trust each other and consider themselves fully equipped to accomplish their communication on their own. There are many examples of this situation.

• Governments assert their right to wiretap (under circumstances they specify) to eavesdrop on certain communications within their jurisdiction.
• Governments, by tradition if not by explicit declaration of privilege, spy on the communications of parties outside their jurisdiction.
• Governments take on themselves the right to control the access of certain parties to certain material. This can range from preventing minors from obtaining pornographic material to preventing citizens from circulating material considered seditious or unwelcome by that government.
• Governments assert their right to participate in specific actions undertaken by their citizens for public policy reasons, such as enforcement of taxation of commercial transactions.
• Private ISPs assert their right to regulate traffic on their networks in the interests of managing load, and in order to segregate users with different intentions (e.g., those who provide or only use certain application services) in order to charge them different amounts.
• Private organizations assert their right to control who gets access to their intranets and to their gateways to the Internet, and for what purposes.
• Private parties assert their right to intervene in certain actions across the network to protect their rights (e.g., copyright) in the material being transferred.

The requirements of private parties such as rights holders may be as complex as those of governments. The end-to-end arguments, applied in a simple way, would suggest that a willing sender can use any software he chooses to transfer material to willing receivers. The holders of intellectual property rights may assert that, somewhat like a tax collector but in the private domain, they have the right to interpose themselves into that transfer to protect their rights in the material (and ability to collect fees), which thus potentially becomes a network issue.[18]

For each of these objectives, there are two perspectives: there are mechanisms that the third parties use to inject themselves into the communication, and there are actions that the end-parties use to try to avoid this intervention. In general, mechanisms with both goals can be found inside networks, representing a dynamic, evolving balance of power between the parties in question.

Different third-party objectives trigger a range of requirements to observe and process the traffic passing through the network. Some objectives, such as certain forms of wiretapping, call for access to the complete contents of the communication. On the other hand, some objectives can be met by looking only at the IP addresses and other high-level identifying information describing the communication. These latter activities, referred to as *traffic analysis*, are common in the communications security and law enforcement communities, where they may be regarded as second best compared to full-content access.

In the contemporary environment, attention to communications patterns extends beyond the government to various private parties, in part because technology makes it possible. A kind of traffic analysis is appearing in the context of large, organizational users of the Internet, where management is policing how organizational resources are used (e.g., by monitoring e-mail patterns or access to pornographic Web sites[19]). Finally, ISPs may use traffic analysis in support of their traffic engineering. ISPs have asserted that it is important for them to examine the traffic they are carrying in order to understand changing patterns of user behavior; with that information they can predict rates of growth in different applications and thus the need for new servers, more network capacity, and so on. The rise of high-volume MP3 file exchanges, boosted by Napster (a directory of individual collections) and Gnutella for peer-to-peer sharing, illustrates the sort of phenomena that ISPs need to track. Normally, they do not need to look at the actual data in messages but only at the identifiers that indicate which application is being used (e.g., whether a message is e-mail or a Web access).

The desire by some third party to observe the content of messages raises questions about the balance of power between the endpoints and the third party. As we detail below, an endpoint may try to prevent any observation of its data, in response to which the third party may try to regulate the degree to which the endpoints can use such approaches. There may be other points on the spectrum between total privacy and total accessibility of information, for example *labels* on information that interpret it or reveal specific facts about it. Labeling of information is discussed below.

One Party Tries to Force Interaction on Another

The example of asymmetric expectations among the end-nodes reaches its extreme when one party does not want to interact at all and the other party wishes to force some involvement on it. This network equivalent of screaming at someone takes many forms, ranging from application-level flooding with unwanted material (e.g., e-mail spam) to what are seen as security attacks: penetration of computers with malicious intent (secretly, as with Trojan horses, discussed below, or overtly), or the anti-interaction problem of denial of service attacks, which can serve to prevent any interactions or target certain kinds.[20]

Even when a user is communicating with a site that is presumed harmless, there are always risks of malicious behavior—classic security breaches and attacks, deception and misdirection of the user, transmittal of viruses and other malicious code, and other snares.[21] The classic end-to-end arguments would say that each end-node is responsible for protecting itself from attacks by others (hence the popularity of anti-virus software), but this may not be viewed as sufficient control in today's complex network.

One classic computer security attack is the so-called Trojan horse, in which a user is persuaded to install and use some piece of software that, while superficially performing a useful task, is in fact a hostile agent that secretly exports private information or performs some other sort of clandestine and undesirable task affecting the recipient's system and/or data. It is not clear how often Trojan horse programs actually succeed in achieving serious security breaches, but there is growing concern that "trusting" browsers may be blind to Trojan horses that can be deposited on end-systems through interactions with server software designed with malicious intent.[22]

Multiway Communication

The examples above are all cast in the framework of two-party communication. But much of what happens on the Internet, as in the real world, is multi-party. Any public or semi-public network offering has a multiway character. Some interactions, like the current Web, use a number of separate two-party communications as a low-level technical means to implement the interaction from a server to multiple users. Others, like teleconferencing or receiving Internet-based broadcast material (audio or video), may also involve multiway communication at the network level, traditionally called multicast.

Part of what makes multiway applications more complex to design is that the multiple endpoints may not function equally. Different participants may choose to play different roles in the multiway interaction, with different degrees of trust, competence, and reliability. Some will want to participate correctly, but others may attempt to disrupt the communication. Some may implement the protocols correctly, while others may crash or malfunction. These realities must be taken into account in deciding how to design the application and where functions should be located.

In general, in a two-party interaction, if one end seems to be failing or malicious, the first line of defense is to terminate the interaction and cease to communicate with that party. However, in a multiway communication, it is not acceptable for one broken endpoint to halt the whole interaction. The application must be designed so that it can distinguish between acceptable and malicious traffic and selectively ignore the latter. It may be possible to do this within the end-node, but in other cases (e.g., when the network is being clogged by unwanted traffic) it may be necessary to block some traffic inside the network. This will require the ability to install traffic filters inside the network that are specific as to source address and application type as well as multicast destination address.

Summary: What Do These Examples Really Imply?

This set of examples is intended to illustrate the richness of the objectives that elements of society may desire to impose on its network-based communication. The existence or identification of such examples does not imply that all of these goals will be accepted and reflected in new technical mechanisms (let alone judgment of their merits). Rather, it shows that the world is becoming more complex than it was when the simple examples used to illustrate the end-to-end arguments were articulated.

Does this mean that we have to abandon the end-to-end arguments? No, it docs not. What is needed is a set of principles that interoperate with each other—some build on the end-to-end model, and some on a new model of network-centered function. In evolving that set of principles, it is important to remember that, from the beginning, the end-to-end arguments revolved around requirements that could be implemented correctly at the endpoints; if implementation inside the network is the only way to accomplish the requirement, then an end-to-end argument isn't appropriate in the first place.[23] The end-to-end arguments are no more "validated" by the belief in end-user empowerment than they are "invalidated" by a call for a more complex mix of high-level functional objectives.

Technical Responses

The preceding section catalogued objectives that have been called for (in at least some quarters) in the global Internet of tomorrow. There are a number of ways that these objectives might be met. In this section, we examine technical responses that have been put forward and organize them into broad categories.

The Different Forms of the End-to-End Arguments

The end-to-end arguments apply at (at least) two levels within the network. One version applies to the core of the network—that part of the Internet implemented in the routers themselves, which provide the basic data forwarding service. Another version applies to the design of applications.

The end-to-end argument relating to the core of the network claims that one should avoid putting application-specific functions "in" the network, but should push them "up and out" to devices that are attached "on" the network. Network designers make a strong distinction between two sorts of elements—those that are "in" the network and those that are "attached to," or "on," the network. A failure of a device that is "in" the network can crash the network, not just certain applications; its impact is more universal. The end-to-end argument at this level thus states that services that are "in" the network are undesirable because they constrain application behavior and add complexity and risk to the core. Services that are "on" the network, and are put in place to serve the needs of an application, are not as much of an issue because their impact is narrower.

From the perspective of the core network, all devices and services that are attached to the network represent endpoints. It does not matter where they are—at the site of the end user, at the facilities of an Internet Service Provider, and so on. But when each application is designed, an end-to-end argument can be employed to decide where application-level services themselves should be attached. Some applications have a very simple end-to-end structure in which computers at each end send data directly to each other. Other applications may emerge with a more complex structure, with servers that intermediate the flow of data between the end-users. For example, e-mail in the Internet does not normally flow in one step from sender to receiver. Instead, the sender deposits the mail in a mail server and the recipient picks it up later.

Modify the End-Node
The approach that represents the most direct lineage from the Internet roots is to try to meet new objectives by modification of the end-node. In some cases, placement of function at the edge of the network may compromise performance, but the functional objective can be met. If spam is deleted before reaching the recipient or afterwards, it is equally deleted. The major difference is the use of resources—network capacity and user time and therefore the distribution of costs—with deletion before or after delivery. The difference, in other words, is performance and not "correctness" of the action.

In other cases, implementation in the end-node may represent an imperfect but acceptable solution. Taxation of transactions made using the Internet[24] is a possible example. Consider an approach that requires browser manufacturers to modify their products so that they recognize and track taxable transactions. While some people might obtain and use modified browsers that would omit that step, there would be difficulties in obtaining (or using) such a program, especially if distributing (or using) it were illegal. One approach would be to assess the actual level of noncompliance with the taxation requirement, make a judgment as to whether the level of loss is acceptable, and develop complementary mechanisms (e.g., laws) to maximize compliance and contain the loss.[25] As we discuss below, a recognition that different endpoints play different roles in society (e.g., a corporation vs. a private citizen) may make end-located solutions more robust and practical.

Control of access to pornography by minors is another example of a problem that might be solved at an endpoint, depending on whether the result is considered robust enough. One could imagine that objectionable material is somehow labeled in a reliable manner, and browsers are enhanced to check these labels and refuse to retrieve the material unless the person controlling the computer (presumably an adult) has authorized it. Alternatively, if the user does not have credentials that assert that he or she is an adult, the server at the other end of the connection can refuse to send the material.[26] Would this be adequate? Some minors might bypass the controls in the browser. Adventurous teenagers have been bypassing controls and using inaccurate (including forged or stolen) identification materials for a long time, and it is hard to guarantee that the person using a given end-system is who he or she claims to be. These outcomes represent leakage in the system, another case where compliance is less than one hundred percent. Is that outcome acceptable, or is a more robust system required?

In other circumstances, it would seem fruitless to depend on end-node modification. As the 1990s debates about government-accessible encryption keys illustrate, if the goal is to eavesdrop on suspected terrorists, there is no way to compel them to use only law-abiding software (a clear illustration of the end-to-end argument that the end-nodes may do as they please in carrying out a transaction). Even if some terrorists communicate "in the clear," it does not give much comfort to law enforcement if there is one encrypted conversation in particular that it wants to listen in on.

Adding Functions to the Core of the Network

Examination of some emerging network requirements has led to a call for new mechanism "in" the network, at the level of the routers that forward packets across the Internet. This outcome is the most explicit challenge to the end-to-end arguments, because it puts function into the network that may prevent certain applications from being realized.

There is an important difference between the arguments being made today for function in the network and arguments from the past. In the past, the typical proposal for network-level function had the goal of trying to help with the implementation of an application. Now, the proposals are as likely to be hostile as helpful—addition of mechanism that keeps things from happening, blocks certain applications, and so on.

Here are a number of examples where this approach is already being adapted today; others are contemplated.[27]

Firewalls

The most obvious example of a node inserted into the Internet today is a security firewall used to protect some part of the network (e.g., a corporate region) from the rest of the Internet. Firewalls inspect passing network traffic and reject communications that are suspected of being a security threat.

Traffic Filters

Elements such as firewalls can perform tasks beyond providing protection from outside security attacks. They can affect traffic in both directions, so they can be programmed to prevent use of some applications (e.g., game playing) or access to inappropriate material (e.g., known pornography sites), as well as a number of other functions. Traffic filters can thus become more general tools for control of network use.

Network Address Translation Elements

Today, devices called Network Address Translation (NAT) boxes are being used in the Internet to deal with the shortage of Internet addresses and to simplify address space management.[28] By modifying the IP addresses in the packets, they may contribute to protecting user identity from other endpoints. These are sometimes integrated in with firewall functions—e.g., as a part of their operation they can limit the sorts of applications that are permitted to operate. NAT boxes are usually installed by managers of organizational networks and some ISPs. There have also been proposals to use address translation on a larger scale, perhaps for an entire country, as a way to control access into and out of that country.

However, the deployment of NAT requires many adjustments elsewhere. An original design principle of the Internet is that IP addresses are carried unchanged end to end, from source to destination across the network. The next level protocol normally used above IP, TCP, verifies this fact. With the introduction of NAT boxes, which rewrite the IP addresses in packets entering or leaving a region of the network, these boxes also had to modify the information sent at the TCP level; otherwise, the TCP error checking would have reported an addressing error. The more difficult problem is that some higher-level protocols (e.g., applications) also make use of the IP address; this implies that for the NAT box to preserve correct operation, it must understand the design of specific applications, a clear violation of the end-to-end arguments. Finally, IP addresses are used in additional ways in practice. For example, some site licenses for software use the IP address of the client to control whether to give the client access to the server. Changing the apparent address of the client can cause this sort of scheme to malfunction.

Design Issues in Adding Mechanism to the Core of the Network

There are two issues with any control point imposed "in" the network. First, the stream of data must be routed through the device, and second, the device must have some ability to see what sort of information is in the stream, so that it can make the proper processing decisions.

Imposing a Control Element into the Path of Communication

Packets flowing from a source to a destination can take a variety of paths across the Internet, since the best routing options are recomputed dynamically while the Internet is in operation. There is no single place in the Internet where a control point can be interposed in an unspecified flow. However, for a known flow, with a given source or destination, there is often an accessible location at which to insert a control point. For most users, access to the Internet is over a single connection, and a control point could be associated with that link. A corporation or other large user normally has only a small number of paths that connect it into the rest of the Internet, and these paths provide a means to get at the traffic from that organization. It is this topological feature that provides a place for an organization to install a firewall. The point where this path connects to an ISP similarly provides a means to monitor the traffic. Thus, the government could implement a wiretap order by instructing the ISP servicing the user to install a control point where the party in question attaches to it—a tack that has been attempted.[29]

Once the traffic has entered the interior of the public Internet, it becomes much more difficult to track and monitor. Thus, the ISP that provides initial access for a user to the Internet will, as a practical matter, play a special role in any mandated imposition of a monitoring device on a user.[30] As governments take increasing interest in what is being transmitted over the Internet, we can expect that the ISPs that provide the point of access for users to the Internet will be attractive to governments as vehicles for implementing certain kinds of controls associated with public policy objectives.[31]

Revealing or Hiding the Content of Messages

Assuming that the network routing problem has been solved and the traffic to be monitored is passing through the control point, the other issue is what aspects of the information are visible to the control device. There is a spectrum of options, from totally visible to totally masked. A simple application of the end-to-end arguments would state that the sender and receiver are free to pick whatever format for their communication best suits their needs. In particular, they should be free to use a private format, encrypt their communications, or use whatever means they choose to keep them private. Encryption can be the most robust tool for those who want to protect their messages from observation or modification. When strong encryption is properly implemented, the control device can look only at source and destination IP addresses, and perhaps other control fields in the packet header. As discussed above, traffic analysis is the only form of analysis possible in this case.

The goal of end-to-end privacy is in direct conflict with the goal of any third party that desires to take some action based on the content of the stream. Whether the goal is to tax an e-commerce transaction, collect a fee for performance of copyrighted music, or filter out objectionable material, if the nature of the contents is completely hidden, there is little the intermediate node can do other than to block the communication all together. This situation could lead to a requirement that the device be able to see and recognize the complete information. Either the outcome of total privacy or total disclosure of content may be called for in specific cases, but it is valuable to identify possible compromises.

Labels on Information

One way to reveal some information about the content of a message without revealing the content itself is to label the message. Labels that would be visible in the network represent one possible compromise between the rights of the end-node parties to transmit anything they want, perhaps encrypted for privacy, and the rights of some third party to observe or act on what is sent. Labels also represent a way to augment the actual information in the message, for example to impose a simple framework of content types on arbitrary application data. For example, a wide range of messages can be described with the simple label "Advertising." California law requires that all unsolicited advertising e-mail have "ADV:" at the beginning of the subject.[32] There is an important duality in the potential use of labels: they could be used to identify both content and users. For example, the transfer of pornographic material might be required to be labeled as "objectionable for a minor," while the request for that material might carry the label of the class of person requesting it. Which scheme is used may depend on where the trust lies and who can be held accountable.[33] Almost of necessity, such labeling schemes will be criticized as lacking generality and expressivity and as constraining all parties in some ways, especially for qualities that go beyond the factual. Labeling places a burden on the content producer or other party to attach accurate labels, and the question becomes whether this requirement is enforceable.[34]

As a practical matter, labels may become commonplace anyway in U.S. commercial communications, as the Federal Trade Commission moves to extend practices and policies associated with preventing deception in conventional media (which have led to the convention of labeling advertisements as such, for example) to the Internet.[35] Also, data labeling is a key building block of many filtering schemes, and it allows the filtering to be done both inside and at the edge of the network.

Labeling schemes sidestep the practical problem of building an intermediate node that can analyze a message and figure out what it means. One could imagine writing a program that looks at the text of mail and concludes that it is bulk advertising, or looks at images and concludes that they are objectionable, or looks at a Web transfer and concludes that it is an online purchase. Although concepts for such programs are being pursued, they raise many troublesome issues, from the reliability of such controls to the acceptability of casting the decision-making in the form of a program in the first place.

There are several proposals for use of labels as a middle point on a spectrum of content visibility, although few are used in practice today.

One of the more visible label schemes in the Internet today is the Platform for Internet Content Selection (PICS) standard for content labeling,[36] which was developed by the World Wide Web Consortium as an approach to identification of potentially objectionable material. The PICS standard is a powerful approach to content labeling, since it permits content to be labeled by third parties as well as the content producers. This generality permits different users of content with different goals and values to subscribe to labeling services that match their needs. The label is not attached to the page as it is transferred across the network, but it is retrieved from the labeling service based on the page being fetched. The content can be blocked either in the end-node (an end-to-end solution) or in an application-level relay, specifically a Web proxy server (an in-the-net solution).[37] While PICS has many interesting and useful features, it has also attracted its share of criticism, most vocally the concern that the "voluntary" nature of the PICS labels could become mandatory in practice under government pressure. PICS might thus end up as a tool of government censorship.[38] This concern would seem to apply to any scheme for labels that can be observed in the network. Labeling schemes should not be seen as a panacea for all content issues, but they are a midpoint on a spectrum between lack of any visibility of what is being carried and explicit review and regulation of content.

Another example of content labels today are the metadata tags that are found on Web pages,[39] used to help guide search engines in their cataloging of pages. Metadata tags can include keywords that do not actually appear in the visible part of the page; this feature can either be used to solve specific cataloging problems or to promote a page to the top of a list of search results. As of today, these labels are not used for control inside the net but only for lookup, and they illustrate some of the problems with the use of labels.[40]

The Internet today provides a minimal label on most communications, the so-called "port number," which identifies which application at the endpoint the message is intended for—Web, e-mail, file transfer, and so on. These numbers can be used to classify the packets crudely, and this ability is used today in a number of ways. ISPs and institutional network managers observe the port numbers to build models of user behavior to predict changes in demand. In some cases, they also refuse to forward traffic to and from certain port numbers, based on the service contract with the user. Some application developers have responded by moving away from predictable port numbers.

Design of Applications: The End-to-End Argument at a Higher Level
The previous discussion concerned augmentation of the core of the network with new sorts of functions that in the current world are more concerned with control and filtering than with enhancing applications. We now look at the design of the applications themselves. There are two trends that can be identified today. One is the desire on the part of different parties, either end-users or network operators, to insert some sort of server into the data path of an application that was not initially designed with this structure. This desire may derive from goals as diverse as privacy and performance enhancement. The other trend is that application requirements are becoming more complex, which sometimes leads away from a simple end-to-end design and toward the use of additional components as a part of the application.

Here are some examples of application-level services that are being employed today to augment or modify application behavior.

Anonymizing Message Forwarders
One strategy for users to achieve anonymity and to protect their communications from third party observation is to use a third-party service and route traffic through it so that possible identification in the messages can be removed. Services that make Web browsing anonymous are popular today,[41] and services with the specific goal of preventing traffic analysis are available.[42] Anonymous mail relays include simple remailers and more complex systems such as the nym server.[43] To use these devices, the end-node constructs the route through one (or usually more) of them to achieve the desired function. It is critical that the user construct the route, because preserving anonymity depends on the data following a path among the boxes that only the user knows; the ISP, for example, or any other third party should not be able to determine the path directly. Careful use of encryption is employed in these schemes to hide the route as well as the identity from unwanted observation.[44]

Helpful Content Filtering
The mail servers in use today can, in principle, be used to perform filtering and related processing on mail. Since the mail is routed through these

devices anyway, server-filtering provides an option to remove spam or other objectionable material before it is even transferred to the receiving host.[45] Filtering can be done in a number of ways, consistent with the spectrum of access to content discussed above: looking at labels on the mail, matching of sender against a list of acceptable correspondents, or processing the content of the message (e.g., to detect viruses).

Content Caches
The World Wide Web, perhaps the most visible of Internet applications today, was initially designed with a simple, two-party end-to-end structure. However, if a number of users fetch the same popular Web page, the original design implied that the page would be fetched from the server over and over again, and transferred multiple times across the network. This observation led to the suggestion that when a page was sent from a server to a user, a copy be made and "cached" at a point near the user, so that if a nearby user requested the page a second time, this subsequent request could be satisfied with the cached copy. Doing so may offer some significant performance advantages, but it does break the end-to-end nature of the Web; for example, the server can no longer tell how many times its pages have been retrieved, nor can the server perform user-specific actions such as advertisement placement.[46]

More Complex Application Design: Using Trusted Third Parties
Many issues in application design today derive in some way from a lack of trust between the users that are party to the application. A fundamental approach is to use a mutually trusted third party located somewhere on the network to create a context in which a two-party transaction can be successfully carried out.[47] In other words, what might have been a simple two-party transaction, conforming to the end-to-end arguments in a straightforward way, becomes a sequence of interactions among the three or more parties. Each interaction is nominally end-to-end (these third parties need not be "in" the network), but its robustness depends on the larger context composed of the whole sequence.

Some simple examples of what a trusted third party might do include signing and date-stamping of messages (even if a message is encrypted, an independent signature can provide protection from some forms of repudiation) or assuring simultaneous release of a message to multiple parties.[48] Another class of trusted third party will actually examine the content of messages and verify that the transaction is in proper form, a role is somewhat analogous to that of a notary public.[49]

Another role of a third party is to provide credentials that serve to give each party in a transaction more assurance as to the identity, role, or level of trustworthiness of the other party. Examples include voter registration, certification of majority (e.g., to permit access to material deemed harmful to minors) and so on. This role of the third party relates to the labeling both of content and users. It may be that a third party is the source of labels that are used to classify material, as discussed above in the context of PICS. There are other forms of tokens, beyond credentials that describe users and content, that can be obtained in advance. For example, anonymous electronic cash from a trusted third party (analogous to a bank) provides a context in which two-party anonymous purchase and sale can be carried out.

Public-Key Certificates

An important role for a third party occurs when public key cryptography is used for user authentication and protected communication. A user can create a public key and give it to others, to enable communication with that user in a protected manner. Transactions based on a well-known public key can be rather simple two-party interactions that fit well within the end-to-end paradigm. However, there is a key role for a third party, which is to issue a Public Key Certificate and manage the stock of such certificates; such parties are called certificate authorities. The certificate is an assertion by that (presumably trustworthy) third party that the indicated public key actually goes with the particular user. These certificates are principal components of essentially all public key schemes, except those that are so small in scale that the users can communicate their public keys to each other one to one in an ad hoc way that is mutually trustworthy.

The act of obtaining the certificate can be done in advance. In most schemes, there is also a step that has to be done after a transaction; this step is tricky in practice. It can happen that a user loses his private key (the value that goes with the given public key) through inadvertence or theft; alternatively, a user may become unworthy in some way relevant to the purpose for which the certificate has been issued. Under such circumstances, the certificate authority (third party) would want to revoke the certificate. How can this be known? The obvious (and costly) approach is for any party encountering a public key certificate to contact the third party that issued it to ask if it is still valid. Although that kind of interaction is seen commonly with electronic credit-card authorization, the potential for more uses of certificates and more users poses the risk of a substantial performance burden on the certifying authority, because it would end up receiving a query every time any of its certificates is used in a nominally two-party transaction and because there are inherent lags in the sequence of events leading to revocation. As a result, it is possible that the complexity may far exceed that associated with, say, invalid credit-card authorization today. There have been proposals to improve the performance implications of this revocation process, the details of which do not matter. But a general point emerges: either the recipient of a public key certificate checks it in "real time," during the process of a transaction with the party associated with that key, or it completes the transaction and then later verifies the status of the party in question, with the risk that a transaction already completed is not appropriate.[50]

In general, in a complex transaction involving multiple parties, there is an issue concerning the timing of the various actions by the parties. Voter registration does not happen at the time of voting, but in advance. However, unless there is periodic checking, one can discover that deceased voters are still voting, as well as voters that have just left town and registered elsewhere. A PICS rating of a page is necessarily done in advance. Even if the PICS rating is checked in real time as the page is retrieved, the rating itself may be out of date because the content of the page has changed. A generalization that often seems to apply is that the greater in time the difference between the preliminary or subsequent interaction with the third party and the transaction itself, the greater the risk that the role played by the third party is less reliable.

The Larger Context

It is important to consider the larger context in which these technical mechanisms exist. That context includes the legal and social structure of the economy, the growing motivations for trustworthiness, and the fact that technology, law, social norms, and markets combine to achieve a balance of power among parties.

Nontechnical Solutions: The Role of Law in Cyberspace

Just because a problem arises in the context of a technical system such as the Internet, it is not necessary that the solution be only technical.[51] In fact, the use of law and other nontechnical mechanisms could be seen as consistent with the end to end arguments at the highest level—functions are moved "up and out," not only from the core of the network but from the application layer as well, and positioned outside the network all together.

For example, to control the unwanted delivery of material to fax machines (spam in the fax world) there are laws that prohibit certain sorts of unsolicited fax transmissions and require that a sending fax machine attach its phone number so that the sender can be identified.[52] Similarly, the growth of computer-based crime has led to criminalization of certain behavior on the Internet: the 1987 Computer Security Act focused on "federal-interest" computers, and, thanks in large part to the proliferating use of the Internet and the associated tendency for computers to be networked, throughout the 1990s there was growing law-enforcement attention, and legislation, relating to abuses of computers in both private and public sectors.[53]

The proliferation of labeling schemes points to the interplay of technical and legal approaches. The network can check the labels, but enforcement that the labels are accurate may fall to the legal domain.[54] This, of course, is the case in a variety of consumer protection and public safety situations; for example, the Federal Trade Commission regulates advertising—including claims and endorsement—in ways that affect content and format generally, and it has begun to examine the need for regulation relating to online privacy protection, while the Securities and Exchange Commission regulates financial claims and the Food and Drug Administration regulates claims relating to food, pharmaceuticals, and medical devices. The FTC and others recognize that labels are an imperfect mechanism in that people may ignore them, they may not apply to foreign sources, and they are subject to legal constraints in the United States as compelled speech, but labeling constitutes less interference with the market than, say, outright banning of products that raise policy concerns.

To date, on the Internet, enforcement has been less formal. The situation is similar to others in which voluntary action by industry may yield "self-regulation" of label content intended to avoid or forestall government regulation. Content ratings for motion pictures, television shows (now associated with the V-chip[55]), and computer games provide examples that have attracted both public and governmental scrutiny; more entrepreneurial examples include the quality labeling emerging for Web sites from the Better Business Bureau and new entities that have arisen for this purpose. In other cases, a more popular vigilantism may be invoked: as the daily news has shown in reporting public outcry against companies misusing personal information (e.g., Amazon.com, RealNetworks, or DoubleClick),[56] public scrutiny and concern itself can have an impact.[57] Overall, mechanisms outside of the Net, such as law, regulation, or social pressure, restrain third parties that turn out to be untrustworthy, systems that turn out to protect one's identity less well than promised, and so on. How satisfactory any of the nontechnical mechanisms may be depends on one's expectations for the role of government (e.g., how paternalistic), the role of industry (e.g., how exploitative or how responsible), and the ability and willingness of individuals to become suitably informed and act in their own defense (in the case of privacy and security concerns) or responsibly (in the case of such concerns as taxation).[58]

There is a philosophical difference between the technical and the legal approaches that have been discussed here. Technical mechanisms have the feature that their behavior is predictable *a priori*. One can examine the mechanism, convince oneself as to what it does, and then count on it to work as described. Legal mechanisms, on the other hand, often come into play after the fact. A party can go to court (a kind of third party) and, as a result of a court order or injunction, achieve change; of course, the existence of a legal mechanism is generally associated with an expectation of deterrence.

For example, the nym server cited above addresses the problem of e-mail anonymity through technical means. By the creative use of encryption, careful routing of data by the communicating application, and absence of logging, it becomes essentially impossible to determine after the fact who sent a message.[59] The result (beneficial in the eyes of the designers) is that one can use the nym server with the confidence that nobody, whether "good guy" or "bad guy," can later come in and force the revelation of the identity. The drawback is that "bad guys" might use cover of anonymity to do really bad things, bad enough to tip the balance of opinion toward response and away from protection of anonymity at all costs. Would society like a remedy in this case?

At a philosophical level, the debate itself represents an important part of finding the right balance. But for the moment, the Internet is a system where technology rather than law is the force most immediately shaping behavior, and until the legal environment matures, there is comparatively less option for remedy after the fact for actions in cyberspace than in real space.[60]

Some argue that law has limited value in influencing Internet-based conduct because the Internet is transborder, sources and destinations can be in unpredictable jurisdictions, and/or sources and destinations can be in jurisdictions with different bodies of law. This argument encourages those who would call for technical controls (which simply work the way they work, independent of jurisdiction and therefore of varying satisfaction to specific jurisdictional authorities) and those who argue for private, group-based self-regulation, where groups of users agree by choice on an approach (e.g., the use of PICS), to create a shared context in which they can function. Because of the limitations of private, group-based regulation, a variety of regulatory agencies are examining a variety of conditions relating to the conduct of business over the Internet and weighing options for intervention, in turn motivating new attempts at self-regulation that may or may not be effected or accepted. Meanwhile, legal solutions are being actively explored.[61]

Assessing Where We Are Today

As noted in the introduction, many forces are pushing to change the Internet today: a greater call (from various voices) for stable and reliable operation, even though we can place less trust in the individual users of the network; new sorts of sophisticated applications driven by new visions of consumer-oriented experiences; the motivation of ISPs to develop into enclaves containing enhanced service to gain competitive advantage; the proliferation of third parties with a range of interests in what the users are actually doing; the proliferation of less sophisticated users for whom "innovation" is a mixed blessing; and new forms of computing and communication that call for new software structures. All of these forces have the consequences of increased complexity, of increased structure in the design of the Internet, and of a loss of control by the user. Whether one chooses to see these trends as a natural part of the growing up of the Internet or as the fencing of the West, they are happening. It is not possible to turn back the clock to regain the circumstances of the early Internet: real changes underscore the real questions about the durability of the Internet's design principles and assumptions.

The Rise of the New Players
Much of what is different about the Internet today can be traced to the new players that have entered the game over the last decade. The commercial phase of the Internet is really less than ten years old—NSFnet, the government-sponsored backbone that formed the Internet back in the 1980s, was only turned off in 1995. At that time, when the commercial ISPs began to proliferate, the number of players was very small and their roles were fairly simple.

The world has become much more complex since that time. One trend is obvious: the changing role of the government in the Internet. The historic role of enabler is withering; comparatively speaking, government contributions to the design and operation of the Internet have shrunk.[62] At the same time, as more and more citizens have started to use and depend on the Internet, government attention to the nature of Internet businesses and consumer issues has grown. This trend was easily predicted, even if viewed by some with regret. In fact, the roles that the government is playing are consistent with government activities in other sectors and with the history of conventional telecommunications, including both telephony and broadcast media: antitrust vigilance, attempts to control consumer fraud, definition of a commercial code, taxation, and so on. There is little the government has done that represents a new role. In the telecommunications area the government has a special set of laws and a special agency, the Federal Communications Commission, to deal with presumed issues of natural monopoly and spectrum scarcity by translating law into regulation and attending to regulatory enforcement.

In the United States, the government has largely refrained from bringing these tools to bear on the Internet, but the potential for doing so is widely recognized (not least because of scrutiny of mergers and acquisitions that bear on the development of the Internet) and has itself influenced the conduct of the players.

The wild card has been the development of the ISP. Its role is less clear and less predefined than that of the government, and it has evolved and become much more complex. Government recognized in the early 1990s that the private sector would build the National (eventually Global) Information Infrastructure, and the gold rush that ensued from commercializing the backbone made the ISP business resemble many others, with ISPs pursuing the most profitable means to define and carry out a business endeavor. Any action that an ISP undertakes to enhance its role beyond basic packet forwarding is not likely to be compatible with end-to-end thinking, since the ISP does not have control over the endpoints. The ISP implements the core of the network, and the endpoint software traditionally comes from other providers.[63] So the ISP is most likely to add services and restraints by modifying the part of the network that it controls. For example, some residential users find themselves blocked from running a Web or game server in their home.[64] Those services are restricted to commercial customers who pay a higher fee for their Internet access. From one perspective, such service stratification is only natural: it is in the nature of private enterprise to separate users into different tiers with different benefits and price them accordingly. Anyone who has flown at full fare while the person with the Saturday-night stay flies for a small fraction of the cost has understood value-based pricing. And yet some Internet observers have looked at such restrictions, when applied to Internet service, as a moral wrong. From that perspective, the Internet should be a facility across which the user should be able to do anything he wants, end-to-end. As a society, much less across all the societies of the world, we have not yet begun to resolve this tension.

Concerns about the final form of Internet service in an unconstrained commercial world are increased by industry consolidation, which raise concerns about adequate competition in local access (as marked by ATT's acquisition of TCI and MediaOne), and by mergers between Internet access providers and Internet content providers (marked by AOL's proposed acquisition of Time–Warner, including all its cable facilities).[65] A related issue is the "open access" debate, which concerns whether ISPs should be compelled to share their facilities. The concern is not just about choice in ISPs, but that if access to alternative ISPs is constrained or blocked, then users would be able to access some content only with difficulty, if at all. There is thus a presumed linkage between lack of choice in access to the Internet and a loss of the open, end-to-end nature of the Internet.[66]

As a broader base of consumers has attached to the Internet, they have sought out very different sorts of experiences. In the competitive world of dial-up Internet access, the company that holds the major share of U.S. consumers is America Online, or AOL. One can speculate about the sorts of experience that the consumer favors by looking at what AOL offers. The emphasis of AOL is less on open and equal access to any activity and destination (what the end-to-end arguments would call for) and more on packaged content (reinforced by the merger with Time–Warner), predictable editorship, and control of unwelcome side effects. Their growing subscribership attests to consumer valuation of the kind of service they offer and the comparative ease of use they provide. Those who call for one or another sort of Internet as a collective societal goal would at least do well to learn from the voice of the consumer as it has been heard so far.

New questions are arising about the legal treatment of ISPs. The rise of ISPs and transformations of historically regulated telephone companies, broadcasters, and more recently cable television providers have created new tensions between a broad goal of relaxing economic regulation —with the goals of promoting competition and such attendant consumer benefits as lower prices and product innovation—and concerns about the evolving structure and conduct of the emerging communications services leaders—factors shaping actual experience with prices and innovation. Although U.S. federal telecommunications regulators have eschewed "regulation of the Internet," topics being debated include whether the legal concept of common carriage that applies to telephone service providers should apply to ISPs.[67] Today's legislative and regulatory inquiries beg the question of whether the ISP business should continue to evolve on its own—whether the transformation of the Internet into public infrastructure calls for some kind of intervention.[68]

The institutional providers of Internet services—the corporations, schools and non-profit organizations that operate parts of the Internet— have also evolved a much more complex set of roles. Employees have found themselves fired for inappropriate use of the corporate attachment to the Internet, and employers have sometimes been much more restrictive than ISPs in the services they curtail and the rules they impose for acceptable use. Users of the Internet today cannot necessarily do as they please: they can do different things across different parts of the Internet, and perhaps at different times of the day.

Finally, one must never lose sight of the international nature of the Internet. As the Internet emerges and grows in other countries, which it is doing with great speed, the cultural differences in different places will be a major factor in the overall shape the Internet takes. In some countries, the ISP may be the same thing as the government, or the government may impose a set of operating rules on the ISPs that are very different from those we expect in the U.S.

The Erosion of Trust

A number of examples in this paper have illustrated that users who do not totally trust each other still desire to communicate. Of all the changes that are transforming the Internet, the loss of trust may be the most fundamental. The exact details of what service an ISP offers may change over time, and they can be reversed by consumer pressure or law. But the simple model of the early Internet—a group of mutually trusting users attached to a transparent network—is gone forever. To understand how the Internet is changing, we must have a more sophisticated consideration of trust and how it relates to other factors such as privacy, openness, and utility.

The spread of the Internet into more and more spheres of economic and social activity suggests growth in its use both among trusting and non-trusting parties. A result is growing individual interest in self-protection, something that may involve, actively or passively, third parties. Against this backdrop arise concerns of specific third parties to meet their own objectives, such as protection of assets, revenue streams, or some form of public safety. That is, trustworthiness motivates both self-protection (which may be end-to-end) and third-party intervention (which appears to challenge the end-to-end principles).

As trust erodes, both endpoints and third parties may wish to interpose intermediate elements into a communication to achieve their objectives of verification and control. For intermediate elements interposed between communicating parties in real time, there is a tension between the need for devices to examine (at least parts of) the data stream and the growing tendency for users and their software to encrypt communication streams to ensure data integrity and control unwanted disclosure. If a stream is encrypted, it cannot be examined; if it is signed, it cannot be changed. Historically, encryption for integrity protection has been accepted more easily by authorities concerned about encryption than encryption for confidentiality, but that may be too glib an assumption in a world with pervasive encryption, where individuals may encounter circumstances when encryption is not an unmitigated good. For example, in the real world, one shows caution about a private meeting with a party that one does not trust. One seeks a meeting in a public place, or with other parties listening, and so on. Having an encrypted conversation with a stranger may be like meeting that person in a dark alley. Whatever happens, there are no witnesses. Communication in the clear could allow interposed network elements to process the stream, which could be central to the safety and security of the interaction. This example of a case where an individual might choose to trade off privacy for other values illustrates the proposition that choices and tradeoffs among privacy, security, and other factors are likely to become more complicated.

At the same time, there are many transactions that the collection of endpoints may view as private, even though there is not total trust among them. In an online purchase, details such as the price or the credit-card number might deserve protection from outside observation, but the fact of the purchase might be a matter of record, to provide a basis for recourse if the other party misbehaves. Such situations may argue for selective use of encryption—not the total encryption of the data stream at the IP level (as in the IPsec proposal), but applied selectively, for example by the browser to different parts of a message. The use of IPsec would most naturally apply to communication among parties with the highest level of trust, since this scheme protects the maximum amount of information from observation.

The use of trusted third parties in the network raises the difficulty of how one can know that third parties are actually trustworthy, or that the endpoints are talking to the third party they think they are. What happens if a malicious "imitation" third party manages to insert itself in place of a trusted agent? Today, Web sites attempt to snare the unwary using names similar to respected ones. How can the users of the Internet be confident that sites that are physically remote, and only apparent through their network behavior, are actually what they claim, actually worthy of trust?[69]

Rights and Responsibilities

The rise of legal activity reflects the rise of debates that center on the relative power (or relative rights, or relative responsibility) that devolves to the end users as individuals and to the network as an agent of the common good (e.g., the state, the group of users served by a given network). Some of these debates are rooted in law of a country or state, some in value systems and ideology. The First Amendment to the U.S. Constitution speaks to a positive valuation of free speech; other countries have different normative and legal traditions. Similarly, societies will differ in how they define accountability and in how they strike a balance between anonymity and accountability. Given differing national contexts, different geographically defined regions of the network may be managed to achieve differing balances of power,[70] just as different organizations impose different policies on the users of their networks. Local control may be imperfect, but it does not have to be perfect to shape the local experience. But if the Internet is to work as an internetwork, there are some limits on just how different the different regions can be.

The end-to-end design of the Internet gives the user considerable power in determining what applications he chooses to use. This power raises the possibility of an "arms race" between users and those who wish to control them. That potential should be a sobering thought, because it would have quite destructive side effects. The cryptography policy debate held that if, for example, controls were put in the network that attempted to intercept and read private communications between parties, the response from users could easily be to encrypt their private communication. The response to that would either be to outlaw the use of encryption, to promote government-accessible keys, or to block the transmission of any message that cannot be recognized, which might in turn lead to messages hidden inside other messages—steganography. It would seem that an attempt to regulate private communication, if it were actually feasible to implement (such controls seem to be getting harder), would result in a great loss of privacy and privilege for the affected individuals.[71] These sorts of controls also serve to block the deployment of any new application and stifle innovation and creativity. Consider what the Internet might look like today if one had to get a license to deploy a new application. This sort of escalation is not desirable.

Perhaps the most critical tension between rights and responsibilities is one that emerges from the erosion of trust—it is the balance between anonymity and accountability. The end-to-end arguments, by their nature, suggest that endpoints can communicate as they please, without constraint from the network. This implies, on the one hand, a certain need for accountability, in case these unconstrained activities turn out to have caused harm. Any system, whether technical or societal, requires protection from irresponsible and harmful actions. The end-to-end arguments do not imply guardrails to keep users on the road. On the other hand, there has been a call for the right of anonymous action, and some sorts of anonymous actions (such as political speech in the United States) are a protected right. Certainly privacy, if not absolute anonymity, is a much-respected objective in many societies. So how can the desire for privacy and anonymity be balanced against the need for accountability, given the freedom of action that the end-to-end arguments imply? This will be a critical issue in the coming decade.

A practical issue in moving forward is the enforceability of a policy. Some kinds of communications, and some kinds of parties, are more tractable when it comes to implementing controls (or behavior that obviates a need for controls in the eyes of those with concerns). For example, there is a distinction that often recurs: the separation between private and public communication. Today, the Internet places few limits on what two consenting end-nodes do in communicating across the network. They can send encrypted messages, design a whole new application, and so on. This is consistent with the simple articulation of the end-to-end arguments. Such communication is *private*. In contrast, *public* communication, or communication *to the public*, has different technical and social characteristics:

• In order to reach the public, one must advertise.

• In order to reach the public, one must use well-known protocols and standards that the public has available.

• In order to reach the public, one must reveal one's content. There is no such thing as a public secret.

• In order to reach the public, one must accept that one may come under the scrutiny of the authorities.

These factors make public communication much easier to control than private communication, especially where public communication is commercial speech (where, to a limited degree, at least in the United States, more rules can be applied than to noncommercial speech). In the case of labels on information that is otherwise encrypted, the authorities may not be able to verify that every label is proper. But authorities can check whether the sender is computing proper labels by becoming a subscriber to the service and seeing if the information sent is properly labeled.[72]

Another pattern of communication that supports enforcement is between an individual and a recognized institution. In many cases, one end of a transfer or the other may be easier to hold accountable, either because it is in a particular jurisdiction or because it is a different class of institution. For example, it may be easier to identify and impose requirements on corporations and other businesses than on individuals. Thus, in a transaction between a customer and a bank, it may be easier to impose enforceable regulation on the bank than the client. Banks are enduring institutions, already subjected to much regulation and auditing, while the individual customer is less constrained. This can create a situation in which the bank becomes part of the enforcement scheme. Similarly, providers of content, if they are intending to provide that content to the public, are of necessity more identifiable in the market than the individual customer, and that makes them visible to enforcement agencies as well as to their desired customers. Even if one cannot check their correct behavior on every transfer from a content provider, the legal authorities can perform a spot check, perhaps by becoming a customer. If the penalties for noncompliance are substantial, there may be no need to verify the accuracy of every transfer to achieve reasonable compliance.[73] Recognition and exploitation of these differing roles for institutions and for individuals may enhance the viability of end-located applications and the end-to-end approach in general.

Conclusions

The most important benefit of the end-to-end arguments is that they preserve the flexibility, generality, and openness of the Internet. They permit the introduction of new applications; they thus foster innovation, with the social and economic benefits that follow. Movement to put more functions inside the network jeopardizes that generality and flexibility as well as historical patterns of innovation. A new principle evident already is that elements that implement functions that are invisible or hostile to the end-to-end application, in general, have to be "in" the network, because the application cannot be expected to include that intermediate element voluntarily.

Multiple forces seem to promote change within the Internet that may be inconsistent with the end-to-end arguments. While concern has been expressed in some quarters about the increasing involvement of governments, the ISP may present a greater challenge to the traditional structure of the Internet. The ISPs implement the core of the network, and any enhancement or restriction that the ISP implements is likely to appear as new mechanism in the core of the network. As gateways to their customers they are an inherent focal point for others interested in what their customers do, too.

The changing nature of the user base is pushing the Internet in new directions, contributing to both ISP and government efforts. At issue is the amount of endpoint software owned and operated, if not understood, by consumers and therefore the capacity of the Internet system in the large to continue to support an end-to-end philosophy. While the original Internet user was technical and benefited from the flexibility and empowerment of the end-to-end approach, today's consumer approaches the Internet and systems like other consumer electronics and services. Low prices and ease of use are becoming more important than ever, suggesting growing appeal of bundled and managed offerings over do-it-yourself technology. Less work by consumers may imply less control over what they can do on the Internet and who can observe what they do; the incipient controversy over online privacy, however, suggests that there are limits to what many consumers will cede for various reasons.

Of all the changes that are transforming the Internet, the loss of trust may be the most fundamental. The simple model of the early Internet— a group of mutually trusting users attached to a transparent network— is gone forever. A motto for tomorrow may well be "global communication with local trust." Trust issues arise at multiple layers: within Internet-access (e.g., browser) and application software (some of which may trigger Internet access), within activities that access content or effect transactions out at remote sites, within communications of various kinds with strangers, and within the context of access networks—operated by ISPs, employers, and so on—whose operators seek to attend to their own objectives while permitting others to use their networks. Growing concern about trust puts pressure on the traditional Internet support for anonymity. The end-to-end arguments, by their nature, suggest that endpoints can communicate as they please, without constraint from the network, and at least in many Western cultures anonymity is valued in many contexts. Growth in societal use and dependence on the Internet, however, induces calls for accountability (itself varied in meaning), creating pressures to constrain what can happen at endpoints or to track behavior, potentially from within the network. One step that can support trust in some contexts is to provide systematic labeling of content. As ongoing experiments suggest, labeling may assist in protection of privacy, avoidance of objectionable material, and anonymity while preserving end-to-end communications, but it still poses significant technical and legal challenges.

More complex application requirements are leading to the design of applications that depend on trusted third parties to mediate between end users, breaking heretofore straightforward end-to-end communications into series of component end-to-end communications. While this approach will help users that do not totally trust each other to have trustworthy interactions, it adds its own trust problems: how one can know that third parties themselves are actually trustworthy, or that the endpoints are talking to the third party they think they are? It doesn't take too many of these options to realize that resolving Internet trust problems will involve more than technology, and the proliferation of inquiries and programmatic actions by governments plus a variety of legal actions combine to impinge on the Internet and its users.

It may well be that certain kinds of innovation would be stifled if the open and transparent nature of the Internet were to erode. Today there is no evidence that innovation has been stifled overall. The level of investment in new dot-com companies and the range of new offerings for consumers, ranging from e-commerce to online music, all attest to the health of the evolving Internet. But the nature of innovation may have changed. It is no longer the single creative person in the garage but the startup with tens of millions of dollars in backing that is doing the innovation. And it may be that the end-to-end arguments favor the small innovator, while the more complex model of today, with content servers and ISP controls on what services can and cannot be used in what ways, are a barrier to that small innovator, but not to the well-funded innovator who can deal with all these issues as part of launching a new service. So the trend for tomorrow may not be the simple one of slowed innovation, but the more subtle one of innovation by larger players backed with more money.

Perhaps the most insidious threat to the end-to-end arguments, and thus to flexibility, is that commercial investment will go elsewhere, in support of short-term opportunities better met by solutions that are not end-to-end, but based on application-specific servers and services "inside" the network. Content mirroring, which positions copies of content near the consumer for rapid, high-performance delivery, facilitates the delivery of specific material, but only material that has been mirrored. Increasing dependence on content replication might reduce investment in general-purpose upgrades to Internet capacity. It is possible that we will see, not a sudden change in the spirit of the Internet, but a slow ossification of the form and function. In time some new network will appear, perhaps as an overlay on the Internet, that attempts to reintroduce a context for unfettered innovation. The Internet, like the telephone system before it, could become the infrastructure for the system that comes after it.

We have painted two pictures of the constraints that technology imposes on the future Internet. One is that technological solutions are fixed and rigid. They implement some given function, and do so uniformly independent of local needs and requirements. They create a black-and-white outcome in the choice of alternatives. Either an anonymizing service exists, or it does not. On the other hand, we observe in practice that there is a continuing tussle between those who would impose controls and those who would evade them. There is a tussle between spammers and those who would control them, between merchants who need to know who the buyers are and buyers who use untraceable e-mail addresses, and between those who want to limit access to certain content and those who try to reach it. This pattern suggests that the balance of power among the players is not a winner-take-all outcome, but an evolving balance. It suggests that the outcome is not fixed by specific technical alternatives, but by the interplay of the many features and attributes of this very complex system. And it suggests that it is premature to predict the final form. What we can do now is push in ways that tend toward certain outcomes. We argue that the open, general nature of the Net, which derived from the end-to-end arguments, is a valuable characteristic that encourages innovation, and this flexibility should be preserved.

Acknowledgments

David Clark's research is supported by the Defense Advanced Research Projects Agency under contract N6601-98-8903, and by the industrial partners of the MIT Internet & Telecom Convergence Consortium. Marjory Blumenthal is an employee of the complex derived from the National Academy of Sciences, and when this paper was framed in 1998 was also an employee of MIT. The views and conclusions contained herein are those of the authors and should not be interpreted as necessarily representing the official policy or endorsements, either expressed or implied, of DARPA, the U.S. Government, or the National Academies.

Notes

1. See Saltzer, J., D. Reed, and D. D. Clark. 1984. "End-to-End Arguments in System Design." *ACM Transactions on Computer Systems*, Vol. 2, No. 4, November, pp. 277–288.

2. See Computer Science and Telecommunications Board. 1999. *Trust in Cyberspace*, National Academy Press.

3. For one view of spam and its control, see Dorn. D. 1998. "Postage due on junk e-mail—Spam costs Internet millions every month." *Internet Week*, May 4, 1998, at ⟨http://www.techweb.com/se/directlink.cgi?INW19980504S0003⟩. For a summary of legislative approaches to control of spam, see Ouellette, Tim. 1999. "Technology Quick Study: Spam." *Computerworld*, April 5, p. 70. The Mail Abuse Prevention System (MAPS.LLC) provides tools for third parties (ISPs) to filter and control spam. Their charter states that their approach to control of spam is "educating and encouraging ISP's to enforce strong terms and conditions prohibiting their customers from engaging in abusive e-mail practices." See ⟨http://www.mail-abuse.org/⟩.

4. There has been a great deal of work over the last decade to define what are called Quality of Service mechanisms for the Internet. See Braden, R., D. Clark and S. Shenker. 1994. *Integrated services in the Internet architecture: an overview*. RFC 1633, IETF, and Carlson, M., et al. 1998. *An Architecture for Differentiated Services*. RFC 2475, IETF. The progress of this work is reported at ⟨http://www.ietf.org/html.charters/intserv-charter.html⟩ and ⟨http://www.ietf.org/html.charters/diffserv-charter.html⟩.

5. See Larson, Gary, and Jeffrey Chester. 1999. *Song of the Open Road: Building a Broadband Network for the 21st Century*. The Center for Media Education Section IV, p. 6, available at ⟨http://www.cme.org/broadband/openroad. pdf⟩.

6. We also discuss other kinds of third parties, whose services may be sought out by the communicating endpoints or whose actions are otherwise tolerated by them. There is growing potential for both kinds of third parties, but this section focuses on the imposition of unwelcome third parties.

7. This trend is signaled by the rise of the Application Service Provider, or ASP, as a part of the landscape.

8. A common method for constructing "configuration-free," or "plug and play," or "works out of the box" devices is to assume that some other element takes on the role of controlling setup and configuration. Of course, centralization raises other issues, such as a common point of vulnerability, and the proper balance is not yet clear between centralization and distribution of security function for consumer networking.

9. For example, see Saltzer, Jerome H. 1999. *"Open Access" is Just the Tip of the Iceberg*. October 22, available at ⟨http://web.mit.edu/Saltzer/www/ publications/openaccess.html⟩. and Lemley, Mark A. and Lawrence Lessig. 1999. Filing before the Federal Communications Commission (In the Matter of Application for Consent to the Transfer of Control of Licenses MediaOne Group, Inc. To AT&T Corp. CS Docket No. 99-251). Available at ⟨http:// cyber.law.harvard.edu/works/lessig/MB.html⟩. Lessig's work can be seen in overview at ⟨http://cyber.law.harvard.edu⟩. For a lightweight example that speaks directly to end to end, see: Lessig, Lawrence. 1999. "It's the Architecture, Mr. Chairman."

10. The Electronic Signatures in Global and National Commerce Act is an indicator of the broadening recognition of a need for tools to support network-mediated transactions, although observers note that it raises its own questions about how to do so—resolving the technology and policy issues will take more work.

11. Chaum, David. 1992. "Achieving Electronic Privacy." *Scientific American*, August, pp. 96–101.

12. It may seem that this attention to protection of identity, especially as it manifests itself in low-level information such as addresses, is exaggerated. The telephone system provides an illustration of how attention to identity has grown and added complexity to communications. For most of the history of the telephone system, the called telephone (and thus the person answering the phone) had no idea what the number of the caller was. Then the "caller ID" feature was invented to show the caller's number to the called party. This very shortly led to a demand for a way to prevent this information from being passed across the telephone network. Adding this capability, which reinstituted caller anonymity at the level of the phone number, led in turn to demand for the feature that a receiver could refuse to receive a call from a person who refused to reveal his phone number. Additional issues have arisen about the treatment of phone numbers used by people who have paid for "unlisted" numbers, which appears to

vary by telephone service provider and state regulatory decision. Given the emergence of this rather complex balance of power in conventional telephony, there is no reason to think that users of the Internet will eventually demand any less. Even if the identity of the individual user is not revealed, this low-level information can be used to construct profiles of aggregate behavior, as in Amazon's summer-1999 publicity about book-buying patterns of employees of large organizations based on e-mail addresses. See Amazon.com. 1999. "Amazon.com Introduces 'Purchase Circles [TM],' Featuring Thousands of Bestseller Lists for Hometowns, Workplaces, Universities, and More." Press Release, Seattle, August 20, available at www.amazon.com; McCullagh, Declan. 1999. "Big Brother, Big 'Fun' at Amazon." *Wired*, August 25, available at ⟨www.wired.com/news/news/business/story/21417.html⟩; Reuters. 1999. "Amazon modifies purchase data policy." *Zdnet*, August 27, available at ⟨www.zdnet.com/filters/printerfriendly/0,6061,2322310-2,00.html⟩; and Amazon.com. 1999 "Amazon.com Modifies "Purchase Circles [TM]" Feature." Press Release, Seattle, August 26, available at ⟨www.amazon.com⟩.

13. An example of this give and take is the popularity of e-mail accounts from a provider such as Hotmail that does not require the user to prove who he really is (as would be required where a financial account is established). This permits the user to send messages with relative anonymity. As a result of this, some online merchants will not accept orders from users on Hotmail accounts.

14. Cookies may be part of a larger class of monitoring software. See, for example, O'Harrow, Jr., Robert. 1999. "Fearing a Plague of 'Web Bugs': Invisible Fact-Gathering Code Raises Privacy Concerns." *Washington Post*, November 13, pp. E1, E8.

15. See O'Harrow, R., and E. Corcoran. 1999. "Intel Drops Plans for ID Numbers." *Washington Post*, January 26. ⟨http://www.washingtonpost.com/wp-srv/washtech/daily/jan99/intel26.htm⟩. Intel backed away from use of the ID as an identifier in e-commerce transactions under consumer pressure. See ⟨http://www.bigbrotherinside.com/⟩.

16. Microsoft implemented a scheme to tag all documents produced using Office 97 with a unique ID derived from the network address of the machine. In response to public criticism, they made it possible to disable this feature. They also discontinued the reporting of the hardware unique ID of each machine during online registration of Windows 98. See ⟨http://www.microsoft.com/presspass/features/1999/03-08custletter2.htm⟩.

17. See Cha, Ariana Eunjung. 2000. "Your PC Is Watching: Programs That Send Personal Data Becoming Routine." *The Washington Post*, July 14, pp. A1, A12–13.

18. See Computer Science and Telecommunications Board. 2000. *The Digital Dilemma: Intellectual Property in the Information Age*, National Academy Press.

19. D'Antoni, H. 2000. "Web Surfers Beware: Someone's Watching." *InformationWeek Online*, February 7, ⟨http://www.informationweek.com/bizint/biz772/72bzweb.htm⟩. Examples of currently available software include SurfWatch, at

⟨http://www1.surfwatch.com/products/swwork.html⟩, and Internet Resource Manager, at ⟨http://www.sequeltech.com/⟩.

20. The rash of denial-of-service attacks on major Web sites in early 2000 illustrates the magnitude of this problem.

21. Moss, Michael. 1999. "Inside the game of E-Mail Hijacking." *The Wall Street Journal*, November 9, pp. B1, B4. "Already, the Internet is awash in Web sites that trick people into clicking on by using addresses that vary only slightly from the sites being mimicked: an extra letter here, a dropped hyphen there. Now, in near secrecy, some of these same look-alike Web sites are grabbing e-mail as well."

22. A series of publicized problems affecting Microsoft's Internet Explorer, and the generation of associated software fixes, is documented on the Microsoft security site: ⟨http://www.microsoft.com/windows/ie/security/default.asp⟩. A similar list of issues for Netscape Navigator can be found at ⟨http://home.netscape.com/security/notes/⟩.

23. Saltzer, Jerome. 1998. Personal communication, Nov. 11.

24. As opposed to taxation of the use of the Internet per se, like taxation of telephone service. This discussion does not address the merits of taxation; it proceeds from the recognition of (multiple) efforts to implement it.

25. For example, independent of technology, income tax compliance is promoted by the practice—and risk—of audits.

26. Practically, many pornography sites today use the combination of possession of a credit card and a self-affirmation of age as an acceptable assurance of adulthood—although some minors have credit cards. Indicating adulthood has different ramifications from indicating minority, as Lessig has noted; the intent here is to contrast identification of content and users.

27. There are other purposes for which a control point "in" the net might be imposed to achieve a supposedly more robust solution than an endpoint implementation can provide. These include facilitating eavesdropping/wiretap, collection of taxes and fees associated with transactions using the network, and so on. One question now being discussed in the Internet Engineering Task Force (IETF) is how, if at all, Internet protocols should be modified to support Communications Assistance for Law Enforcement Act of 1995 (CALEA) wiretap regulations. See Clausing, Jeri. 1999. "Internet Engineers Reject Wiretap Proposal." *The New York Times*, November 11, p. B10. The current sentiment in the design community is that this is not an appropriate goal for the IETF. However, there appears to be some interest from equipment vendors in conforming to CALEA, given interest expressed by their customers, so the outcome of this discussion remains unclear.

28. It is possible that the introduction of the new Internet address space, as part of the next-generation Internet protocol called IPv6, with its much larger set of addresses, will alleviate the need for NAT devices. There is much current debate on whether NAT devices are a temporary fix or now a permanent part of the Internet.

29. As this paper was being completed, news broke about the FBI's "Carnivore" system, characterized as an "Internet wiretapping system" that is deployed at an ISP's premises. See King, Neil, Jr., and Ted Bridis. 2000. "FBI's Wiretaps To Scan E-Mail Spark Concern." *The Wall Street Journal*, July 11, pp. A3, A6. Also, note that users who move from place to place and dial in to different phone numbers do not use the same physical link for successive access, but since they have to authenticate themselves to the ISP to complete the connection, the ISP knows who is dialing and could institute logging accordingly.

30. Similarly, if an organization has any requirement imposed on it to control the behavior of its users, it will be at the point of egress that the control can best be imposed.

31. Of course, this sort of control is not perfect. It is possible for a creative user to purchase a number of ISP accounts and move from one to another in an unpredictable way. This is what is happening today in the battle between spammers and those who would control them, another example of the dynamic tussle between control and avoidance.

32. California Assembly Bill 1676, enacted 1998.

33. For a detailed discussion of labels on content and on users, see Lessig, Lawrence, and Paul Resnick (1999). "Zoning Speech on the Internet: A Legal and Technical Model." *Michigan Law Review* 98(2): 395–431.

34. This is a critical issue for the viability of industry self-regulation. That topic, given the looming prospect of government regulation, is the subject of much debate. Major industry players and scholars, for example, participated in a 1999 international conference organized by the Bertelsmann Foundation, which cast labeling approaches as user-empowering and urged government support for private filtering based on labeling. See Bertelsmann Foundation. 1999. *Self-regulation of Internet Content*. Gutersloh, Germany, September, available at ⟨http://www.stiftung.bertelsmann.de/internetcontent/english/content/c2340. htm⟩.

35. See, for example, U.S. Federal Trade Commission. 1998. *Advertising and Marketing on the Internet: Rules of the Road*. Washington, DC, August, available at ⟨www.ftc.gov⟩.

36. The PICS web site maintained by the World Wide Web Consortium is ⟨http://www.w3.org/pics⟩.

37. There are a number of Web proxy servers that implement PICS filtering. See ⟨http://www.n2h2.com/pics/proxy_servers.html⟩.

38. For a discussion of concerns aroused by PICS, see ⟨http://rene.efa.org.au/ liberty/label.html⟩. For a response to such concerns by one of the PICS developers and proponents, see Resnick, Paul, ed. 1999. "PICS, Censorship, & Intellectual Freedom FAQ." Available at ⟨www.w3.org/PICS/PICS-FAQ980126. HTML⟩.

39. The Metatdata web site maintained by the World Wide Web Consortium is ⟨http://www.w3.org/Metadata/⟩.

40. For example, there have been lawsuits attempting to prevent the use of a trademark in the metadata field of a page not associated with the holder of the mark. A summary of some lawsuits related to trademarks in metadata can be found at ⟨http://www.searchenginewatch.com/resources/metasuits.html⟩.

41. Examples of anonymizing browser services can be found at ⟨http://www.anonymizer.com⟩, ⟨http://www.idzap.net/⟩, ⟨http://www.rewebber.com/⟩, ⟨http://www.keepitsecret.com/⟩, ⟨http://www.confidentialonline.com/home.html⟩, and ⟨http://www.websperts.net/About_Us/Privacy/clandestination.shtml⟩. The last of these offers a service in which the anonymous intermediate is located in a foreign country to avoid the reach of the U.S. legal system. The quality of some of these services is questioned in Oakes, Chris, 1999. "Anonymous Web Surfing? Uh-Uh," *Wired News*, Apr. 13, ⟨http://www.wired.com/news/technology/0,1282,19091,00.html⟩.

42. For one example of a system that tries to provide protection from traffic analysis, see Goldschlag, David M., Michael G. Reed, and Paul F. Syverson. 1999. "Onion Routing for Anonymous and Private Internet Connections." *Communications of the ACM*, Vol. 42, No. 2, February. For a complete bibliography and discussion, see ⟨http://onion-router.nrl.navy.mil/⟩.

43. Mazières, David, and M. Frans Kaashoek. 1998. "The design, implementation and operation of an e-mail pseudonym server." *Proceedings of the 5th ACM Conference on Computer and Communications Security* (CCS-5). San Francisco, California, November, pp. 27–36.

44. The outgoing message is prefaced with a sequence of addresses, each specifying a relay point. Each address is encrypted using the public key of the prior hop, so that the relay point, and only the relay point, can decrypt the address of the next hop the message should take, using its matching private key. Each relay point delays the message for an unpredictable time, so that it is hard to correlate an incoming and an outgoing message. If enough hops are used, it becomes almost impossible to trace the path from destination back to the source.

45. For a review of tools currently available to filter spam in mail servers, see ⟨http://spam.abuse.net/tools/mailblock.html⟩.

46. More complex replication/hosting schemes for controlled staging of content provide features to remedy these limitations, in return for which the content provider must usually pay a fee to the service.

47. This topic has been receiving more analysis in different contexts. For a legal assessment, see, for example, Froomkin, A. Michael. 1996. "The Essential Role of Trusted Third Parties in Electronic Commerce," *Oregon Law Review* 75: 29, available at ⟨www.law.miami.edu/~froomkin/articles/trustedno.htm⟩.

48. For example, see the mutual commitment protocol in Zhou, Jianying, and Dieter Gollmann. 1996 "A Fair Non-repudiation Protocol." *Proceedings of the 1996 Symposium on Security and Privacy*, Oakland, May 6–8.

49. A notary is "[a] responsible person appointed by state government to witness the signing of important documents and administer oaths." See National

Notary Association. 1997. "What is a Notary Public?" Chatsworth, CA, at ⟨http://www.nationalnotary.org/actionprograms/WhatisNotaryPublic.pdf⟩. Recognition of this role has led to the investigation of a "cyber-notary" as a useful agent within the Internet. This has been a topic of study by the American Bar Association, but there does not appear to be an active interest at this time.

50. There is a partial analogy with payment by check, where the bank balance is normally not verified at the moment of purchase. However, the taker of the check may demand other forms of identification, which can assist in imposing a fee for a bad check. If a certificate has been invalidated, the recipient cannot even count on knowing who the other party in the transaction actually is. So there may be fewer options for later recourse.

51. We emphasize the broader choice of mechanism out of the recognition that technologists often prefer technical solutions. The Internet philosophy acknowledged early in the paper argues for the superiority of technology over other kinds of mechanisms. See, for example, Goldberg, Ian, David Wagner, and Eric Brewer. 1997. "Privacy-enhancing technologies for the Internet," available at ⟨www.cs.berkeley.edu/~daw/privacy-compcon97-222/privacy-html.html⟩. Those authors observe that "[t]he cyperpunks' credo can be roughly paraphrased as 'privacy through technology, not through legislation.' If we can guarantee privacy protection through the laws of mathematics rather than the laws of men and whims of bureaucrats, then we will have made an important contribution to society. It is this vision which guides and motivates our approach to Internet privacy."

52. There is no technical verification that this number is indeed sent (fax is, like the Internet, very much an end-to-end design), but the presumption is that the law can be used to keep unwanted faxes at an acceptable level. Note also that this law, which had the goal of controlling receipt of unwanted material, outlaws "anonymous faxes," in contrast to telephone calls, where one can prevent the caller's phone number from being passed to the called party.

53. This trend was emphasized by the mid-1999 establishment, by executive order, of a federal task force concerned with illegal conduct on the Internet: President's Working Group on Unlawful Conduct on the Internet. 2000. *The Electronic Frontier: The Challenge of Unlawful Conduct Involving the Use of the Internet.* March. Available at ⟨http://www.usdoj.gov/criminal/cybercrime/unlawful.htm⟩.

54. The authors recognize that today on the Internet various labels are associated with voluntary schemes for content rating, etc.; illustrations of the complementarity of law or regulation come, at present, from other domains. Note, however, that the Bertelsmann Foundation conference summary cited above specifically cast law enforcement as a complement to voluntary labeling. It observed (p. 45):

Law enforcement is the basic mechanism employed within any country to prevent, detect, investigate and prosecute illegal and harmful content on the Internet. This state reaction is essential for various reasons: It guarantees the state monopoly on power and public order, it is democratically legitimized and directly enforceable and it secures justice, equity and legal certainty. However, a mere system of legal regulation armed with law enforcement would be ineffective because of the technical, fast-changing and global nature of the Internet. In a coordinated approach, self-regulatory mechanisms have to be combined with law enforcement as a necessary backup.

55. U.S. Federal Communications Commission, "V-Chip Homepage," available at ⟨http://www.fcc.gov/vchip/⟩.

56. Information on Amazon.com was cited above. On RealNetworks, see: Clark, Don. 1999. "RealNetworks Will Issue Software Patch To Block Its Program's Spying on Users." *The Wall Street Journal*, November 2, p. B8. That article explains, "Unbeknownst to users, the [Real-Jukebox] software regularly transmitted information over the Internet to the company, including what CDs users played and how many songs were loaded on their disk drives." DoubleClick presented a broader privacy challenge because it tracked consumer movement across sites and products; the controversy it caused precipitated broad reactions, including government investigation due to a complaint made to the Federal Trade Commission. See: Tedeschi, Bob. 2000. "Critics Press Legal Assault on Tracking of Web Users." *The New York Times*, February 7, pp. C1, C10.

57. Simpson, Glenn R. 2000. "E-Commerce Firms Start to Rethink Opposition To Privacy Regulation as Abuses, Anger Rise." *The Wall Street Journal*, January 6, p. A24.

58. What individuals can do for themselves, and what industry does, depends, of course, on incentives, which are a part of the nontechnical mechanism picture. Recent controversy surrounding the development of UCITA illustrates differing expectations on and interpretations of who incurs what costs and benefits. An issue with these evolving frameworks is the reality that consumers, in particular, and businesses often prefer to avoid the costs of litigation.

59. The operators of the server are happy to provide what information they have in response to any court order, but the system was carefully designed to make this information useless.

60. This tension among technology, law, and other influences on behavior is at the heart of the much-discussed writing of Lawrence Lessig on the role of "code" (loosely, technology). See his 1999 book, *Code and Other Laws of Cyberspace*, Basic Books, New York. Critical responses to *Code* … note that technology is malleable rather than constant—a premise of this paper—and so are government and industry interests and motives. See, for example, Mann, Charles C. 1999. "The Unacknowledged Legislators of the Digital world." *Atlantic Unbound*, December 15, available at ⟨www.theatlantic.com/unbound/digicult/dc991215. htm⟩.

61. What is known as "conflict of laws" provides a set of principles and models for addressing legal problems that span at least two jurisdictions. Resolving such problems is hard in the context of real space, and cyberspace adds additional challenges, but progress under the conflict-of-laws rubric illuminates approaches that include private agreements on which laws will prevail under which circumstances, international harmonization (difficult and slow but already in progress), and indirect regulation, which targets the local effects (e.g., behavior of people and equipment) of extraterritorial activity. For an overview, see Goldsmith, Jack

L. 1998. "Against Cyberanarchy." *The University of Chicago Law Review*, 65: 4, Fall, pp. 1199–1250. Among other things, Goldsmith explains that: "Cyberspace presents two related choice-of-law problems. The first is the problem of complexity. This is the problem of how to choose a single governing law for cyberspace activity that has multiple jurisdictional contacts. The second problem concerns situs. This is the problem of how to choose a governing law when the locus of activity cannot easily be pinpointed in geographical space" (p. 1234). Case law shows that these issues are being worked out (or at least worked on). See, for example: Fusco, Patricia. 1999. "Judge rules ISP, Server Location May Determine Jurisdiction." ISP–Planet, June 11, available at ⟨www.isp-planet.com/politics/061199jurisdiction.html⟩; and Kaplan, Carl S. 1999. "Judge in Gambling Case Takes On Sticky Issue of Jurisdiction." *The New York Times*, August 13, p. B10. The latter addressed the interplay of state law with federal law, which proscribes gambling via the Wire Act (18 USC 1084) and the Travel Act (18 USC 1952) and the Interstate Transportation of Wagering Paraphernalia Act (18 USC 1953). Some of these issues have been attacked by the American Bar Association's Internet Jurisdiction Project; see ⟨http://www.kentlaw.edu/cyberlaw/⟩.

62. See Computer Science and Telecommunications Board. 1994. *Realizing the Information Future: The Internet and Beyond*, National Academy Press, and Computer Science and Telecommunications Board. 1999. *Funding a Revolution: government Support for Computing Research*, National Academy Press.

63. Large ISPs such as AOL have attempted to attain control over the end nodes by distributing their own browser, which they encourage or require the user to employ. This approach has proved successful to some extent. In the future, we can expect to see ISP interest in extending their control over the endpoint to the extend possible, for example by means of added function in Internet set-top boxes and other devices they install in the home.

64. For example, see the Appropriate Use Policy of Excite@Home, at ⟨http://www.home.com/aup/⟩, which specifically prohibits the operation of servers over their residential Internet service.

65. For an assessment of possible outcomes, see Saltzer, Jerome. 1999. "'Open Access' is Just the Tip of the Iceberg," essay prepared for the Newton, MA Cable Commission, October 22, at ⟨http://mit.edu/Saltzer/www/publications/openaccess.html⟩. After succinctly commenting on a number of possible outcomes that he finds undesirable, Saltzer notes that the most dire possible outcome of today's open-access tussle, without open access and stifled competition and innovation, "is looking increasingly unlikely, as customers and cable competitors alike begin to understand better why the Internet works the way it does and the implications of some of the emerging practices."

66. See material cited in note 10 above. Note also the concerns raised under the rubric of "peering." See, for example, Caruso, Denise. 2000. "Digital Commerce: The Internet relies on networks' passing data to one another. But what happens if one of them refuses?" *The New York Times*, February 14, p. C4.

67. Common carriage implies certain rights and certain responsibilities, such as the provider's obligation to serve all comers while being protected from liability

if those subscribers use the network for unacceptable purposes. The fact that the Internet has been designed such that (by the end-to-end arguments) ISPs cannot easily control the content sent over their networks and the fact that ISPs appear to serve all comers have caused some to suggest that ISPs be treated as common carriers; the suggestion also arises from those who perceive a greater ability of ISPs to control content than their nominal business and technology would suggest.

68. The late-1990s development of concern about "critical infrastructure" intensifies the attention and concern associated with growing reliance on the Internet, with explorations by the government and some industry leaders of new programs and mechanisms for monitoring use or "abuse" of the Internet and for increasing its robustness against malicious or accidental disruption. See Blumenthal, Marjory S. 1999. "Reliable and Trustworthy: The Challenge of Cyber-Infrastructure Protection at the Edge of the Millennium," *iMP Magazine*, September, ⟨http://www.cisp.org/imp/september_99/09_99blumenthal.htm⟩.

69. The popular fictional character Harry Potter receives some advice that might apply equally to his world and the Internet: "Never trust anything that can think for itself if you can't see where it keeps its brain." Rowling, J.K. 1998. *Harry Potter and the Chamber of Secrets*. Bloomsbury Publishing, London, p. 242.

70. Pomfret, John. 2000. "China Puts Clamps on Internet; Communists Seek Information Curb," *The Washington Post*, January 27.

71. See Computer Science and Telecommunications Board. 1996. *Cryptography's Role in Securing the Information Society*. National Academy Press.

72. Already today regulatory agencies (e.g., the Federal Trade Commission) are doing spot-checks of actual Web sites.

73. This approach is somewhat similar to the practice in some parts of the world of not always checking that passengers on public transit have the proper ticket in hand. Instead, roving inspectors perform spot-checks. If the fine for failing to have the right ticket is high enough, this scheme can achieve reasonable compliance.

5

The InterNAT: Policy Implications of the Internet Architecture Debate

Hans Kruse, William Yurcik, and Lawrence Lessig

1   Introduction

There are two classic models for intelligence within networks [LEAR00]. The first is an end-system model. Under this design, end-devices have no intelligence; the network devices to which they connect provide all the services. The telephone system is an example of just such a network. End-systems have well-known benefits and costs. The absence of intelligence in end-devices makes them inexpensive to manufacture and manage, but network devices (central-office switches) in turn become expensive and complex to maintain.

The second model for intelligence within networks is end-to-end.[4] First proposed by Saltzer, Reed, and Clark in 1981, the end-to-end model is a set of architectural principles that guide the placement of functions within a distributed system [SALTZER81]. According to the argument, lower layers of a distributed system should avoid providing functions that can be implemented in higher layers (end-systems), especially if (1) the function cannot be completely implemented in lower layers and (2) all applications would not benefit from such functions.

End-to-end thus shifts intelligence in a network to the application hosts. It therefore also shifts cost and management complexity from routers and switches to hosts. This is a benefit for those maintaining the network. Another benefit is that congestion control can be managed between hosts; it is therefore not required that state information be kept within routers to optimize performance.[5] In the end-to-end design the network simply acts as a transparent transport mechanism for individual packets with each packet being labeled by globally unique source/destination addresses.

This notion of "transparency" implicit within an end-to-end design has a number of technical and policy consequences. It demands that network devices between two end-systems not modify information within the packet above the data link layer, except under well-defined circumstances.[6] Changing IP addresses is not viewed as acceptable, nor is any change to the transport layer (layer 4) or above.

2   The Problem: Unexpected Protocol Interactions

The New York City Board of Education is using network address translators as a security measure to keep their 1000 + schools off the public network (Internet). Teachers are reporting that the networks are unusable because of them. Many of the educational benefits that the schools want to gain from being connected to the Internet are inaccessible because of the limitations network address translators place on the type of connections that may be made (and accepted).[7]

The end-to-end model is a choice, not a necessity, in the Internet's design. The Internet Engineering Task Force (IETF) has traditionally been instrumental in supporting end-to-end with "rough consensus and working code."[8] In fact, one of the authors of the original end-to-end model paper, David Clark, chaired the Internet Activities Board (IAB) overseeing the IETF from 1981 to 1989. But the design is increasingly under threat. In reflecting on the state of the Internet in late 1999, a current member of the IAB and present/past chair of numerous IETF working groups, Steve Deering,[9] summarized his thoughts on intelligence within networks with a slide called "Internet is Losing?"[10] The examples he used included:

· Unique IP addresses are no longer necessary.
· The Internet is not always on (many users log on via America Online, etc.).
· End-to-end transparency is often blocked behind network address translators and firewalls.

While the intelligence in the existing Internet remains concentrated in end-systems, users are increasingly deploying more sophisticated processing within the network for a variety of reasons including security, network management, e-commerce, and survivability. The following are some specific examples:

· The use of network address translators to solve IP address depletion problems.

- The use of performance-enhancing proxies to tune protocols on links with unusual characteristics, e.g. in terrestrial and satellite-based wireless systems.
- The use of tunneling and other virtual private network techniques to provide secure connectivity over the Internet to an organization's intranet/extranet.
- The use of firewalls and intrusion detection to prevent and respond to malicious attacks.
- The deployment of quality-of-service mechanisms to provide delay, delay jitter, and packet loss guarantees to applications and network services.

Our point is not to question the need that has led to each of these devices. No doubt each addresses important network needs that demand resolution. Rather than debate the benefit of each such device and their legitimacy with the network, we accept the notion that such technologies are here to stay, at least for the short term. End-to-end will not be reestablished by banishing such devices. But the presence of such devices threatens the existing end-to-end Internet. The problem is acerbated in the present context by the inability of hosts and applications to detect intelligent network devices.

While the next generation of the Internet Protocol, IPv6, has been designed to solve many of these problems, migration will take time. Not only must protocol stacks and routers be upgraded, but applications must be changed to conform to the new structure of the IPv6 addresses. The good news is that IPv6 has been designed so that IPv4 and IPv6 can coexist while IPv6 is deployed gradually. The bad news is that this coexistence means that there will be less pressure to move from IPv4 to IPv6. In addition, devices designed to provide network security, improved performance, and network monitoring will continue to "break" the end-to-end model even in the IPv6 network.

In the meantime, there are significant costs to the end-to-end Internet. Applications and application-layer protocols interact in unexpected ways with intelligent network devices within the current IPv4 Internet model. This is a consequence of intelligent network devices reducing the transparency of the network. The critical element of transparency is some ability to predict how the network will behave [CHEN98]. To quote from a 1998 paper by the original authors of the end-to-end model [CHEN98]:

Since lower-level network resources are shared among many different users with different applications, the complexity of potential interactions among independent users rises with the complexity of the behaviors that the users or applications can request. For example, when the lower layer offers a simple store-and-forward packet transport service, interactions take the form of end-to-end delay that can be modeled by relatively straightforward queuing models. *Adding priority mechanisms (to limit the impact of congestion) that are fixed at design time adds modest complexity to models that predict the behavior of the system. But relatively simple programming capabilities, such as allowing packets to change priority dynamically within the network, may create behaviors that are intractable to model.*

The network therefore faces an important trade-off. Maintaining the largest degree of network transparency constrains interactions among different users of a shared lower level so that network behavior can be predicted, but it also creates performance and security problems that cannot be easily solved. Therefore, deployment of some of the features required by the network users requires the use of devices that violate end-to-end transparency; this diminishing transparency increases unexpected interactions between protocols.

We have identified three distinct types of unexpected protocol interactions that have been introduced by the diminishing of transparency due to the deployment of intelligent network devices:

• Some network devices attempt to read or modify portions of transmitted packets that the sending system assumes fixed (e.g., performance enhancing proxies, network address translators).

• The use of IP tunnels creates the design issue of how to construct the second "outer" IP header upon tunnel ingress,[11] and the more complicated issue of whether the original "inner" IP header needs to be modified upon tunnel egress,[12] based on changes that intermediate nodes made to the outer header [e.g., tunneling and virtual private networks].

• Some devices, deliberately or due to limits in their design, prevent some packets from traversing that device (e.g., firewalls, intrusion detection).

In this chapter we examine these protocol interactions in a effort to understand recent protocol design decisions and their effect on the transparency provided by the end-to-end Internet model. We are particularly interested in examining the protocol structures involved to determine why the traditional protection against protocol interactions inherent in the layered protocols could not prevent the observed problems. The remainder of this chapter is organized as follows: section 3 describes the use and interaction of network address translators and other network devices that destroy transparency. Section 4 states the policy implications of these challenges to the end-to-end Internet model. In section 5 we close with a summary and directions for future work.

3   Layer-Violation Network Devices

One of several design philosophies behind the Internet protocols is to provide a variety of services based on the concept of layers [CLARK95]. This layered design is intended to provide needed information to each type of network device independent of the information required for other devices. A network device should normally operate at or below the network layer of the protocol stack, e.g., the IP layer in TCP/IP. End-systems rely on the end-to-end Internet model to provide transparency to layer information (IP layer and above) such that this layer information remains unchanged or invisible. However, a number of special circumstances have led to the creation of layer-violation (LV) network devices that rely on information from protocol layers they would not normally access [KRUSE99].

3.1   Network Address Translators (NATs) and Performance-Enhancing Proxies (PEPs)

There is no longer a single Internet address space. We're going to have to call it the InterNAT.[13]

NATs allow the use of private IP addresses in a private intranet while maintaining connectivity to the Internet through one or more global IP addresses. Since many applications assume that the end-system address is globally unique, NAT usually require application-level gateways that modify application-specific sections of the packet where the end-system address has been embedded. These gateways cause changes in the packet that are unanticipated by the end-systems [HAIN00, HOLDREGE00]. A Network Address and Port Translator (NAPT) cannot forward a connection request from the Internet to a private network unless an administrative mapping has been provided for the port requested in the incoming packet. Other packets may be dropped or misrouted because the NAPT does not have the appropriate application-level gateway and thus fails to make corrections in the packet to allow the application's peer to respond.

It should also be noted that with the advent of dial-up Internet users whose IP address is allocated at dial-up time, the actual IP addresses of such users is purely transient. During their period of validity they can be relied upon end-to-end, but these IP numbers have no permanent associations with the domain name of any host and are recycled for reuse at the end of every session. Similarly, LAN-based users typically use DHCP[14] to acquire a new address at system restart.

PEPs are used in networks with unusual link characteristics [ALLMAN99]. These proxies may attempt to read transport-level information in the packet or they may add and delete packets from the flow. Many of these proxies can be bypassed by flows that do not permit such interactions, at risk of suffering from poor performance. Both NAT and PEP devices vastly complicate the deployment of IP-level security between end-systems [KRUSE99], and they may cause other failures that can be difficult to diagnose [CARPENTER00]. For instance, both the NAT and PEP devices usually do not report the fact that they failed to correctly handle a packet, were bypassed, or dropped a packet they could not process due to insufficient information. Encrypted packets will be examined by the security software at the receiving end where modifications made by the NAT or PEP device will be interpreted as illegal tampering and the packet will be discarded by the security software. While dropping packets is an auditable event, the sender of the packet is usually not notified.

3.2   Tunneling and Virtual Private Networks (VPNs)

IP tunnels are defined as a section of the network in which IP packets are encapsulated inside a second IP header (often called the "outer header"). The tunnel is designed to transport packets between two intermediate points in the network, without making reference to the actual IP packets during the tunnel section of the packet's path. Tunnels can serve a number of purposes, including:

• Transport of multiple protocols over an IPv4 router infrastructure (i.e., IPv6, IPX, AppleTalk) as well as service types not supported by intermediate nodes (i.e., multicast backbone or MBONE).

• Secure passage between two nodes at the edges of trusted domains. Inside the tunnel, original IP packets are encrypted and therefore completely inaccessible.

• Creation of VPNs. In this scheme, packets between two sites are carried over IP tunnels to provide isolation from the addressing and routing requirements of the Internet. A similar type of tunnel can be used to connect an off-site user to the corporate network.

The use of tunnels creates specific types of protocol interaction problems. Specifically how should the outer IP header be constructed at the tunnel ingress point? In general, it seems reasonable to copy fields from the original IP header; however, this is not always the correct approach. In networks that provide quality-of-service control through resource reservation [TERZIS00] or differentiated service [BLAKE98], the tunnel may be used to traverse a portion of the network that cannot provide these services, and therefore requires that some of the original IP settings not be copied. In other cases [FLOYD00], the ability of the tunnel egress point to provide certain types of processing will determine how to construct the outer IP header.

By far the more complicated issues arise upon tunnel egress. Some portions of the outer IP header may have been modified during tunnel traversal. Examples include updating of header fields that mark the packet as being in a particular differentiated service group, or updating of fields designed to provide explicit congestion notification to endpoints. The tunnel egress node must merge the original IP header with the—possibly modified—outer IP header. The rules for doing this are ambiguous and different procedures may emerge. For example, from a performance and application perspective, one would wish to propagate congestion notification information across security tunnels. From a security perspective, one may wish to discard the entire outer IP header, regardless of its content, to prevent attacks based on the ability of hostile systems to modify the unprotected outer IP header inside the tunnel.

3.3 Firewalls, Intrusion Detection, and IPsec
Several devices can discard packets before they reach the end-system destination address. Most prominently, firewalls are designed to do just that for all packets that have not been entered in a permission list. Firewalls, by their very nature, fundamentally diminish transparency. Typically the source is not notified of the fact that the packet was dropped (although auditing of dropped packets can be performed at the firewall). In order

to prevent attacks, many corporate firewalls will not permit network-management packets (e.g., ICMP) to pass through.

Intrusion detection (ID) is a monitoring and auditing system for attempted and successful system breaches with the goal of detecting and ultimately preventing such activity. Because many attacks can be recognized by their signature (headers), the best place to process information is at the network layer. Since ID is based on algorithms that correlate network layer information with signatures, they require large amounts of storage. The state of the art is reactive offline processing. ID systems are currently maturing and the next generation will rely on integration with routers to monitor activity proactively in real time. One example of a transparency issue related to ID systems is fragmentation. While fragmentation is a useful method for supporting various media on internetworks, it may mean caching packets at the ID system to reassemble for inspection—a process that destroys transparency and could be a performance bottleneck.

At the other end of the spectrum from filtering and correlating packets is security. IPsec is actually an architecture—a collection of protocols, authentication, and encryption mechanisms—as described in [KENT98]. The loss of transparency is both a bug and a feature from the security standpoint [CARPENTER00]. To the extent that it prevents the end-to-end deployment of IPsec, it damages security and creates vulnerabilities. For example, if a NAT is in the path, the best that can be done is to decrypt and re-encrypt IP traffic in the NAT with the traffic momentarily in plaintext. Since NATs are prime targets for attack already, this is unacceptable. Indeed, NATs break other security mechanisms as well, such as Kerberos and DNSSEC, since these rely upon address values. In a weaker sense, the loss of transparency at an intranet/Internet boundary may be considered a security feature since it is a well-defined point to enforce security policy. However, such a security strategy is vulnerable to insider attack and boundary penetrations that expose the entire intranet to trivial attack. Lastly, where cryptographic algorithms are used, protocols should be designed to permit alternative algorithms to be used. There have been several efforts by corporations to embed their own patented cryptographic algorithms within a protocol to capture a market while at the same time severely limiting end-to-end transparency.

Electronic commerce applications commonly require the implementation of procedures to insure confidentiality (usually via encryption), authentication, non-repudiation, and availability (especially the prevention of denial-of-service attacks). In many cases these systems are based on end-to-end semantics that rely on the transport-layer information remaining unchanged within the network. LV network devices also hinder the deployment of this security infrastructure [KRUSE99].

3.4   Quality-of-Service (QoS) Mechanisms

Classically, the end-to-end model views the network as a monolithic entity that provides a single QoS to all users, best-effort delivery. The Internet has expanded to incorporate applications with requirements for guarantees on network behavior beyond best-effort delivery. In the case of mechanisms such as RSVP, the host signals to the network the level of service it requires, whereas with differentiated services (DIFFSERV) the network prioritizes traffic without the host's knowledge or consent [BRADEN97, BLAKE98]. Both end-systems and LV network devices cooperate to provide deterministic and statistical QoS guarantees on metrics such as delay, delay variation, and packet loss rates. It is an open problem how to provide QoS guarantees over the Internet, but the proposed schemes incorporate LV network devices that will introduce unexpected protocol interactions.

4   Policy Implications

Technical architectures embed policy choices. Changes in those architectures change those policy choices. The architecture of end-to-end is no exception. The issues that end-to-end affects reach beyond the value of any particular LV technology. Compromising end-to-end thus creates externalities. Changes may render the Internet more subject to private or state control [LEMLEY99]. Successful analysis of such changes therefore demands an ability to synthesize both the technology and policy issues.

Our aim in the sections that follow is to identify some of the policy issues implicated by changes in the end-to-end architectures. We begin by identifying analogies to end-to-end architectures in other contexts of social policies. We then consider the social risks that changes might present.

4.1   End-to-End Analogies

There is an analogy between the values that an end-to-end architecture embeds and the values exemplified in other familiar social systems. The essence of this value vests power in end users. End-to-end is a structure for assuring the bottom-up control over the evolution of the Internet. Like a competitive market setting prices or a federated republic preserving free trade, end-to-end minimizes both the control a central actor might have and the opportunity for control that particular individual actors might have.

These two effects are distinct, and their difference can be seen in relation to the constitutional design of the American republic. Like an end-to-end system, the U.S. Constitution minimized the power vested in a central authority. (The states, and the people, retained all power not granted to the federal government; the power originally granted was minimal.) But not all choices were originally left to the states. In some respects, states under the original design were constrained. In particular, states were restricted in their power over interstate commerce. A state could not, consistent with the Constitution, discriminate against commerce flowing from outside its borders; it could not burden interstate commerce more than necessary to achieve legitimate state ends.

These restrictions on state freedom serve an important national goal. They assure the free flow of commerce within the United States, and thereby spur greater and more diverse commerce. Like the effect of end-to-end, this guarantee of a neutral market induces more innovation; innovators know that their efforts will have the benefit of a large national market. Both the commitment to a decentralized regulatory regime and a restriction on the scope of that regulatory regime therefore advance the national market.

End-to-end in network design functions in a similar way. By pushing "intelligence" in the network to the application layer, the system decentralizes control over network use and functionality. The network thus develops as users of the network choose. But end-to-end also limits in certain respects how the network can develop. By limiting the functions at the network level, the design assures neutrality in how the network will develop. Innovators need not fear that powerful actors within the network will bias the network against their developments. If users of the network demand it, then the network will provide it.

The end-to-end design also mirrors the values implicit in the common law structure of "common carrier" regulation. Like states with respect to interstate commerce, a common carrier must remain neutral about the service it provides. A common carrier must take all comers if it takes any. This neutrality assures entrepreneurs that they will not be vulnerable to at least this dimension of strategic cost. This in turn can lower the cost of innovation [LEMLEY99].

4.2   Open Access

While the end-to-end Internet model was first adopted for technical reasons, it has important policy consequences as well [LEMLEY99]. The plug-and-play nature of Internet interoperability enables a wide variety of applications to connect; it therefore is architected to maximize the number of entities that can compete for the use of the network [LEMLEY99]. The Internet supports a complex and dynamic industry structure—one that offers market opportunities for many different companies. Although the overall industry structure can be quite hierarchical (because there is opportunity for specialized companies of many different sizes), individual management of each company can be flat and therefore able to rapidly respond to changing market conditions [SALTZER99]. By keeping the network simple and its interactions neutral, the Internet has facilitated applications that could not have been envisioned. [LEMLEY]

One consequence of the end-to-end design is that the network weakens the opportunity for strategic behavior by particular actors on the network and by owners of the network. If control is vested in the ends, then choke points on the network are eliminated. Network owners cannot control how the network will develop. The advent of layer-violating network devices, however, makes interoperability problematic in a growing number of cases. Internet Service Providers (ISPs) would like to bundle access to the Internet with a collection of other services such as e-mail, Web-page hosting, storage, etc. For many customers this bundling is convenient. But technologically bundling these services can give a dominant ISP an anti-competitive motivation to use LV network devices to deny customers open access to the Internet for competing services.

Here we report five examples of potentially anticompetitive behavior enabled by deviating from end-to-end design: (summarized from [SALTZER99])

1. *Fixed Backbone Choice.*   ISPs connect with international backbone networks (similar to long-distance carriers in the telephone analogy)

based on economic incentives, availability, and often cross-ownership. Besides a potential conflict of interest, an ISP backbone may prevent users from getting better service from another backbone.

2. *Filtering.*   Several ISPs have begun to examine packets that they carry and discard those with certain purposes. Again there is a conflict of interest in that the ISP has an incentive to find technical or political logic to filter out competing services.

3. *No Home Networks.*   In refusing to attach home networks, ISPs are actually protecting their ability to assign the IP address of the customer. By refusing to carry traffic to IP addresses they did not assign, the access provider can prevent the customer from contracting for a competing service from another ISP.

4. *Server Restrictions.*   Some ISPs impose an "acceptable use policy" that forbids customers from operating an Internet service such as a Web site. The technical excuse is that Web sites attract traffic and the provider has limited capacity. However, again the ISP has a conflict of interest because it offers a Web site hosting service.

5. *Content Limits.*   Some ISPs either limit the number the number of minutes or outright deny customers the use of "streaming video/audio" or download of MP3 audio (e.g., Napster). The technical excuse for these restrictions is capacity constraint but the ISP has a conflict of interest and will restrict new services that may sometime in the future become a competing services.

These five examples conflict with the Internet value of transparency. Saltzer reinterprets his end-to-end argument in this policy context [SALTZER99]:

The end-to-end argument says don't force any service, feature, or restriction on the customer; his application knows best what features it needs, and whether or not to provide features itself.

4.3   Risks

No one can accurately predict the effect of increasing deployment of LV devices on the end-to-end Internet model. Our aim in this paper is not to claim that these threats will be realized, but simply to identify some of these potential costs. To the extent that these costs exist, they evince the externality created by compromising on the end-to-end design. These potential risks include the following:

1. *ISP Market Concentration.*   Compromising on end-to-end would increase the ability of content providers to discriminate in the content they offer. The ability to facilitate discrimination in the access to content

across the Internet may facilitate concentration in what is currently a highly competitive ISP market. If service providers can guarantee premium access to certain "channels" bundled with a dominant form of access, this can increase market concentration.

2. *Control Innovation.* By gaining control over Internet infrastructure, traditional companies are in a position to protect existing markets from a threat the Internet might create. For example, to the extent that broadband service on the Internet might be a threat to the existing market for cable services, cable companies would have an interest in protecting cable services from a broadband threat. To date, the behavior of some cable providers is consistent with the hypothesis that they would architect the network to protect their legacy monopoly. The MediaOne Internet service systems restrict customers to 10 minutes of video-streaming content at a time. When asked whether AT&T would permit streaming generally, an AT&T executive responded that it didn't spend $56 billion to get into the cable business "to have the blood sucked out of our veins" [USA 1999].

3. *Threat to Innovation.* To the extent that any actor can intervene to protect an existing technology by blocking competing technologies or by discriminating against them, this will increase the costs to innovators within that market. The threat of strategic action against new innovation will weaken the incentive for such innovation. (This, for example, was the theory of the government's case against Microsoft corporation.) Compromising end-to-end can increase the risk of such strategic action. If the network can be architected to embed and protect one form of content distribution, for example, that will stifle innovation in other forms of distribution.

In all three ways, compromising on the principle of end-to-end presents risks to competition, and hence innovation, on the network. The change thus affects interests beyond the narrow interests at stake when any particular decision to implement a LV device is made. Some of the costs, in other words, of a LV device are born by the network. These costs, like pollution, are externalities to the network.

4.4 Governance
Our aim so far has been to suggest that compromising end-to-end as a principle of network design may have effects upon innovation and efficiency. It may also affect Internet governance. To the extent that changes in network design concentrate power in network owners, those changes will increase the power of individual actors to determine the evolution of network design. Such changes will thus increase the "governance" of the

Net, but not through institutions of traditional governance. In the world of perfect end-to-end design, no single institution could exercise power over how the network would develop. In a world where end-to-end is compromised, the potential for large institutions controlling the use of aspects of the network increases.

The compromise of end-to-end may also induce the emergence of institutions of traditional governance, ICANN in particular. This is because of the costs that LV devices impose on the existing Internet. LV devices increase the coordination costs for deploying new technologies to the existing Internet. With every new LV device, new applications must take account of the standards for those devices before they can be certain to run on the Internet generally. These coordination costs may be reduced if the network were to move to an IPv6 standard. The slowness of existing systems to move to the IPv6 standard, however, may induce governments to support organizations (such as ICANN) in their efforts to advance the network standard. This in turn may increase the jurisdiction of these international "governance" bodies, as they work to secure international network standards.

While the emergence of solutions to the costs imposed by LV devices through governance organizations may well be an improvement, one must also take into account the risks that any governance organization will present beyond the specifics of this one case. Governance structures concentrate power in ways that may well stifle innovation and liberty on the net. These unintended consequences are another potential cost of deviating from the original network standard [RESNICK 99].

5   Summary

In this paper we have presented the evolving challenges to the overall transparency of the end-to-end Internet model as proposed by Saltzer, Reed, and Clark. It can be argued that the transparency inherent to the end-to-end model is in many ways responsible for the engineering success of the Internet. However, with unprecedented growth of the Internet has come pressure to violate the end-to-end model. We have documented examples in which Internet protocols designed for end-to-end transparency will not work in a world where packets have to traverse LV network devices such as NATs and firewalls. The large investment in LV network devices has been made for valid reasons and this installed infrastructure will not be easily changed.

The trend continues toward incorporating more processing within the network. Active network research ranges from packets programming routers to routers making pre-programmed decisions based on packet content.[15] [TENNENHOUSE97] In response to recent denial-of-service attacks, the IETF is convening an itrace BOF[16] to process reverse path state information on packets within intermediate routers using ICMP traceback mechanisms. A tension is building between providing end-systems knowledge of network conditions for enhanced services versus increased security vulnerabilities based on this knowledge.[17] An example of this is the ongoing discussion within the IETF of an Internet draft on "Fog Lamps" to improve *visibility* of network devices to end-systems, a view directly opposed to the *transparency* view of the end-to-end Internet model [LEAR00].

No one can predict the ultimate effects of layer violations on the Internet [LESSIG99]. In one scenario, a complete migration to IPv6 potentially allows the restoration of a global address space and end-to-end transparency, albeit with firewalls and PEPs still remaining. At the other extreme, only a partial IPv6 deployment leads to fragmentation of the network layer, with global connectivity resembling islands of connectivity. The Internet architecture has helped fuel the greatest economic boom in recent history; we should be skeptical of changes in its design [LESSIG99, LEMLEY99]. The strong presumption should be in favor of preserving the architectural features that have produced this extraordinary innovation [LEMLEY99].

Acknowledgment

This research was supported in part by a grant from NASA #NGT-30019 and the John Deere & Company.

Notes

1. We use the term "end-to-end model" while acknowledging that the original authors prefer the terminology "end-to-end arguments".
2. Noted Internet researcher Van Jacobson is quoted as stating, "Very simple. A router has only three choices when presented with a packet. It can transmit the

packet. It can delay (queue) the packet. Or it can throw the packet away" [CHEN98].

3. Network devices routinely update a "hop" counter in the network layer, and may record the route taken by a packet. Routers may also alter the content of one or more quality-of-service label fields in the network-layer portion of the packet.

4. Jeffery Altman, e-mail posted to the IETF mailing list, December 1999.

5. Motto of the IETF.

6. Steve Deering is also the inventor of IP multicast and lead designer of the next-generation Internet Protocol (IPv6).

7. Closing talk of *Networked Group Communications Conference* (NGC'99), Pisa, Italy, Nov. 19, 1999.

8. Ingress is a path going *into* a network.

9. Egress is a path *exiting* from a network.

10. Lloyd Wood, IETF mailing list February 17, 2000; Wood goes on to say, "Hey, that means the Internet is InterNATional."

11. DHCP is the Dynamic Host Control Protocol.

12. While some researchers have attacked "active networking" as not scalable and destabilizing, it is premature to make such determinations.

13. ICMP Traceback (itrace) Birds-of-a-Feather (BOF) at the 47th IETF meeting, Chair: Steve Bellovin, 3/30/00, 15:30–17:30.

14. Increased knowledge of conditions within the network may make additional diagnostic information available to interloping devices.

References

[ALLMAN99] Allman, M. et al., *Enhancing TCP over Satellite Channels Using Standard Mechanisms*, RFC 2488, 1999.

[BLAKE98] Blake, S. et al., *An Architecture for Differentiated Service*, RFC 2475, Dec. 1998.

[BRADEN97] Braden, R. et al., *Resource ReSerVation Protocol—Version 1 Functional Specification*, RFC2205, Sept. 1997.

[CARPENTER00] Carpenter, Brian, *Internet Transparency*, RFC 2775, 2000.

[CHEN98] Chen, Thomas M., and Jackson, Alden, et al., "*Commentaries on Active Networking and End-to-End Arguments*," IEEE Network Magazine, May/June 1998.

[CLARK95] Clark, David D., "*The Design Philosophy of the DARPA Internet Protocols*," ACM Comp. Comm. Review, Vol. 25, No. 1, Jan. 1995, pp. 102–111.

[DEERING00] Deering, Steve, personal communications, Cisco Corp., March 2000.

[FLOYD00] Floyd, S. et al., *"IPsec Interactions with ECN"* (work in progress), ⟨http://www.ietf.org/internet-drafts/draft-ipsec-ecn-00.txt⟩.

[HAIN00] Hain, T., *"Architectural Implications of NAT"* (work in progress).

[HOLDREGE00] Holdrege, M. and P. Srisuresh, *Protocol Complications with the IP Network Address Translator (NAT)* (work in progress, March 2000). ⟨http://www.ietf.org/internet-drafts/draft-ietf-nat-protocol-complications-02.txt⟩.

[KENT98] Kent, S. and R. Atkinson, *Security Architecture for the Internet Protocol*, RFC2401.

[KRUSE00] Kruse, Hans, *"The Pitfalls of Distributed Protocol Development: Unintentional Interactions Between Network Operations and Applications Protocols,"* 8th Int. Conf. on Telecom. Systems (ICTS), Nashville, TN, March 2000, pp. 289–293.

[KRUSE99] Kruse, Hans. *"Protocol Interactions and Their Effects on Internet-Based E-Commerce,"* 2nd Int. Conf. Telecom. and E-Commerce (ICTEC), Nashville, TN, Oct. 1999.

[LEAR00] Lear, Eliot. *NAT and Other Network 'Intelligence': Clearing Architectural Haze Through the Use of Fog Lamps* (work in progress, December 1999), ⟨http://www.ietf.org/internet-drafts/draft-lear-foglamps-01.txt⟩.

[LEMLEY99] Lemley, Mark A. and Lawrence Lessig, *Ex Parte Comments in the Matter of Application for Consent to the Transfer of Control of Licenses MediaOne Group, Inc. to AT&T Corp.*, FCC CS Docket No. 99-251. ⟨http://cyber.law.harvard.edu/works/lessig/cable/fcc/fcc.html⟩.

[LESSIG99] Lessig, Lawrence, *"It's the Architecture, Mr. Chairman."* ⟨http://cyber.law.harvard.edu/works/lessig/cable/Cable.html⟩.

[RESNICK99] Lessig, Lawrence, and Paul Resnick, *Zoning Speech on the Internet: A Legal and Technical Model*, 98 Mich. L. Rev. 395 (1999).

[SALTZER99] Saltzer, Jerome H., *"'Open Access' is Just the Tip of the Iceberg"* Oct. 22, 1999. ⟨http://web.mit.edu/Saltzer/www/publications/openaccess.html⟩.

[SALTZER84] Saltzer, Jerome H., David P. Reed, and David D. Clark, *"End-to-End Arguments in System Design,"* ACM Trans. Comp. Systems, Vol. 2, No. 4, Nov. 1984, pp. 277–288 (an earlier version appeared in 2nd Int. Conf. on Distr. Computer Systems, April 1981, pp. 509–512).

[TENNENHOUSE97] Tennenhouse, D. et al., *"A Survey of Active Research Network Research,"* IEEE Communications Magazine, Vol. 35, No. 1, 1997.

[TERZIS00] Terzis A. *RSVP Operation Over IP Tunnels*, RFC 2746, 2000.

6

The Potential for Scrutiny of Internet Peering Policies in Multilateral Forums

Rob Frieden

As the Internet matures and commercializes,[1] it has become more hierarchical,[2] particularly regarding the terms and conditions for network interconnection between Internet Service Providers (ISPs). The previous "democratic" Bill and Keep/Sender Keep All (SKA) system[3] promoted positive networking externalities,[4] but also generated free-rider[5] opportunities and great potential for network congestion. The individual networks that make up the Internet remain well integrated, but a more hierarchical pricing arrangement has developed. Now only the largest ISPs continue to "peer"[6] on a SKA basis, while demanding payment from smaller operators.[7]

Requiring smaller ISPs to pay for access to larger ISPs' networks constitutes a rational business transaction and reflects a maturing, more businesslike attitude among ISPs. However, it constitutes a substantial change in circumstances and imposes substantial new costs on smaller ISPs, some of which object to what they consider a one-sided exploitation of superior bargaining power. No matter how justified and efficiency-enhancing on a macro level, the commercial, unregulated nature of ISP interconnection negotiations now requires sizeable transfer payments where none previously existed. Much of the payment flows to Tier-1 ISPs located in North America, leading some ISPs and their governments in other locales to claim that the transfer payments violate international trade, antitrust, and economic development policies.[8] North American ISPs and governments have responded by emphasizing the commercial nature of Internet peering and the rationale for not extending burdensome, unnecessary, and archaic "legacy regulation."

This chapter explores the nature of the Internet interconnection dispute with an eye toward the strategies used to raise the issue in multilateral telecommunications and trade policy forums like the International Telecommunication Union and the World Trade Organization. The paper also will offer a prediction whether the problem will abate or grow acute. This consideration involves an assessment whether Internet traffic flows and content will more substantially diverge from a North American centrality and whether interconnection arrangements will become even more finely calibrated.

Marketplace Consequences of a Hierarchical Internet

As Internet industry segments mature, many governments wind down and eventually terminate their role as incubator and anchor tenant. In many nations, including the United States, governments helped promote Internet use and proliferation of the Internet infrastructure.[9] Having concluded that the Internet has reached a critical mass, most governments now endorse the view that a largely commercial and private environment will best serve the national interest. Most governments now favor a privatized Internet, but not an environment that one could deem completely unregulated. As the Internet becomes a major medium for a variety of private and commercial transactions, activities previously considered illegal or warranting government oversight similarly will trigger such government involvement when the Internet provides the medium or conduit.

The privatized, commercial Internet has evidenced similar economic characteristics to telecommunication networks.[10] Tier-1 ISPs have accrued favorable economies of scale and scope through growth in terms of both customer base and the inventory of bandwidth available for service. Having made the investment to accommodate burgeoning demand, Tier-1 ISPs must find new profit centers in addition to monthly subscriptions. These operators have found they can efficiently provide many Internet-mediated services, including electronic commerce and advertiser-supported access to desirable content, and also force smaller ISPs, which have not achieved similar growth or expanded their bandwidth inventory, to pay for access and transit services.

To accrue positive economies of scale and scope, telecommunications and Internet operators alike have worked to expand their customer base, available bandwidth, number of interconnection sites, and the content they host, as opposed to providing access to content hosted elsewhere.

Massive, multi-billion-dollar mergers and acquisitions evidence the desire to achieve scale and scope economies in a speedy fashion: by acquiring the market share of a competitor, rather than migrating customers and revenues from competitors.

The quest to accrue scale and scope economies constitutes one of the major reasons the Internet has become more hierarchical,[11] with a small set of major carriers operating the key backbone routes and capturing a large market share however measured (e.g., by bandwidth, number of subscribers, minutes of use, revenues, number of discrete "hits" to internal Web sites, number of discrete Domain Numbering System sites internal to ("hosted" by) the network, etc.). The small number of major backbone ISPs, coupled with an increasingly commercial orientation, has made it possible for the Tier-1 ISPs to demand and secure payments from smaller ISPs for access to their networks and the content they host.

Without concluding whether a more hierarchical Internet promotes greater efficiencies, the concentration of Tier-1 ISPs' market share, however measured, has made it possible to secure a superior bargaining position vis à vis smaller ISPs:

As the cooperative, nonprofit ethos of the Internet began to fade, however, some providers began to have second thoughts about connecting directly to one another [through open peering]. Today, large backbone providers such as AT&T, Cable & Wireless, GTE, PSINet, Sprint, Qwest Communications and UUNET consider one another peers and don't hesitate to connect to each other. However, they often spurn smaller ... ISPs.[12]

While technical and operational factors do impact the Tier-1 ISPs' interconnection decision-making process, the "main reason for not peering, however, is economic."[13] While one can suggest that marketplace-driven negotiations never should trigger government scrutiny, others would argue the legitimacy of antitrust/competition policy analysis[14] when assessing the terms and conditions for Internet access.

Does a Small Set of Tier-1 ISPs Reduce Consumer Welfare?

A key question in for assessing whether Internet access pricing triggers the need for government involvement involves an examination whether consumers suffer when a small number of backbone ISPs agree to restrict SKA "true peering." Such an assessment involves an examination of ISP market share and the state of competition over all components in a complete Internet link, viz., local access to the subscriber's ISP and the local ISP's links with other ISPs for access to the rest of the world, both in terms of telecommunications carriage and content creation/dissemination. In general, a healthy and efficiently operating Internet industry operates[15] even under a hierarchical structure coupled with a limited number of Tier-1 ISPs.[16] However, this finding requires some qualification because bottlenecks can exist in the Internet topology within a region. Likewise, the potential does exist for price squeezes, i.e., the ability of one competitor to raise the costs of others for a service element needed by all competitors and supplied by one or few operators.

It is important to recognize that a hierarchical Internet industrial structure results in different types of ISPs incurring different costs for access to both content and carriage. Such price differentials have triggered the Internet access pricing dispute, because some stakeholders consider pricing differences clear evidence of price gouging by the Tier-1 ISPs, while others consider them the logical and reasonable consequence of unequal bargaining power. Without offering an opinion on the equities involved in different access terms and conditions, several major causes for the difference exist:

• The facilities-based, long-haul telecommunications transmission marketplace has such substantial market entry and operational costs that relatively few operators can efficiently and effectively enter and remain in the market. This view, supported by our empirical analysis of the telecommunications infrastructure and its ownership, contrasts with the comparatively low costs and low barriers to market entry in reselling the long-haul services of a Tier-1 ISP;[17]

• The nature of Internet access, from a consumer (end-user) point of view, seamlessly blends access to content and the telecommunications transport needed to acquire and deliver the content. Users expect their ISPs to deliver content quickly and effectively regardless of where the content is physically hosted; ISPs recover the cost of Internet-mediated content and the telecommunications transport costs without separately itemizing or disaggregating these costs. With the proliferation of Internet-mediated services triggering the need for ever-increasing telecommunications transport costs, ISPs have augmented revenues from end-user subscriptions with revenue streams from advertisers, a share of electronic commerce revenues, and, where possible, payments from other ISPs for transiting their networks; and

• Traffic flows and, more importantly, end-user demand for content and Internet-mediated services directly impact the terms and conditions for Internet access. ISPs offering superior content and/or content delivery options can demand and fetch premium compensation, the product of commercial negotiation that factors in demand and supply elasticities as well as consumer expectations regarding quality of service.

Subjecting the Internet Market Structure to Traditional Antitrust/Competition Policy Analysis

Traditional antitrust/competition policy analysis[18] considers individual firms in the context of the markets within which they operate with an eye toward determining whether and how a firm might engage in anticompetitive and market-distorting behavior. This analysis has two major tasks: (1) the macro-level definition of the relevant product/service and geographical markets; and (2) the micro-level assessment of individual firm market share and potential to engage in practices that harm competitors and consumers.

Defining the Relevant Product/Service and Geographical Market

How one defines the market for Internet access and Internet-mediated services directly affects conclusions whether the market is robustly competitive or subject to market power and domination by the Tier-1 ISPs. Any definition of Internet markets should consider the functional equivalency or substitutability of a product or service in determining the "relevant" product or service market.[19] Markets can be defined as including all goods and services considered by consumers to constitute an alternative to the others. Economists measure the substitutability of products and services in terms of cross-elasticities.[20]

Internet access and Internet-mediated services constitute elements of the single, broader market for bandwidth capable of transporting digital bitstreams. Digitization makes it possible to assemble and deliver a variety of different types of services. While all bits do not have the same function or value, a data-transport pipe like that owned and operated by the Tier-1 ISPs (or their telecommunications carrier parent or affiliate) can serve as the medium for delivering a variety of Internet-mediated services and the bitstreams they generate. Accordingly, an appropriate market definition considers long-haul data transport via telecommunications.

Given the international nature of the Internet topology, a global geographical market seems appropriate for purposes of assessing the potential for market domination and anticompetitive practices.

Individual or Collective Behavior of Firms—Evidence of Market Power
Having defined the overall service market and the geographical nature of the market, antitrust/competition policy then requires an examination of the companies serving these markets. This examination considers whether and how one or more firms have market power, the ability to affect the price or supply of one or more elements that make up international data transport services. The appearance of market power correlates with firm size and market penetration, but a finding of market power does not result simply because one firm has a large market share and has a large capitalization.[21] Some markets operate efficiently and competitively despite the fact that a few quite large enterprises have captured the dominant market share. On the other hand, one small, thinly capitalized enterprise might have a near monopoly in a market narrowly defined by type or locality.

In examining the international data transport marketplace, one can see that a dichotomy in terms of market entry costs and opportunities exists between local and regional ISPs, on one hand, and long-haul national and international ISPs on the other hand. This dichotomy underscores the importance of the baseline market definition exercise, because one might infer market power based on high market share in narrowly defined markets, while another might infer no market share based on a diluted market penetration when using a larger market definition.

Perhaps the commercial aviation marketplace provides a helpful example of a similarly dichotomous market. Few financial or other barriers exist to foreclose the creation of a new airline. With a handful of airplanes leased by a fully leveraged venture, a new airline can enter the marketplace. Absent barriers to accessing airport terminal and landing space, the airline can serve a few routes and provide significant competition to incumbents. However, no one would mistake this small and incremental competition as coming close to fostering robust and full competition to what a major incumbent carrier provides. A nation like the United States might have hundreds of national airlines, but nevertheless have only six major carriers controlling over 70 percent of the total market as measured by industry-appropriate criteria, e.g., "revenue miles" and "seat miles."

Depending on one's perspective and market definitions, the commercial aviation marketplace in the United States can be characterized as robustly competitive or oligopolistic, notwithstanding low barriers to market entry and a general downturn in overall rates since deregulation stimulated market entry. Despite the absence of bottlenecks in terms of access to capital, airport terminal space, and runway landing slots, few airlines compete for long-haul traffic or offer a thoroughly national and international route system.

One would have a harder time justifying the view that a few ventures dominate the market for Internet access and Internet services if these markets were defined in the context of the total number of ventures pursuing some aspect or element of the multifaceted international data-transport marketplace. Conversely, a narrower definition of the Internet marketplace, emphasizing the market share held by Tier-1 ISPs, could support the view that these operators share market power and the ability to extract high rates ("monopoly rents" in economics) and impose "unfair" terms.

The Internet marketplace does appear to evidence parallels to commercial aviation. While a nation might have hundreds if not thousands of ISPs, the overall market segments into a large percentage of total ISPs serving single localities or regions, with a quite limited number of ISPs operating the major long-haul backbone networks needed for national and international services. The startup costs for a local ISP evidence quite limited barriers to market entry. A new ISP can enter the marketplace simply by leasing a few local trunks from the local exchange carrier to provide subscribers with access to a modem bank for access to and from the Internet secured by the interconnection of those local lines with a few interexchange carrier lines that access the transit services of a larger ISP.

On the other hand, a major backbone Internet operator does not appear overnight. These Tier-1 operators must have the financial and operational wherewithal to construct or lease and manage a nationwide network of high-capacity lines. Few enterprises can amass the needed investment and skills. Accordingly, it should come as no surprise that most of the Internet Tier-1 ISPs are subsidiaries or affiliates of major telecommunication carriers.

If we use the global geographical market definition and characterize the relevant service market as one involving data transport, the existence of a small number of Tier-1 ISPs can raise questions about the potential for the exercise of market power. However, no empirical evidence supports the view that such market power exists. A unilateral decision by one or more Tier-1 ISPs to eliminate open, public peering by itself does not constitute an exercise of market power or anticompetitive practices. While such a decision raises the cost of doing business for smaller ISPs, it may reflect legitimate business judgment rather than evidence a concerted effort to drive smaller ISPs out of the market, thereby reducing the supply of ISP services despite the growing demand for Internet services and bandwidth. The decision whether and how to peer does not necessarily reflect the exercise of market power. Likewise, the peering decisions of Tier-1 carriers does not directly impact the supply of bandwidth. A peering decision typically does not directly impact a telecommunication carrier's decision whether and when to deploy additional satellite or submarine cable transmission capacity. It may have a direct impact on the price of Internet services to consumers, but many factors impact pricing decisions and one would need to conduct further analysis to conclude that a change in peering policy constituted the primary reason for an increase in end-user prices.

Exercise of Market Power in Anticompetitive Ways
We have seen that dominant market share serves as a primary potential indicator of market power. However, other indicators exist that may contribute to a finding of market power, even if the computed market share typically would not point toward monopolization or market domination. A firm may exercise market power by engaging in practices that adversely impact competitors, the robustness of competition, and consumer welfare. The potential for such adverse impacts grows when competitors need to collaborate in the joint provision of a service, or when competitors need to rely on access to the facilities or services of another competitor to assemble all the elements needed to provide a complete service. Internet service provision requires both collaboration, e.g., net-

work interconnection, and cooperation, e.g., access by small ISPs to the backbone trunks of Tier-1 ISPs on fair, cost-based terms and conditions.

Decisions by Tier-1 ISPs not to collaborate or to cooperate may result from legitimate business decisions or may constitute an anticompetitive practice. The refusal to interconnect facilities may constitute a "concerted refusal to deal."[22] In antitrust jurisprudence this practice refers to an attempt to drive a competitor out of business or to raise its cost of doing business with the impact of reducing its marketplace attractiveness. Even if a Tier-1 ISP continued to permit lesser ISPs to interconnect, the terms and conditions might constitute a "price squeeze,"[23] i.e., an attempt to raise competitors' costs and lower their marketplace attractiveness by increasing the cost of an essential facility, bottleneck, or service element needed by the lesser ISP to provide a complete end-to-end service. ISPs having superior bargaining power may also leverage this power to extract concessions from lesser ISPs, including agreements not to compete in certain service or geographical markets, setting a price floor on the service offered by the lesser ISP, or tying access to a desired service (e.g., long-haul backbone trunks) with a commitment to buy or lease less desired and competitively provisioned services. Tier-1 ISPs may attempt to enforce these anticompetitive restraints by threatening to drive noncompliant, lesser ISPs out of business with predatory prices, deliberate, below-cost rates, or with the threat to raise or eliminate access opportunities.

The potential for anticompetitive practices and leveraging bottlenecks exists in both aviation and Internet industries. In aviation, absent government ownership or effective regulation, an airport operator could discriminate in favor of one particular airline in the manner in which it assigns (or denies) access to space in the airport terminal and opportunities to take off or land aircraft. Access to the local loop and the backbone networks of Tier-1 carriers may be viewed as constituting essential facilities in terms of Internet access, because the terms and conditions for such access can thwart or stimulate competition. To the extent that smaller ISPs do not have alternatives to Tier-1 ISPs' backbone trunks, they may have to comply with unilateral or collective policies designed to "manage competition." However, Tier-1 ISPs can exercise market power only if their single or collective (collusive) behavior forecloses competitive alternatives. Whether Tier-1 ISPs can discipline lesser ISPs into submission and acquiescence to unilaterally set terms and conditions on such key matters as interconnection and transit pricing depends on whether and how the lesser ISPs can resort to alternatives, including self-help, the construction and operation of their own backbone facilities, or the lease of such facilities from telecommunication carriers that do not also operate as Tier-1 ISPs.

How Might Anticompetitive Practices Occur? Tier-1 ISPs Bear Limited Regulatory Burdens

Tier-1 ISPs might have the opportunity to engage in anticompetitive practices because of lax antitrust/competition policy enforcement and a generate predisposition not to regulate the Internet.[24] Additionally, governments might not consider matters like interconnection and peering policy as constituting anticompetitive practices. In this examination of how extensive governments engage in regulatory oversight, our analogy between ISPs and commercial airlines breaks down somewhat.

ISPs incur substantially less government oversight than their airline counterparts for four primary reasons:

1. governments regulate the telecommunications transport function performed by the carriers that lease facilities to Tier-1 ISPs;[25]

2. notwithstanding its growing importance, the Internet has not approached the status of public utility or functional equivalent to telecommunications;[26]

3. most governments have purposely embraced a hands-off strategy with an eye toward promoting entrepreneurialism and private initiatives; and

4. until recently ISPs themselves have emphasized connectivity and global reach even if the network interconnection, access, and pricing policies employed to reach that goal, e.g., open peering and Sender Keep All, reduced profitability and resulted in the possibility that some ISPs would bear disproportionately greater financial burdens to build out the network infrastructure than others.

Rationale for Regulatory Asymmetry Between Telecommunications Regulation and Internet Unregulation

Heretofore national regulatory authorities have adopted an inconsistent and dichotomous regulatory regime between the Internet and telecommunications. Internet access issues currently lack a regulatory forum, because governments have largely refrained from interfering with a commercial, self-regulating system. Accordingly, the national telecommunications regulatory authority lacks jurisdiction to adjudicate an Internet access dispute containing an allegation of marketplace abuse or anticompetitive practices. Other adjudicators, including courts, may provide a substitute forum, but it may prove helpful to explore the reason governments have refrained from creating a uniform regulatory regime and forum for addressing both telecommunications and Internet disputes.

The Internet Is Considered a Contestable or Competitive Market

Simply put, governments have not installed a regulatory regime for the Internet because they believe one is not needed. Advocates for regulatory relief on Internet access issues will dispute this by emphasizing the need for closer antitrust/competition policy scrutiny using a better calibrated market definition. Advocates for Internet access relief allege that the consolidation in the long-haul market segment accords the Tier-1 ISPs the power to distort the bargaining process and to extract "supracompetitive," overly generous compensation for access to, and transit through, their networks. These advocates believe the competitive playing field has tilted in favor of the Tier-1 ISPs that can exploit the inelastic demand for their transport service and the content they have available. Some Internet access relief advocates would characterize the Tier-1 ISP networks as "essential facilities"[27] and "bottlenecks,"[28] because all long-haul Internet traffic must traverse these facilities, in much the same way as this traffic might have only one local loop-routing option provided by an incumbent local exchange carrier monopoly. If governments adopt the view that Tier-1 ISPs networks constitute essential facilities or bottlenecks, then these governments have an economic and legal rationale for applying regulatory instruments aimed at "improving" the terms and conditions for access, including the interconnection/access charges imposed by Tier-1 ISPs on smaller ISPs.

Notwithstanding market consolidation by the Tier-1 ISPs, governments have yet to adopt the view that the long-haul Internet access marketplace is oligopolistic and uncontestable. First, absolute denials of access to Tier-1 ISP facilities apparently have not occurred. Advocates for government intervention dispute the terms and conditions for such access, not that they lack access opportunities. Similarly, no evidence exists to support the view that Tier-1 ISPs have conspired or coordinated efforts to fetter smaller ISPs with discriminatory Internet access terms and conditions. Tier-1 ISPs operating in the United States now require access and transit payments from smaller ISPs, regardless of their location. However, the higher distance-sensitive charges on ISPs operating outside of North America and far from a Tier-1 ISP's Point of Presence impose a comparatively greater financial burden than that borne by closer ISPs. Lastly, no indication exists that Tier-1 ISPs have engaged in a strategy to raise smaller ISPs' costs of doing business with an eye toward driving them out of the market. Tier-1 ISPs have not entered markets with lower predatory rates. In fact, the prevailing market entry strategy of Tier-1 carriers in the region involves acquisitions on terms deemed quite generous, e.g., America Online's acquisition of the Australian ISP OzMail.

The strongest case for government intervention lies where self-correcting marketplace outcomes cannot be relied upon to remedy short-term problems. A "cautious approach would be to reject any possibility of mandatory access except where it is 'essential' to the existence of competition. If applicants for access can plausibly invent around the network monopoly, establish their own competitive networks, or join other networks that may not be equivalent but are acceptable alternatives to the dominant network, that arguably might eliminate any consideration of court-ordered access."[29]

Advocates for a "hands-off" approach to Internet access issues emphasize the suitability of marketplace remedies, i.e., discriminatory or unfair access terms and conditions should generate incentives for smaller ISPs to set up their own competitive networks or collectively join with other smaller ISPs to create a rival long-haul network. Likewise, they consider the profits accruing to Tier-1 ISPs appropriate rewards for risk taking and achieving marketplace success. Expropriating some or all of the monetary fruits of Tier-1 ISPs' labors simply rewards free-riders and risk-averse players. Also, a hands-off approach frees governments of the difficult if not impossible task of resolving equity and operational issues.[30]

Applying Antitrust/Competition Policy to Three Near-Term Marketplace Scenarios

Three near-term marketplace outcomes may occur in the Internet access dispute: (1) extension of the status quo; (2) Tier-1 ISPs consolidate network management in ways similar to how telecommunication carriers manage deployment of international satellite and submarine cables; and (3) rapid deployment of additional long-haul transmission capacity leads to a robustly competitive marketplace making bandwidth a tradable commodity. Each scenario will be subject to antitrust/competition policy scrutiny.

Scenario 1: The Status Quo Continues

Reasonable people can disagree whether the status quo raises legitimate antitrust/competition policy concerns. Concentration of ownership and control over long-haul bandwidth can create both incentives and opportunities for operators of such essential facilities to act in a cartelized and anticompetitive way. However, no coordinated behavior has become evident, nor does it appear that the unilateral decision of any one or more Tier-1 ISP can have a markedly anticompetitive impact on the market for Internet transport and access to Internet-mediated services and content.

One might conclude that Tier-1 ISPs have raised the cost of an essential service element to competitors, thereby demonstrating that the Tier-1 ISPs have engaged in an illegal price squeeze. However, one could just as well conclude that the international data-transport marketplace segments into backbone, long-haul carriage and regional or local carriage. Under this sort of market segmentation, Tier-1 ISPs in effect do not compete with smaller ISPs such that the decision to raise access and transit fees does not constitute a price squeeze. In a nutshell, the status quo has generated major disputes, because different stakeholders perceive the Internet marketplace differently. Without a shared baseline in terms of market definitions, inferences and extrapolations will differ, particularly as to whether universally understood anticompetitive practices have occurred.

Arguments That Anticompetitive Practices Have Occurred

Proponents of regulatory and other types of relief to Tier-1 ISP peering policies argue that prices to smaller ISPs have increased without justification. Tier-1 carriers need not meet in a smoke-filled room to collude. The term "conscious parallelism" refers to the uncoordinated but identical pricing decisions by erstwhile competitors.[31] This practice frequently occurs in commercial aviation as carriers signal pricing strategies implicit through their ticket reservation systems. A carrier seeking to raise rates hopes that competitors will match the fare increase, thereby making the initiating carrier's rate increase "stick." Should the other carriers not follow through with the same rate hike, the initiating carrier typically lowers its rates to the previous level.

Tier-1 ISPs can collude and conspire to raise the costs of their data transport access and transit service though a series of seemingly unilateral decisions. While one Tier-1 ISP may have initiated the decision to abandon public peering, it could not have made this decision stick unless and until all other Tier-1 ISPs executed the same change in peering policy. Absent a cost-based or demand-based justification, the decision to change peering policies may evidence a decision by the Tier-1 ISPs to foist costs onto other ISPs with an eye toward bolstering the Tier-1 ISPs' profitability and market dominance. This attempt to dominate if not monopolize the data transport marketplace should trigger antitrust/ competition policy safeguards designed to protect consumers and competitors from attempts to tilt the competitive playing field in favor of one select group of market player.

Arguments That Anticompetitive Practices Have Not Occurred

Tier-1 ISPs justify their revised peering policy as a rational and cost-based response to changed circumstances. The Internet has largely made the transition from infant industry incubation to a maturing, commercializing private industry. The largest Tier-1 ISPs can no longer ignore differences in ISP size, traffic streams, amount of bandwidth available, subscriber population, number of peering or interconnection sites, and scope of content hosted. ISPs have had to wean themselves from government subsidies and must as well pay greater attention to the requirements and expectations of their investors.

Greater sensitivity to the bottom line requires ISPs to scrutinize telecommunication transport costs and to determine whether they have borne a fair and not excessive share of costs. This attention has triggered greater vigilance against free ridership, which in this context refers to the previous ability of smaller ISPs to exploit public peering for access to bandwidth, content, network functionality, and transit services in excess of what they contribute for use by other ISPs and their subscribers. The decision to change peering policies and to shift the financial burden responds to the legitimate and reasonable rebalancing of the data-transport financial burden. Because North American ISPs have contributed to the creation and hosting of keenly desired content, and have upgraded their networks to provide pathways capable of handling multimedia applications, they have a commercial opportunity to recoup their investment and to capture the fruits of their labor. Accordingly, a change in peering policy reflects the need to recover ever increasing network infrastructure upgrade costs and to charge what the market will bear, given the inelastic demand for the content Tier-1 ISPs host and the network access and transit services they offer.

Scenario 2: Tier-1 ISPs Behave Like Their Telecommunications Carrier Counterparts

The second near-term scenario involves cartel-like behavior much the same as international telecommunication carriers have engaged in historically, albeit at a decreasing and unsustainable level. This view sees an ironic outcome: just as the international telecommunications marketplace grows increasingly competitive, robust and open consolidation among Tier-1 ISPs makes the backbone data-transport market increasingly concentrated, managed, and cartelized. While market concentration and high market share by itself does not necessarily evidence an anticompetitive market, the incentive and perhaps the opportunity to engage in such practices increase.

Tier-1 ISPs may choose as a frame of reference the "old school" and "clubby" international telecommunication environment that served as the predominant industrial model from the onset of telegraphy to the late 1980s.[32] During that time period, international submarine cable consortia and international/regional satellite cooperatives largely managed the telecommunication marketplace. Carriers collectively made facilities deployment decisions, going so far as to allocate usage between cable and satellites. This management process emphasized carrier convenience, conservation of capital, and risk sharing over consumers' interests, entrepreneurship, and the considerable benefits of competition.

Centralized management may seem anachronistic and ludicrous in this time of privatization, liberalization, deregulation, competition, and globalization. But one should note that these descriptive characteristics of the telecommunication marketplace have appeared only recently. Few incumbents willingly part with guaranteed market share and a quiet life for potentially greater upsides, but drastically more volatility, risk, uncertainty, and hard work. Tier-1 ISPs have managed to acquire market share though superior business skills, efficient operations, the first-to-market ("early mover") advantage, and access to plenty of capital to fund growth. Additionally, these ventures have benefited from opportunities to buy market share through strategic mergers and acquisitions. Having secured a dominant market share, the Tier-1 ISPs surely have every incentive to try to sustain their comparative advantage and to perpetuate their market dominance.

Arguments That Anticompetitive Practices Have Occurred

The rationale that Tier-1 ISPs will sustain their marketplace dominance lies primarily in the view that they must take affirmative and anticompetitive steps to forestall outsiders and smaller ISPs from bringing technological and other innovations to market. This view parallels the charge that the Microsoft Corporation violated antitrust/competition policies to sustain its monopoly.[33] Faced with the potential for lost market dominance in either its core market, i.e., personal computer operating systems, or developing markets, i.e., World Wide Web browser software, Microsoft allegedly engaged in predatory and strong-arming tactics. The company offered free of charge a Web browser where consumers previously had to buy it, possibly evidence of predatory pricing. The company also allegedly forced personal computer manufacturers to feature this software as a condition for the opportunity to buy the more intensely desired Windows operating system. Collectively the alleged activities of Microsoft worked to extend its market dominance by leveraging inelestic demand for access to its computer operating system to secure market dominance in a new and heretofore separate market for Web browsers.

Tier-1 ISPs can sustain their market dominance by leveraging the inelestic demand for the content they host. One could argue that Tier-1 ISPs tie this demand with somewhat more elastic demand for data-transmission capacity, with the result that smaller ISPs incur a comparatively higher financial burden. But even if a tying arrangement[34] does not exist, because Internet charging blends access to data transport and content, Tier-1 ISPs have every incentive to press their marketplace advantage by managing deployment of Internet backbone routes and controlling access to these essential and possibly bottleneck facilities.

Arguments That Anticompetitive Practices Have Not Occurred

The strongest argument that Tier-1 ISPs cannot operate as a cartel, now or in the future, lies with the reasons that telecommunications carriers can no longer do so. The Intelsat, Inmarsat, Intersputnik, and Eutelsat cooperatives face robust, facilities-based competition from in-orbit satellites operated by private entrepreneurial ventures.[35] The traditional submarine cable consortia comprised of the incumbent carriers face direct competition from new carrier ventures lacking the incumbency advantage but nevertheless finding ample demand for their state-of-the-art fiber-optic cable technology. Simply put, even if the Tier-1 ISPs could manage to discipline each other to engage in cartel-like behavior, the market entry barriers they would attempt to erect would prove unable to thwart newcomers.

With the proliferation of routing options worldwide, Tier-1 ISPs will not have the ability to discipline the marketplace. At least in theory, smaller ISPs, displeased with new peering policies of one or more incumbent Tier-1 ISPs, should have the opportunity to secure backbone datatransmission services from new carriers, e.g., Global Crossing, Level Three, 360 Networks, Gateway Exchange, FLAG Telecommunications, etc.

Scenario 3: Long-Haul Data Transmission Becomes a Fungible Commodity

Scenario 3 extends the currently experienced extraordinary demand for bandwidth with equally impressive rollouts of new capacity using state-of-the-art circuit multiplication technologies. While one side of the calculus may skew the supply of data-transmission capacity temporarily toward glut or scarcity, this scenario involves a fundamental reshaping of the industry and the manner by which carriers provision capacity and reseller/endusers acquire it.

In this scenario, telecommunications transport capacity becomes fungible and tradable, like bushels of corn and other commodities. A spot market for data-transmission bandwidth means that the market has become robustly competitive and that all suppliers become "price takers," with no single supplier or group, including the Tier-1 ISPs, in a position to set prices. Market price setting in real time juxtaposes with the current model that relies largely on direct negotiations, and significant price differentials based on volume requirements, traffic route, and consumer/reseller demand elasticities. In this current environment, suppliers can price-differentiate based on user characteristics and general market conditions. A commodity market environment operates more dynamically and in closer relation to immediate marketplace conditions.

Arguments That Anticompetitive Practices Have Occurred

Few situations exist where one or more suppliers can successfully "corner" or "manipulate" a commodity market. However, this does not suggest that players do not attempt to affect the market or that such endeavors do not have some kind of impact. The anticompetitive practices that generate an impact do not eliminate supply, but create temporary negative impacts on supply that can quickly trigger a price increase. Attempts to coordinate supply of a commodity, like oil, do not always work, as individual suppliers or governments have incentives to "cheat" and capture market share at higher per-unit prices. However, efforts to discipline suppliers can work, particularly when the number is manageable, as is the case with the Tier-1 ISPs.

Even in a commodity market, suppliers may attempt to collude and operate a cartel. The anticompetitive practices exercised represent attempts to fix prices, often by setting a price-floor target with supply geared to sustain that level. Suppliers may have some success to calibrating supply to a target price, but such management typically cannot work over the long term, as evidenced by the fluctuations in commodities over time.

Antitrust/competition policy agencies may have difficulty in policing telecommunication bandwidth markets, in much the same way as commodities futures and stock market trading creates incentives for fraud and other deceptive tactics. Tier-1 ISPs may try to run up prices in a commodity trading marketplace, but the success of such activities depends largely on whether they can control the options available to resellers and end users. For example, effective price fixing in the submarine cable marketplace will prove unsustainable unless equally effective price fixing takes place in satellite markets, since most Internet applications can use either transmission medium.

Arguments That Anticompetitive Practices Have Not Occurred

In a market able to reflect nearly instantaneous changes in prices, any significant impact on price can trigger close scrutiny. What Tier-1 ISPs may be able to achieve in closed-door negotiations and nondisclosure agreements they cannot achieve when the spot market offers such quick responsiveness. Under these conditions, Tier-1 ISPs should be disinclined to risk exposure and potential civil/criminal culpability for attempts to fix prices and to collude with other suppliers.

Scenario 2 offers Tier-1 ISPs some degree of legitimacy to meet and manage the marketplace in ways similar to what cooperatives do to ensure the supply of some commodities, e.g., milk. A dairy board can attempt to "stabilize" the price of milk complete with price floors, ostensibly to promote the widespread availability of such an essential product and as well to promote the apparent public benefit of sustaining family farms. In Scenario 3 no such legitimate forum exists and presumably each and every supplier must respond to marketplace conditions.

An Assessment of Outcomes in the Near Term

In the near term a dichotomy of outcomes may occur. On one hand, stakeholders may pursue a course of action in multilateral forums to redress grievances. On the other hand, stakeholders may opt to rely on technological and marketplace factors to remedy existing problems.

Do-Nothing Scenarios

Several near-term scenarios involve significant change affecting Internet stakeholders even without seeking redress in multilateral forums. The volatility of the Internet and the pace of change in Internet market segments means that a "do-nothing" approach will nevertheless result in stakeholders facing significantly different conditions in the months ahead. The robustness of the Internet economy means that what had appeared unimpeachable and unchangeable may become dislodged and upended. Dominant market shares may become unsustainable as incumbents fail to sustain their technological and marketplace leadership in the face of innovations and the next "killer application." Already in the short history of the Internet, ventures as large as IBM and as small but promising as Pointcast (first mover in "push" technologies delivering massive amounts of mostly unsolicited content to Internet subscribers) have lost their opportunity to extract monopoly rents, or at least to capitalize on first-to-market advantages.

Internet Access Issues May Become Less Troublesome

The matter of Internet access has presented a problem to some ISPs primarily because the access and transit services provided by Tier-1 ISPs constitute a significant portion of the smaller ISPs' operating expenses compared to other ISPs. Small ISPs and ones operating in localities far from North America have incurred substantially higher overall costs in doing business relative to similarly situated ISPs in other regions. One near-term scenario presents the Internet access problem as temporary and solvable because the solution is available to ISPs, their government and the marketplace.[36]

Changes in Traffic Flows and Market Conditions Support Better Peering Terms and Conditions

Regardless of their geographical location, ISPs smaller than the Tier-1 operators incurred higher telecommunication transport costs when Tier-1 ISPs replaced open peering with access for compensation. The Tier-1 ISPs could get away with changing the fundamental terms and conditions for network connectivity, because smaller ISPs needed them more than they needed the smaller ISPs. Any change in the balance of power and network access need over time will translate into different Internet access terms and conditions.

Asia/Pacific ISPs can secure better Internet access terms and conditions when and if demand elasticities and traffic flows trend more closely toward parity for inbound and outbound traffic flows. The move toward parity can occur primarily when in-region content grows in availability and popularity and when ISPs opt to host that content in region. Currently the desirability of content hosted in North America places ISPs located elsewhere in a demand-inelastic position. However, this situation does not mean that ISPs subscribers in Asia/Pacific purposely eschew indigenous, non-North American content. Cable television network programmers in the region have found that their subscriber prefer both kinds of content. For example, the launching of MTV Asia resulted from the failure of the standard North American version of the popular music video network to gain significant market share. To the extent that a market opportunity exists for indigenous content, then over time local programmers will attempt to satisfy market demand.

However, Internet access issue relief will not necessary result simply because of less reliance on North American content. ISPs must locate the content closer to subscribers and outside North America. As anomalous as it may seem, currently non-North American ISPs incur a cost penalty for locating content closer to their subscribers. Despite the burden of self-provisioning lines all the way to North America, the cost of such routing can undercut shorter and more direct routing in-region. A recent article in *The Industry Standard*, a widely read Internet news magazine, reported that an Australian-based content provider has opted to locate its content in North America because it could save forty percent in hosting and telecommunications costs.[37] Lower Internet access costs *to North America* would only bolster the incentive to host content there.

One can conclude that, even if Internet access terms and conditions more closely approximated a telecommunications model of line cost sharing on a 50/50 basis, telecommunication transport providers outside North American would continue to offer comparatively less attractive and more expensive rates. Surely economies of scale and scope contribute to a North American carrier's comparative cost advantage. But pricing policies, particularly for local loop access, and the comparatively less robust degree of competition factor prominently as well.

Accordingly, changes in pricing policies and the scope of competition might drive rates closer to North American levels. Quite possibly carriers outside of North America can unleash pent-up demand for Internet services by lowering access costs. Empirical evidence supports the view that a reduction in end user rates, and intermediate pricing factors like international accounting rates, tend to stimulate substantial increases in consumer demand, so much so that operators can make up in volume what they lose in margins.

Lower Transmission Costs Reduce Significance of the Issue

Much of the Internet access dispute stems from the comparatively greater percentage of total operating costs allocatable to the telecommunication transport portion in Asia/Pacific and other locations outside North America. According to John Hibbard, Telstra's Managing Director of Global Wholesale Business, up to "70 percent of an Australian ISP's costs are due to the international segment to the U.S.... [thereby] loading up the domestic cost structure."[38] The Internet access dispute can grow less troublesome thanks to the benefit of lower per-unit transmission costs to North America coupled with the proliferation of in-region ISPs and transmission options. Despite the seemingly unquenchable demand for ever-expanding bandwidth, one can envision a near-term future where the variety of new extremely high-bandwidth, Dense Wave Division Multiplexing fiber optic cable projects actually changes the region's infrastructure supply from one of scarcity to one of a possible glut. Even if Asia/Pacific subscribers persisted in their preference for North American content, with commensurate traffic routing by their ISPs, the cost of such a routing topology would decline on a per unit of capacity basis. Reduction in reliance on North American content and routing options would contribute to reaching closer parity in demand elasticities.

A Contrary View: Internet Access Issues May Become More Troublesome

Despite optimism that conditions may improve and at least partially abate Internet access concerns, the potential exists for the status quo to extend into the future. The financial burden borne by smaller ISPs may grow more acute if demand for high-bandwidth applications stimulates ever increasing requirements, offsetting even large reductions in per-unit costs. Under this scenario, Tier-One ISPs can maintain or increase their market power and demand even greater compensation. At the very least, leaving Internet access to commercial negotiations will result in some degree of lag as contracts may have long terms before coming up for renewal and renegotiation. As well, the negotiation process and the balance of power in them may heavily weight other factors in addition to traffic flow and transmission costs.

Do-Something Scenarios

Several near-term scenarios involve significant change affecting Internet stakeholders because they have engaged in "self-help" and/or resorted to multilateral forums for redress. Smaller ISPs can take affirmative steps to improve their negotiating leverage with Tier-1 ISPs. Additionally, they can attempt to ventilate Internet access issues in a number of bilateral and multilateral forums, regardless of whether these issues lend themselves to examination, much less resolution, in these forums.

Aggrieved ISPs Pursue "Self-Help"

Smaller ISPs have every financial incentive to find ways to minimize their reliance on Tier-1 ISPs for Internet connectivity. They can enhance their bargaining leverage to seek better terms and conditions at contract-renewal time by pursuing alternatives to contract renewals. To achieve this end, smaller ISPs should exploit their affiliation or subsidiary relationship with a facilities-based carrier. Integrated international carriers with an ISP affiliate or subsidiary can efficiently load voice, data, and Internet traffic on self-provisioned and leased lines. Additionally, the burden of whole-circuit provisioning does accrue some operational advantages. For example, in some nations, including the United States, the self-provisioning of circuits to a foreign point provides greater opportunities for low-cost access to the public switched telephone network in the foreign country without toll revenue-sharing or an accounting rate settlement.

Self-help also includes the use of technological remedies, including a recalibration of bandwidth sizing for outbound and inbound traffic. The asymmetrical nature of Internet traffic lends itself to different-sized transmission pathways to and from North America. Smaller ISPs need not provision an identical amount of bandwidth when outbound traffic to North America might require substantially less bandwidth than the return flow: a file request of a few bytes outbound to North America can trigger an onslaught of several hundred thousand bytes representing the requested content augmented by advertisements and other commercial inducements that help support the availability of the content. Caching of the most frequently viewed World Wide Web pages in local servers and other technological options can help conserve bandwidth.

Self-help involves both unilateral and jointly undertaken efforts by smaller ISPs. In the latter category, Asia-Pacific ISPs can coordinate more closely to aggregate traffic for efficient long-haul loading to North America. As well, they could pursue alternative peering opportunities in-region and with other ISPs in North America willing to provide better Internet access terms and conditions.

Stakeholders Seek Redress in Multilateral Forums

The Internet access matter may become a subject for examination by multilateral trade telecommunications and regional development forums because some stakeholders have failed to secure what they consider suitable resolution in the context of commercial negotiations between ISPs. Under circumstances where a matter has become a chronic irritant and financial drain, it follows that these stakeholders would seek new forums for resolution.

Stakeholders Seek Redress at the ITU

The International Telecommunication Union (ITU) provides a forum primarily for standard setting, allocating spectrum, registering spectrum and satellite orbital arc usage and recommending policies and procedures in telecommunications.[39] This specialized agency of the United Nations lacks enforcement powers, but has proven effective because most nations recognize the value in achieving uniform "rules of the road." Over the years the ITU has lent its "good offices" to addressing and attempting to resolve complex and contentious issues.

In October, 2000 the ITU's World Telecommunications Standardization Assembly (WTSA)[40] considered the Internet traffic settlements issue. The WTSA delegates agreed to a "Recommendation"[41] concerning the need for providers of direct international Internet connections to take into account, in their commercial arrangements, the "possible need for compensation between them for the value of elements such as traffic flow, geographic coverage, number of routes, and international transport, amongst others."[42]

While nonbinding and having rather general language, the existence of any Recommendation evidences a how important this issue is to many nations. Nations like the U.S. objected to any official consideration of the issue in view of the belief that Internet peering involves a commercial bilateral relationship. Nevertheless, a compromise was drafted in the waning hours of the Assembly:

The discussions on this very contentious issue found a positive outcome on the last day of the Assembly. The purpose of the recommendation is to set out the principle according to which there should be bilateral agreement when two providers establish a circuit between two countries for the purpose of carrying Internet traffic. The possible need for compensation between the providers has also been recognized. At present, when providers install Internet circuits, they generally have a choice between the "sender-keeps-all" or peering system of bilateral connections when traffic is more or less balanced, or the asymmetrical system whereby the initiating provider pays for the whole connection with the other country (full-circuit cost).[43]

Stakeholders Seek Redress at the WTO

The World Trade Organization (WTO) provides a forum primarily for shaping trade policy and for resolving trade disputes. Internet access issues may not fit within the scope of responsibilities conferred to the ITU by treaty, although we should note that such a limitation may not stop stakeholders from trying to recast the matter into one that does. The nature of this assignment does not require the consultants to analyze thoroughly whether and how the WTO would accept an invitation to examine Internet access issues. As a threshold matter, a number of different outcomes might result:

· The WTO Directorate rejects application as outside reach of the WTO;
· Representatives might not reach a consensus for even limited WTO study; and
· As in the case of international accounting rates, a "gentlemen's agreement" might forestall involvement in the short term.

Stakeholders Seek Redress in National Forums

Stakeholders might also pursue national forums in tandem with a multilateral forum campaign. Even if the ITU and WTO do not address Internet access issues, a national regulatory authority might, despite the difficulty in asserting extraterritorial jurisdiction on ISPs not operating domestically. National regulatory authorities might attempt unilaterally to remedy perceived problems by ordering structural and regulatory remedies, perhaps in manner similar to how the U.S. Federal Communications Commission prescribed benchmark settlement rates for telecommunication carriers.[44] Alternatively, national regulatory authorities might pursue liberalization, privatization and deregulatory initiatives that could stimulate competition, resulting in downward pressure on local loop and long-haul rates. Lower telecommunication costs should reduce Asia/Pacific ISPs' costs and narrow the financial penalties and comparative disadvantages they face. Yet another scenario involves adjudication by a national court on competition policy/antitrust claims.

Conclusion

The Internet access dispute provides a timely case study of how important the Internet has become in terms of both communications and commerce. Concerns about the digital divide have triggered a multi-billion-dollar campaign to subsidize telecommunications and Internet access in the United States and elsewhere. ISPs incurring higher access charges and their customers want to shape the issue in terms of equity and universal service, and not in terms of commercial negotiation and a maturing, commercializing Internet.

Higher access costs may have the potential to disadvantage smaller ISPs and ones far from North American and other concentrated sources of desired content. But the nature and scope of such disadvantage largely depends on what percentage of the total cost it constitutes for ISPs and their customers. No one likes to incur new and sizeable expenses without much warning and seemingly without adequate explanation why the prior pricing regime created free-rider opportunities that unfairly burdened large ISPs. But absent evidence that accepted competition policy and trade principles have been violated, the imposition of new charges does not warrant intervention by multilateral forums.

Notes

1. "When the National Science Foundation commercialized the Internet between 1992 and 1994, it took what might be called a minimalist approach, allowing market forces to develop the technology. It was a grand experiment with markets, and, by some perspectives, an unusual way to develop infrastructure." Shane Greenstein, "On the Net: The Recent Commercialization of Access Infrastructure—The NSF Got it Right, but They Also Got Quite Lucky. Why? And Can it Work Again?," *iMP Magazine* (rel. Dec. 22, 1999), available at ⟨http://www.cisp.org/imp/december_99/12_99greenstein.htm # Clemente⟩.

2. From Constance K. Robinson, "Network Effects in Telecommunications Mergers MCI Worldcom Merger: Protecting the Future of the Internet," in *Telecom Deals: M&A, Regulatory and Financing Issues 2000*, Practicing Law Institute Corporate Law and Practice Course Handbook Series, PLI Order No. B0-00N5, 1192 PLI /CORP.517, 535–536 (July, 2000) [hereinafter cited as Protecting the Future of the Internet]:

[T]he providers of Internet connectivity ... [can] be classified as a loose hierarchy broken down into roughly four tiers. At the top are nationwide (or worldwide) Internet backbones, which provide nationwide Internet services using extensive owned or leased fiber facilities. They generally have peering arrangements or private peering connections with the other national backbone providers and are "transit-free," so they do not have to rely on transit agreements.... The second group of providers are national Internet backbone networks that use facilities leased from underlying fiber telecommunications providers, but which pay transit fees to one or more national backbone providers. A third group comprises the Regional or local ISP Internet connectivity providers, which lease some regional or local network fiber facilities and equipment and interconnect with other small providers at the public NAPs make up another category. They typically purchase transit backbone services from any of the national backbone providers. The last group is made up of ISPs that do not have a network, but instead rely on others for wholesale Internet connectivity services. Small "Mom & Pop" ISPs are typical of this type.

From Seth A. Cohen, "Deregulating, Defragmenting & Interconnecting: Reconsidering Commercial Telecommunications Regulation in Relation to the Rise of Internet Telephony," 18 J. L. & COM. 133, 147 (Fall, 1998):

The result of technological advancement in telephony markets is a regulatory gap between conventional service providers and service providers that use new Internet technologies. As the technologies mature, both traditional market issues and concerns regarding regulatory controls are increasingly raised by competitors as well as regulatory agencies. The reluctance to regulate the new telecommunications technologies is based in the fear that the technology is not mature enough to bear the burden of regulation.

3. Sender Keep All and Bill and Keep arrangements refer to the absence of a monetary transfer when ISPs agree to route the traffic of another ISP to yet another ISP (also known as transiting), or to the final recipient. These terms also refer to a business relationship among telecommunications carriers: "Each carrier sets consumer collection rates and keeps 100%. This allows new entrants, but it does not encourage operators to receive calls because no compensation is given to allow incoming calls over their system." Taunya L. McLarty, "Liberalized Telecommunications Trade in the WTO: Implications for Universal Service Policy," 51 FED. COM. L.J. 1, 41, n. 203 (Dec. 1998). ISPs may use the term "peering" or "true peering" to identify a Sender Keep All, Bill and Keep Arrangement. Currently peering typically occurs only when ISPs of equal size expect to route roughly equivalent traffic streams. In practice, peering now occurs only among large ISPs with extensive transmission facilities and traffic volumes.

4. A positive network externality exists when the cost incurred by a user of the Internet does not fully reflect the benefit derived with the addition of new users and points of communications. See, e.g., Joseph Farrell and Garth Saloner,

"Standardization, Compatibility and Innovation," 16 RAND J. ECON. 70 (1985); Michael L. Katz and Carl Shapiro, "Network Externalities, Competition and Compatibility," 75 AM. ECON. REV. 424 (1985). Positive network externalities refer to an accrual in value, including increased access to information, increased ease of communication, and a decrease in a variety of transaction and overhead costs. *See* Carl Shapiro and Hal R. Varian, *Information Rules: A Strategic Guide to the Network Economy*, 183–84 (Cambridge, MA: Harvard Business School Press, 1999); see also Carl Shapiro, "Exclusivity in Network Industries," 7 GEO. MASON L. REV. 673 (Spring, 1999); Peter S. Menell, "An Analysis of the Scope of Copyright Protection for Application Programs," 41 STAN. L. REV. 1045, 1066 (1989) (" 'network externality' describes a class of goods for which the utility ... derived from the good's consumption increases with the other persons consuming the good"). See also Mark A. Lemley and David McGowan, "Legal Implications of Network Economic Effects," 86 CAL. L. REV. 481, 483 (1998); United States v. Microsoft Corp, 84 F. Supp. 2d 9, 20 (D.D.C. 1999) (findings of fact) ("A positive network effect is a phenomenon by which the attractiveness of a product increases with the number of people using it."), 87 F. Supp. 2d 30 (D.D.C.) (conclusions of law), 97 F. Supp. 2d 59 (D.D.C. 2000) (final judgment), *petition for cert. filed*, 69 U.S.L.W. 3111 (U.S. July 26, 2000) (No. 00-139).

5. Free ridership refers to the ability to tap into valuable services without having to pay. In some instances service providers consider free ridership unavoidable and even a social benefit, e.g., advertiser-supported commercial television makes possible the consumption of high-cost content without a direct payment and without indirect payment through consumption of the products and services advertised. However, digital technology greatly exacerbates the free-ridership problem as one can cheaply and easily make perfect duplicates of valuable intellectual property not intended for free use. The Internet provides a cheap medium for widespread dissemination of purloined content. "Bringing social order to the Internet thus requires overcoming free rider problems similar to those necessary to bring order to the west." Andrew P. Morriss, "Miners, Vigilantes & Cattlemen: Overcoming Free Rider Problems in the Private Provision of Law," 33 LAND & WATER L. Rev. 581, 688 (1998); See also Alvord-Polk, Inc. v. Schumacher & Co., 37 F.3d 996 (3d Cir. 1994) (denying summary judgment for defendants on antitrust claims that wallpaper vendors accessible by toll-free telephone numbers constituted "free-riders" of full-service vendors who incur the cost of creating and distributing wallpaper sample books, salesperson advice and showroom displays) *citing* Continental T.V., Inc. v. GTE Sylvania Inc., 433 U.S. 36, 55, 97 S.Ct. 2549, 2560, 53 L.Ed.2d 568 (1977); Big Apple BMW, Inc. v. BMW of North America, Inc., 974 F.2d 1358, 1376–77 (3d Cir.1992).

6. "A peering arrangement describes the situation where firms exchange data traffic without charging one another (bill-and-keep). A local peering arrangement is when the exchange occurs at a site close to the end-users. This proximity essentially improves the performance and speeds of the Internet connection, as data traffic travels less distance." Federal Communications Commission, Cable Services Bureau, Deborah A. Lathen, Chief, *Broadband Today—Staff Report to*

Chairman William E. Kennard, Federal Communications Commission—on Industry Monitoring Sessions Conducted by Cable Services Bureau, at n. 128 (Oct. 1999) available at ⟨http://www.fcc.gov/Bureaus/Cable/Reports/broadban.pdf⟩.

7. *Protecting the Future of the Internet* at 530–531:

At the beginning of [Internet] privatization, most of the networks had peering agreements with each other. With the massive growth of the Internet, the … [public peering points also known as Network Access Points] became congested, slowing down the speed of the connection and resulting in more lost data, and lowering the quality of connection to the rest of the networks. The larger networks responded to this problem by investing in private dedicated connection points which provide faster and more accurate connections. Generally, only the big national networks have these private peering connection points. Over time, as individual networks grew, large nationwide backbone providers began to complain that small local or regional ISPs were free riding on the large providers' substantial network investments. To deal with the free-riding issues, the larger network providers began to create policies to restrict future peering arrangements with small and regional ISPs that had not invested in growing their networks. They stopped peering and entered into transit agreements where the national backbones charged the small network or ISP "transit fees" for carrying and terminating their traffic.

8. For example, at the request of several Asia-Pacific governments, the Asia Pacific Economic Cooperation Telecommunications Working Group initiated an inquiry into International Charging Arrangements for Internet Services (ICAIS). Representatives of the Australian government and commercial Internet ventures asserted the need for "equitable distribution of costs and benefits, including return on investment. The model should encourage effective working of open markets in the relevant services and facilities. It should also work in situations where closed markets interconnect with open markets." APEC TEL19, PLEN/G/03, International Charging Arrangements for Internet Services, Australia's Objectives for the Project, available at ⟨http://www.apii.or.kr/apec/atwg/⟩. On the other hand, representatives of the United States government and commercial Internet ventures stated that "cost efficient arrangements for Internet traffic will continue to be worked out most quickly if the Internet market is left unhampered." United States Government, International Charging Arrangements for Internet Services, U.S. Background Paper, PLEN/G/03, AT&T Position Regarding Internet Charging Mechanisms and the Development of the Asia-Pacific Internet Infrastructure, submitted by the United States of America, PLEN/G/02, available at ⟨http://www.apii.or.kr/apec/atwg⟩.

9. From American Civil Liberties Union v. Reno, 929 F.Supp. 824, 831 (E.D. Pa. 1996), *aff'd.*, Reno v. American Civil Liberties Union, 521 U.S. 844, 117 S.Ct. 2329 (1997):

The Internet had its origins in 1969 as an experimental project of the Advanced Research Projects Agency (ARPA), and was called ARPANET. This network linked computers and computer networks owned by the military, defense contractors, and university laboratories conducting defense-related research. The network later allowed researchers across the country to access directly and to use extremely powerful supercomputers located at a few key universities and laboratories. As it evolved far beyond its research origins in the United States to encompass universities, corporations and people around the world....

From *Id.* 521 U.S. at 849–850:

The Internet is an international network of interconnected computers. It is the outgrowth of what began in 1969 as a military program called "ARPANET," which was designed to enable computers operated by the military, defense contractors, and universities conducting defense-related research to communicate with one another by redundant channels even if some portions of the network were damaged in a war. While the ARPANET no longer exists, it provided an example for the development of a number of civilian networks that, eventually linking with each other, now enable tens of millions of people to communicate with one another and to access vast amounts of information from around the world.

10. From Aileen A. Pisciotta, "Regulation of International Communications in the Age of the Internet: Lagging Behind the Future," 33 INT'L Law 367, 371 (Summer, 1999):

Over the near term, the Internet and the PSTN will begin to look increasingly similar with overlapping functions. As the Internet matures, ISPs will become more diversified and universal peering arrangements will become less practicable. The need for "settlements," at least with respect to some functions, will arise. Universal service contributions will be difficult to escape, particularly for phone-to-phone ... [Internet-mediated telephony] that utilizes IP-based packet-switching over dedicated facilities, but does not necessarily actually utilize the public Internet. Over the long term, however, the real issue is not whether IP telephony and basic voice telephony are consistently regulated according to familiar PSTN concepts.

11. For additional background on the impact of a hierarchical Internet industry structure on universal service policy objectives, see Rob Frieden, "Last Days of the Free Ride? The Consequences of Settlement-Based Interconnection for the Internet," 1 INFO No. 3, 225–238 (June, 1999); Rob Frieden, "Without Public Peer: The Potential Regulatory and Universal Service Consequences of Internet Balkanization," 3 VA. J. of L. & TECH. 8 (Fall, 1998) available at ⟨http://vjolt. student.virginia.edu/⟩.

12. Jonathan Angel, "Toll Lanes on the Information Superhighway," 15 NETWORK MAGAZINE, No. 2, 42, 44 (Feb. 2000).

13. *Id.* at p. 46.

14. For background on United States antitrust law and policy applied to telecommunications see Georges J. Alexander, "Antitrust and the Telephone Industry after the Telecommunications Act of 1996," 12 SANTA CLARA COMP. & HIGH TECH. L. J. 227 (1996). For background on antitrust and telecommunications-specific rules in the European telecommunications markets, see Paul Nihoul, "Convergence in European Telecommunications—A Case Study on the Relationship Between Regulation and Competition Law," 2 INT'L. J. Com.L. & POL. 1 (1998/99).

15. See Tom Downes and Shane Greenstein, "Do Commercial ISPs Provide Universal Access?" in Sharon Gillett and Ingo Vogelsang, eds., *Competition, Regulation and Convergence: Selected Papers From The 1998 Telecommunications Policy Research Conference* (Lawrence Erlbaum Associates, 1998).

16. From Michael Kende, The Digital Handshake, at 22:

In conclusion, the presence of a large number of top-tier backbones can prevent any anti-competitive actions. In a competitive backbone market, no large backbone would unilaterally end peering with another, as it has no guarantee that it will benefit from such an action. Furthermore, there would be no insurmountable barrier to entry or growth of smaller backbones. Larger top-tier backbones would continue to compete to provide transit services to smaller backbones. These smaller backbones would be able to resell these services to their own customers, and would not seem to face any barrier to acquiring either the infrastructure or customer base that could enable them eventually to join the ranks of the larger backbones and qualify for peering. Actual, as well as potential, entry by new backbones would act to constrain the actions of larger incumbent backbones, keeping prices at competitive levels.

17. See Jonathan Weinberg, "The Internet and 'Telecommunications Services,' Universal Service Mechanisms, Access Charges, and Other Flotsam of the Regulatory System," 16 YALE J. REG. 211 (Summer, 1999).

18. Section 2 of the Sherman Act, 15 U.S.C. §2 (2000), prohibits monopolization, attempts to monopolize, and conspiracies to monopolize. No evidence exists that any single Tier-1 ISP has market power, or has conspired with other Tier-1 ISPs to achieve market domination collectively by coordinating a single peering policy.

19. See Robert Pitofsky, "New Definition of Relevant Market and the Assault on Antitrust," 90 COLUM. L. REV. 1805, 1831–33 (1990); *see also* U.S. Department of Justice & Federal Trade Commission, *Horizontal Merger Guidelines* (1992, as amended 1997), reprinted in 4 Trade Reg. Rep. (CCH) par. 13,104.

20. See Satellite Television v. Continental Cablevision, Inc., 714 F.2d 351, 255 (4th Cir, 1983), *cert. den.*, 465 U.S. 1027 (1984).

21. Low barriers to market entry may overcome evidence of market anticompetitiveness. See, e.g., FTC v. Cardinal Health, Inc., 12 F. Supp. 2d 34, 55 (D.D.C. 1998) ("A court's finding that there exists ease of entry into the relevant product market can be sufficient to offset the government's prima facie case of anticompetitiveness."); United States v. Long Island Jewish Med. Ctr., 983 F. Supp. 121, 149 (E.D.N.Y. 1997) ("A merger is not likely to cause an anticompetitive effect if other participants can enter the relevant markets and reduce the likelihood of a price increase above competitive levels."); United States v. United Tote, Inc., 768 F. Supp. 1064, 1071 (D. Del. 1991) ("United Tote's second argument is that it is so easy to enter the totalistor market that high market share does not accurately reflect an ability to exercise market power."); McCaw Personal Communications, Inc. v. Pacific Telesis Group, 645 F. Supp. 1166, 1174 (N.D. Cal. 1986).

22. A boycott or company-organized refusal to deal constitutes one of the core anticompetitive practices deemed illegal by Section 1 of the Sherman Act, 15 U.S.C. §1 (2000).

23. A price squeeze involves "a situation where a firm manipulates the input and output prices faced by a competitor to prevent that firm from competing." William B. Tye, "The Price of Inputs Sold to Competitors: A Response," 11 YALE J. REG. 203, 212, n. 24 (1994). In telecommunications and Internet markets, some competitors may need to lease the facilities or services of a competitor. For example, a small ISP typically secures long-haul, broadband

transmission capacity used for transit services from a larger, Tier-1 ISP. If the larger ISP raised its transit charges but did not raise rates for similar services it provides directly to end users, it might be deemed to have engaged in a price squeeze by deliberately raising the costs incurred by rivals. See also Debra J. Aron and Steven S. Wildman, "Effecting a Price Squeeze Through Bundled Pricing," in Sharon Gillette and Ingo Vogelsang, eds. *Competition, Regulation, and Convergence: Current Trends In Telecommunications Policy Research* 1 (Lawrence Erlbaum, 1999).

24. See, e.g., Jason Oxman, Federal Communications Commission, Office of Plans and Policy, *The FCC and The Unregulation of the Internet*, OPP Working Paper No. 31, available at ⟨http://www.fcc.gov/opp/workingp.html⟩; President William J. Clinton and Vice President Albert Gore, Jr., *A Framework For Global Electronic Commerce* (1997), available at ⟨http://www.ecommerce.gov/framewrk. htm⟩ (articulating principles including the view that the private sector should lead; governments should avoid undue restrictions on electronic commerce, and, where governmental involvement is needed, its aim should be to support and enforce a predictable, minimalist, consistent and simple legal environment for commerce).

25. For example, in the European Union, Council Directive No. 90/387/EEC, art. 3, O.J. L. 192/1, at 2 (1990) establishes baseline principles that facilities-based telecommunication carriers must apply when leasing lines and interconnecting with enterprises providing value-added services. While the carriers do negotiate terms and conditions in a commercial, arm's-length atmosphere, Open Network Provision principles direct the providers of the underlying transmission capacity to offer access on terms and conditions based on objective criteria that must be transparent and published in an appropriate manner and that guarantee equal and non-discriminatory access in accordance with Community law. See Gunter Knieps, "Interconnection and Network Access," 23 FORD. INT'L L.J. 90 (2000).

26. Regulatory asymmetry can work when the products or services involved do not constitute functional equivalents. However, proliferating and developing Internet services have begun to include features that consumers may consider as unregulated substitutes for regulated telecommunication services, e.g., Internet telephony. "In general terms symmetric regulation means providing all suppliers, incumbents and new entrants alike, a level playing field on which to compete: the same price signals, the same restrictions, and the same obligations.... But all forms of asymmetric regulation contain an intrinsic bias toward some firms or technologies...." Mark Schankerman, "Symmetric Regulation for Competitive Telecommunications," 8 INFO. ECON. & POL'Y. 55 (1996).

27. The "essential facility" doctrine in antitrust/competition policy supports government intervention to mandate access by competitors to a facility or service provided by one competitor based on the following assumptions: 1) that the competitor has the ability to exert monopoly power over the essential facility, i.e., to deny access, or provide discriminatory access including the imposition of higher access rates on competitors, thereby leading to a price squeeze; and 2) that competitors cannot practically or reasonably duplicate the facility. *See* Daniel

Glasl, "Essential Facilities Doctrine in EC Antitrust Law: A Contribution to the Current Debate," 6 EURO. COMP. L. REV. 306 (1994); William B. Tye, "Competitive Access: A Comparative Industry Approach to the Essential Facility Doctrine," 8 ENG. L. J. 337, 346 (1987). But compare with Phillip Areeda, "Essential Facilities: An Epithet in Need of Limiting Principles," 58 Antitrust L. J. 841 (1989); Allen Kezsbom and Alan Goldman, "No Shortcut to Antitrust Analysis: The Twisted Journey of the 'Essential Facilities' Doctrine," 1996 COL. BUS. L. Rev. 1 (1996).

28. A bottleneck constitutes a potential choke point in the flow of commerce. In telecommunications and Internet traffic a bottleneck exists where traffic tends to back up due to congestion or limitations in the ability of the facility to handle the volume of traffic sent. *See* Robert B. Friedrich, "Regulatory and Antitrust Implications of Emerging Competition in Local Access Telecommunications: How Congress and the FCC Can Encourage Competition and Technological Progress in Telecommunications," 80 CORNELL L. Rev. 646, 659 (1995); Michael T. Osborne, "The Unfinished Business of Breaking up 'Ma Bell': Implementing Local Telephone Competition in the Twenty-First Century," 7 RICH. J. L. & TECH. 4 (Fall, 2000); Mark Cooper, "Open Access to the Broadband Internet: Technical and Economic Discrimination in Closed, Proprietary Networks," 71 U. COL. L. REV. 1011 (Fall, 2000).

29. Robert Pitofsky, "Antitrust Analysis in High-tech Industries: A 19th Century Discipline Addresses 21st Century Problems," 4 TEX. REV. L. & POLITICS 129, 138 (Fall, 1999); see also David J. Teece and Mary Coleman, "The Meaning of Monopoly: Antitrust Analysis in High-Technology Industries," 43 ANTI. BUL. 801 (1998).

30. See Leonard W.H. Ng, "Access and Interconnection Issues in the Move Towards the Full Liberalization of European Telecommunications," 23 N. C. J. INT'L L. & COMM. REG., 1 (Fall 1997).

31. From Conrad M. Shumadine, Walter D. Kelley, Jr., and Frank A. Edgar, Jr., *Antitrust and the Media*, 582 PLI/Pat 229, 418 (November, 1999):

Basically, the doctrine of conscious parallelism establishes a means by which a tacit agreement or understanding in restraint of trade may be proven. Under this doctrine, if certain competitors engage in a course of conduct that would be detrimental to any one of the competitors if such competitor acted alone and is beneficial to all of the competitors if such conduct is undertaken by all, then it may be inferred that the competitors agreed to undertake such conduct. Frequently, this commonality of interest in all competitors undertaking the same course of conduct is referred to as 'interdependence.'

See also Patrick Bolton, Joseph F. Brodley and Michael H. Riordan, "Predatory Pricing: Strategic Theory and Legal Policy," 88 GEO. L.J. 2239 (August, 2000); James E. Meeks, "Predatory Behavior as an Exclusionary Device in the Emerging Telecommunications Industry," 33 WAKE FOREST L. REV. 125, 131 (1998) (viewing predatory pricing in strategic terms; dominant-firm price cutting that raises entry barriers and harms potential competition is anticompetitive when it appears probable that the low pricing will not be maintained if entry is deterred).

32. For comprehensive background on international telecommunications and the impact of new factors like the Internet see Rob Frieden, *Managing Internet-Driven Change in International Telecommunications* (Newton, MA: Artech House, 2001).

33. United States v. Microsoft Corp. (Microsoft III), 84 F. Supp. 2d 9, 19 (D.D.C. 1999 (findings of fact); see also Thomas A. Piraino, "Identifying Monopolists' Illegal Conduct Under the Sherman Act," 75 N.Y.U. L. Rev. 809 (Oct. 2000).

34. "A tying arrangement arises when a seller conditions the sale of one product or service (the tying product) on the purchase of a separate product or service (the tied product)." Dustin Rowles, "Is it a Tie-in or an Integration? U.S. v. Microsoft Weighs In," 6 B.U. J. SCI & TECH L. 12, *4 (West Law pagination) (June, 2000).

35. Inmarsat was privatized in April, 1999 having previously spun off ICO, Ltd., a mobile satellite service venture currently under bankruptcy reorganization. See Requests for Special Temporary Authority To Change Points of Communications from Inmarsat to Inmarsat Limited, 14 FCC Rcd. 6283 (1999). Intelsat has taken steps toward privatization, including the spinoff in 1989 of New Skies, Ltd., a commercial venture operating six of Intelsat's satellites. Congressional and stakeholder concerns about a level competitive playing field slowed the process of further privatization until a compromise was reached reflected in the Open-Market Reorganization for the Betterment of International Telecommunications Act (the ORBIT Act) enacted into law (Pub. L. No. 106-180, 114 Stat. 48) on March 17, 2000. The ORBIT Act amends the Communications Satellite Act of 1962 to establish a statutory framework for the privatization of INTELSAT and Inmarsat and directs the President to report to Congress concerning the progress of privatization in relation to certain objectives, purposes and provisions.

36. See James Savage, Robert Frieden, and Timothy Denton, ICAIS Module 3, Final Report (April 2000) available at ⟨http://www.tmdenton.com⟩ (third report of a comprehensive analysis of international charging arrangements for Internet access performed for the Telecommunications Working Group of the Asia Pacific Economic Cooperation organization).

37. Stewart Taggart, "Fed Up Down Under," 3 THE INDUSTRY STANDARD No. 5, 260 (Feb. 14, 2000).

38. Ibid., at 265.

39. See Jannat C. Thompson, "Space for Rent: The International Telecommunications Union, Space Law, and Orbit/Spectrum Leasing," 62 J. AIR L. & COM. 279, 286 (1996).

40. The World Telecommunications Standard Assembly, previously known as the World Telecommunication Standardization Conference, addresses a wide variety of issues relating to setting standards and uniform "rules of the road" in telecommunications. See International Telecommunication Union, World Telecommunication Standardization Assembly (WTSA-2000), Structure of the Assembly, available at ⟨http://www.itu.int/ITU-T/wtsa/wtsa_structure.html⟩.

41. ITU Recommendations do not generate a binding treaty commitment. "The Recommendation, which is voluntary, suggests that parties involved take into account the possible need for compensation for elements such as traffic flow, number of routes, geographical coverage and the cost of international transmission among others when negotiating such commercial arrangements. In addition, the Assembly agreed that while international Internet connections remain subject to commercial agreements between operating agencies, there is a need for ongoing studies in this area." International Telecommunication Union, WTSA 2000 Outcome, Report on the Outcome of the Assembly, Montreal, 6 October 2000 available at ⟨http://www.itu.int/newsroom/press/documents/wtsa2000rep.htm#International⟩.

42. The text of the Recommendation issavailable at ⟨http://www.itu.int/newsroom/press/documents/diii.htm⟩.

43. WTSA 2000 Press Release.

44. See 1998 Biennial Regulatory Review Reform of the International Settlements Policy and Associated Filing Requirements, IB Docket No. 98-148, Report and Order and Order on Reconsideration, 14 FCC Rcd. 7963 (1999) (largely abandoning accounting rate scrutiny for traffic to World Trade Organization Member nations). *See also* Policy Statement on International Accounting Rate Reform, 11 FCC Rcd. 3146 (1996) (stating intent to update accounting rate policies to encourage competition and technological innovation); International Settlement Rates, IB Docket No. 96-261, Report and Order, 12 FCC Rcd. 19806 (1997) (creating four transition periods for compliance with benchmarks and responding to the potential for expanded opportunities for one-way bypass of an accounting rate settlement created by the Basic Telecommunications Service Agreement) (proposing Rob Frieden, "Falling Through the Cracks: International Accounting Rate Reform at the ITU and WTO," 22 T. P., No. 11 (December 1998).

7

Wireline vs. Wireless Internet Access: Comparing the United States and Japan

Emily Moto Murase

Introduction

The Internet has enjoyed rapid growth in both the United States and Japan. In the year 2000, over half of the U.S. population accessed the Internet, up from 40% in 1999.[1] In Japan, Internet usage grew from 12% in 1999 to 15% in the year 2000.[2] While access to the Internet is primarily through personal computers in the United States, a different picture is emerging in Japan, where many have begun to access the Internet through cellular phones. For example, in the 12 months since service was inaugurated in February 1999, the Nippon Telegraph & Telephone (NTT) DoCoMo i-Mode cellular Internet service garnered 5.2 million subscribers. Subscribership has since tripled, with no sign of slowing.[3] What explains the difference in the emerging Internet infrastructure?

Some argue that the preference for wireless Internet access in Japan is the direct result of cultural factors. It is cumbersome to type Japanese characters on a computer keyboard. Rooms in Japanese homes are multifunctional and do not lend themselves to dedicated space for a home office that includes a personal computer. While these explanations may have face validity, cultural outcomes can be viewed as inevitable and unquestionable. Alternative explanations, based on institutional factors, allow decision makers options to consider in seeking particular, though not necessarily inevitable, outcomes. The central argument of this paper is that wireline telecommunications policies, technological comparative advantage, and wireless market structure, not cultural factors, are key factors that explain the divergent outcomes.

In Japan, government policies to protect NTT's monopoly over local telephony gave rise to opportunities for wireless service providers to offer a substantial price advantage to consumers. The Japanese comparative advantage in the manufacture of consumer products such as cellular phones gave the wireless Internet infrastructure additional momentum. The Japanese government also carefully managed entry into the wireless market, creating regional service blocks that could easily be leveraged into national wireless networks.

In the United States, the industry pricing policy of unlimited local calling has been a key, albeit unintended, contributing factor to the explosion in wireline Internet access. The U.S. comparative advantage in computer hardware and software has reinforced personal computer-based Internet access. And the market structure for digital cellular operators was designed to maximize competition, not necessarily national networks.

This chapter concludes with a discussion of future directions for Internet infrastructure in the United States and Japan. Understanding the divergent paths by which Internet access in Japan is increasingly wireless while access in the United States remains primarily wireline will provide insight into alternative paths for the future development of the Internet infrastructure in the two countries.

Differences in Internet Infrastructure

What are the key differences in Internet infrastructure in the United States and Japan? Before answering this question, it is instructive to review a few milestones in Internet history. The purpose here is not to provide a comprehensive history of the Internet in the two countries. However, the timeline in table 7.1 shows that residential availability of the Internet in Japan was not far behind the United States.[4] Since 1992, Japan has lagged behind the United States by only about a year in key milestones.

Despite the fact the direct Internet access became available in Japan within a year it was offered in the United States, Internet penetration rates have been far lower in Japan than in the U.S. (see table 7.2).[5]

What explains this difference? Let us examine the penetration rates of communication and Internet terminals in the two countries. Telephone penetration in both Japan and the United States is virtually universal, making dial-up access widely available. Part of the explanation lies in the level of personal computer penetration, which lags in Japan compared

Table 7.1
Milestones in Internet history

Year	Place	Event
1969	U.S.	The Advanced Research Projects Agency (ARPA) at the Department of Defense creates the ARPANET, linking several research universities.
1971	U.S.	An ARPA contractor invents an electronic mail program.
1982	U.S.	ARPA adopts the Transmission Control Protocol (TCP) and Internet Protocol (IP).
1984	Japan	Japanese universities create the Japan Unix Network, JUNET.
1986	U.S.	The National Science Foundation creates the NSFNET.
1990	U.S.	Dial-up Internet service first becomes available in the United States.
1991	Europe	Researchers at the European Organization for Nuclear Research (CERN) develop the World Wide Web.
1992	U.S.	Researchers at the National Center for Supercomputing Applications at the University of Illinois pioneer Web browser technology.
1993	U.S.	The White House launches an official Web site. The Internet becomes commercially available in Japan.
1994	Japan	The Japanese Prime Minister launches an official Web site.
1995	U.S.	The major online service providers (e.g., America Online, Compuserve, Prodigy) offer direct (dial-up) Internet access in the U.S.
1996	Japan	The major online service providers (Nifty-serve, NEC) offer direct (dial-up) Internet access in Japan.
Feb 1999	Japan	NTT DoCoMo introduces the *i-Mode* service, enabling Internet access on cellular telephones.
Sept 1999	U.S.	Sprint introduces Sprint PCS Wireless Web, enabling Internet access on cellular telephones.

Sources: Intern Society, Ministry of Posts and Telecommunications, TKAI, Sprint

Table 7.2
Internet penetration rates in Japan and the U.S., 1999 and 2000

	Japan	U.S.
1999	15 million (12% of population)	106 million (39%)
2000	19 million (15%)	144 million (52%)

Sources: Access Media International, Nua Research

Table 7.3
Penetration rates of communication and Internet appliances in the U.S. and Japan, 1999 (by percent of all households)

	Japan	U.S.
Telephony (% households)	98%	94%
Personal computers (% households)	38%	54%
Cellular phones (% population)	38% (46% as of July 2000)	32% (37% as of August 2000)

Sources: Ministry of Posts and Telecommunications, *Nikkei Shimbun*, Federal Communications Commission, Cellular Telecommunications Industry Association, and National Science Foundation

to the U.S. However, the penetration rate of cellular phones in Japan has outpaced that in the U.S. Table 7.3 summarizes this comparison.[6] The Internet penetration gap is rapidly closing as increasing numbers of Japanese have begun to access the Internet through their cellular phones (see table 7.4).[7]

The typical Internet connection via personal computer, modem, and telephone line operates at a data transmission speed of 33 kilobits per second (K/bps).[8] Although electronic mail over cellular phones has been available in Japan since 1997, it was not until February 1999 that NTT DoCoMo, through its i-Mode service, enabled cellular phone users to access websites via the Internet, albeit at the relatively slow rates of 9.6 K/bps–14.4 K/bps.[9] NTT DoCoMo dedicated an existing packet-switching network to the data transmissions of its i-Mode users, thereby making the Internet available to users at all times and obviating the need

Table 7.4
Method of accessing the internet, 1999 (by percent of all households)

	Japan	U.S.
Personal computer	25%	46%
Cellular phone	9%	N.A.
	(41% as of September 2000)	

Sources: Ministry of Posts and Telecommunications, *Nikkei Shimbun*, Federal Communications Commission, Cellular Telecommunications Industry Association, and National Science Foundation

to dial into the network at each use.[10] While the AT&T PocketNet Phone offered limited Internet access to U.S. business customers as early as 1996, Sprint was the first to announce nationwide availability of digital wireless Internet access for residential customers in September 1999.[11] Public data on the numbers of cellular Internet users in the United States are not yet available.

What explains these outcomes? The different Internet infrastructure landscapes in the United States and Japan should be understood as a manifestation of differences in wireline telecommunications policy, technological comparative advantage, and wireless market structure.

Wireline Telecommunications Policy

The different outcomes can be explained by examining their historical antecedents. A central feature of Japanese telecommunications policy has been the ability of NTT to remain a monopolistic player in domestic telephony despite the efforts of the Ministry of Posts and Telecommunications (MPT) to introduce competition into the market. This policy orientation has resulted in prohibitively high prices for wireline Internet access in Japan. In contrast, early policies of tariff rebalancing in the United States created a flat-rate pricing structure in local telephony that has had the unintended effect of creating a compelling incentive for wireline Internet access.

Until 1985, NTT was a state-run monopoly provider of local and domestic long-distance telephony. As part of the 1985 Telecommunications Business Law, NTT was partially privatized. As an additional step toward market liberalization, the law authorized MPT to license "new common carriers" or NCCs to compete against NTT in the domestic long-distance market. NCC competition over the last 15 years has dramatically driven down prices for inter-prefectural calls. For example, in 1985, NTT charged about $4.00 for a three-minute weekday call between Tokyo and Osaka (roughly 311 miles, about the distance between Philadelphia and Boston). In 1998, competitor TTNet charged only $.63, or roughly 15% of the 1985 NTT monopoly price. Under such pressure, NTT lowered its rates by over 75%, charging roughly $.90 for the same call.[12] As of 1998, the NCCs had captured nearly 50% of all inter-prefectural calls. However, because the NTT monopoly over local telephony remains, the NCC share of all domestic calls was only 16%.[13]

For years, there was discussion of a "break-up" of NTT along the lines of the 1982 break-up of AT&T. At the time of the 1990 review of NTT's status, the MPT sought NTT break-up to increase competition in the domestic telecommunications market that extended beyond domestic long-distance services and into local telephony. However, NTT was able to resist the forces of divestiture with the support of a powerful lobby that included the *Zendentsu*, the influential labor union of NTT employees, the *Keidanren* (Federation of Economic Organizations), politicians who relied on NTT patronage, the Ministry of Finance, and the Ministry of International Trade and Industry.[14]

As one of the largest labor unions in the country, the *Zendentsu* did not have much to gain from a break-up. The *Keidanren* counted among its members the so-called "NTT family suppliers" Fujitsu, NEC, Oki, and Toshiba, who were financially dependent on NTT patronage, as were a number of politicians. The Ministry of Finance was concerned about a potential price drop in the now partially publicly owned NTT stock, negatively affecting the national budget. Others within the Japanese government, including the Ministry of International Trade and Industry (MITI), believed that divestiture would hinder NTT's eventual entry into global markets.

In 1997, the MPT and NTT reached an agreement to reorganize the company into a holding company and several subsidiaries, including two local operating companies, NTT East and NTT West.[15] The reorganization was completed in July 1999 and is notable for its continued preservation of the local monopoly. The NTT monopoly over local telephony

Table 7.5
Average installation and monthly fees for residential local telephony, 1999

	Japan	U.S.
One-time installation fees	$742.00	$44.00
Monthly fees	$15.00 for metered local calling + $.10 for every 3-minute daytime local call	$20.00 for unlimited local calling

Sources: InfoCom research, Federal Communications Commission

has resulted in extraordinarily high prices for local service.[16] U.S. prices are included in table 7.5 for comparative purposes.[17]

The implications of the Japanese pricing structure for local telephony on wireline Internet access are clear. First, given the exorbitant installation fee per line, few can afford to install a second telephone line dedicated to Internet access. Second, metered local calling means that for a one-hour session on the Internet, a user can expect to pay $1.80 in phone charges alone.

In contrast, the United States witnessed a boom in second-line installations as the demand for residential access to the Internet grew in the late 1990s. Industry estimates placed the percentage of households with second telephone lines at 17% in the California-Nevada region and 10% in the Colorado area.[18] Unlimited local calling is a major incentive for residential wireline Internet access in the United States. However, this was not an explicit policy goal at the time flat-rate local service was instituted.

The unlimited local calling pricing structure had its origins in the tariff rebalancing that occurred in the 1980s. Prior to that, the pricing structure for telephony rested on a series of subsidies: from business to residential, from long distance to local, and from urban to rural service. The Federal Communications Commission introduced an Access Charge Plan in 1982 that called for flat monthly charges to both residential and business customers. By addressing the discriminatory pricing and subsidy system that had distorted supply and demand patterns, the tariff rebalancing effort contributed to greater economic efficiency in telephony.[19] But no one could have anticipated the effect that flat-rate pricing of local telephony would have on the diffusion of the Internet.

Today, typical residential wireline Internet access is provided by Internet service providers who offer local access numbers so that consumers can avoid paying toll charges for dialing up to the network. Industry reports suggest that 47 million people rely on dial-up Internet access.[20] Who could have envisioned that an entire industry, dial-up Internet service provisioning, would build a business model based on unlimited local calling?

In Japan, the high prices for local calling, and therefore wireline Internet access, provided an opportunity for wireless services to offer an alternative. As in the United States, however, cellular telephony was initially very expensive and limited primarily to business customers. A deposit that was nearly double the exorbitant installation fee for wireline telephony was required of cellular subscribers until the early 1990s, when the introduction of the Personal Handyphone System (PHS) put severe pressure on the cellular industry to restructure prices.

In 1994, the Ministry of Posts and Telecommunications authorized up to three carriers for each of 10 regional blocks to operate PHS systems. Through the deployment of outdoor cell stations, the PHS system operated as a cordless telephone network that could be used outdoors. The service, inaugurated in July 1995, reached a peak subscription level of 7.1 million in September 1997.[21]

PHS was cheap and easy to use. In 1998, PHS subscribers paid a one-time fee of about $30 and another $27 as a basic monthly charge.[22] Yet the functionality was limited. Subscribers would often experience service interruptions as they moved out of range of the outdoor cell stations. And the PHS handsets did not function in moving automobiles or subways trains.

Competitive pressure from the expanding PHS market forced cellular service providers to lower prices. As prices dropped, many PHS subscribers migrated to cellular service, including digital cellular service, which was becoming widely available. This explains the rapid rise in Japanese cellular telephone subscribers that characterized the latter half of the 1990s, in contrast to the flat growth in the preceding years. By 1998, 46% of the Japanese population owned a cellular telephone.

In these ways, divergent wireline telecommunications policies have led to different pricing outcomes. These pricing outcomes have had an important influence on penetration rates of telephony, both wireline and wireless.

Technological Comparative Advantage

Technical interrelatedness also helps to explain the differences in emerging Internet infrastructure. In the 1970s, as the computer industries in both the United States and Japan were rapidly innovating and expanding, the two countries began to develop different comparative advantages: the United States in personal computers and Japan in consumer electronics. This difference has had important implications for the emerging Internet infrastructure.

Beginning in the 1950s, IBM established itself as the global leader in the computer industry. IBM had set the world standard for medium-sized mainframe computers and successfully pioneered mass production of small business computers.[23] In response, MITI in Japan embarked on a major effort to promote Japanese computer technology. And, by the late 1970s, Japanese manufacturers were competing with IBM for dominance in the Japanese mainframe computer market. For example, Fujitsu overtook IBM's position as the leading computer manufacturer in Japan in 1979.[24]

Yet, with the notable exception of microcontrollers, simple versions of microprocessors that are embedded in consumer electronic products such as video and audio equipment, Japanese technology has been focused on the domestic market.[25] Japanese microprocessors are produced primarily for domestic consumption, as is Japanese software. In contrast, U.S. chip manufacturers have maintained global dominance in microprocessors ever since Intel developed the first microprocessor in 1971, capturing just over 50% of global market share in 1999.[26]

Economist Martin Fransman attributes this difference to differing domestic demand patterns. In the United States in the early 1990s, the domestic demand for semiconductors came primarily from the computer industry, while, in Japan, the greatest demand for semiconductors came from consumer electronics. During the same period, personal computer penetration rates in Japan remained low, 17% compared to 24% in the United States in 1994.[27]

Another reason for the lack of success of Japanese personal computer manufacturers has been their tendency to rely on proprietary standards and technology. For example, when NEC introduced the first Japanese microprocessor, the PD700, in 1972, it was compatible with the Intel line of microprocessors. However, NEC turned to a proprietary system in the late 1970s as a way to control the entire supply chain, from the microprocessor to customer sales of computers to software. While NEC would soon become the number-one producer of personal computers in Japan, U.S. computer manufacturers were dominating the global markets for hardware and software. It was not until 1994 that NEC abandoned its proprietary strategy in favor of interoperability with other hardware and software, including those originating in the United States.[28] And the market for personal computers in Japan has remained relatively small. For example, more households in Japan feature warm-water bidets (42%) and video cameras (40%) than personal computers (38%) as of 1999.[29]

Without a large domestic market and no real global market, Japanese manufacturers of high-technology products have had little incentive to invest heavily in developing hardware and software for personal computers. The comparative advantage Japan has had in consumer electronics, on the other hand, leads logically to heavy investment in the design and manufacture of feature-rich cellular handsets capable of Internet access. U.S. computer manufacturers, in contrast, have large domestic and global markets that provide incentives to develop personal computers designed to take full advantage of the Internet, such as the 1998 Macintosh i-Mac.

Wireless Market Structure

Divergent market structures in wireless telecommunications in the United States and Japan further account for the differences in the emerging Internet infrastructure. Initially, both the United States and Japan closely managed competitive entry into the first-generation analog wireless market. The United States adopted a duopoly structure while Japan allowed a few "new common carriers" to compete against the monopoly provider NTT. However, as so-called second-generation digital wireless technology became available, the United States pursued a policy of market-driven competition while Japan continued to manage competitive entry in the wireless market.

In the mid-1970s, the Federal Communications Commission (FCC) envisioned a single national cellular system. However, in 1981, in order to promote competition in cellular telephony, the FCC adopted a duopoly structure in each of 734 geographically defined market segments. The United States was divided into 306 Metropolitan Statistical Areas (MSAs) and 428 Rural Statistical Areas (RSAs). Block-A cellular licenses were awarded to companies not affiliated with the local Bell operating company, while Block-B licenses were awarded to local Bell operating companies.[30] Yet cellular telephony remained expensive and limited to business customers. For example, in 1987, the average local monthly bill was close to $100.00.[31]

Through an act of Congress in 1993, the FCC was authorized to allocate an additional 153 megahertz of radio spectrum for Personal Communication Services (PCS), defined as "a wide array of mobile, portable, and ancillary communications services to individuals and businesses."[32] Of this total, 120 megahertz was dedicated to broadband PCS, which encompassed digital wireless telephony.

The design of the spectrum auctions was crafted to maximize competition. The broadband spectrum was divided into six blocks: Blocks A, B, and C, representing three bands containing 30 megahertz each, and Blocks D, E, and F, representing three bands of 10 megahertz each.[33] Licenses for Blocks A and B covered 51 Major Trading Areas. Intended for incumbent cellular operators, these licenses sold for $7 billion in March 1995.[34] Licenses for Block C, covering 493 (smaller) Basic Trading Areas, were awarded to entrepreneurs, including women-owned and minority-owned businesses as well as rural telephone companies, who paid a total of $11 billion.[35] The licenses for the 10-megahertz Blocks D, E, and F numbered 1,472 and cost a total of $2.5 billion.

The market-driven approach in the United States, as manifested in the spectrum auctions, opened up the licensing process to historic numbers of applicants from a diversity of backgrounds. Moreover, by awarding licenses to the highest bidders, the auctions generated $20.5 billion, unprecedented revenue for the federal government. But the resulting digital wireless market is fragmented. Not only are there three technological standards, the Global System for Mobile Communications (GSM),

Time Division Multiple Access (TDMA) and Code Division Multiple Access (CDMA), but large and small operators alike face coordination problems as they attempt to create a cohesive "footprint" of coverage regionally and nationally. Potential wireless subscribers face a menu of complex pricing schemes that include differential rates for weekday use, weekend use, roaming, and Internet access.

In contrast, the about 40 wireless carriers in Japan rely primarily on NTT proprietary analog and digital technology.[36] This reflects carefully restricted entry into the market. NTT first offered cellular telephony in 1979, as a monopoly provider. In 1988, the Ministry of Posts and Telecommunications permitted the entry of Idou Tsushin Corporation (IDO) in the Tokyo cellular market.[37] Just over six months later, the Kansai Cellular Telephone Company, a member of the DDI Group, introduced service in the Osaka area.[38] NTT spun off NTT DoCoMo to handle cellular telephony in 1992 and a year later, the company was divided into nine regional entities. The Ministry of Posts and Telecommunications licensed up to four carriers in each of 10 regional blocks in 1994, just as some cellular providers were beginning to offer digital services.

According to basic economics, the severely limited number of wireless service providers should result in exorbitantly high prices. However, competition from the Personal Handyphone Service described above has sharply reduced prices, making cellular telephony affordable for a large segment of the Japanese population (see table 7.6).[39] In fact, as table 7.7 shows, both fixed and variable costs tend to be lower in wireless than wireline telephony in Japan.[40]

Despite initial fragmentation, the U.S. wireless market has rapidly consolidated. AT&T Wireless, Sprint PCS, and Verizon Wireless have emerged as leading national carriers.[41] Intense price competition has resulted in lower prices for wireless telephony than wireline for some usage patterns (see table 7.8).[42] Yet, despite the cost advantage of wireless telephony, adoption has been slower in the U.S. than in Japan. While the number of Japanese who have cellular phones has likely surpassed 50% today, figures cited earlier suggest that the number in the United States is only approaching 40%.

In comparing the wireless market structures of the United States and Japan, there are notable differences. In Japan, competition in the wireless

Table 7.6
Wireless telephony charges in Japan, 1985, 1998, and 1999

	1985 Analog cellular	1998 PHS	1999 Digital cellular
Deposit	$2000	$30	None (as of October 1993)
Subscription fee	$800	None (as of February 1997)	None (as of December 1996)
Monthly charge	$300	$27	$41
Total fixed charges	$3100	$57	$45 (decline of 98.5% from 1985 levels)
Cost of a 3-minute local daytime call	$2.80	$.30	$.95

Sources: Ministry of Posts and Telecommunications, InfoCom Research

Table 7.7
Telephony costs in Japan, 2000

	Wireline (NTT)	Wireless (NTT DoCoMo)
One-time fee	$728	$30
Monthly fee	$15	$45
Total fixed charges	$742	$75
Cost of a 3-minute local daytime call	$.10	$.90

Source: InfoCom Research

Table 7.8
Telephony costs in the U.S., 2000

	Wireline (Pacific Bell)	Wireless (Pacific Bell Wireless)
One-time fee	$33	None
Monthly fee	$11	$40
Total fixed charges	$44	$40
Cost of a 3-minute local daytime call	Free, unlimited	Up to 125 minutes included in monthly fee; $.35 thereafter.

Source: Pacific Bell

market is severely restricted and carefully managed. Given monopoly prices for wireline communication, wireless telephony offers a substantially less expensive alternative and an impetus for widespread adoption. Meanwhile, the U.S. wireless market has been designed for maximum competition, first for wireless licenses, then for acquisitions and partnerships to increase wireless coverage or "footprints." Given historically low rates for wireline telephony, U.S. consumers are just now seeing attractive wireless telephony rates resulting from price competition.

A Word on Culture

It would be a gross overstatement to say that culture has had no influence over the emerging Internet infrastructure in the United States and Japan. Differences in lifestyle, home life, and language can guide some technology choices.

In evaluating the emerging Internet infrastructure, especially related to residential access, discretionary time available to users is an important consideration. Even casual observers of Japan will recognize that the Japanese tend to spend longer at the office than Americans. Unlike in the United States where discretionary time spent on the Internet generally comes in the evening after work, typical employees in Japan will remain at the office through the evening hours on a regular basis. For them, discretionary time is primarily limited to the commuting hours, when many travel great distances between their homes in the outlying areas and their downtown workplaces on public transportation. Waiting for the train or bus is an ideal time to access the Internet to check for e-mail or a stock update. And, while growing numbers of home offices are boosting personal computer sales in the United States, severely limited living space and rooms designed to be multifunctional makes such dedicated space an impossible luxury for most people in Japan.[43]

Many cite the difficulty of typing the Japanese language as a key factor in the low penetration rate for wireline Internet access. It is true that the complex Japanese writing system, which includes two phonetic alphabets, *hiragana* and *katakana*, and Chinese characters called *kanji*, is not easily input using the standard English keyboard. However, this difficulty has not prevented the Japanese word-processor manufacturing industry from achieving a household penetration rate of 45%.[44] Anecdotal evidence suggests that the younger generation in Japan has little trouble using the typewriter keyboard.

While differences in lifestyle, home life, and language may contribute something to the divergent Internet infrastructures that are evolving in the United States and Japan, these factors alone are not sufficient to explain the origins, rate, and direction of technological change. The institutional factors discussed above play a defining role in what technologies have emerged, how they have succeeded or not succeeded and, importantly, why.

Implications

Wireless Internet access is growing at a phenomenal rate in Japan. Currently, 15.6 million, or 1 in 10, Japanese subscribe to the NTT DoCoMo i-Mode service, inaugurated in February 1999.[45] The closest U.S. comparison to this remarkable diffusion is, perhaps, the popularity of America Online. Following the release of the Windows version in January 1993, it took America Online 18 months to reach 1 million subscribers. In comparison, it took NTT DoCoMo i-Mode only 6 months. Four years after the Windows release, America Online announced a membership of 10 million. In comparison, NTT DoCoMo i-Mode reached that number in under 18 months.

Wireline telecommunication policies, technological comparative advantage, and wireless market structure have contributed to a cost structure for Internet access that helps to explain the surge in wireless Internet access in Japan (see table 7.9).[46] Wireline Internet access requires a

Table 7.9
Internet access costs in Japan, 2000

	Wireline (NEC Biglobe)	Wireless (NTT DoCoMo i-Mode)
One-time fee	$728	$348
Monthly fee	$20	$3
Per-Message fee	None	$.04/e-mail ($.003/data packet)
Telephony charge	$15/month + $1.80/hour	None

Source: InfoCom Research, NEC, Nikkei Mobile

Table 7.10
Internet access costs in the U.S., 2000

	Wireline (Pacific Bell)	Wireless (Pacific Bell Wireless)
One-time fee	$33 (phone line)	$40
Monthly fee	$22 (Internet access)	$5 (PCS e-mail)
Per-message fee	None	First 300 messages included in monthly fee; $.10/message thereafter
Telephony charge	$11/month (basic monthly phone charge)	Up to 125 minutes included in monthly fee; $.35 thereafter.

Source: Pacific Bell

sizable upfront investment, not to mention purchase of a personal computer equipped with a modem. Moreover, monthly costs starting at $34 plus a couple of dollars per hour can add up quickly. Although the Internet-ready handset is not inexpensive, the incremental costs for wireless Internet access are much lower than those for wireless access in Japan. While data for the United States also shows that wireless Internet access may be less expensive, the service has only recently begun to be marketed widely (see table 7.10).[47]

What are the implications of Japan's increasingly wireless Internet infrastructure for the United States? Will the United States and Japan eventually converge on wireless Internet technologies, or will the United States diverge and continue along a wireline trajectory?

The conventional wisdom is that the infrastructures will converge. As wireless Internet access grows in Japan, users will become frustrated with the limitations of the small screen size on cellular handsets and migrate to personal-computer-based wireline access. There is some indication that the Ministry of Posts and Telecommunications as well as other government agencies in Japan are anxious to see greater Internet-based activity. As part of the Third Info-Communication Reform effort begun in July 1999, MPT has pledged to examine a flat-fee pricing structure for Internet access and price reductions for short-distance leased circuits.

Meanwhile, wireless Internet access is becoming increasingly available in the United States. Sprint and AT&T are just now aggressively marketing cellular Internet access nationwide. Online bookseller Amazon. com now offers its products and services to cellular Internet subscribers not only in the United States, but in Canada, the United Kingdom, and Germany as well. Yet the adoption rate for wireless Internet access in the United States is not nearly as rapid as that demonstrated in Japan.

Alternatively, the Internet infrastructure in the United States and Japan may diverge, with the United States remaining largely wireline– and personal–computer-based. Given the continued dominance of the U.S. software and hardware industries, the personal computer is likely to remain an important part of the typical U.S. household. Despite the fact that wireless telephony has become widespread in Latin America, Europe, and Asia, telephony in general has remained largely wireline in the United States.

NTT DoCoMo has embarked on a major effort to shape the global standard for the third-generation (3G) of wireless telephony. According to industry reports, NTT DoCoMo is investing roughly $7.1 billion annually in wideband code-division multiple-access (W-CDMA) technology, including handsets, base stations, and network control systems.[48] In 1998, the Ministry of Posts and Telecommunications proposed to the International Telecommunications Union that W-CDMA be adopted as the wireless transmission technology for the IMT-2000 (3G) mobile communication system.[49]

To advance the adoption of W-CDMA, NTT DoCoMo has forged a host of strategic alliances with telecommunications operators around the world. Currently field trials of the technology are underway in Malaysia, Singapore, Indonesia, South Korea, and China. Cooperative agreements to promote W-CDMA have been concluded with operators in Italy, Finland, the United Kingdom, the Philippines, and Thailand. In July 2000, NTT DoCoMo purchased a 15% equity stake in KPN, Royal Dutch Telecom, which has operations in the Netherlands, Germany, Belgium, Hungary, the Ukraine, and Indonesia and a total of 10.2 million subscribers.[50]

Yet NTT DoCoMo's drive to shape global standards has had little attention from U.S. policy makers. Instead, the current focus of U.S. policy toward telecommunications in Japan has been on lowering NTT interconnection rates. The policy objective is ostensibly to make the Japanese telecommunications market open to greater competition, including expanded opportunities for foreign service providers. However, the Japanese telecommunications market has been extremely resistant to such pressure in the past. It would be a mistake to devote too much effort to this area. Instead, crucial battles are currently underway in the much more important global telecommunications market. As global industry and markets organize around a wireless Internet infrastructure, will the United States be left behind? Will Japan succeed in its determination to shape a global wireless standard based on NTT DoCoMo technology?

Based on the phenomenal success of the NTT DoCoMo i-Mode service, it appears that Japan is poised to take the lead in developing and exploiting wireless Internet infrastructure overseas as well. That the United States will be in a position to challenge Japan's efforts appears unlikely, given the nascent domestic demand for wireless Internet access. Current efforts in the United States to make broadband Internet access widely available will certainly have an influence over the direction of Internet infrastructure development. But will a new technology emerge to make current forms of Internet infrastructure obsolete?

Just as policy, technology, and market structure have influenced the evolution of Internet infrastructure to this point, these factors will continue to be influential. They will largely determine the future trajectory of Internet infrastructure development in Japan and the United States.

Notes

1. Nua Internet Surveys for July 1999 and July 2000; available at ⟨http://www.nua.ie/surveys/how_many_online/n_america.html⟩.

2. Japan Internet Association, *Internet White Paper 2000* (in Japanese), Japan Internet Association (Tokyo, Japan: Impress Publications, 2000), 30–31.

3. The number of i-Mode subscribers as of March 19, 2000 was 5.2 million. NTT DoCoMo maintains a regularly updated website on i-Mode subscribership, available at ⟨http://www.nttdocomo.com/i/inumber.html⟩.

4. The timeline is primarily excerpted from Robert H. Zakon, "Hobbes' Internet Timeline," which is hosted at the Internet Society website available at ⟨http://www.isoc.org/zakon/Internet/History/HIT.html⟩. Japan-specific dates are from the Ministry of Posts and Telecommunications (MPT) *White Paper 1999*, 26, available at ⟨http://www.mpt.go.jp⟩ and the TKAI *Japan Internet Report*, February 1996, available at ⟨http://www.tkai.com⟩. Sprint press release, "Sprint Announces 'Grand Opening of the Wireless Internet' with Nationwide Availability of the Sprint PCS Wireless Web," September 20, 1999; available at ⟨http://s2.sprintpcs.com/news/1999/09_20_99.html⟩.

5. Figures for Japan as cited in Access Media International press release, "Internet Users in Japan Total 15.1 Million in February 1999," June 22, 1999, available at ⟨http://www.ami.co.jp⟩, and *Internet White Paper 2000*, 30–31. To calculate percent of Japanese population, I relied on census data and projections from the Statistics Bureau of the Management and Coordination Agency, available at ⟨http://www.stat.go.jp/english/1-2.htm.⟩. The agency reported that the Japanese population as of October 1, 1999 was 126,686,000. The projected figure for the year 2000 was 126,892,000. U.S. figures came from the Nua Internet Surveys for July, 1999 and July, 2000.

6. I use household penetration rates for personal computers and telephones because they are generally shared communication media within a household. Since cellular phones are essentially communication media for individuals, I have cited these penetration figures based on percent of total population. The MPT reports that household telephone subscribership as of September 1999 was 41.3 million (*MPT White Paper: Communications in Japan 2000*; available at ⟨http://www.mpt.go.jp/eng⟩). According to the Statistics Bureau of the Management and Coordination Agency, the population of Japan as of October 1, 1999 was 126,686,000 and the average number of persons per household was 3.3 (*Annual Report on Current Population Estimates* for October 1, 1999 and the 1999 figures included in the *Family Income and Expenditure Survey* of May 2000; available at ⟨http://www.stat.go.jp/english/1-2.htm⟩). Thus, I calculate the total number of households to be 42.2 million, and the household penetration rate to be 98%. The household penetration rates of 38% for personal computers was reported by the Management and Coordination Agency in the *Nikkei Shimbun* newspaper, July 12, 2000, morning edition, p. 5. The figure for the cellular phone penetration rate came from the MPT press release "Prompt Report on the Number of Subscribers of Cellular Telephone and Personal Handy-phone System (PHS)," September 7, 2000; available at the MPT website cited above. To get the penetration rate, the total subscribers of cellular telephone and PHS services, 60,894,000, was divided by the estimated year-2000 population figure of 126,892,000 (according to the Management and Coordination Agency). Telephone penetration rate for the U.S. is taken from the U.S. Federal Communications Commission (FCC) Report, *Telephone Subscribership in the United States*, Washington, DC, June 26, 2000; available at ⟨http://www.fcc.gov/Bureaus/Common_Carrier/Reports/FCC-State_Link/fcc-link.html⟩. The figure for the personal computer penetration rate is from the National Science Foundation Report, *Science & Engineering Indicators—2000 Report*; available at ⟨http://www.nsf.gov/sbe/srs/seind00/frames.htm⟩; see chapter 8, "Use of Computers and Computer Technology in the United States." The source for the cellular phone penetration rate is the *FCC Fifth Annual Report and Analysis of Competitive Market Conditions with Respect to Commercial Mobile Services*, Washington, DC, August 18, 2000, p. 4, available at ⟨http://www.fcc.gov/wtb/reports/fc000289.pdf⟩.

7. According to the MPT, the number of dial up Internet subscribers was 10.59 million and the number of mobile Internet subscribers 3.673 million as of December 1999. In press releases from August and September 2000, the top three

mobile Internet services, NTT DoCoMo i-Mode, DDI/TU-KA/IDO EZweb, and J-Phone J-Sky had 12 million, 3 million, and 2.5 million subscribers, respectively, amounting to an overall total of 17.5 million (reports in Nikkei BP AsiaBizTech; available at 〈http://www.nikkeibiztech.asiabiztech.com〉). I divided this figure by the number of households in Japan, 42.2 million, to get the final percentage. According to the National Science Foundation *Science & Engineering Indicators Report*, 46% of U.S. households have modem-equipped computers. Since demand for cellular Internet services has been very limited in the U.S., penetration figures were unavailable. For example, the Cellular Telecommunications Industry Association has not made such figures publicly available.

8. U.S. Department of Commerce, *Advanced Telecommunications in Rural America* (Washington, DC, April 2000), p. 6; available at 〈http://www.ntia.doc. gov/reports/ruralbb42600.pdf〉.

9. Harumi Yasui and Yoshi Takatsuki, "Te no hira ni noru Intanetto" [The Palmtop Internet]," *Nikkei Communications* (in Japanese), March 1, 1999, p. 99.

10. The NTT DoCoMo packet-switching network relies on the NTT proprietary Personal Digital Cellular (PDC) system. See Yasui and Takatsuki (note 9), 114. An alternative to this technology is the Code Division Multiple Access (CDMA) standard adopted by competitor KDDI, the merger of new common carriers DDI and IDO, plus regional carrier Tu-Ka, and international provider KDD.

11. AT&T press release, "AT&T PocketNet Phone Ushers in New Wireless Internet Era," July 11, 1996; available at 〈http://www.att.com/press/0796/ 960711.pca.html〉. Sprint press release, "Sprint Announces 'Grand Opening of the Wireless Internet' with Nationwide Availability of the Sprint PCS Wireless Web," September 20, 1999; available at 〈http://www3.sprint.com/PR/CDA/ PR_CDA_Press_Releases/1,1697,,00.html〉. Wireless Internet infrastructure standards in Japan are discussed in Izumi Yuasa, *NTT DoCoMo no Chosen* (The challenge of NTT DoCoMo) (Tokyo, Japan: Kou Business, 2000), pp. 236–238.

12. MPT, *Outline of the Telecommunications Business in Japan* (Tokyo, Japan, January 2000), 10; available at 〈http://www.mpt.go.jp/whatsnew/yellowbook/ index.html〉.

13. MPT, *Outline of the Telecommunications Business in Japan*, p. 9.

14. Steven K. Vogel, "International Games with National Rules: Competition for Comparative Regulatory Advantage in Telecommunications and Financial Services," Working Paper 88 (Berkeley, CA: Berkeley Roundtable on International Economics, June 1996); available at 〈http://socrates.berkeley.edu/ ~briewww/pubs/wp/wp88.html#RTFToC3〉.

15. For a schematic diagram of the reorganization, refer to the MPT *Outline of the Telecommunications Business in Japan*, January 2000, p. 18.

16. For wireline installation, NTT charges a $720 connection charge and an $8 subscription fee. The average monthly fee is about $15. For simplicity, I use the exchange rate of 100 yen/US$1. NTT DoCoMo requires a subscription fee of about $30. The standard monthly fee is $45. InfoCom Research, *Information & Communications in Japan 2000* (Tokyo, Japan: InfoCom Research Inc., 2000), pp. 45–46, 62.

17. FCC, *First 2000 Trends in Telephone Service Report* (Washington, DC, March 2000), p. 14–3; available at ⟨http://www.fcc.gov/Bureaus/Common_Carrier/Reports/FCC-State_Link/fcc-link.html⟩.

18. IDC report as cited in the *Tampa Tribune*, "2nd Phones in Home Grow 20%," August 5, 1997.

19. See Richard H. K. Vietor, *Contrived Competition: Regulation and Deregulation in America*, Cambridge, MA: Belknap Press, 1994, pp. 215–216.

20. *ISP Planet*, "Report Shows Internet Approaching Oligopoly," May 3, 2000; available at ⟨http://www.isp-planet.com/research/census_q12k.html⟩.

21. MPT, *White Paper 1999*, p. 150.

22. These figures are based on NTT DoCoMo's Personal Handyphone Service, standard plan in the Tokyo metropolitan area. InfoCom Research, *Information and Communication in Japan 1999* (Tokyo, Japan: InfoCom Research, Inc., 1999), p. 61. These rates have remained the same for 1999. InfoCom Research, *Information and Communication in Japan 2000*, p. 67.

23. Martin Fransman, *Japan's Computer and Communications Industry: The Evolution of Industrial Giants and Global Competitiveness* (Oxford, UK: Oxford University Press, 1995), 139.

24. Fransman, p. 154.

25. Fransman, pp. 5, 127.

26. See "World Market Sales and Shares, 1991–1999," at the Semiconductor Industry Association Web site; available at ⟨http://www.semichips.org/⟩.

27. Management and Coordination Agency, "IT Penetration Market Study," as cited in the *Nikkei Shimbun* newspaper, July 12, 2000. U.S. Department of Commerce, *Falling Through the Net: Defining the Digital Divide* (Washington, DC, July 1999), p. 10; available at ⟨http://www.commerce.gov⟩.

28. Fransman, (note 23), p. 193.

29. *Nikkei Shimbun*, July 12, 2000.

30. FCC, *Annual Report and Analysis of Competitive Market Conditions with Respect to Commercial Mobile Services* (Washington, DC, August 18, 1995), pp. 3–5; available at ⟨http://www.fcc.gov/Bureaus/Wireless/Reports/fcc95317.txt⟩.

31. Cellular Telecommunications Industry Association, *Annualized Wireless Industry Survey Results* (Washington, DC, December 1999); available at ⟨http://www.wow-com.com/wirelesssurvey/⟩.

32. FCC, *Second Annual Report and Analysis of Competitive Market Conditions with Respect to Commercial Mobile Services* (Washington, DC, March 25, 1997), p. 18; available at ⟨http://www.fcc.gov/wtb/reports/cmrscomp.pdf⟩.

33. FCC, *Second Annual Report*, 19.

34. Jeffrey Silva, "Group Seeking Federal Inquiry, Try to Stop PCS License Awards," *Radio Communication Report*, June 5, 1995.

35. FCC, *Second Annual Report*, p. 19.

36. According to the Ministry of Posts and Telecommunications, there were nine NTT DoCoMo companies, 21 other cellular phone carriers and nine Personal Handyphone Service carriers in the wireless as of January, 2000. MPT, *Outline of the Telecommunications Business in Japan*, 5.

37. Toyota Motor Corporation is a majority shareholder of IDO. See the IDO corporate Web site at ⟨http://www1.ido.co.jp/company_e/index_e.html⟩.

38. The Kyoto-based Kyocera Corporation has a 25% ownership interest in DDI. See the DDI corporate Web site at ⟨http://www.ddi.co.jp/index-e.html⟩.

39. Figures are for NTT DoCoMo cellular services. MPT, *Outline of Telecommunications Business in Japan*, p. 21. PHS figures as cited in InfoCom, *Information & Communications in Japan 1999*, p. 60.

40. InfoCom Research, *Information & Communications in Japan 2000*, pp. 45–46, 62–63.

41. The AT&T Wireless network employs TDMA technology while the Sprint PCS system relies on the competing CDMA wireless standard. See ⟨http://www.attws.com, http://www.sprint.com⟩. Verizon Wireless, created in 2000 through a merger of Bell Atlantic Mobile, GTE, Vodaphone/Air Touch Cellular, and PrimeCo, also relies on CDMA technology. See ⟨http://www.verizon.com⟩.

42. Figures from Pacific Bell are cited because the company operates both wireline and wireless networks. The wireless network is based on GSM wireless technology. See ⟨http://www.pacbell.com⟩. Many of the wireless carriers offer service plans as low as $20 per month, but usage during peak times for these plans is limited to 30–60 minutes per month. The service plan Pacific Bell Wireless offers for $40 includes 250 peak minutes, 1,000 off-peak minutes, and free unlimited long distance. The leading national carriers also offer free unlimited long distance, which is a strong incentive to subscribe to wireless services.

43. Remarks by Professor Richard Dasher, Stanford University, "The Impact of the Internet: How Lifestyles Will Change," for the Electronic Messaging Symposium sponsored by the Electronic Messaging Industry Organization and the Multimedia Cooperation Center, Tokyo, Japan, October 28, 1999.

44. *Nikkei Shimbun*, July 12, 2000.

45. This number is current as of December 3, 2000. Updated figures available at ⟨http://www.nttdocomo.com/i/inumber.html⟩.

46. While Internet service providers in Japan have generally charged by the hour or other time interval, NEC Biglobe began to offer a plan with unlimited Internet access in September, 2000. See ⟨http://www.biglobe.ne.jp/⟩ (in Japanese). InfoCom Research (2000) reports that most Internet providers charge roughly $10–$30 for 15 hours per month usage, not including telephone charges, which are billed separately by NTT. The handset price is the average of the 10 Internet ready models offered by NTT DoCoMo. See *DoCoMo Monthly*, a catalog of NTT DoCoMo handsets and service packages (in Japanese). E-mail transmission in the NTT DoCoMo i-Mode system is charged by the packet. The maximum length of an e-mail message in the i-Mode system is 250 characters. According to the October 2000 issue of *Nikkei Mobile* magazine (in Japanese, p. 23), a 250-character e-mail costs roughly 4 yen.

47. Prices for Internet access can be found at the Pacific Bell Web site: ⟨www.pacbell.com⟩.

48. Nikkei BP Asia BizTech, "NTT DoCoMo Makes Public IMT-2000 Procurement Specifications," January 26, 1999; available at ⟨http://www.nikkeibp.asiabiztech.com/⟩.

49. Nikkei BP Asia BizTech, "Japan's Telecom Ministry Proposes Wideband CDMA to ITU," July 3, 1998.

50. NTT DoCoMo press release, "NTT DoCoMo Concludes Investment Agreement with KPN Mobile," July 12, 2000; available at ⟨http://www.nttdocomo.com/pr/000712.htm⟩.

III

Dilemmas in Development of
Communications Infrastructures

8

Developing Telecommunications Infrastructure: State and Local Policy Collisions

Sharon Strover and Lon Berquist

Ever since the 1996 Telecom Act became law, state and local governments have endeavored to implement and adapt to its pro-competitive thrust. Most of the research addressing the near-term outcomes of the 1996 Act focuses on issues of unbundling, on the Regional Bell Operating Companies (RBOCs') entrance into long-distance services, or on reformulating universal service requirements. Little work has addressed other aspects of state and local roles in fulfilling the promises of the 1996 Act.

While attempting to promote telecommunications competition, the Act makes clear that states have a substantial role in preserving the longstanding aims of universal service. Many states have laboriously overhauled their universal service programs even as they grapple with the array of demands and conflicts among the vendors moving into new competitive positions. Attempts to "level the playing field" for new entrants challenging incumbents have sometimes faced state or local obstacles. The newest wave of CLECs and broadband connectivity/advanced services providers are challenging the abilities of cities and state utility commissions to treat all vendors equitably while at the same time guaranteeing comparable services for urban and rural populations as well as all corners of towns and cities.

Multiple systems of regulatory authority have created dilemmas for cities in particular. In some states, cities are encouraged to develop their own telecommunications infrastructures. In others, they are expressly forbidden to own or manage telecommunications facilities or services. On the front lines of vendors clamoring for more access to rights of way and lower fees to use those resources, cities often are not well equipped to evaluate and adjudicate the competing claims of telecommunications service providers. The political structure of cities generally demands equal treatment throughout all parts of a city region when it comes to the city sanctioning services, while service providers' business demands typically focus on just a subset of a city's constituencies. This balancing act mirrors the situation faced by state regulators, as on the one hand they smooth the way for businesses that might desire to serve only the most lucrative areas of a state while on the other they uphold the need to fulfill universal service obligations.

Several state and local governments have launched public and private-public projects that foster advanced telecommunications infrastructure as a strategic investment, their justifications being that such initiatives will encourage economic development, strengthen education, enhance governmental services and information, revitalize the role of libraries, advance telemedicine, and bolster universal service. Incumbent industries, whether telephone companies or cable operators, have objected strenuously to many of those projects and in a few cases have successfully derailed them. Many economists argue that public investment in infrastructure distorts normal marketplace operations and therefore destroys the positive effects of competition, the core of the 1996 Act. Nevertheless, those projects *do* exist, some of them directly extending or embedded in the spirit of universal service.

Given competing claims and a fundamental belief in and legal commitment to competition, how do states and cities grow into their new roles? This research seeks to investigate three basic questions: (1) Under what circumstances are state and local investments in telecommunications infrastructure undertaken? (2) What are the economic and political factors that explain the outcome of such investments? (3) How do their universal service policies or interests in service parities intersect the dynamics of telecommunications competition?

Methods

This study consists of a review of current literature and an analysis of existing data that document federal, state, and local policies directed at influencing the development of telecommunications infrastructure. Most of the data and information were collected in 1998 and the first half of 1999. Information was gathered from a variety of existing research reports, telecommunications trade publications, and state and municipal web sites. Follow-up e-mail and phone interviews with selected individuals were conducted to clarify and expand on collected data.

This review allowed us to discover the varying regulatory actions of state governments in promoting competition. This process also identified the innovative programs that encourage regional telecommunications infrastructure development. Finally, details about state and municipally sponsored telecommunications projects and networks were collected.

Two databases collected data on (1) state policies for all 50 states, including a summary of innovative policies or legislation dealing with telecommunications competition, universal service, and regional telecommunications development; and (2) telecommunications networks, including innovative state- and city-sponsored telecommunications networks.

In the State Policy Database, legislative Web site searches were conducted to discover recent bills that promote competition among telecommunications carriers and offer innovative programs or policies affecting telecommunications services within each state. Each state's utility commission Web site also was visited to discover additional regulatory issues affecting competition. Follow-up e-mail and phone interviews were conducted with state staff to clarify state policy or to obtain the status of pending legislation.

For the Network Database, initial data were gathered from existing publications listing public managed networks—primarily the American Public Power Association's 1999 *Annual Directory & Statistical Report* and the National Association of State Telecommunication Directors' 1998 *State Report*. Information from various articles in trade publications and Web site searches of home pages for state municipal associations, utility associations, and states and cities provided the bulk of information. E-mail and phone interviews clarified collected data. Data on cities likewise came from secondary literature as well as some interviews.

Here we organize findings around three general areas: (1) cities and advanced telecommunications, (2) state policy towards municipalities, and (3) statewide infrastructure development. Together they illustrate some of the contradictions in how competition policy is implemented across the country.

Findings

Cities and Advanced Telecommunications

Municipal Telecom Initiatives

The vision of an information superhighway promulgated by the National Information Infrastructure initiative pronouncements and the promise of competition through the Telecom Act have prompted many states and municipalities to explore creating government-owned or public-private partnered advanced telecommunications networks.

In the most common model, cities like Glasgow, Kentucky have simply extended the technological capabilities of their existing municipal cable systems to allow high-speed Internet service or provide other conventional cable services. Other cities have sought a more advanced telecommunications system such as a switched broadband network providing two-way voice, data, and video. Currently a number of localities (see table 8.1 below) have developed or are considering entirely new city-initiated telecommunications networks or advanced municipal cable systems.

There are several explanations for the increasing number of municipal telecommunications infrastructure projects. For cities, the expanding telecommunications market has potentially enormous consequences. Cities tend to be the electronic hubs for telecommunications networks and they often are concentrated centers of business and communication that demand advanced telecommunications systems and services. Telecommunications infrastructure long has been considered a strategic tool for economic growth, and in today's information economy rural towns as well as urban cities are well aware of the potential benefits that might be gained by possessing an advanced telecommunications network.[1]

Moreover, in many communities local government is the biggest user of telecommunications service and often has existing telecommunications infrastructure in place for city telephony and data needs in the form of city-run municipal power utilities. These typically have supporting telecommunications infrastructure with abundant unused capacity. Cities also utilize networks for internal governmental purposes, whether for simple telephony or for data networking. Some cities, particularly those that manage their own utilities, have developed or are considering advanced telecommunications systems in direct competition with their local telephone company or cable system. Leveraging existing telecommunications infrastructure makes it far easier and efficient for cities to develop an advanced telecommunications network for the entire community.[2]

Finally, universal service is not exclusively a federal or state government interest. Cities desire telecommunications services (particularly advanced telecommunications services) for every residence, business, and institution in the city in order to realize economic development possibilities. However, the Telecommunications Act of 1996, while maintaining universal service goals and promoting Internet connection discounts to schools and libraries, does little to promote access to *advanced* telecommunications services for residences or businesses, nor does it adequately make provisions for regions in which normal market forces of supply and demand translate into a paucity of services or service choices.[3] So, for example, several small cities dissatisfied with the local cable operator have created local, city-sponsored competitors.

Most municipal telecommunications initiatives fall into two categories: (1) cities issuing Requests for Proposals (RFPs) to partner with private firms in developing broadband networks to serve institutions, residents, and businesses, or (2) cities expanding their current public telecommunications infrastructure (a municipal utility network or municipal cable system providing cable TV and Internet services) to serve residents, sometimes in response to perceived poor cable service by incumbent operators. These categories reflect very different goals and opportunities, and successful implementation appears to be dependent on city size, complexity of local politics, state policy, and civic entrepreneurship.

City Public-Private Partnerships

Attempts to attract private investors to partner in the building of municipal networks have had limited success. Most cities attempting to partner are larger, and have a longstanding interest in having up-to-date telecommunication capabilities. Of the cities highlighted in table 8.1 below, Anaheim offers the only successful case of actual implementation of a public-private telecommunications network (though it has recently filed a lawsuit against the private partner). The examples noted below tend to be large cities that attract considerable attention when governmental action is initiated, leading to intense lobbying and political pressure from established private telecommunications firms. The rarefied political process these cities face is directly related to the lack of success they have had with these partnerships. A few highlights follow.

Anaheim, California.   The City of Anaheim, with a municipally run electric utility and its own internal telephone system, has developed a public/private network with First World Communication that connects Anaheim's businesses, schools, residents, and government buildings, utilizing 50 miles of the Public Utility Department's existing fiber-optic cable. As mentioned, litigation with the partner ensued.

Austin, Texas.   The City of Austin explored the possibility of building its own telecommunications network in 1994; however, in response, the Texas Legislature passed a comprehensive telecommunications bill that prohibited "direct or indirect" municipal involvement in the provision of telecommunications services. Responding in turn to this legislation, the City issued a Request for Strategic Partners (RFSP) for a public/private partnership with hopes that a private firm would offer advanced broadband services. A handful of firms expressed interest.

In April, 1996, the City Council voted to negotiate a franchise with CSW Communications to build a hybrid fiber-coax (HFC) network to interconnect all homes, businesses, and institutions in the city. However, the network never developed into a sophisticated broadband system, and CSW sold the system to another company, ICG, which currently offers only limited, competitive telephone service.

In 1999, three private telecommunications providers sought and received cable franchises to offer voice, video, and high-speed data services in competition with the existing phone company and cable operator. Essentially, the advanced services model had changed by late 1999: the new companies did not want partnerships, they just wanted to operate private businesses without the complication of a city partnership.

Los Angeles, California.   In 1996, the City of Los Angeles issued a request for information to build a public/private telecommunications infrastructure. They expected to build an advanced fiber optic network to serve internal city government needs as well as schools, businesses, and homes. In 1999, a Master RFP was released seeking private partners to expand the city's fiber-optic network with the possibility for partners to utilize a portion of the network for their own private ventures.

San Diego, California.   In 1996, San Diego issued an RFP to encourage private firms to partner with the city in building a "community-wide information infrastructure." During its deliberations, however, the Telecommunications Act of 1996 passed, and the city abandoned the process with the hope that competition among private sector telecommunications firms, touted by sponsors of the Act, would accomplish the goals expressed in the original RFP.

Seattle, Washington. Seattle issued an RFP seeking investors/developers interested in building an information highway in Seattle in 1995, but abandoned the process when Viacom sold its Seattle cable franchise to TCI, and the city was able to leverage a major part of its stated goal, residential high-speed Internet access, in negotiations with TCI. Seattle's later contestations with its cable company garnered a great deal of press coverage, and the case illustrates the difficult situation a municipal "voice" faces in attempting to embed its values (open access in this case) in local, privately provided infrastructure.

Leveraging Existing Infrastructure

Most successful city telecommunications initiatives occur in smaller cities and towns with established municipal cable systems or municipally owned utilities. This allows for upgrading existing networks with marginal investment. Often, newer municipal cable system development (with added high-speed Internet connectivity) occurs in reaction to the public outcry against poor service or high rates of incumbent private cable operators. We observe that these smaller venues are better able to manage the political problems that occur when industry performance does not meet public expectations. Many initiatives illustrate a high degree of utility company involvement, and we note that the public utilities often insure open access of their infrastructure to various ISPs, a point of contention for privately held cable systems offering modem service.

Cedar Falls, Iowa. Voters approved Cedar Falls' utility-based telecommunications efforts in 1994. The municipally owned utility has built a hybrid fiber-coax system that can provide video, voice, and data services to every resident and business in the town.

Eugene, Oregon. The Eugene Water & Electric Board plans to contract with a private company to install fiber-optic lines to municipal buildings, the University of Oregon, public schools and other institutions. The municipal utility added telecommunications to its service charter in May 2000, its long-term plans based on improving its own telecommunication capabilities and then exploiting unused capacity.

Glasgow, Kentucky. Since 1990, the Glasgow Electric Plant Board has offered a combined service (4 Mbps Internet link and 52-channel cable television) over its coaxial cable system. Primarily built to service

Glasgow's utility, the coax system subsequently offered service to compete with the cable operator.

Palo Alto, California. The City of Palo Alto is developing a 26-mile fiber-optic ring to serve the City's internal needs as well as to connect schools, libraries, and medical clinics. The city also initiated a Fiber-to-the-Home trial in 1998–99.

Tacoma, Washington. City-owned Tacoma City Light is building a fiber-optics network throughout the city that will compete head-to-head with the existing cable operator and telephone company. Anticipated services include high-speed data transport, electronic meter reading, and a 65-channel cable television system. Its facilities are open for use by competing ISPs.

Springfield, Oregon. The Springfield Utility Board began work in the summer of 1997 on an initial $1.5-million project to lay fiber-optic cable, with plans to spend $20 million to connect every home and business in town.

Table 8.1 lists cities providing data services through existing utility telecommunications networks, municipal cable service, or city-initiated public-private networks, current as of 1999.

State Policy and Cities

The Telecommunications Act of 1996 presented a unique challenge for federal, state and local governments to work cooperatively on telecommunications policy issues. State public utility commissions are required to open the local telecommunications market and encourage the deployment of telecommunications infrastructure, which forces them to create a balance between promoting a business environment that is conducive for private investments and fostering competition among providers. At the same time, vendors anxious to enter new lines of business (especially local exchange companies desiring to enter long distance) chafe under regulatory scrutiny and attempt to insure that their barriers to entry are as low as possible. As will be evident, competition *from* the public sector (such as in the case of city-owned infrastructure) is sometimes seen as threatening to incumbent industries. How states have dealt with their own cities' attempts to obtain telecommunications infrastructure illustrates strong divergences around the country. In several states this sort of potential competition has been stymied from the outset, while some other states encourage it.

State telecommunications or utility commissions routinely engage in arbitrations and mediations, order unbundling and interconnection agreements between incumbents and new entrants, and provide incentives for deployment of telecommunications infrastructure. Most state policies (at the legislative or agency level) establish rules for competition through the removal of traditional price regulation combined with incentives to spur local competition.

FCC studies undertaken since 1996 have looked at competition in terms of the presence of competing local exchange companies as well as in terms of the deployment of advanced infrastructure around the country. Their studies have shown that the initial effect of deregulatory policies has been a small gain in market share by competitive local exchange carriers (CLECs): their presence is recorded as only about 6% of local access lines at the end of 1999. However, such competitive services typically target businesses, not residential users, and CLECs have not moved rapidly in developing their own infrastructure—most of their business entails the resold capabilities of incumbents' networks. As of 1998, CLECs provided a total of between 4 and 5 million switched lines in 1998, which is less than 3% of nationwide switched access lines.[4] This percentage grew slightly to 3–4% of local switched access lines by the close of 1999.

The FCC reports on local competition, however, fail to offer detailed data on competition *within* markets. Because their studies concentrate on the number of CLEC entrants within each state (or within a Local Access and Transport Area (LATA), often a rather large geographic region), they do not offer insight into head-to-head competition that might be developing within markets. They also do not provide detailed data on residential as opposed to business offerings. Some of the ways that state legislation or regulation has dealt with municipalities wishing to influence their local telecommunications merit attention against this backdrop in which competition is fostered but rather poorly realized three or four years after the Telecom Act's implementation.

States vary quite a bit in how they have implemented policies allowing or encouraging public initiatives in local telecommunications infrastructure development. Several public telecommunications initiatives are developed in response to the lack of private investment in advanced telecommunications infrastructure, and some infrastructure initiatives

Table 8.1
City-initiated networks

City (by state)	Network
Alabama	
Scottsboro	Scottsboro Electric Power Board
Paragould	City, Light, Water, and Cable
Conway	Con.nect
California	
Alameda	Alameda Fiber Network
Anaheim	Anaheim Universal Telecommunications System
Palo Alto	Palo Alto Fiber Backbone
San Bruno	San Bruno Municipal Cable TV
Colorado	
Longmont	Longmont Power & Communications
Florida	
Gainesville	GRUcom (Gainesville Regional Utilities)
Ocala	Ocala Electric Utility Fiber Network
Georgia	
Fairburn	Fairburn City Utilities
Newnan	Newnan Utilities Cable
La Grange	La Grange Advanced Telecommunications
Marietta	Marietta FiberNet
Tifton	City-Net
Thomasville	Community Network Services
Iowa	
Cedar Falls	CFU Net
Coon Rapids	Coon Rapids Municipal Cable
Harwarden	Harwarden Integrated Technology
Harlan	Harlan Municipal Utilities
Indianola	Indianola Municipal Utilities
Lenox	Lenox Municipal Utilities
Kentucky	
Barbourville	Barbourville Online
Glasgow	Glasgow Electric Plant Board (HomeLAN)
Massachusetts	
Braintree	BELD.net
Easton	Easton Online
Holyoke	HEG Net
North Attleborough	North Attleborough Electric Fiber Services
Shrewsbury	Shrewsbury Community Cablevision
Michigan	
Coldwater	City One Cable
Sturgis	Digital Community

Table 8.1 (continued)

City (by state)	Network
Minnesota	
Alexandria	Alexandria Light & Power
Moorhead	Moorhead Public Service
Nebraska	
Lincoln	Lincoln Fiber Network Study (proposed)
North Carolina	
Cary	Fiber Optic Overlay Project
Ohio	
Bryan	Bryan Fiber Optic Network
Lebanon	Lebanon Electric Bureau
Wadsworth	Wadsworth Electric and Communications
Oregon	
Ashland	Ashland Fiber Network
Eugene	Eugene Fiber Optic Network
Springfield	Springfield Fiber Optic Network
Tennessee	
Chattanooga	EPB Telecommunications
Tullahoma	Tullahoma Network Resource Center
Virginia	
Abingdon	Electronic Village of Abingdon
Blacksburg	Blacksburg Electronic Village
Lynchburg	Lynchburg Fiber Optic Cable
Washington	
Tacoma	Click Network

are developed in order to meet the needs of particular constituencies, whether governmental, educational, or institutional. (As our next section indicates, many states have formed special commissions or panels to examine broadly the statewide telecommunications needs of government, education, business, and citizens in terms that go beyond the narrow regulatory mission of utility commissions.) The FCC's attention to broadband deployment under section 706 also appears to have encouraged some states to adopt measures that facilitate more municipally based telecommunications infrastructure development.[5] To promote advanced broadband services, the FCC convened a Federal-State Joint Conference to provide a forum for ongoing dialogue between the FCC, state utility commissions, and local and regional entities regarding the deployment of advanced telecommunications.[6] That Joint Conference appears to have

Table 8.2
States with legislation or utility policy promoting local telecommunications competition

State	Policy
Alabama	Allows electric cooperatives to provide rural telecom service
Florida	Counties and cities can provide telecom services in some instances
Georgia	Allows municipalities to overbuild private cable systems
Indiana	Allows rural electric cooperatives to furnish telecom services
Iowa	Municipally owned utilities allowed to offer telecom services
Kentucky	Permits some cities with municipal utilities to provide telecom services
Maine	Allows water utilities to provide fiber optic telecom services

succeeded in putting the issue of broadband deployment before the individual legislatures or utility commissions of several states, often framed in terms of combating a "digital divide." The Commission also issued a second report, "Deployment of Advanced Telecommunications Capability," which notes a great deal of growth in high-speed connection options around the country, clustered particularly in metropolitan regions.[7]

Table 8.2 illustrates the handful of state policies that have promoted *local* telecommunications competition, that is, the building of additional infrastructure at the municipal level.

There is a much longer list of generally competitive (i.e., rate-relaxation) measures adopted by states that demonstrate the broad extent of such initiatives, and most of these target rate reform of some sort. However, the small list here that speaks directly to *promoting* competition in cities is striking. Most such initiatives encourage market competition by allowing cities' municipal utilities or utility cooperatives to provide telecommunications service. This particular remedy is not widely popular among private sector competitors, and the product of some of that distaste appears in table 8.3.

Table 8.3 illustrates the states that expressly prohibit cities from developing their own telecommunications services. Some states, such as Ohio, have failed to pass bills prohibiting public telecommunications networks, but it is likely many states will initiate or reintroduce these bills in future

Table 8.3
States prohibiting or limiting municipal telecom networks

State	Policy
Arkansas	Government entity may not provide basic local exchange service directly or indirectly
Florida	Cities and counties must separately account for telecom services and are subject to same requirements as private firms
Missouri	Prohibits local governments from selling or leasing telecommunications services to the public or to other telecommunications providers
Nevada	Prohibits cities with over 25,000 residents from offering telecommunications service
Texas	Prevents cities from direct or indirect involvement in providing telecommunications services
Virginia	Generally prohibits municipalities from offering telecommunications service or infrastructure

sessions. Not surprisingly, telephone companies and cable operators are alarmed by the growing interest in public telecommunications systems and they have been active claimants in the legislative or regulatory processes behind the decisions to prevent city-based telecom initiatives. Despite the evidence that Congress clearly expected municipal power utilities to be among the entrants in a competitive telecommunications market, several recent court battles and regulatory conflicts have decided against or have inhibited municipal telecommunications efforts.[8] Incumbent telephone operators have successfully lobbied state legislatures to pass bills preventing or limiting municipal involvement in telecommunications services.[9]

Florida appears in both lists because on the one hand it does allow for some municipal telecommunications services, but its rules on how those operations must conform to typical firms' accounting practices effectively erode the benefits of municipal utility involvement. While municipal utilities make the same arguments concerning achieving efficiencies and economies of scope that any business might make, they are limited by such rules from implementing services in such a way that realizes substantial consumer savings.

Justifications for prohibiting cities from offering or being involved in providing telecommunications services typically are absent from legislation, although hearings and legislative histories reveal strongly worded opinions from incumbent vendors.

State Investments in Infrastructure

As more states awaken to the potential economic gains associated with advanced telecommunications infrastructure and as popular emphasis on broadband deployment penetrates political circles, more states are attending to targeted infrastructure building plans. The intrinsic problem with such plans, of course, is that they muddy the hand of the market: to the extent that government loans, incentives, and grants tip the hand of competition, they eliminate precisely the "self-righting" forces worshipped in the 1996 Telecommunications Act. In effect, many such infrastructure plans implicitly or explicitly acknowledge that some areas, or some applications, are "less economic" than others. However, carrying this argument to its logical conclusion is not popular.

For example, we found that several states have established specific rural telecommunications policies or funding programs that encourage rural infrastructure development. Table 8.4 highlights those states with specific programs meeting the needs of rural areas. The intended role of utilities is particularly notable in some of these programs.

Another tier of programs has begun to emerge in 2000, epitomized by the recently announced agreement between North Carolina and BellSouth, Sprint, and GTE. In that plan, the telecommunications vendors will provide affordable, high-speed Internet access to all areas of the state by 2003 in exchange for various tax incentives. Georgia's similar program with BellSouth would deliver high-speed Internet access to rural Georgia residents and all of Georgia's K–12 schools through funding provided by the company as well as tax incentives. These programs illustrate a contrast with those noted in table 8.4 insofar as having regional utilities provide services in rural areas constitutes a small competitive threat and consequently is less problematic to large incumbents. Plans for *statewide* Internet access, however, if not controlled by the dominant LECs, could easily grow into unwelcome competition. By working with state government, the LECs eliminate that prospect while the states gain statewide coverage.

In another type of infrastructure program, nearly every state sponsors some sort of educational telecommunications network, although the

Table 8.4
States with funds earmarked for rural telecommunications

State	Rural Initiative
Alabama	Electric cooperatives can offer telecom service in rural areas
Colorado	Colorado High Cost Fund and Colorado Rural Technology Project funds rural areas
Georgia	Municipal cable possible in small rural towns neglected by private firms
Idaho	Limits interconnection requirements for rural operators
Indiana	Allows rural electric corporations to furnish telecommunications services
Iowa	Municipal utilities (including rural) allowed to offer telecom services
Kentucky	Permits cities (including rural) with municipal utilities to provide telecom services
New Hampshire	Legislative oversight committee will examine issue of rural access and delivery
Oregon	Infrastructure fund targets rural areas of state
South Carolina	State Rural Infrastructure Fund provides telecommunications funding for rural cities
Texas	TIF specifically targets underserved rural regions of state

nature of that network can be quite different from state to state, with some supporting data communications and other supporting radio, television, and even satellite networks for distance education. Likewise, governments support networks for their own agency uses, often linking state agencies and offices across huge distances. Our database documents various aspects of these networks, particularly those dedicated to advanced telecommunications applications. We discover that major issues for state network development include (1) when to use public or private ownership and management; (2) offering "postalized" telecommunications services based on specific, distance-insensitive use rates across the state; and (3) determining how advanced the technological capabilities of networks should be. Highlights of representative statewide networks follow.

CALNet.   CALNet is the statewide, publicly managed network (though operated by private telecommunications firms) that serves California state agencies with voice and data needs. Previously operated exclusively by the state, CALNet follows a trend among many states to outsource network operations to private carriers, and its transition to private operations highlights some of the questions states ask in deciding who should own and manage such facilities dedicated to public use.

Iowa Communications Network.   ICN is a state-managed and -operated fiber optic network with full motion capabilities for connecting government, education, and medical facilities. It has come under fire for years from the private sector as an instance of unfair competition in telecommunications by virtue of the state "doing business" with its own programs. ICN carries a great deal of state-originated traffic.

Connecting Minnesota.   Connecting Minnesota is a public/private partnership initiated by the Departments of Transportation and Administration to bring fiber-optic communications to significant portions of greater Minnesota and to increase telecommunications capacity in the Twin Cities metro area. The state contracted with a single vendor to build the network in return for exclusive use by the vendor of a number of fiber strands.

North Carolina Information Highway.   The North Carolina Information Highway (NCIH) provides state government entities with a broadband network for high-speed data, voice, and video. One of the first statewide fiber optic networks, its early users complained that little money was earmarked for "last mile" costs, which hindered many institutions' ability to connect to the backbone.

TEX-AN 2000.   TEX-AN 2000 is the statewide consolidated telecommunications network for telephone, video, and data serving government and education in Texas. The state establishes the specifications for the network and allows the private vendor community to come up with infrastructure solutions to meet the demands of state agencies. For telecommunications services, the state has contracted for "postalized" rates through a bid process. This means that the state will pay a set price for designated circuits (56 kbps, T1, etc.) ordered from the vendor (currently AT&T) within a LATA (a geographic region that defines the boundaries of local versus long distance services). These contracted rates offer savings to the state and, significantly, may provide opportunities for local government and educational districts to enter the statewide "cloud" of services at steep discounts.

Texas Telecommunications Infrastructure Fund.   The byproduct of 1995 telecommunications deregulation legislation largely focused on Southwestern Bell, the Telecommunications Infrastructure Fund in Texas is the country's largest such program dedicated to providing high-speed connectivity to K–12 schools, public libraries, higher education and rural, not-for-profit hospitals. It is supposed to be a 10-year, $1.5-billion program. While the program's emphasis on funding T-1 connectivity brings some of its revenue back to local exchange carriers, it has been criticized for putting state money where private investment should be fostered and also for investing in "stovepipe" networks of T-1s. Nevertheless, Internet connectivity is now enjoyed by nearly every school and library in the state.

NET.WORK.VIRGINIA. NET.WORK.VIRGINIA is an advanced broadband network delivering ATM (asynchronous transfer mode) service statewide. In addition to serving government and education, private industry and other entities can connect directly to NET.WORK. VIRGINIA for the purpose of participating with educational programs.

This list represents a range of statewide infrastructure programs, but the controversies behind some of them are telling. Constructing specific state-provided programs that target users, regions, or functionalities runs the risk of alienating would-be private sector providers. Unfortunately, the transition to competition has not provided clear markers for those occasions when competition will be slow or when it will not materialize at all, and those hazy domains are precisely the regions where state intervention is generally requested. The more recent crop of collaborations between states and dominant private vendors such as BellSouth may represent the politically and economically expedient way of solving this dilemma: such programs do not create competition for incumbents. In fact, they enable the state to actually invest in already large and local providers.

Conclusions

We have briefly reviewed the patterns of telecommunications deregulation as they are unfolding at the local and state levels. Three primary areas were addressed: the role of municipalities in drawing or creating new infrastructure; the actions and incentives of states in either limiting or encouraging municipal-level telecommunications involvement; and the configuration of statewide infrastructure programs.

Role of Municipalities

As noted above, issues of public network ownership need to be explored that recognize the growing role of city and regional attempts to develop advanced telecommunications networks to meet the needs of local government, education, business, and residents. Although the nationwide residential deployment of broadband services through the private sector's cable modem and DSL services continues to grow, it offered an unimpressive penetration rate of approximately 0.3% of U.S. households according to early 1999 estimates, which tripled to a still rather low figure of about 1% by the end of 1999 (high-speed plus advanced services are estimated to have penetration of 1.6%).[10] To the extent that cities' own efforts in developing infrastructure are encouraged, such penetration rates could rise more quickly. Anchor tenants and collaborations are two strategies cities may use where not prohibited by the state.

Anchor Tenants

Increasingly, city and county governments have economic incentives to develop internal communications networks to save taxpayer dollars. Local government's abilities to provide public information more efficiently online are enhanced with advanced telecommunications capabilities, and government units are consistently held to private sector standards in terms of efficiency and performance. Cities with municipal utilities have existing telecommunications networks for utility management purposes, and as the primary tenant of a public network, cities have the ability to share excess network capacity with other institutions, businesses, or residents. As anchor tenants in a telecommunications venture, they would perform much as any business would in maximizing the use of their resources and making additional investment more cost-efficient.

Collaborations

The ability to share excess capacity with other institutions often leads to regional collaborations among local government, school districts, and other government agencies, as well as businesses. This can be particularly important in rural areas where aggregate demand can draw services that single smaller users could not command. If competition among private carriers fails to offer advanced telecommunications at affordable rates, it is likely that collaborative public and public-private telecommunications networks will continue to grow as long as policymakers allow them to do so. Some programs, such as Texas' Telecommunications Infrastructure Fund, are deliberately encouraging this.

States and Municipalities

As interest in publicly funded networks grows, competitive concerns among private carriers also will grow. As has been the case in many state legislatures, more states will see legislation introduced in an attempt to limit or prohibit cities and other governmental bodies from developing telecommunications networks.

Most states concede they must take a much more active role in promoting competition, developing advanced infrastructure, and ensuring that telecommunications services continue to be available to all. It is much too early to declare which state policies will lead to achieving the goals set out by the Telecom Act, but the data offered in this report suggest that creating competition is tricky, uneven, and subject to highly political interpretations and actions.

Who should be allowed to compete and on what terms constitutes a thorny area: should all types of utilities be able to go "head to head" with conventional telecommunications providers? Should local ISPs be able to offer their services on cable modem networks, whether they are privately or publicly owned? As utilities continue to be deregulated, their legitimate role in providing telecommunications services should be addressed by state policy. The differences and similarities between public and privately owned utility systems with respect to providing advanced telecommunications infrastructure should be addressed.

What type of regulation yields the best competitive outcomes? Comparing alternative state regulatory policies and infrastructure outcomes should provide answers as to what models are most effective at enhancing competition, holding down prices, and encouraging investment in advanced telecommunications capabilities.

What sorts of infrastructure investments are optimal? In addition to comparing state regulatory policies' impact on infrastructure development in terms of what incentive regulations, price caps, or rate moratoria lead to greater infrastructure investment, exploring the outcomes associated with increasing public investment in *state* networks offers an opportunity to evaluate private versus public investment in telecommunications infrastructure and how states may benefit from either approach.

As the United States attempts to develop its Information Superhighway, researchers and policymakers need to focus on the regulations and policies of the federal government and the states as well as the infrastructure projects of states, regions and cities. While the federal government has a continuing and important role in developing information infrastructure, a great deal of policy and infrastructure development must occur at the state and local level. Too often states are unaware of other states' efforts and whether they succeed or fail; states generally lack the resources to undertake their own broad-ranging studies, and certain parochial attitudes may hold sway. There is the additional problem at the state level of political influence by large industries. More shared information across states and across localities can yield a better understanding of the most viable approaches, and produce a pool of experts who can work with one another in crafting the most effective programs.

Notes

1. Stephen Graham and Simon Marvin, *Telecommunications and the City: Electronic Spaces, Urban Places* (London: Routledge, 1996).

2. Lon Berquist and August E. Grant, "The Emerging Municipal Infrastructure: The Austin Experience," in Debra Hurley and James H. Keller, eds., *The First Hundred Feet: Options for Internet and Broadband Access* (Cambridge, MA: MIT Press, 1999).

3. Miles Fidelman, "The New Universal-Service Rules: Less than Meets the Eye," *Civic. com*, Vol. 1, No. 7 (1997), pp. 30–33.

4. Federal Communications Commission, "Local Competition," Industry Analysis Division, December, 1998. See also see "Trends in Telephone Service", Industry Analysis Division, March, 2000.

5. Federal Communications Commission, "Report on the Deployment of Advanced Telecommunications Capability to All Americans," CC Docket No. 98–146, 1999.

6. Federal Communications Commission, "In the Matter of Federal-State Joint Conference on Advanced Telecommunications Services," CC Docket No. 99–294, Order (released October 8, 1999). This item can be found at ⟨http://www. fcc.gov/Bureaus/Common Carrier/Orders/1999/fcc99293.txt⟩.

7. Federal Communication Commission. "Deployment of Advanced Telecommunications Capability: Second Report." CC Docket 98–146, 2000, released 8/21/00.

8. James Baller and Sean Stokes, "The Public Sector's Authority to Engage in Telecommunications Activities," *Journal of Municipal Telecommunications,* Vol. 1, No. 1 (1999), ⟨http://www.munitelecom.org⟩. The authors argue Section 253(a) of the Telecommunications Act of 1996 makes clear that no state or local law may prevent "any entity" from providing telecommunications services—suggesting that cities, as "any entity," may provide telecommunications services.

9. Blake Harris, "Telecom Wars," *Government Technology,* Vol. 11, No. 3 (1998), pp. 38–39, 72.

10. According to the FCC, early 1999 figures estimate 350,000 cable modem subscribers and 25,000 DSL subscribers. Late 2000 figures found 875,000 cable modem subscribers and 115,000 DSL subscribers. From Federal Communications Commission, "Deployment of Advanced Telecommunications Capability: Second Report," CC Docket No. 98–146 (2000).

9

From C to Shining C: Competition and Cross-Subsidy in Communications[1]

Gregory L. Rosston and Bradley S. Wimmer

Introduction

Many predicted that 1996's passage of the Telecommunications Act would usher in a new era of competition in telecommunications. Even with the breaking down of legal barriers to competition, market forces still obey the laws of economics: firms tend to enter markets where they can make money and stay away from those where they cannot. By examining the combination of market and regulatory factors that determine the potential profitability of entry in different markets, we can better understand the competitive implications of the Act. Using data on where competition is developing, estimates of costs, and incumbent revenues, we test these predictions. One important aspect of the introduction of competition is regulators' responses to it. For example, some regulators may find that competition undermines their social-pricing policies. We might, therefore, expect to find that regulatory efforts to maintain and protect implicit cross-subsidies will have a large impact on the development of competition.

In this chapter, we begin by attempting to quantify the size of the implicit subsidies in the current setting. We extend the results of Rosston and Wimmer (2000) in three significant ways. In that paper we estimated the tax rates state regulators would have to impose to maintain various benchmark rate levels. We also showed that increasing the benchmark reduces tax rates substantially without seriously reducing subscribership. We add to these results by incorporating data on local telephone service rates. In addition, we examine data on collocation agreements in Bell Atlantic's wire centers. By using these additional data, we examine how much rate rebalancing is necessary to move towards an efficient and competitive local rate system. We can also make some predictions about where competition is likely to arise and, subsequently, test these assertions with data on competition by wire center. Finally, we also test the effectiveness of explicit and portable universal service funding on inducing competitors to enter rural settings.

The chapter is organized in the following manner. Section 1 describes the data and the assumptions underlying some of the variables generated with these data. In section 2, we examine the relationship between rates, costs and other characteristics of wire centers. Section 3 discusses universal service and the divergence of rates and costs. Section 4 examines how competition is developing. Specifically, we use data on costs, demographics, and whether or not competition, as measured by the presence of a collocation agreement, exists in a particular wire center. Generally, we find that large differences between costs and revenues in a particular wire center, as expected, attract competitors. In addition, we examine whether the presence of explicit federal subsidies increases the probability that competitors have entered a market. Section 5 discusses our conclusions.

1   Data

We use the forward-looking cost model developed by the FCC in connection with its universal service proceedings. The FCC (with significant input from interested parties) has developed a model that estimates the cost of providing local telephone service. The Hybrid Cost Proxy Model (HCPM) divides regions served by non-rural carriers into roughly 12,493 geographic areas based on the current location of incumbent local exchange carrier wire centers (or switches and those served by a particular switch). For each wire center, the model estimates the cost of the various components used to provide local telephone service: loop, switching, signaling, transport, etc. Based on the differences in local conditions, population density and other factors, the model estimates the cost of providing local service in each wire center.

The recent 8th Circuit Court decision on forward-looking costs[2] appears to do two things: (1) it blesses the use of forward-looking cost models for the pricing of unbundled elements; and (2) it disallows the use of a *hypothetical* network architecture in determining these forward-looking prices. While this decision was made in the context of the FCC's Local Competition orders dealing with unbundled network element pricing, it may also apply to the use of the HCPM for universal service. Despite these possible problems, we feel comfortable using the results of the cost model for two reasons. First, the HCPM is still the model adopted by the FCC and is currently in use. Second, and more important, most parties claim that models that adopt a more embedded network approach yield higher costs. As a result, any rate rebalancing needed using the HCPM model would be a lower bound on the magnitude of the problem facing state regulators.

The wire centers included in the HCPM serve approximately 161 million switched-access lines. We limit our attention to the lines served by the original Regional Bell Operating Companies (hereafter RBOCs). These carriers account for over 80% of the lines in the HCPM. Focusing our attention on the RBOCs provides significant insight into the competitive considerations facing state regulators as they attempt to move towards explicit universal service funding.

We have complemented the results of the cost model with two additional sets of data. The first is demographic data from PNR and Associates, a consulting company that is involved with several aspects of the cost modeling effort. PNR matched demographic data from the 1990 Census with the wire center boundaries used by the HCPM. From PNR we were able to obtain, among other things, the number of households in each wire center that were headed by people of different races or ethnic groups, a breakdown by income, family type, and several other factors.[3]

We also include data on local exchange-service prices for each wire center. We used posted tariff data for each state for each RBOC. Information on rate centers, localities and switch location were obtained from the Local Exchange Routing Guide (LERG). We were able to match the wire centers in the HCPM with the wire centers in the tariff data in 8,026, or about 98%, of all wire centers in RBOC territories.

We were unable to match 185 (about 2%) of the 8,211 RBOC wire centers with information on rates. In general, while we have not substantiated this, we believe a portion of the exchanges may have been sold since the HCPM was developed and account for the majority of our missing exchanges. Additionally, we also suspect that several of the wire centers located on state borders may have been difficult to match with rate information.[4] Nonetheless, we lost very little information. Of those matched, over 99% were matched using either the LERG's rate center or locality (we used the switch location in less than 1% of the cases).

For each wire center, we obtained the rate for unlimited local residential and business calling, when available.[5] While nearly every state offers measured-rate service for business and residential calling, we used the flat-rated option with unlimited calling when it was available. This was done to keep the analysis tractable. Each state has its own discount plans for measured service, making cross-state comparisons difficult. We also identified any differences between multiple-line and single-line business rates when the tariffs made a distinction. In the majority of states, the multiple-line and single-line business rates are the same.[6] The rates used are for the local calling area only. We do not include any additional charges for extended area of service, where customers increase the size of their local calling area by paying a small fee. In approximately 3.8% of the wire centers, there are multiple rate centers, with different rates, for residential and business customers, accounting for almost 7% of the total lines.[7] In these cases we take a simple average of the rates for the wire center.[8]

In two states, Illinois and Wisconsin, only measured service is available for residential users.[9] Both offer customers plans where they pay a flat-rated charge for a minimum number of calls and a per-call rate for additional calls. Wisconsin includes 75 calls, while the Illinois plan includes 100. In eleven states, business customers are not offered an unlimited calling option, at least in the most urban areas of the state.[10] As in the case of measured residential service, business customers are able to choose a plan where they pay a flat fee for a minimum number of calls and a charge for each additional call.[11] For these states, we were required to estimate total charges based on an estimate of the number of calls. This was accomplished using information contained in the FCC's Monitoring Report as used by the HCPM.[12]

The HCPM estimates the average number of residential and business dial equipment minutes, along with the percentage of completed calls, to determine the size of switches placed in wire centers. Using dial equipment minutes, we estimated the number of 4- and 5-minute calls for the average business line to estimate total revenues from business lines in wire centers. In addition to the dial-equipment-minute method, we also assumed 100 calls per residential line and 200 calls per business line, which follows assumptions made by the FCC in its reports on business usage.[13] In our analysis, we use 4-minute business calls and 5-minute residential calls; the number of calls used is consistent with the HCPM. Overall, our results are not highly sensitive to the number of calls assumed.

We included data on the federal subscriber-line charge (SLC or EUCL) as well as the primary interexchange carrier charge (PICC) to obtain the total revenues for local service, since these federal charges are independent of the number of local or long-distance calls.[14] We obtained these data for the most recently completed tariff period (July 1, 1999 to July 1, 2000) and the most recent (July 1, 2000) change in access charges due to the CALLS program.[15]

We also obtained data on collocation arrangements by wire center for Bell Atlantic, which includes the original Bell Atlantic and NYNEX territories, as of early August 2000. Bell Atlantic provides a list of collocation arrangements by wire center. We do not distinguish between the type of collocation, although these data are available, but simply use the fact that collocation has been requested. While not a perfect measure, the presence of a collocation agreement indicates that the local market served by a particular wire center has a degree of competition.

2   Relationship between Rates and Costs

There has been much discussion about the implicit subsidies in local telephone rates. We showed in Wimmer and Rosston (2000) that density alone explains about 80 percent of the variation in local telephone costs in the HCPM model. Despite the strong negative relationship between density and costs, a large number of states adopt so-called "value-based" pricing plans. Value-based pricing is a system where rates are positively related to the number of customers within a local calling area. For example, in South Carolina, there are seven different rate groups (see table 9.1). As the table shows, the rates go down as density decreases, which is exactly the opposite of cost-based pricing.

We have constructed a set of variables from the rate data to examine further the relationship between prices and costs. First, we have

Table 9.1
Example of rate schedule: South Carolina residential rates

Rate group	Number of lines	Basic local rate
1	7,000	$12.70
2	15,000	$13.15
3	28,500	$13.60
4	50,000	$14.05
5	78,000	$14.50
6	125,000	$14.95
7	Unlimited	$15.40

Table 9.2
National average revenue per line

	Total lines	Average revenue (4)[1]	Average revenue (5)[2]
Business lines	46,809,464	$39.14	$38.20
Residential lines[3]	85,371,680	$18.29	$18.29
Overall	132,181,124	$25.67	$25.34

Notes: 1. Indicates that measured calls average 4 minutes per call.
2. Indicates that measured calls average 5 minutes per call.
3. Does not differ because number of residential calls is assumed to be constant.

calculated average local revenue per line, which is equal to the sum of local rates, SLCs, and PICCs. To calculate the average revenue per line, we simply total revenues by type of line (i.e. multiple- and single-line businesses, and primary and nonprimary residential lines multiplied by the appropriate rates[16]) and take the ratio of total revenue to total residential and business lines.

In addition to the average revenue per line, we have also estimated the average revenue per business and residential line. We find that the national average revenue per line, including federal PICCs and SLCs and our estimate of any variable revenues associated with measured service, is higher for business lines than for residential lines.[17] Table 9.2 summarizes these results.

Our results verify what is widely recognized: business rates are higher than local residential rates. Our data show that this difference is statistically significant. In an effort to avoid, or minimize, the debate about common-cost recovery, we take the entire amount of revenue from local service for both business and residential customers and assume that per-minute access is priced at cost.[18] Some parties may argue that residential lines should be treated as incremental in wire centers with primarily business lines. Under this assumption, the price of residential service needs to cover only its incremental cost. To avoid this problem, we examine total revenues to see if they cover the total cost of providing service within a wire center. For wire centers that do not cover costs, an infinite number of price changes, and various combinations of prices, could be used to allow full recovery of costs.[19]

After calculating the local revenue per line, we estimated the following equation:

$$\ln(\textit{Average Revenue}_i) = \alpha_{1n} + \alpha_2 \ln(\textit{Average Cost}_i) + \alpha_3 \textit{Measured Service}_i + \alpha_4 \textit{Percent Business Lines}_i + \varepsilon_i$$

Average Revenue is the average revenue earned per line and is calculated as discussed above. To account for state-specific fixed effects we include a vector of constants, α_{1n}, that are allowed to vary across states. *Average Cost* is the HCPM's estimate of the average cost per line. *Measured Service* is a qualitative variable that is set equal to one if unlimited calling is not available to business or residential customers. Finally, *Percent Business Lines* is simply the ratio of total business lines to total residential and business lines, multiplied by 100.[20] The αs are the respective coefficients and ε_i is the random disturbance term.

Because we use average revenue per line as the dependent variable, we hold constant for the percentage of lines that are business lines.[21] As shown above, we find that the average revenue per business line, for local services only (not including any CLASS features or hunting), is substantially higher than the average revenue per residential line. Measured business is included for two reasons. First, we might expect to see differences in rates in areas depending on the rate structure. Because we base the number of calls and their length on actual dial-equipment minutes, we might expect to see fewer calls, and perhaps lower revenues, in these areas. In any event, it is important to hold constant for the presence of measured service to find the relationship between average revenue and average cost. Table 9.3 contains the results for regressions where we include and do not include state-specific fixed effects.[22]

Table 9.3
Relationship between average revenue per line and average cost (absolute value of *t*-statistics in parentheses, using White's (1980) heteroscedastic standard errors)

	ln(Ave Rev) (4 min)	ln(Ave Rev) (5 min)	ln(Ave Rev) (4 min) Fixed	ln(Ave Rev) (5 min) Fixed
ln(Cost)	−0.075	−0.076	−0.064	−0.066
	(13.73)	(14.01)	(15.75)	(15.63)
Measured	−0.052	−0.075	−0.123	−0.144
	(11.06)	(16.20)	(4.08)	(5.06)
Percentage business	0.007	0.007	0.009	0.008
	(33.02)	(31.52)	(53.24)	(48.63)
Constant	3.232	3.240	3.177	3.190
	(138.36)	(138.8)	(151.33)	(149.6)
R^2	0.40	0.39	0.86	0.85
N Obs	8,026	8,026	8,026	8,026

The first two columns in table 9.3 give the results of the regressions where state-specific fixed effects are not included. The final two contain those with fixed effects. We find that we can reject the null hypothesis that the fixed effects are jointly insignificant.[23] In all the specifications, we find an inverse relationship between average revenue and average cost. This relationship is statistically significant at standard levels in all specifications. In the case of average revenue, we find that a 10 percent increase in average costs is associated with approximately a 0.65 percent decline in average revenues, when we account for state-specific fixed effects. The magnitude of the relationship is even greater when we do not account for fixed effects.

The results also show that the average, and thus total, revenue received in a wire center is affected significantly by the percentage of business lines. Again, concentrating on the fixed-effects model, we find that increasing the percentage of business lines by 10 percent increases average revenue per line by approximately 0.09 percent. Finally, measured rates in both the business and residential cases lead to a reduction in average revenue when either 4- or 5-minute calls are assumed. These results are consistent with the results we estimate using the assumption that measured business call users make 200 5-minute calls per month.

3   Subsidies

For each RBOC wire center in the HCPM, we calculate the difference between the rate for flat-rate local residential service and the cost reported in the model. There is a wide dispersion in the differences between these numbers, both within and across states.

The weighted average cost per line for providing local service is $22.74.[24] At the same time, the weighted average revenue for local residential telephone service (including SLCs and PICCs) is $18.28, not including any federal subsidy dollars. If we include federal subsidy dollars, average revenue increases to $18.51. The explicit universal service funding applies to the high-cost wire centers according to a FCC formula. These dollars are added to the rates charged to consumers to determine overall revenue received in each wire center.[25]

The difference between the residential revenues and costs can be large and varies across states. For example, in Vermont, we estimate that the average line falls over $10 short in terms of flat-rated revenues. We estimate that, in the aggregate, 17 states do not cover their costs for basic local service, as modeled by the HCPM, with revenues from local rates, federal SLCs, PICCs, and subsidies. The differences are even more pronounced when we examine revenue per residential line and compare this with estimated costs. Using this measure, only five states have a positive differential.[26]

While it is interesting to see the results on a statewide basis, and this may be very important for state regulators in understanding the problems or lack of problems they face, competitors are more likely to look at the results on a narrower basis. Competitors are likely to target rate centers where they can charge prices that cover costs. We have examined the results on a wire-center basis to understand the number of wire centers that have rates covering the cost of local service.

Overall, only 31% of the 8,026 wire centers have estimated revenue streams that exceeds their estimated costs. In 15 states, over 80% of the wire centers are estimated to have a shortfall, while only three states have over one-half of their wire centers covering estimated costs.[27] Such a simple comparison, however, may be misleading. As discussed above, costs are inversely related to density, while revenues are positively related to density. Thus, it is more reasonable to examine the number of lines receiving and contributing to our measure of implicit subsidy.

Overall, 30% of lines are in wire centers that are estimated not to generate enough revenue to cover their costs. In Vermont, 73% of the lines are in wire centers where the contribution is negative. Nine states have more than half of their lines in wire centers where the contribution is negative. By contrast, in 38 of the 47 states examined, over half of the lines in the state have revenues that are sufficient to cover costs; and 22 have over 75% of their lines covering costs. According to these figures, the cross-subsidy problem, when the measure is based on total wire-center local revenue (i.e., including both business and residential lines), is concentrated in a relatively small number of states.

Simply counting the number of lines where revenues exceed or fall short of costs hides the magnitude of the problem because it may reflect only small differences. We therefore calculated these numbers using larger hurdles. First, to examine the source of cross subsidies, we estimated the number of lines where revenues are greater than 125% of costs. This calculation shows that about 44% of the lines are in wire centers where revenues are greater than 125% of costs. On the other side, about 10% of the lines are in wire centers where revenues are less than 75% of costs. Again, the cross-subsidy problem is most severe in only a few states. Only five states have more than 25% of their lines in wire centers where revenues fall short of 75% of the costs. As in the early cases, the problem is most severe in Vermont, where 38% of the lines reside in wire centers where less than 75% of costs are recovered through local charges (including federal flat-rated charges).

These wide divergences mean two things. First, it is unlikely that competition will come to the wire centers where rates are below costs unless subsidies are made explicit and competitively neutral, rates change, or additional revenue sources are sufficient to make up the difference. But, because there are other rate centers where rates are above costs, we would expect to see them be the targets of competitive entry.

4   Competition

It is a basic tenet of economics that competitors enter markets when they expect to earn a profit. Typically, this leads to the result that the most efficient firms serve consumers. However, in the market for local telecommunications, the use of implicit cross subsidies makes entry into many local markets untenable because prices are held below cost by regulatory fiat. To ensure that firms are fully compensated, regulators require firms to hold rates well above cost in other markets. It is not surprising, therefore, that anecdotal reports on the development of competition note that residential consumers are being passed over by competitors in favor of dense urban business districts. In this section of the paper, we examine how these factors, and others, are influencing the development of competition. To accomplish this we use data on the presence of collocation arrangements in the original Bell Atlantic and NYNEX service areas (hereafter Bell Atlantic).

When entering a market, a competitor must interconnect with the incumbent's network. This may be accomplished in a number of ways, one of which is to place equipment in an incumbent's wire center. Such arrangements are known as collocation agreements. Collocation agreements are also required if the entrant is going to purchase unbundled loops or provide competitive high-speed digital services. Thus, one measure of competition is the presence of a collocation agreement. While this measure is somewhat broad (it does not measure the number of lines captured by a competitor or whether the entrant is serving business or residential customers), it does indicate whether or not a competitor has begun, or is planning, to offer service in an area.

Bell Atlantic has collocation agreements in place in approximately 57% of the 2,332 Bell Atlantic wire centers in our data set. These wire centers, however, account for over 90% of all the lines in the territory. Thus, while nearly a majority of the wire centers still do not have collocation, the vast majority of lines are served by wire centers that do have collocation.

Entrants using unbundled loops to provide service gain access to all the customers served by a particular wire center when they collocate. Using the FCC cost model data, the number of lines in a wire center, including special access and public-telephone lines, ranges from 11 to 407,207 lines. The average number of lines served in a wire center is 20,000, with a median of 6,735. In urban areas, several wire centers, many of which contain multiple switches, are used to serve a local area.[28] In more rural settings, a single switch is used to serve an entire town and its surrounding areas. Presumably, local phone companies locate their switches in a manner that minimizes the cost of serving the local populace, which allows it to serve clusters of customers efficiently.

Using wire-center boundaries allows us to gather data on several characteristics of the local telephone market. As discussed above, the FCC's cost model estimates costs based on current wire-center boundaries. This gives us information on the average cost per line, number of lines, and the breakdown of the number of business and residential lines. Moreover, as part of its high-cost proceeding the FCC made available information on the amount of federal subsidy dollars targeted to individual wire centers. The new high-cost program requires that subsidy dollars be portable. That is, the subsidy is available to any company that wins a customer if that company has been deemed *eligible* by the state commission. These data, therefore, allow us to examine the effect the federal high-cost program is having on the development of competition in outlying areas.[29]

We have augmented these data with demographic information from the 1990 census. In particular, we include data on the percentage of households in the census's top income category, those with an income in excess of $45,000 annually, in 1990 dollars. Finally, as discussed above, we have gathered price data on a wire center basis. These data, combined with data on whether or not a particular wire center has a collocation agreement with an entrant, allows us to begin to examine the factors affecting the development of competition.

We begin our analysis by presenting basic summary statistics. The data in table 9.4 are presented according to the presence, or lack, of a collocation agreement.

The average cost per line in the wire centers without collocation ($40) is more than double the cost ($19) of those with a collocation agreement. This is an indication that these are less densely populated areas. This is confirmed by the difference in wire center size. In the data, the average number of households in wire centers with a collocation agreement is over seven times greater than those without. In addition, we have calculated that the average wire center with a collocation agreement has ten times as many lines as the average wire centers without a collocation agreement (35,000 vs. 3,000). Also, the percentage of total lines that are business lines in wire centers without collocation is significantly lower than in those with a collocation agreement (11% compared to 31%).

Table 9.4
Summary statistics for the Bell Atlantic region (with standard deviations in parentheses)

Variables	Collocation	No collocation
Average cost per line	$19.41 (3.89)	$40.16 (21.75)
Average revenue per primary residential line	$19.17 (4.36)	$17.71 (5.82)
Average revenue per multiple business line	$41.60 (10.89)	$43.70 (8.98)
Percentage of wire centers receiving federal support	4% (0.19)	23% (0.42)
Average number households in wire centers	15,483 (14,337)	2,204 (1,730)
Average percentage of business lines in wire centers	31% (0.15)	11% (0.12)
Switching access charge (interstate)	$0.0056 (0.002)	$0.0056 (0.002)
Average percentage of households in top income group in wire center[1]	39% (0.16)	24% (0.13)
Percentage of wire centers with measured business rates	44% (0.50)	37% (0.48)
Observations	1,341	991

Note: 1. Because we use 1990 census data, two wire centers were listed as having no households in the census data. These wire centers are excluded from the analysis.

In order to gain an understanding of the demographic makeup of our data, we have included data on the percentage of households earning more than $45,000 annually, according to the 1990 Census. We find that in wire centers with a collocation agreement the percentage of households in the top income category (above $45,000) is much higher than in those wire centers without collocation.

Finally, we have calculated the difference between our calculation of revenues (as described above) and the cost per line in these wire centers. Not surprisingly, we find that in wire centers with a collocation agreement the average differential is a positive $8.26, while those without have an average differential of negative $17.66. This difference is driven by three factors. First, the average cost is higher in wire centers without a collocation agreement. Second, while multiple business lines earn a slightly higher amount, primary residential-line revenues are lower in wire centers without collocation agreements. Finally, the percentage of business lines is much lower in wire centers without collocation agreements. In general, these data are consistent with the notion that competitors are taking advantage of the pricing structure in local telecommunications and are concentrating their entry in relatively dense, urban areas.

To gain a clearer understanding of the factors that lead a competitor to enter a local market, as measured by the presence of a collocation agreement, we estimate the factors that affect the probability that a competitor will enter a particular market. Define Π_i to be the level of profits an entrant expects to earn if it enters a particular local market. Let X_i be a vector of variables that affect the expected revenues and costs of entry. Thus, expected profitability is given by $\Pi_i = X_i\beta + \varepsilon_i$, where β is a vector of coefficients and ε_i is a normally distributed random disturbance term. We are unable, however, to observe the expected profitability of the entrant. What we can observe is whether or not an entrant has entered a particular market, or:

Entry $= 1$ if $X_i\beta + \varepsilon_i > 0$

Entry $= 0$ if $X_i\beta + \varepsilon_i < 0$

Thus, the probability of entry is given by $\mathrm{Prob}(\varepsilon_i > -X_i\beta)$. The empirical analysis focuses on market entry. A logit model is specified relating the probability of entry to a set of variables that approximate the expected cost of serving customers and the amount of revenue an entrant can be expected to earn.[30] A dichotomous $(0,1)$ variable is used to classify whether a firm has entered an area served by a wire center, as measured by a collocation agreement (Entry $= 1$), or has not (Entry $= 0$). The model is of the following form:

$P_i = F(X_i\beta) + \varepsilon_i,$

where P is the probability of entry, X is a vector of variables that captures information on the expected profitability of entry, $F(.)$ is the logistic distribution and ε_i is a random disturbance term.

To estimate the logit model we consider entry to have occurred when a collocation agreement is present. On the right-hand side we employ variables that measure the expected cost of serving customers in a particular market and factors that should be correlated with the amount of revenue an entrant could expect to earn.

To measure the costs of serving customers we include the FCC's cost model estimates of average cost per line in each wire center. To the extent that rates do not reflect costs, a decrease in costs should increase the likelihood that entry occurs in a particular wire center.

To measure potential revenues, we include the total revenue, as measured by the sum of local rates and federal flat-rated charges from the tariff period of July 1, 1999 to July 1, 2000, on a per-line basis for both primary residential and multiple-line businesses.[31]

To capture the effect of a large gap between revenues and costs on potential entry, we include a variable, Per-Line Difference, which is equal to the average difference between revenues and costs in a separate specification of the model. While one specific factor may not dominate the entry decision, we expect that as this differential grows, the probability of a collocation agreement should increase.

We also consider demographic factors. Competitors may enter local markets where incumbents do not adequately supply advanced services, such as high-speed Internet connections. Eisner and Waldon (1999) find that the demand for online services is positively related to income. Therefore, we might expect that competitors are more likely to enter markets where average income is relatively high, and include the percentage of households with an average income in excess of $45,000 as measured by the 1990 census. We expect the probability of entry to be positively related to income. We also include the tariff year 1999–2000 interstate switching rate in the regressions. High access charges have traditionally been used to cross subsidize local rates. We expect the probability of entry to be positively related to interstate switching access rates.

Finally, we consider the impact the federal high-cost program is having on competition. While the FCC has delayed the targeting of high-cost support until the third quarter of 2000,[32] we include the original estimates of which wire centers will receive a subsidy in our specifications. Even in the face of the delay, competitors may have taken steps to begin providing service in anticipation of receiving support once it is targeted to high-cost areas.

In the absence of increasing rural rates towards costs, it is unlikely that competitors will enter such markets. This is likely to be the case even when new entrants could provide service more efficiently than the incumbent. The federal high-cost program (and similar state programs) was introduced to address such problems by providing a portable subsidy, in

Table 9.5
Marginal effect of costs, revenues, and other factors on the probability of collocation; evaluated at the sample mean[1] (absolute value of z-statistics in parentheses)

	No state fixed effects		State fixed effects	
Average cost per line	−0.037 (14.90)	—	−0.038 (12.96)	—
Multiple business line rate	0.003 (1.93)	—	0.001 (0.35)	—
Residential line rate	−0.0005 (0.078)	—	0.064 (4.59)	—
Difference in revenues and costs	—	0.029 (14.62)	—	0.033 (14.10)
Business measured[1]	—	—	−0.16 (0.53)	−0.03 (0.09)
High-cost support[1]	0.32 (4.53)	0.26 (4.08)	0.24 (2.35)	0.28 (2.80)
Percentage top income group (× 100)	0.01 (8.03)	0.01 (8.57)	0.007 (5.63)	0.007 (5.59)
Local switching rate (× 100)	0.46 (4.66)	0.22 (2.78)	—	—
Log likelihood	−804.65	−815.27	−733.68	−730.18

Note: 1. For discrete variables we report the effect of a discrete change (0 to 1) on the probability of collocation.

part, to entice entry into rural settings.[33] We therefore examine the impact the high-cost subsidy is having on the incidence of collocation agreements. To do so, we include High Cost, an indicator variable, which is equal to 1 if lines in the wire center are subsidized and 0 otherwise.

The first two columns of table 9.5 give the results for the model as discussed above. We report the marginal effect a change in the independent variable has on the probability that entry will occur. The marginal effects reported are evaluated at the sample mean. The second two columns include a set of state dummy variables.[34] Because federal access charges are constant within an entire state, the switching rate is not included in the regression that includes the state dummies.

In the first set of results, we do not include the dummy variable, Business Measured, which is set equal to 1 if business customers are offered only measured rate local service, and 0 otherwise. Because five states and the District of Columbia in the Bell Atlantic territory have measured rates, the inclusion of the Business Measured dummy variable appears to pick up both the impact of measured offerings and other factors that may be specific to these states.[35] We therefore present a second set of results that include Business Measured and state-specific dummy variables.

The first and third columns in table 9.5 give the results when rates and estimates of costs are used. The second and fourth columns report the results when the difference between rates and costs is used in lieu of the individual elements.

Overall, our results are consistent with the notion that competitors are more likely to enter densely populated regions. In all of our estimates, the marginal effect of a decrease in cost, or an increase in the revenue-cost margin, increases the probability of entry. In all four regressions, average cost and revenue-cost difference receive the expected signs and are highly significant. Concentrating on the results included in the third column, we find that a one-dollar decrease in costs increases the probability of entry by about four percent. A similar result is found in the regression without state fixed effects.

Our results concerning rates are less clear. In the regressions that do not include state fixed effects, multiple-line business rates are positively correlated with the likelihood of entry. The estimated effect is statistically significant at conventional levels. When state-specific and the measured dummies are included, however, this relationship becomes insignificant.

In contrast to our results concerning business rates, we find that residential rates are positively correlated with the probability of a collocation arrangement in the fixed-effects regression, but are insignficant when we do not account for fixed effects. Because rates do not vary greatly within states and the states with measured service, on average, have lower business rates, the inclusion of the dummies has a large effect on our results. We therefore tested the joint significance of the state-specific fixed effects and find that we cannot reject the null hypothesis that they equal zero. This result implies that more work is needed to understand the effect that different regulations imposed by state regulatory agencies are having on the development of competition.

In addition to examining the individual effects of rates and costs, we examined the effect that the difference between rates and costs, which is a proxy for profitability, has on the probability of entry. As expected, as the gap grows the probability of entry increases. Our results indicate that a one-dollar increase in the revenue-cost gap increases the probability of entry by about 3 percent. The estimated marginal effect is highly significant. This result suggests that rebalancing rates so that they reflect costs will lead to entry is less urban areas.

Perhaps the most interesting results concern the effect the presence of federal high-cost support has on the probability of entry. In both sets of results, the marginal effect of the high-cost program is positive and statistically significant. It appears that, even before federal support is targeted to high-cost wire centers, the prospect of federal dollars is having an impact on the development of competition after accounting for all of the other factors. Finally, we also find that the presence of high-income consumers and high interstate access rates lead to a higher probability of entry.

Overall, the results of our analysis suggest that regulatory policies that keep rates artificially low in rural settings make entry into such areas less attractive. Similarly, artificially high rates for business customers, and in urban areas, attract competitors. Our analysis shows that as competition develops regulators will be forced to address the web of implicit subsidies that were put in place under a regime of regulated monopoly.

5   Conclusions

In this paper we have taken the first steps to evaluate the effect that different policies are having on the development of competition. As expected, we find that large gaps between costs and revenues exist across a carrier's region. In several states, a relatively small number of lines are priced well in excess of estimated costs, while others are well below costs. We then show that, as expected, competitive entry is driven by the size of the gap between revenue and costs. We also examined the effect the new federal high-cost subsidy program is having on entry, and found, somewhat surprisingly, that the presence of a yet-to-be-targeted subsidy appears to lead to a higher probability of entry.

The size of a state's implicit pricing problems may affect its decisions concerning competitive entry. We might expect to see differences in regulators' decisions depending on the state's reliance on implicit cross subsidies.

Notes

1. We would like to thank Rich Lerner, Tracy Waldon, and Jim Zolnierek of the FCC for their help in gathering information on rates. We would also like to thank Rich Clarke and Ed Lowry, along with Robert McNary, for help provided on this project. All mistakes are, of course, ours alone.

2. *Iowa Utilities Board v. FCC*, July 18, 2000.

3. For a fuller discussion of our use of the PNR data see Wimmer and Rosston (2000).

4. The missing wire centers are typically smaller and more costly than those included.

5. In one case, Michigan, we used a plan that did not have unlimited calling but included a large number of local calls (400).

6. While many business customers may purchase "trunks" for use with PBXs and hunting service, we report only multiple-line and single-line rates. Additionally, many states explicitly note that, for two-way service, the business line rate is the same regardless of whether or not it is connected to a PBX. In short, we attempted to match rates to the cost of services modeled by the HCPM.

7. This generally occurs in large wire centers serving both central cities and suburbs where the rates differ.

8. We take the simple average because, at this time, we do not have data on the number of lines within the wire center serving different rate centers.

9. In Michigan, the plan that allows customers up to 400 calls per month, where calls in excess of 400 require a small per-call charge, is significantly less expensive than the unlimited calling option for the average consumer. We therefore used the 400-call rate rather than the unlimited-calling option.

10. These states include California, the District of Columbia, Illinois, Massachusetts, Maryland, Michigan, New Jersey, Ohio, Rhode Island, and Wisconsin.

11. California and New York do not offer per-call charges. Business customers are required to pay for each minute of use. In addition, in several states, e.g., Wisconsin and New Jersey, the rates for multiple business lines is higher than that charged to single-line businesses.

12. We would like to thank Bill Sharkey for his help in identifying this aspect of the model.

13. We have rerun the regressions using a 4-minute duration and the results are very similar.

14. Even though the PICC charge is not charged directly to the end-user customer, we adopt the assumption that competition will force the consumer ultimately to pay this charge.

15. We report the results for rates before the CALLS program. Among other things, the CALLS program, at this time, reduces per-minute access charges and PICCs and increases SLCs. Thus, the overall change in flat-rated revenues, our concern in this study, is not large.

16. We have estimated the number of second lines in each wire center. This was completed by first multiplying the HCPM's estimate of households by the penetration rate reported by the FCC in its *Penetration Report for 1999* to estimate the number of primary residential lines. We then used the difference between primary residential lines and total residential lines to estimate nonprimary lines. In five cases, this approach yielded more nonprimary lines than primary lines appropriate nonprimary lines; the vast majority of the remaining wire centers are estimated to have less than 40 percent nonprimary residential lines. On average, we estimate that approximately 16% of all lines are nonprimary lines. The appropriated SLCs and PICCs are assigned to lines based on these calculations.

17. In this calculation, we aggregate across primary and nonprimary residential lines, along with single and multiple business lines.

18. We realize that access is currently priced above cost, but the divergence has been narrowing significantly. Moreover, artificially high access charges are a source of implicit subsidy. Their inclusion would, therefore, interfere with our attempt to estimate the size of implicit-subsidy problems.

19. To avoid cross-subsidy, we could consider constraints that require that each line cover its incremental cost and that no price exceed its stand-alone cost.

20. We omit special access lines and the cost of special access lines.

21. Percentage of business lines is calculated by taking the ratio of total business line to total lines (not included special access lines) and multiplying this ratio by one hundred.

22. We also ran, but do not report, regressions for residential and business revenues separately. These results are consistent with those reported.

23. In all cases, the F-statistic for this test exceeds 500.

24. This number differs slightly from the $23.84 reported in Rosston and Wimmer (2000) because the sample in this paper is restricted to RBOC wire centers for which we were able to obtain rate data. The earlier paper included all nonrural incumbent LECs and all RBOC wire centers.

25. The FCC will start targeting dollars to specific high-cost wire centers beginning in the third quarter of 2000.

26. While our data focuses exclusively on RBOCs, this does not mean that other states do not have significant rate-cost imbalances. States where the RBOC prices are close to costs may have service provided by other carriers that have significant imbalances.

27. We remind the reader that our data do not include revenues from CLASS features such as call waiting or any interstate or intrastate per-minute access charges.

28. For example, in the state of New York, in the Local Exchange Routing Guide, 12 wire centers list their locality as New York and 16 list Brooklyn.

29. The FCC has delayed the targeting of high-cost support to high-cost wire centers until the third quarter of 2000. Thus, inclusion of these data serve to estimate the effect support is having on entrants who are currently serving customers in high-cost areas or intend to do so once subsidy dollars are targeted.

30. For comparison purposes, we also ran a probit model. The results of the probit model are consistent with those reported here.

31. In the results reported, we use the measure of business line revenue assuming 4-minute calls. Regressions assuming 5-minute calls or 200 calls produced rates that were consistent with those reported below. Since there are fixed costs associated with entering a local market, we also ran a specification that included the number of households in a wire center. As expected, we found a positive relationship between the number of households and the probability of entry. Because of the close correlation among costs, rates, and density, it is difficult to separate the effects of costs and number of customers to which an entrant gains access when entering a dense area.

32. In the Matter of Federal-State Joint Board on Universal Service; CC Docket No. 96-45 Nineteenth Order On Reconsideration; Adopted: December 17, 1999, Released: December 17, 1999.

33. Perhaps more importantly, as competition develops the sources of implicit cross subsidies will wither away as competition forces rates towards costs.

34. We do not report the estimates for the state effects.

35. Specifically, examination of our measure of per-line revenue for multiple business lines is, on average, lower for wire centers with measured service than in those without. In regressions where we did not hold constant for state-specific effects, the measured business coefficient is negative and the coefficient on multiple-line business revenue is also negative. While this may be the result of a causation problem—regulators may have allowed Bell Atlantic to drop rates in areas where it is facing competition—we prefer to report the results with the state-specific effects. In the future, we hope to expand the data set in order to isolate the effect measured rates have on the probability of entry.

References

Eisner, James, and Tracy Waldon, "The Demand for Bandwidth: Second Telephone Lines and On-Line Services," unpublished manuscript, 1999.

Federal Communications Commission, "In the Matter of Federal-State Joint Board on Universal Service"; CC Docket No. 96-45 Nineteenth Order On Reconsideration; Adopted: December 17, 1999, Released: December 17, 1999.

Rosston, Gregory L., and Bradley S. Wimmer, "The 'State' of Universal Service," *Information Economics and Policy* 12 (2000), pp. 261–283.

White, H. "A Heteroscedasticity-Consistent Covariance Matrix Estimator and a Direct Test for Heteroscedasticity," *Econometrica* 48, 1980b, pp. 817–838.

Wimmer, Bradley S., and Rosston, Gregory L., "Winners and Losers in the Universal Service Battle," in Compaine and Vogelsang (eds.), *The Internet Upheaval: Raising Questions, Seeking Answers in Communications Policy* (TPRC Proceedings). Cambridge: MIT Press and TPRC (2000), pp. 387–412.

IV

The End of the Digital Divide?

10

Unexpected Outcomes in Digital Divide Policy: What Children Really Do in the Public Library

Christian Sandvig

Introduction

In the last five years, major policies to promote access to new communication technologies have been enacted and debated.[1] In the United States, the debate has often been framed by the unfortunate term the "digital divide," a term suggesting that access to technology is the most worrisome problem, that this paucity of access is somehow isolated from other social problems and socioeconomic factors, and that access can be described using a binary distinction between "have" and "have not." Policy mechanisms meant to address the digital divide (such as the Federal Communications Commission E-Rate program in the United States) have focused on children as a key population—subsidizing access initiatives in schools and libraries.

Over the last century, communication technologies have transformed childhood. Both the form and offerings of communication media have proliferated, and overall use of communication technology among children has steadily increased. The complexity, fidelity, and in some cases the interactivity of communication technology have also increased (Roberts et al. 1999). Mediated communication has become one of the primary socializing agents for children. At the same time, communication technology has come to occupy an increasingly important role in other aspects of everyday life—particularly in the economic. Society is increasingly dependent on skilled labor (Bell 1999, pp. 212–265), and access to and familiarity with computers is now seen as essential for participation in economic and social life. Policies focusing on children are important in understanding communication policy generally. Laws that benefit children may be enacted before similar policies that would apply to adults because children as a group are seen as unable to demand benefits or protection for themselves, because children may require benefits and protection that adults may not (the younger the children, the greater the concern), or for no other reason than that appeals on the behalf of children are rhetorically powerful.

Digital divide policy mechanisms intended to benefit children occupy an uneasy space between conflicting impulses: while they appear to be simply about access, they represent a desire both to empower children and also to restrict them. A Children's Partnership report expresses this tension well when it unselfconsciously explains: "because some young people are drawn to online activities that are not always healthy, it is essential that they receive guidance and training to use the medium productively" (The Children's Partnership 2000, p. 20). It is provocative to try to imagine what a child "productively" using the Internet would be doing. From earlier reports on the possible benefits of community technology centers we can gain some clues: skill acquisition, job training, and technological literacy are typically emphasized as positive outcomes by proponents (Mark, Cornebise, and Wahl 1997).

One might suspect that, left to their own devices, children would be unlikely to sit down in front of the computer for an afternoon of job training. Subsidized access in libraries is a setting where children are often left to their own devices: much of the access is unstructured, which may not be the case at school. Indeed, Lentz et al. found that children using the public access sites in Austin tended to engage in "game playing and other entertainment activities" (2000, p. 18). Two studies of Internet access in public libraries in Canada found that Internet gaming and chat were the most popular uses, particularly among children (Balka and Peterson 2000; Gorgeç, Lew, and Curry 1999). As one author commented, "[o]ur data suggest that even if all ... citizens have access to the Internet, few of them will engage in the sorts of activities that the access strategies have been designed to support" (Balka and Peterson 2000, p. 101).

While previous research has examined use of public access centers, this study attempts to confront more clearly policy initiatives with empirical measures of use. It attempts to build on earlier work by comparing the assumptions and goals of digital divide policies to user behavior, in a sense attempting to move beyond a surprise that children play games to better understand public access sites as objects of public policy. In this, it will consider three policy initiatives affecting access centers, where each initiative envisions children as the primary beneficiary. The first initiative deals with access, the second and third deal with content regulation. Although only the first is labeled by the term "digital divide" in public discourse, all initiatives together aim to shape the use of communication technology, especially at public access centers.

Initiative One: Ensuring Access for the Underprivileged

Telecommunications are used not to link all places, but to link "valuable places in a non-contiguous pattern," allowing the "reconfiguration of metropolitan areas around selective connections of strategically located activities, bypassing undesirable areas" (Castells 1998, p. 144). It is true that technology can solve problems, but it may also reinforce the problems of inner cities, depressed areas, and the poor by excluding them. This potential exacerbation of social inequality can produce what some have called the "information poor" (Graham and Marvin 1996, pp. 37, 190–206) and others the "digital divide" (National Telecommunications and Information Administration 1999).

A number of government programs seek to combat this problem by introducing technology centers in depressed areas and targeting children as primary beneficiaries. The predominant model for this type of access is an institutional one. The Telecommunications Act of 1996 is the most prominent recent policy initiative to address the access issue. It explicitly expanded the concept of *universal service* to include such new technologies as the Internet.[2] Traditionally, universal service has referred to programs designed to ensure widespread use of telephony through subsidy.[3] The 1996 Act proposed an institutional model in which children are key: schools and libraries serve as the principal place for the otherwise disenfranchised to use advanced communication technology. These institutions receive substantial public funding to provide this service through subsidies to carriers (1996). At the present funding level, up to $2.25 billion will be disbursed per year under this program (Universal Service Administrative Company 1999), which has lately changed its terminology to universal *access* in many circles to better reflect the institutional access model as opposed to the previous subsidy for every home. Other federal programs have also endorsed institutional models for access: e.g., Department of Education grants to Community Technology Centers (CTCs, see U.S. Department of Education 1999) and Department of Commerce grants to Community Access Centers (CACs) from the Telecommunications and Information Infrastructure Assistance Program.[4]

It has been argued that universal service as a concept was originally unique to the United States, in that the rationale given for universal service is unlikely to be based on equity or welfare (Rapp 1996)—many rationales are economic and focus instead on system benefits. In this manner, arguments for universal service are very comparable to those for universal education (Sawhney 1994). In the United States, this policy represents not a belief that all should have access because equity is necessarily a noble goal, but rather an expectation that these technology centers will be used for educational (hence the emphasis on schools) and ultimately economically productive purposes.[5]

Initiative Two: Privacy and Protection from Advertisers

A 1998 Federal Trade Commission survey found that 89% of Web sites "directed to children" collect personal information, but that only 24% of these sites have a privacy policy available for viewing, and as few as 1% to 8% attempt to involve parents in their children's information disclosure—e.g., through consent or notification (Federal Trade Commission 1998, pp. 31, 35, 38). The FTC presented this as a case where technology had created new dangers: the harmful disclosure of personal information by children that could not be addressed by existing law (pp. 40–41). On the recommendation of the FTC, Congress subsequently passed the Children's Online Privacy Protection Act (COPPA) in 1998.[6] The Act regulates sites that are directed toward children or have "actual knowledge" that children under age 13 are users. It requires these sites to obtain "verifiable parental consent" in order to collect or disclose personal identifying information from children, to state what information is collected and how it will be used, and to protect the confidentiality and security of personal information collected. Further, sites may not collect more information that is "reasonably necessary" for a particular activity, and parents must be able to request the information that has been gathered and revoke permission to use it at any time (Children's Online Privacy Protection Act of 1998; Federal Trade Commission 1999).

During the policy debate leading up to the Act's passage, it was at times referred to as an effort to protect children from online marketers[7] and the debate was often framed in terms of advertising (cf. American Advertising Federation 1999). In fact, COPPA addresses all data collection from children and regulates any type of site (commercial or otherwise). While it is true that advertisers are a primary interest group in this area, the Act does not address advertisements directed at children as such.[8]

Initiative Three: Protection from Indecent Material

Concern about pornography on the Internet may have entered mainstream public debate in 1995 when *Time* published a cover story on the results of a (now discredited) study with the headline "CYBERPORN" (Elmer-DeWitt 1995). The policy problem asserted has typically been that changes in technology provide easier access to indecent material, and that children must be prevented from obtaining such material. Numerous policy efforts have sought to restrict obscene or pornographic material on the Internet itself, the most prominent being the failed Communications Decency Act (CDA) and its successor[9] the Child Online Protection Act (COPA).[10] Other efforts have focused on restricting institutional modes of access to the Internet (i.e., schools and libraries), where children presumably may not be watched by parents. For example, at the end of the first legislative session of the 106th Congress, four acts requiring some form of library filtering were pending.[11] The youngest children are often portrayed as the most "at risk."[12]

The Case of the San Francisco Electronic Discovery Center

Each of these debates assumes an answer to the question: How do children use public computers and Internet access? Initiative one assumes that an institutional access point is essentially the same as home access, and that what transpires there will be economically productive, broadly construed. Initiative two assumes that children disclose identifying information that may place them in danger, and that when they do they use services directed to children. Initiative three assumes that young children seek pornographic material, and proposed filtering legislation implies that they do so from public places. It is the purpose of this paper to assess whether or not these assumptions have any basis in human behavior.

To do this, we conduct an empirical investigation of Internet use by children at a public library in an underprivileged area. Let us now turn from the policies about children to the children themselves.

Setting

This study considers a library program in San Francisco called the Electronic Discovery Center (EDC).[13] An EDC is a cluster of computers[14] in a library branch equipped with broadband Internet access[15] and children's software titles. These clusters are available to use for no charge, and are reserved exclusively to serve children under the age of 14 and the adults who accompany them. This study analyzes the EDC at the Main Library.[16]

The ultramodern architecture of what librarians call the "New Main" library is an impressive sight, but more impressive is the contrast between the pristine library building and the adjacent neighborhood of the Tenderloin, one of San Francisco's poorest. Those living near the library have a median family income of $12,754, with 27.5% of the population in the library's census tract in poverty by Census Bureau definitions (U.S. Census 1991).[17] The median family income is below $30,000 in eight of the nine adjacent census tracts (U.S. Census 1999). In comparison, San Francisco as a whole averaged 12.3% of the population in poverty, and a median family income of $37,854 (U.S. Census 1991; U.S. Census 1999).

Within the library, the Fisher Children's Center is an airy, brightly colored series of rooms on the second floor providing comfortable furniture sized to the dimensions of small children, exhibition space for reading stories and meeting authors, large windows, and sunny spots to play and read. The Center houses the New Main's collections of books, periodicals, and videos for children in several languages. These surround a long, curving wooden librarian's desk, usually occupied by two children's librarians.

The EDC consists of three "islands" of computers in the Fisher Center (see figures 10.1 and 10.2). These islands are located on one side of the wide entryway and fenced by a wall to one side (containing the Fisher Center's bulletin board), half-height book stacks to the front (picture books and videos) and rear (foreign language books), and the librarian's station. Each square pedestal supports four computers arranged two per side, and each group of two computers has an attendant collection of

Figure 10.1
Electronic Discovery Center (EDC). Note that there are three chairs for every two computers.

Figure 10.2
A partial view of the EDC. There are four computers per "island;" two islands are shown.

three child-sized chairs.[18] The library does not employ filtering software; instead, each computer is marked with a warning notice posted by the library cautioning that the library does not control the content of the Internet. Two round child-sized tables are nearby, as are two adult-sized well-cushioned chairs for larger visitors. The space of the EDC is not closed off on any side, and there is always a steady flow of people moving near and sometimes through the area. No partitions separate computers, and while the space of the EDC is loosely demarcated by half-height shelving, the EDC is very much a public part of the Center.

Method

A previous study in the EDC presented the findings of 10 weeks of qualitative nonparticipant observation and open-ended interviews of children, parents, and librarians in early 1999 (Sandvig 2000). This paper instead presents quantitative data on Internet use in the EDC, but draws upon data from the previous study for context.

Over a 16-week period (August 28 to December 17, 1999), researchers unobtrusively monitored the library's computer network for requests using the relevant Internet protocols[19] originating from a computer in the EDC.[20] As this was overwhelmingly Web use, we restricted further analysis to Web traffic. Typically, researchers analyzing network data about the Web rely on logs kept by the Web server—providing the ability to answer some research questions about requests to a particular site (McLaughlin et al. 1999). In contrast, this study gathers data at the gateway from the EDC to the Internet in order to answer questions about Internet use from the EDC.[21] We installed a caching proxy[22] and modified it to observe all transactions in detail.[23]

The caching proxy saved all Web addresses and an assortment of information about each request. We then discarded requests that were not for Web pages[24] and malformed requests,[25] leaving 203,647 page requests.[26] To bring the sample to a manageable size for coders, a subsample of 1,000 page requests was randomly drawn from across all 16 weeks.

For the content analysis, it is impossible for coders to revisit the Web pages as users saw them. Many Web pages change frequently, are personalized for a particular user, require a signin/password, or contain information that is confidential and would violate the anonymity of users (e.g., pages allowing access to Web-based e-mail). While the sampling unit discussed so far was the page request, for the coding unit the addresses requested were truncated to the smallest number of workable significant characters, hereafter called the "site."[27] The "site" was defined as the address produced by concatenating the hostname and domain: i.e., "fantasybasketball.yahoo.com" would be distinct from "chat.yahoo.com."[28] A computer script to truncate addresses reduced the subsample of 1,000 to 235 distinct sites. After these stems were viewed by researchers from February to March 2000, a computer script applied the 235 codings back to the sample of 1,000, eliminating problems of intracoder reliability—often referred to in this context as stability (Weber 1990, p. 17). In other words, while the same site might appear multiple times in the sample, it was coded only once.

Participants

Approximately 110–200 children use the computers at the EDC each day (Sandvig 2000, p. 11).[29] This means that over the 16 weeks of data collection, a conservative estimate would be that over 12,000 visits by library patrons were recorded and analyzed in this study (it is not known, however, how many of these visits represent regular patrons vs. one-time events). About one child in ten also brings along an older sibling, parent, or other adult (p. 11). Users in the EDC are restricted to a half-hour time period because of the high demand for computer time. As spaces in the EDC are almost always full, more than one child usually uses each computer, allowing them to stay longer (p. 15). The clientele of the EDC contains a mixture of children from the surrounding (poorer) neighborhoods and children who come from the suburbs to visit the New Main (p. 18).

Data collection purposely began after school had started in the local school district and ended before winter break: this study presents activity that occurred while school was in session. That is, patron visits to the EDC were heaviest after school on weekdays and all day on weekends,[30] and any use of the EDC for school projects or assignments would be expected to occur during this period (as opposed to the summer).

Measures

Measures fall into two groups: those coded by researchers and those computed by software. For the first group, researchers coded *symbolic* measures (judgments about the content). For the second, computer scripts computed *behavioral* measures (activity of the users) from values saved by the caching proxy software.[31]

Symbolic Measures

To address the question of how children use public computers and Internet access, the first symbolic measure is a functional assessment of the *primary purpose of the site* visited. The primary purpose indicated by the site itself was determined to be one of nine mutually exclusive and exhaustive categories. While most sites might allow several kinds of activity, coders were asked to select the "most prominent" or "most fundamental" category. Categories were derived from extensive pretesting and revision, but were also chosen to be roughly comparable to other recent studies of Web use by children (particularly Roberts et al. 1999, Appendix C, p. 31).

1. *Full-Page Advertising.*   Separate Web pages exclusively containing promotion for a product or service, a way to purchase, provide information or obtain more information (often called "pop-ups").[32]

2. *Play Games.*   Provide online games. Typically, graphical Java applets are featured, but textual word games, quiz games, and puzzles would also apply. Games may be played alone, against the computer (e.g., the applet), or across the network.

3. *Communicate with Individuals.*   Facilitate communication between individual Internet users or small groups by providing real-time chat, instant messaging, asynchronous bulletin-board discussions, Web-based greeting cards, invitations, home-page hosting services, and/or e-mail services. They may cater to a general audience or a more specific group.[33]

4. *Find Other Sites.*   Provide a means to find other sites, either for a general audience or more specific group. These sites include "portals" and may provide keyword search services, recommendations/reviews of other sites, and/or lists of links to other sites.

5. *Purchase or Research Purchases.*   Provide product information and may allow online purchases. They may bear the name of a manufacturer or a retail store, or they may aggregate information from these sources.

6. *Learn about Famous Celebrities and the Events Where They Appear.* Information about film or television celebrities (or their characters and shows), famous animated characters, sports stars, and/or musical groups—or about shows, films, concerts, or sporting events that feature these celebrities. This category requires mention of celebrity, e.g., not

television schedules alone, but schedules that emphasize "fan" information or interviews with stars.

7. *Learn about a Topic or Subject.*   Information, facts, listings, commentary, or a reference source on a topic that may be narrowly (fishing, employment) or broadly (current events, art, politics) defined—including journalism online and classified ads.

8. *Unclassifiable.*

9. *Unreachable.*[34]   Only 1% of page requests in the content analysis were coded into the unclassifiable category, and only 1% were unreachable.

After coding each site by functional category, coders answered a series of binary (does/does not) questions about content contained on the site; the positive conditions are described below.

Targets Ethnic Community.   May contain the words "Asian," "Latino/a," "Vietnamese," "Chinese," "Black," or similar words.

Targets Children.   May be described by the words "children's," "teen's," "kid's," "for kids," "for children," or "for teens," or the site may contain a subsection labeled this way.

Contains Non-English Content.   A language other than English appears on the page, or another version of the page is offered in a language other than English.[35]

Contains Advertising.   Any explicit advertising (sometimes known as "banner ads") that promotes something *other* than the site itself.[36] The ad need not be contained in a graphic (but most ads found were). In many cases, these ads were marked by the words "ad," "advertising," or "sponsor," and were in a demarcated area of the page. Note that this variable measures explicit advertising within a page.[37]

Makes Educational Claims.   Coders were not asked to judge whether or not content *was* in fact educational (by any definition), but rather to determine if the site *promoted* any of its own content as educational (e.g., may use the words "education," "educational," "reference," "learn," "learning").[38]

Contains Pornography.   Has any content that is sexually explicit, sexually arousing, offensive to moral standards, or depicts sexual acts. This definition is a combination of the concepts of pornography, obscenity, and erotica as described by Linz and Malamuth (1990, p. 2). Nudity must occur in an arousing, sexual or offensive context to be coded (e.g., anatomical diagrams in a biology site would not be included). It is worth noting that content fitting any definition of pornography (or even nudity) was very rare in the data.[39] Pornography was not included as a category in the measure of the site's primary purpose because these are conceptually distinct.[40]

Behavioral Measures

Behavioral measures are calculated by software, and describe the Internet activity in the EDC or actions of particular users.

Duration of Page View.   Subtraction of two consecutive time stamps on a page request that originated from a particular computer. Time was measured with a precision of one-tenth of a second.[41]

Frequency of Viewing a Type of Site.   Previous research has tended to measure frequency of viewing one particular category of content over another by using the number of page requests (generally because this is simple). Instead, where discussions of frequency appear in this study, an analysis unit was computed by multiplying the number of page views by the duration measure to provide a more valid measure of *time spent* on one type of page vs. another. This measure might seem problematic because it confounds the time required to download the page with the time the user spends viewing it, but studying sites that use a caching proxy reduces this problem if the universe of content viewed is relatively homogeneous. In the 16-week sample, the latency of all requests was very low.[42] The median latency was .05 seconds (mean = .22, S.D. = .85). 71.2% of the content was retrieved over the Internet; the rest was served from the cache on the library's network.

Simultaneous Viewing.   An estimate of the number of users in the EDC who are viewing the same site at the same time, in addition to the computer that requests the page. For each page request, a computer script compared the site requested with the last requests made by the other computers in the lab. The script then summed the number of computers (beyond the requesting computer) that requested the same site. While it might seem difficult to defend two computers located at opposite sides of the room as being related in a meaningful way, patrons at the EDC were commonly observed walking around to look at other computers for ideas about where to go and what to do. This measure then provides a crude metric for this type of sharing. While there are twelve computers in the lab, this measure ranged from 0 to 8.[43]

Intercomputer Sharing Statistic.   A more defensible measure of sharing that likely did involve interpersonal contact; this measure adjusts simultaneous viewing to account for the distance between the computers viewing the same site. Observations in the EDC indicated that sharing computers while talking was quite common; the configuration of the room allowed each user to easily see his or her computer and the adjacent computer on the island. Users could also easily see the person using the computer opposite theirs by leaning slightly to the left or right to make eye contact (see figure 10.2 above).[44] This measure accounts for the distance between the computers by arranging them on a coordinate grid and then computing equation 1, an intercomputer sharing statistic:

$$\sum_{c=1}^{n} \left(\frac{1}{d_c}\right) \tag{10.1}$$

Here n indicates, for each page request, the number of computers simultaneously viewing same site, where the previous measure summed instead the distance d between each computer c and the computer making the request. This measure is then the sum of one over the distance between each computer and the requesting computer. It has no natural scale, and is generally suitable only for comparison, not direct interpretation.[45] This measure ranged from 0 to 3.5, and the mean was .46 (S.D. = .69).[46]

As several of the measures in this study involve latent content as opposed to manifest content, a second coder analyzed 400 sites randomly selected from the 1,000-site content analysis sample.[47] Coders used a detailed, step-by-step protocol containing examples for each decision. Cohen's κ for intercoder reliability was then computed (cited in Riffe, Lacy, and Fico 1999). Cohen's κ was significant ($p < .01$) and above .70 for every measure except "makes educational claims" ($\kappa = .42$). Cohen's κ was not computed for the "contains pornography" measure because content in this category was so infrequent that the portion of the data that was coded by two coders produced zero instances of it.[48]

Results and Analysis

Although the Internet is often presented as containing a vast amount of information, use of the Internet at the EDC was highly concentrated among just a few sites. While pages from hundreds of Internet domain names were accessed over the 16 weeks, the top 25 domains accounted for 77% of the traffic. Domain names accounting for over 1% of total traffic are presented in table 10.1.

As can be seen from table 10.2, game-playing sites was the most popular use of Web in the EDC (37% of time spent). Java-based game sites such as bonus.com, cyberjoueur.com, and javagameplay.com predomi-

Table 10.1
Domains accounting for more than 1% of total page requests from the EDC over 16 weeks (fall 1999)

		%	Cum. %
1.	bonus.com	28.5	28.5
2.	yahoo.com	12.8	41.3
3.	sfpl.lib.ca.us*	5.9	47.2
4.	doubleclick.net	5.7	52.9
5.	cyberjoueur.com	2.6	55.5
6.	msn.com	2.3	57.8
7.	geocities.com	2.0	59.9
8.	passport.com	1.7	61.6
9.	alloy.com	1.4	63.0
10.	javagameplay.com	1.4	64.3
11.	pokemon.com	1.1	65.5
12.	communityconnect.com	1.1	66.6
$N = 203,647$			

Note: * The large amount of traffic to this domain is an artifact, as the EDC home page is in this domain.

Table 10.2
Primary purpose of sites used by children in the EDC

Primary purpose of site	% of time spent
Play games	37[a]
Communicate with individuals	26[b]
Find out about a topic/subject	12[c]
Full-page advertising	10[c]
Find other sites	6[d]
Find out about celebrities/events	5[d]
Purchase/research purchases	2[e]
Unclassifiable/other	1[e]
Unreachable	1[e]
Total	100%
Cohen's $\kappa = .82$**	

Notes: Figures with different superscripts are statistically different, $p < .05$.
** $p < .01$.

nated in this category. Communicating with individuals was also popular (26%). Within this category chat sites predominated (such as chat.yahoo.com and the chat service at alloy.com), but Web-based e-mail services such as hotmail.passport.com were also significant, accounting for over a quarter of interpersonal communication sites (about 6% of the total). Personal home-page hosting sites such as geocities.com (whose specific content would vary widely by page, and whose page-by-page content would thus not be shown by this measure) accounted for the remainder.

When visiting a site to find out about a topic or subject (12%), the most likely topics of interest were cheat codes for games (e.g., bestcheats.com) and learning more about the Pokémon trading-card game (pokemon.com, pokemon-trade.com). Beyond this, topics were highly varied. While many online magazines targeted toward a child audience exist and would likely have been included in this category by coders,[49] children at the EDC did not visit these sites (with one exception: teenmag.com was visited once).

Full-page (or "pop-up") advertising was remarkably common (10%). Recall that this category indicates pages that contained only advertising, and does not indicate the prevalence of advertising ("banner" ads) on other kinds of pages. Because pop-up advertisements may appear on the screen with other pages, the time-spent measure is somewhat problematic for this category, as it cannot be determined what the user is actually looking at. As an alternative, the content percentages were recomputed using number of page requests. This produced the same figure: 10% of the total.

When searching for other sites (6%), yahoo.com was overwhelmingly the most popular. Yahoo's alternative directory that is explicitly for children (yahooligans.com) was not popular (0.2%), despite being prominently linked from the library's start page during the study.

The celebrities and events (5%) of interest to children in the EDC were typically the television celebrities (e.g., the World Wrestling Federation at wwf.com), musical groups (e.g., the Back Street Boys at backstreetboys.com), and information about current movies (pokemonthemovie.com).

Purchasing or researching purchases (2%) was uncommon. When it did occur, children were usually interested in purchasing game consoles

Table 10.3
Site features by primary purpose of site

Primary purpose of site	Advertising present	Targets children	Educational claims	Non-English content	Targets ethnic com.
Play games	92%	88%		7%	
Communicate with individuals	86	1		18	9%
Find out about a topic/subject	62	51	12%	1	3
Find other sites	93	84	89	2	7
Find out about celebrities/ events	86	37		1	3
Purchase/ research purchases	33	48	3	3	3
Unclassifiable/ other	54				
Overall	70%	51%	11%	7%	3%
Cohen's κ	.88***	.71***	.42***	1.0***	.96***

Notes: Blank cells indicate zeros. Sites whose purpose was "full-page advertising" were excluded from this analysis.
*** $p < .01$.

or cartridges (nintendo.com), other toys (etoys.com, hasbro.com), and tennis shoes (footaction.com).

Content features of the sites visited by children are summarized in table 10.3. Advertising was present on 70% of all sites. Explicit advertising was least common on sites where children could make purchases—because the site is itself advertisement: the general goal of advertising on the Web (to bring customers to a purchasing site) has in this case already been achieved.[50] We can then state that 10% of all Web pages viewed were full-page advertisements (see table 10.2), and of the remaining sites, 70% contained banner advertisements.

Although the definition used for "targets children" was very broad (any mention of children would suffice), visits to sites that target children were rare or a minority in several categories of content. Although many sites exist on the Internet that allow chat specifically for children (often requiring parental consent), they were not visited by the children in the EDC, who preferred adult fora.

Similarly, the definition of "makes educational claims" was very broad (any education-related word), yet sites explicitly containing educational content were extremely rare. Search sites commonly have a section labeled "education" (or, if they target children, they often use the word "learning"), and they account for most content that makes educational claims.

The viewing of non-English content was generally not very common overall (7%), although this may reflect a limit on the ease of finding non-English content on the Internet as a whole. Yet a surprisingly large number of sites whose purpose was communication with individuals did feature non-English content (18%). These were typically chat sites.

Chat sites were also the most likely category of content to target ethnic communities within the category "communicate with individuals." While overall content targeting ethnic communities was rare (3%), it is interesting to note that children seemed drawn to ethnic communities for purposes of chat (9%), more so than for any other type of site.

The relationship between the measures in table 10.3 was analyzed using chi-square tests. The presence of advertising (χ^2 [6, $N = 813$] = 118.0) and content targeting children (χ^2 [6, $N = 813$] = 443.4) varied significantly by content category. Content targeting an ethnic community, presence of educational claims, and non-English content occurred too infrequently to analyze using a chi-square test.

The measure of pornographic content is not displayed in table 10.3 because it accounts for less than one percent of the total. Eight sites were classified by coders as pornographic. An examination of the sites, however, reveals that one (peep.com) is a misspelling of the 25th most popular site (peeps.com, a music site). A second contains a misleading URL (cartoonheaven.com)—while many sites accessed at the library were about children's cartoons, this one contains pornographic cartoons. In the remaining six sites, only the first page of the site was accessed. The first page in each case contained nudity of some sort, but the bulk of the page contained a warning cautioning minors not to enter the site. In each case, it appears that no further pages were viewed after this point. We conclude that at most 0.6% of the visits were to sites containing pornographic content.

Table 10.4
Mean simultaneous viewing and sharing by primary purpose of site

Primary purpose of site	Additional users viewing simultaneously	Intracomputer sharing statistic
Play games	1.7	.78
Communicate with individuals	.6	.27
Find out about a topic/subject	.3	.14
Find other sites	.7	.20
Find out about celebrities/events	.2	.16
Purchase/research purchases	.2	.13
Overall	1.0	.46

Table 10.4 summarizes the two measures of sharing by purpose of site. The concentration of visits to a few sites is reflected here, as on average when a page was requested one additional user in the EDC was already viewing the same site at the same time. That is, the mean number of other computers viewing was 1: at any given time, on average two computers (the computer requesting it and one other computer) in the EDC would be looking at the same site (median = 0, S.D. = 1.4). Qualitative information suggests that the children in the EDC are highly influenced by the content viewed by other children, and this finding appears to support that conclusion. The intracomputer-sharing statistic, while not directly interpretable by itself, controls the simultaneous viewing measure for distance. This indicates that game playing (.78) was more commonly viewed on computers that were near each other than were other activities. Communicating with individuals (the second highest at .27) was also observed to be a collaborative activity in the EDC, with friends signing on to a chat channel at the same time from nearby computers, then coordinating chatting activities by speaking to each other while typing.

While the sharing variables were interval measures, assumptions for parametric tests were not met and Kruskal–Wallace tests were performed to analyze the relationship between sharing and purpose of site. Simultaneous viewing ($\chi^2[6, N=813]=215.0$) and sharing ($\chi^2[6, N=813]=196.7$) differed significantly as a function of the primary purpose of the site ($p < .01$).

Discussion

Revisiting Initiative One: Success for an Active Medium of Play

While justifications for Internet access in inner cities often rest on claims of educational benefit, in the EDC content that is explicitly educational was often avoided. In the EDC the Internet appears to be used most often as an active medium of play and leisure. This is consistent with qualitative observations at the same site, where children often explained their use of Internet access at the library as "fun" and rarely arrived at the EDC with a specific informational need in mind or a fact that needed to be looked up (Sandvig 2000, p. 17). Children reported in interviews that one attraction of the EDC is the unrestricted nature of the time spent there: they can choose to look at whatever they want, and they do not tend to choose the explicitly educational.

In this, the EDC is very comparable to children's use of computers in other contexts. For instance, the distribution of the type of sites visited in the EDC is comparable to other recent data on children's Web use in the home and at school. In a nationally representative 1999 survey of 3,155 children aged 2–18, the most frequently reported type of site visited was "gaming" by a large margin, then "sports," and "entertainment" (Roberts et al. 1999, Appendix C, p. 31).[51] In addition, 13% of children surveyed reported visiting chat rooms the previous day (p. 52). The EDC is then achieving the public policy goal of access to the Internet for the underprivileged in that the type of content accessed from the EDC is similar to that accessed in the home of those who own computers and Internet connections. If equality is a goal, then this is success by one measure for programs like the E-Rate, but it is a success that does not sit well with many.

Some librarians, volunteers, and parents are unsettled by the use of computers in the EDC for games and chat, and express emotions from disdain to outrage at this "misuse" of the computers. As one volunteer explained while referring to Internet games: "I try to stop them." This is reflective of the place of the Internet in society and the predominance of metaphors such as the "information infrastructure," "digital library," and "electronic marketplace" (cf. Stefik 1996). Agre calls part of this "the individualistic conception of computing" and points out that it is often not a valid one, yet this debate rests on it (Agre 1997, p. 243). By and large, the children at the EDC show little interest in "information" as it is often conceived: they want to neither look things up nor transact purchases. Rather, they want to use the network to play and to communicate with others. Although this conflicts with some visions of the network, this is what children like to do. Despite the outrage of a few parents and the seeming shock of other studies of libraries, it should come as no surprise to us that children play. A more useful avenue to pursue would be to consider what might be achieved with access policies given that children play.

An insight of computer game manufacturers has been that the games most likely to be acceptable to parents (often the purchasers) and to children (the users) are those that take a playful approach to learning—combining arcade-style action with mathematics, for instance. For the Internet to be realized as a tool for education that is voluntarily used by children, this struggle remains to be grappled with in the area of Internet applications.

Sharing as Unanticipated Benefit

As evidenced by the sharing measures, children often share the computers at the center. Qualitative data indicates that they watch other users (e.g., see figures 10.1 and 10.2 above). In doing so, they learn about computers from strangers, yet this benefit is not part of the policy debate about public access centers. Observations of children in the EDC confirm that children often learn how to use the computer by watching others or by asking them questions (Sandvig 2000). It is then a key insight that it is games and chat that are more likely to be shared.

In the early days of the telephone, users would often first encounter the device in a public place such as at a demonstration at a church, or later installed in a business such as a drug store for the public's use (Fischer 1992). With the telephone, learning about a new communication technology occurred in public places; knowledge about computers can be similarly conceptualized. If a policy goal is the building of computer skills in a particular community, a public access center is a nexus around which the community property of knowledge about computers can be built through a mixing of the more and less skilled (Agre 1997, pp. 244–245). Universal access policies that address the "digital divide," on the other hand, rely on public places as the primary point of access for the disadvantaged because subsidy to every home was thought to be too expensive for advanced information technology.

Revisiting Initiative Two: Will the Real Adults Please Stand Up?

Children like to chat and exchange e-mail with friends. Many very young children observed in the EDC have (one or more) Web-based e-mail accounts. Over a quarter of all time spent at the EDC was spent at a site that allowed communicating with other individuals (table 10.2), yet only 1% of these sites were explicitly for children (table 10.3). Protecting children from information disclosure via chat and e-mail is the focus of the recently enacted privacy law COPA, discussed earlier. While the data for the present study were collected before recent restrictions went into effect, it is still clear by analyzing the law and the sites coded in this study that only the most obviously exploitative sites collecting personal information explicitly from very young children will be affected. While the policy initiative was based on research that conceived the target of policy to be *sites directed to children*, children do not prefer to visit these sites for e-mail and chat.[52]

For instance, one of the most frequently visited places to chat found in this sample was alloy.com (a fashionable teen culture site). Alloy.com does collect personal information, but the privacy policy points out that "Alloy.com is not directed to children under the age of 13" and "prohibits registration" by them,[53] yet most users of the EDC were under 13, and alloy.com accounted for 1.4% of all page requests.

The remedy advanced by regulations so far is chiefly parental consent. At the time of data collection for this study, many children's sites on the Web required parental consent before participation. These sites do not appear in our sample, however, and it seems that children in the EDC do not visit them. Nine of the ten top chat sites in this sample did post privacy policies,[54] but from an examination of the data it does not appear that the children read them. Over the 16 weeks, nine requests for privacy policies of any kind were found in the 203,647 pages requested.[55] Finally, observations of children in the EDC indicate that lying about name, age, and other personal information occurs in during the majority of data collection from young children in public places (Sandvig 2000, pp. 14–15). In this manner, the law does not apply to most of the sites visited by children, and even the consent requirements that will exist under the law are easily circumvented. It is not known from these data if the problem of harmful information disclosure by minors exists, but if it does exist, the privacy initiative will not address it because the policy is not written to apply to actual use by children.

Revisiting Initiative Three: The Absence of Indecency

The viewing of pornographic material in the EDC was rare to nonexistent. This is substantiated by interviews conducted in the EDC: while all of the library volunteers interviewed had heard stories about pornographic material being viewed in the EDC, only one volunteer had personal experience, and this was on one occasion. Interestingly, it appears that the public nature of the EDC discourages such viewing, as computer screens are visible to passers-by. Several volunteers recounted the perception that pornography was most likely to be viewed on the screen that was the most hidden from other patrons because of a pillar.

The six instances found in which only the first (warning) page of a pornographic site was visited seem explainable by children seeking the thrill of transgression. It is not that the warning notices on the first page work, but rather that the purpose is of the visits was transgression—not to actually view pornographic images but to demonstrate courage in violating a well-known social norm. This low (less than 1%) level of pornography in public libraries is comparable to other reports.[56]

Here it appears that the overwhelming policy focus on indecent material is erroneous. While young children are portrayed in policy debates as the most in need of protection from pornography, they are also likely to be the least interested in it. Although policy debate has focused on preventing access to indecent material from public places via filtering requirements, interviews indicate that the more public an area is, the less likely it is that indecent material will be accessed. Again, the social problem presented by this policy is not grounded in real life.

Conclusion

In the end, Internet policies to date in the three areas examined seem to have notable lacks. Content regulation, be it concerning decency or privacy, appears unlikely to resolve the problems it claims to address. Indeed, content regulation initiatives to date do not seem clearly tied to actual problems in an empirical sense. Access policy is achieving some desired results but also producing unexpected ones. On the whole, all of the policies considered here appear to be somewhat disconnected from the material conditions that they attempt to regulate. To express surprise at this result, as other studies in this area have done, is to employ a straw man. The explanation for this disconnection lies in an understanding of policy as a symbolic and political activity.

Concerns about content place government in an ideological dilemma between responsiveness to concerns of the public on one hand and a commitment to a free enterprise system of control on the other. Much like other political debates about communication (Rowland 1983, p. 297), the underlying pressure of a minimalist regulatory ideal and the actions of interest groups committed to the protection of corporate rights produce policies that are, on the whole, ineffectual. No politician is afraid of alienating the pedophile vote and the pro-pornography lobby, leaving a policy debate dominated by politically safe topics—and even privacy is politically safe compared to, say, restrictions on advertising. Internet content is then debated as though the chief dangers presented by the network were a shadow land of nasty, lurking strangers (or a child's own dirty urges). Concerns about the digital divide are drawn from a policy vision containing unrealistic conceptions of children busily striving to become better educated workers suited for skilled jobs—all regardless of any grounding in fact—because such is a politically expedient effort that allows politicians to engage in symbolically rewarding efforts to (1) help children, (2) help the poor, and (3) appear familiar with high technology.

The broader implications from here are somewhat contradictory. In one sense, these results call for an improved effort to ground policy initiatives in a realistic understanding of lived existence, but at the same time they imply that the chances of this happening are low. Internet content and access policymaking for children are so far primarily responsive to entrenched interests, and debates center on topics that are largely free of pressure from them. The practical implications from here, however, are striking. Sharing computers between strangers is an avenue of interaction possible with public access centers in libraries that is impossible with other policy mechanisms, such as subsidy to the home. While play and chat are not socially legitimate needs that are seen to require public funding, it is precisely these activities that are the most likely to promote sharing—a promising avenue for learning about technology, and a promising mode of learning about content that is, as yet, underutilized. In the final analysis, the promise of digital divide policies for children is the promise that eventually we will not shun playful behavior, but accept it as human and harness it where appropriate.

Notes

1. This material is based on work supported by the National Science Foundation under Grant No. REC 9603344.

2. The terminology public, universal, service and access is very confused in this debate: Public Internet access sites are supported by the public via universal service policies (also called universal access policies) in the U.S., and public service policies in European countries provide universal access. This paper will refer to the policy in question as "universal access" and the centers in question as providing "public access," although other literature may refer to such differently.

3. The phrase "traditional" is somewhat problematic here, as this definition has gradually evolved from subsidy actions of the FCC, and before 1996 had not been codified in law. Some analysts argue that the definition here called "traditional" is invalid, as it is not supported by any initial legislative intent (Mueller 1997). For a clear discussion of recent policy, see Aufderheide (1999).

4. Now the Technology Opportunities Program (TOP).

5. For an overview of competing policy visions for the Internet, see Stefik (1996).

6. Not to be confused with the Child Online Protection Act (COPA), discussed later as initiative three.

7. E.g., the FTC initiative was a product of the Division of Advertising Practices, Bureau of Consumer Protection.

8. Unless data collection is involved.

9. Sections of the CDA enacted within §223 of the Telecommunications Act of 1996 were struck down by the U.S. Supreme Court as unconstitutional in 1997 (Aufderheide 1999, pp. 183–185). Enforcement of the subsequent Child Online Protection Act is presently blocked pending litigation over its constitutionality (Mendels 1999).

10. Not to be confused with the Children's Online Privacy Protection Act (COPPA), discussed previously as initiative one.

11. H.R. 896: Children's Internet Protection Act, H.R. 2560: Child Protection Act of 1999, S. 97: Children's Internet Protection Act, and S. 1545: Neighborhood Children's Internet Protection Act (American Library Association 1999).

12. For instance, the *Time* cover pictured a very young child (Elmer-DeWitt 1995).

13. For an overview of the Electronic Library Project, under which the EDC program was partially developed, see Murase, Boutilier, and Sandvig (1999).

14. EDC computers at the main library have Pentium 166 MHz processors and are running Windows 95. Each computer is equipped with a Microsoft EasyBall

mouse, a keyboard, headphones, and a 15″ monitor. Computers are connected via an Ethernet LAN to a Windows NT server that provides access to CD-ROM towers containing children's software.

15. The main library is connected to the Internet via a T-1 line.

16. The EDC program predates the implementation of subsidies to libraries for universal access under the 1996 Telecommunications Act, but it is exactly the type of program intended to receive funding under the Act, and indeed the library has applied for subsidies and expects to receive them (Boutilier 1998).

17. Of course, those living near the library are not the only patrons. As the flagship of a large library system, the New Main draws patrons from throughout the city.

18. When ordering chairs for the center, library planners toured another nearby computer center at the San Francisco Exploratorium (a hands-on museum of science and art) and noticed that groups of children tended to cluster around the few available computers. Anticipating this demand, they placed three chairs in front of every two computers at the EDC (Boutilier 1998).

19. Requests using the HTTP, FTP, and Gopher protocol were monitored. A telnet application was also provided in the EDC, but observation indicated that telnet use was comparatively rare.

20. The caching proxy did not collect data because of network problems on two occasions during this period, once for one hour (December 7) and once for three hours (November 9).

21. Thanks to Jason Coffer, Steve McMahon, and François Bar for proposing and refining this method.

22. The Squid Internet Object Cache provided by the National Laboratory for Applied Network Research. Thanks to NLANR for providing this tool; if an open-source object cache had not been available, this research would not have been possible (see ⟨http://squid.nlanr.net/⟩).

23. The source code of v.1.1 was modified slightly to cause the logging of all headers for each transaction. Thanks to Guillaume Vambenepe for assistance in this effort.

24. Web pages were identified by selecting for the MIME type "text/html".

25. That is, requests containing an error code from the caching proxy (generally mistyped or unreachable hosts).

26. This is analogous to what are often termed "page views."

27. For sampling units vs. coding units, see Riffe, Lacy, and Fico (1999, ch. 4).

28. Initially, the stem also included the first directory in the path after the domain name in cases where this resulted in a page that could be retrieved. By this scheme, "⟨http://dir.yahoo.com/Education/⟩" would be distinct from "⟨http://dir.yahoo.com/Reference/⟩". However, in the majority of cases pretested, this did not result in a different functional coding, so this practice was dropped for the simpler (but slightly cruder) hostname and domain.

29. The extent to which this consists of repeat visitors is not known.

30. On public school holidays during this period (Labor Day, Columbus Day, Veterans' Day, and Thanksgiving Day), the EDC was also closed.

31. As an aside, this form of traffic analysis also provides ready access to extensive *structural* measures (features of the content: page size, number of images, etc.), but as these are not of theoretical interest they are not included here.

32. Once a site was coded as full-page advertising, no further coding of the content was done for that site, as the content viewed by the original users was often not available (that is, it can not be determined what ad was viewed by what user).

33. Note that many sites offer some of these features (e.g., free Web-based e-mail), but only sites whose primary purpose is one of these services were coded in this category.

34. Unreachable during coding—as previously discussed, requests unreachable by participants were initially discarded.

35. Note that many of the pages coded "does contain" for this measure contained some non-English content and some English content together—with this method it is impossible to determine which language was read by the user.

36. E.g., a publisher's site may have information about books that they produce, but this would *not* be categorized as "does contain advertising" because it is not advertising for a topic other than books.

37. This measure is distinct from entire pages ("pop-ups") whose primary purpose is advertising, which is in the functional category described previously.

38. This is in no way a learning measure: it is a measure of sites that self-label as education.

39. We opted for a broader definition than found in other literature because of this.

40. E.g., there could be a site that lets you find other sites (primary purpose category 4) that are pornographic ("does contain pornography").

41. Page views of duration longer than 300 seconds were excluded as outliers—researchers watching children observed no page views of this length on these computers.

42. The time elapsed from a request from an EDC computer to the completion of the transfer of the content, measured with a precision of one thousandth of a second. This is measured by the caching proxy software as a performance metric.

43. Note that this measure is subject to influence by the frequency of the type of site requested; more popular sites would tend to appear simultaneously more often, regardless of any sharing behavior by users. It is presented primarily as descriptive of the atmosphere of the lab as a whole.

44. The observation of sharing in these two configurations was quite common, although only those children on the same side of the island could see one anothers' screens, and only those children on the opposite side of the island could easily see one anothers' faces. Children would often attempt to get their friends seated either next to them or directly across from them, but if this was not possible, they would also speak to strangers.

45. As an aside, due to the layout of the lab, the computers of interest directly next to the requesting computer and across from the requesting computer are one foot apart, resulting in a sharing statistic of over 1 if either of these two computers of interest were viewing the same page.

46. It is worth noting that intracomputer sharing (several people sharing the same computer) was extremely common as well but cannot be measured using this study design.

47. Thanks to Emily Murase for her assistance in this effort.

48. Although both coders agreed that zero instances appeared.

49. The site alloy.com, mentioned earlier, is an online teen magazine site. Children in the EDC visited only the chat area, however, so visits were categorized as "communicate with individuals".

50. Note that this measure is distinct from full-page advertising, described earlier.

51. Each child could indicate more than one answer.

52. One clause of the Act provides that operators with "actual knowledge" of visits by children are also obligated, but it is seems that as long as operators do not monitor their own sites, this will exempt them from any obligation (1999).

53. See ⟨http://www.alloy.com/a2k/privacyterms/privacy.html⟩.

54. Presence/absence of privacy policy was not initially coded in the content analysis; a May visit to the top ten chat sites in the sample produced this estimate.

55. This is a rough estimate based on the observation that Web addresses for privacy policy often contain the word "privacy." The full sample was screened for URLs containing this word, and nine of the resulting pages were privacy policies of some sort (that is, they were titled "privacy policy").

56. Surprisingly, replication for this finding comes from a bombastic pro-filtering organization. In an examination of the output of filtering software installed at three public libraries, a Family Research Council booklet emphasizes raw numbers, anecdotes, and graphic news reports. Yet dividing the number of estimated pornographic sites by the number of total requests yields a percentage ranging from .002% to .53% for each library examined (Burt 2000, pp. 1, 39–45). The booklet concedes "0.53 percent of all web accesses may not sound significant, this translates into thousands of separate incidents" (p. 44).

References

Agre, Philip E. 1997. Building Community Networks. In *Reinventing Technology, Rediscovering Community: Critical Explorations of Computing as a Social Practice*, edited by P. E. Agre and D. Schuler. Greenwich, CT: Ablex.

American Advertising Federation. 1999. Comments to the Secretary of the Federal Trade Commission Re: Children's Online Privacy Protection Rule, P994504. San Francisco: American Advertising Federation.

American Library Association. 1999. End of Session Legislative Summary, 106th Congress, First Session. *ALA Washington Office Newsline* 8(22).

Aufderheide, Patricia. 1999. *Communications Policy and the Public Interest: The Telecommunications Act of 1996.* New York: Guilford.

Balka, Ellen, and Brian J. Peterson. 2000. Moving Beyond the Field of Dreams: Citizenship and the Use of the Internet at Vancouver Public Library. Paper read at Directions and Implications of Advanced Computing Symposium, May 20–23, at Seattle, WA.

Bell, Daniel. 1999. *The Coming of Post-Industrial Society.* Rev. ed. New York: Basic Books.

Boutilier, Sybil. 1998. Grants and Special Projects Director, San Francisco Public Library System.

Burt, David. 2000. Dangerous Access: Uncovering Internet Pornography in America's Libraries. Washington, DC: Family Research Council.

Castells, Manuel. 1998. *The Information Age: Economy, Society, and Culture: End of Millennium.* 3 vols. Vol. 3. Oxford: Blackwell Publishers.

Children's Online Privacy Protection Act of 1998. 15 USC 6501–6506.

Cohen, J. A. 1960. Coefficient of Agreement for Nominal Scales. *Educational and Psychological Measurement* 20: 37–46.

Elmer-DeWitt, Philip. 1995. On a Screen Near You: Cyberporn. *Time*, July 3.

Federal Trade Commission. 1998. Privacy Online: A Report to Congress. Washington, DC: Federal Trade Commission.

Federal Trade Commission. 1999. Children's Online Privacy Protection Rule. *Federal Register* 64(212): 59887–59915.

Fischer, Claude S. 1992. *America Calling: A Social History of the Telephone to 1940.* Berkeley, CA: University of California Press.

Gorgeç, A., S. Lew, and A. Curry. 1999. An Analysis of Internet Use in the Public Library. Vancouver, BC: School of Library, Archival, and Information Studies, University of British Columbia.

Graham, Stephen, and Simon Marvin. 1996. *Telecommunications and the City: Electronic Spaces and Urban Places.* London: Routledge.

Lentz, Becky, Joseph Straubhaar, Antonio LaPastina, Stan Main, and Julie Taylor. 2000. Structuring Access: The Role of Public Access Centers in the "Digital Divide." Paper read at International Communication Association, at Acapulco, Mexico.

Linz, Daniel, and Neil Malamuth. 1990. *Pornography.* Newbury Park, CA: Sage.

Mark, June, Janet Cornebise, and Ellen Wahl. 1997. Community Technology Centers: Impact on Individual Participants and Their Communities. Waltham, MA: Education Development Center, Inc.

McLaughlin, Margaret, Steven B. Goldberg, Nicole Ellison, and Jason Lucas. 1999. Measuring Internet Audiences: Patrons of an On-Line Art Museum. In *Doing Internet Research*, edited by S. G. Jones. Thousand Oaks, CA: Sage.

Mendels, Pamela. 1999. Judge Delays Online Pornography Law. *The New York Times: Cybertimes*, February 1.

Mueller, Milton. 1997. *Universal Service: Competition, Interconnection, and Monopoly in the Making of the American Telephone System.* Cambridge, MA: MIT Press.

Murase, Emily M., Sybil Boutilier, and Christian Sandvig. 1999. Strategies for Promoting Access to the Internet Among Children and Youth: A Case Study of the San Francisco Public Library's Electronic Library Project. Paper read at INET 99: The Internet Global Summit, at San Jose, CA.

National Telecommunications and Information Administration. 1999. Falling through the Net: Defining the Digital Divide, A Report on the Telecommunications and Information Technology Gap in America. Washington, DC: GPO.

Rapp, Lucien. 1996. Public Service or Universal Service? *Telecommunications Policy* 20(6): 391–397.

Riffe, Daniel, Stephen Lacy, and Frederick G. Fico. 1999. *Analyzing Media Messages: Using Quantitative Content Analysis in Research.* Mahwah, NJ: Lawrence Erlbaum Associates.

Roberts, Donald F., Ulla G. Foehr, Victoria J. Rideout, and Mollyann Brodie. 1999. Kids & Media @ the New Millennium: A Comprehensive National Analysis of Children's Media Use. Menlo Park, CA: Henry J. Kaiser Family Foundation.

Rowland, Willard D. 1983. *The Politics of TV Violence: Policy Uses of Communication Research.* Beverly Hills, CA: Sage.

Sandvig, Christian. 2000. The Information Apologue: Play and Internet Access in the Children's Library. Paper presented to the annual meeting of the International Communication Association, June, at Acapulco, Mexico.

Sawhney, Harmeet. 1994. Universal service: Prosaic motives and great ideals. *Journal of Broadcasting and Electronic Media* 38(4): 375–395.

Stefik, Mark, ed. 1996. *Internet Dreams: Archetypes, Myths, and Metaphors.* Cambridge, MA: MIT Press.

Telecommunications Act of 1996. Pub. LA. No. 104-104, 110 Stat. 56 (1996).

The Children's Partnership. 2000. *Online Content for Low-Income and Underserved Americans: The Digital Divide's New Frontier.* Santa Monica, CA: The Children's Partnership.

Universal Service Administrative Company. 1999. Federal Universal Service Programs Fund Size Projections and Contribution Base for the Second Quarter 1999. Madison, WI: USAC.

U.S. Census. 1991. 1990 Decennial Census Summary Tape File 3A. Washington, DC: US Census.

U.S. Census. 1999. Model Based Income and Poverty Estimates for San Francisco County, California. Washington, DC: US Census.

U.S. Department of Education. 1999. Community Technology Centers. Washington, DC: Department of Education.

Weber, Robert Philip. 1990. *Basic Content Analysis.* 2nd ed. Newbury Park, CA: Sage.

11

Accessibility of Broadband Telecommunication Services by Various Segments of the American Population[1]

David Gabel and Florence Kwan

Introduction

The latest figures published by Department of Commerce show that in August 2000, 51 percent of American households owned computers and 41.5 percent of all households were connected to the Internet.[2] However, as any casual reader of the daily news knows, more and more information is being digitized and made available via "packet-switched" networks such as the Internet. The vast increase in the amount of digital information available, the growing numbers of telecommuting employees in the economy, and the increasing dependence of businesses on "packet-switched" networks for communication among employees, customers, service providers, and business units, have made high-speed, advanced services access[3] to these networks an important ingredient for economic advancement.[4]

As companies race to roll out technology solutions such as cable modem or xDSL hookups to satisfy the burgeoning demand for high-speed, high-capacity access to advanced data networks,[5] there is a growing national concern about the ability of all segments of American society to have access to, and benefit from, these solutions. According to the Chairman of the Federal Communication Commission,

The most important issue on our agenda today is broadband. This debate that we are having in our country about broadband—that we must have about broadband—is an important debate. Broadband is going to change America in wonderful ways that no one in this room can predict, certainly not myself.... Fundamentally, we want four things for consumers in the broadband world. We want fast deployment. We want ubiquitous deployment. We want competitive deployment. And we want open deployment.[6]

Just prior to the speech, the FCC adopted rules requiring the further unbundling of network elements by the nation's incumbent local telephone companies.[7] These rules essentially rely upon marketplace forces to create an environment in which new broadband service providers will be encouraged to enter the local exchange market.[8] In a related proceeding,[9] the Commission stated that its market-based approach to stimulating new market entry promotes the goal of Section 706 of the Telecommunications Act of 1996[10] (i.e., the deployment of advanced services to all Americans on a reasonable and timely basis). The FCC has reconfirmed its commitment to a market-based approach in its recent *First Report and Order and Further Notice of Proposed Rulemaking; In the Matters of Deployment of Wireline Services Offering Advanced Telecommunications Capability*, where it has adopted "measures that we consider critical steps in encouraging the competitive provision of advanced services."[11]

Congress and the FCC have placed great reliance upon marketplace forces to achieve the dual goals of advanced service competition and universal access. FCC staff, however, have acknowledged the "virtual consensus" that local telephone competition mostly takes place in urban business districts and that "competitors are more likely to enter highly populated urban areas."[12] Given this inconsistency in current policies regarding broadband services, research is warranted to provide a better understanding of the factors that influence providers' decisions to offer advanced services. The study presented here is offered as a step in the development of that understanding.

In designing this study we were interested in examining where advanced service is and is not available. In addressing this matter we recognized that we needed to look at what is happening in different markets. We also recognized that, to be done properly, the analysis should be careful in defining what constitutes access. Some published data report access at a high level of aggregation, such as the state or city level of observation.[13] We have used a level of granularity that is finer than the city. This is necessary because, as the map from Time Warner's Web site illustrates, there can be a lot of variation within a city (see figure 11.1).[14]

One could say that Manhattan has cable modems, but this misses the distinctions that are reflected in the map. Firms are making decisions about where to roll out service first and where subsequent investments

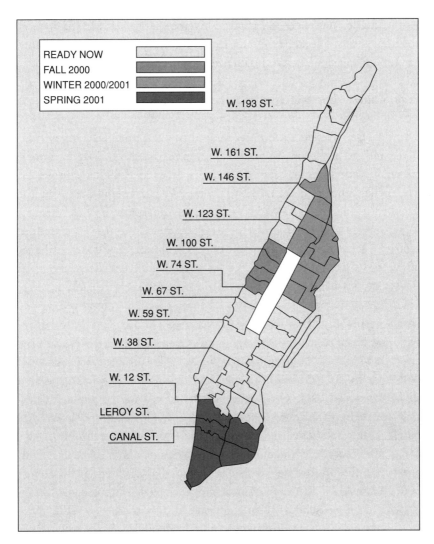

Figure 11.1
Cable modem availability in Manhattan, June 2000.
Source: Time Warner

will be made. We have undertaken this analysis to see what influences such factors as income, race, and regulation may have on the availability of high-speed access to the Internet for residential customers.

Prior Studies That Addressed Access to the Internet

The U.S. Department of Commerce and the National Telecommunications and Information Administration have been tracking computer ownership and Internet usage since the emergence of these technologies. The earlier reports of their *Falling through the Net* series presented the problem of the "digital divide", that is, the difference in rates of access to computers and the Internet between segments of society. The third report concluded that at the end of 1998, only about a quarter of U.S. households had connection to the Internet, and that those segments of the society least likely to be connected to the Internet are "low-income, Black, Hispanic, or Native American, senior in age, not employed, single-parent (especially female-headed) households, those with little education, and those residing in central cities or especially rural areas."[15] The latest in the series, *Falling through the Net: Toward Digital Inclusion*, finds that by August 2000, "a digital divide remains or has expanded slightly in some cases, even while Internet access and computer ownership are rising rapidly for almost all groups."[16] The study shows that "divides still exist between those with different levels of income and education, different racial and ethnic groups, old and young, single and dual-parent families, and those with and without disabilities".[17] In August 2000, 51 percent of American households owned computers, and 41.5 percent of all households were connected to the Internet.[18] While these studies provide us with information about who is less likely to be using the Internet, it does not tell us whether this outcome is affected by the availability of service. "Internet connection" is the embodiment of both demand and supply factors. On the demand side, households choose whether or not to buy a computer, and then choose whether to subscribe to Internet service. Households with computers may or may not want to subscribe to Internet services, due to their preference and ability to pay, but Internet access is in their choice set only if Internet service is available to them. The *Falling through the Net* series provide insights as to the demand characteristics that may be associated with usage, but no supply-side or availability information is included.

According to a study by Downes and Greenstein (1998), "over ninety-two percent of the U.S. population has easy access to a competitive Internet access market."[19] While this finding may suggest close to universal access for traditional narrowband Internet access, the same cannot be suggested for broadband access, such as that via Digital Subscriber Line (DSL) and cable modem. Narrowband Internet access (traditional dial-up) piggybacks on top of traditional phone networks to connect households to the ISPs. Hence, the availability of ISP service can be translated into the availability of narrowband Internet service.[20] Unlike narrowband dial-up access, high-bandwidth technologies can require costly and time-consuming upgrades. For DSL, service availability is dependent on engineering around bridge taps, load coils, and digital loop carrier configurations,[21] which are currently not compatible with DSL technology. Furthermore, the quality of service degrades with distance from the customer's premises to the central office. For example, a customer must be within approximately 18,000 feet of the carrier's central office for ADSL service to be deliverable.[22] For cable modem, the upgrade process often includes extending optical fiber closer to the end user and improving system quality to reduce signal leakage. The cable system's transmission capacity needs to be upgraded to 750 MHz to allow greater flexibility in allocating bandwidth for two-way high-speed services.[23] Equipment that enables the transmission of digital data packets such as routers, switches, and a cable modem termination system need to be installed for high-speed Internet service. Further, amplifiers and optical lasers need to be installed in both downstream and upstream directions in order to allow bidirectional transmission. Without such equipment, providers typically can provide high-speed service only in the downstream direction and must rely on a telephone-line return path.[24] Because infrastructure rollout is still in its nascent stage, the availability of Internet service via these technologies is growing but is far from universal.[25] Because consumers are limited by inadequate infrastructure, we believe that it is important to understand the factors that affect the availability of these services.

Limited research on broadband usage and access is available. The 2000 *Falling through the Net* report provides data on high-speed Internet connection for the first time. In August 2000, 10.7 percent of online U.S. households (about 4.5% of all U.S. households) had broadband-speed access.[26] Among total broadband households, the majority procure either cable modems (50.8%) or DSL (33.7%). The data show that the digital divide exists for broadband connection as well as for general Internet connection. Rural areas, for example, are now lagging behind central cities and urban areas in broadband penetration at 7.3% compared to 12.2% and 11.8%, respectively. Disparities are also found between different income, education, and age groups. Again, these figures are on broadband usage but do not provide explicit information on the availability of services.[27]

The Federal Communications Commission announced the completion of a study of the availability of high-speed and advanced telecommunications services in August 2000. The data used in the study is based largely on the first systematic, nationwide "Broadband Survey" of subscription to high-speed and advanced services, begun by the Commission earlier in 2000. The Commission's nationwide "Broadband Survey" required any facilities-based company that provided 250 or more broadband service lines (or wireless channels) in a given state to report basic information about their service offerings and customers. The Commission found that "advanced telecommunications capability is being deployed in a reasonable and timely fashion overall, although the Commission identified certain groups of consumers that are particularly vulnerable to not receiving service in a timely fashion." The Commission identified six groups as particularly vulnerable to not having access to advanced services, if deployment is left to market forces alone:

1. rural Americans, particularly those outside of population centers
2. inner city consumers
3. low-income consumers
4. minority consumers
5. tribal areas
6. consumers in U.S. territories.[28]

Our study attempts to complement the existing research by investigating the availability of broadband services to residential subscribers, focusing on the choice of providers to deploy cable modem and DSL technology. We have focused on these two technologies because, as recently reported by the federal government, only these two technologies are rapidly being deployed to provide two-way, high-speed access to the Internet.[29] Both cost and socio-economic factors are taken into account as determinants of availability. This not only allows us to look at cost issues that may affect a provider's decision to deploy advanced technology, it also helps to identify segments of society that are disenfranchised from *advanced* communication services.

Objectives

In this chapter we examine providers' choice to deploy advanced technology, hence the choice to make broadband services available to different segments of the population. The question of access is analyzed in the context of federal policy favoring reasonable and timely access for all Americans. We look at residential broadband services offered by telephone and cable television operators, with a focus on high-speed Internet access via xDSL and cable modems. Although cable television operators have not been traditionally viewed as competitors in the telecommunications market, there is an increasing trend towards cable operators offering the same services as local exchange carriers—telephony and high-speed Internet access. There were an estimated 2.3 million cable modem subscribers in the United States by June 30, 2000. Cable modem service was commercially available to 48 million homes in the United States and Canada, equal to 44 percent of all cable homes passed.[30]

Based on our understanding of the telecommunications network, a few crucial factors impact the decision to offer service. First, there is the cost of supplying the service. Whereas there are sizeable fixed costs associated with establishing service, a firm needs to estimate the potential size of the market. We use two types of data to control for the size of the market: the number of customers that can be reached and the economic and demographic characteristics of the population. We would expect that, all else equal, the older and poorer the customer base, the lower the forecast interest in the service, and therefore there is a reduced likelihood that service will be introduced.[31] Furthermore, the more telecommunications users per square mile of service territory, the greater the likelihood that advanced telecommunications services will be made available.

The decision to roll out high-speed access is also influenced by the cost of reaching the Internet backbone. The cost of a link to the Internet backbone increases with distance. The mileage transport rate to the Internet backbone is also a function of population density. For a given distance, fiber transport rates are lower in urban areas because of the greater degree of rivalry between telecommunications suppliers. There-fore there is a need to control for the cost of connecting customers to the Internet backbone. Based on our conversations with industry suppliers as well as other published research, we have estimated the cost of transport from the local market to the Internet backbone by estimating the cost of connecting to the nearest interexchange carrier's point of presence.[32]

We also test if the regulations imposed on Regional Bell Operating Companies impedes the rollout of advanced telecommunications services to residential customers. Under the Telecommunications Act of 1996, the Regional Bell Operating Companies (RBOCs) are prohibited from providing interLATA (long-distance) services until they have satisfied a competitive list of conditions established by Congress and monitored by the Federal Communications Commission.[33] We test to see if residential customers in areas served by RBOCs, all else equal, are less likely to have high-speed access to the Internet.

Utilizing a statistically valid sample of customer locations,[34] logistic regression techniques are used to estimate the following relationship:

Availability = f(economic and demographic variables,
        teledensity, area served by incumbent RBOC).

The modal specification outlined above addresses the availability of high-speed access. The dependent variable is binary—service is or is not avail-able to a household.

Data

We examine the availability of broadband services at the wire center level of observation.[35] For our estimation, we used data from three dif-ferent sources. First we obtained data on the number of access lines at a wire center, as well as the size of its service territory, and the type and name of the company that owns the wire center. DSL and cable modem service availability data were collected from various company and tech-nology Web sites, which we were able to map to wire center locations. For a few locations, additional data was obtained by calling service providers. We use the 1990 census data for the economic and demo-graphic characteristics of various areas of the country. Census block group data were aggregated to the level of the wire center and merged with the availability data. The resulting database contains the following variables:

• *Switch Identity.*   To determine the geographic boundaries and demographics of a wire center service area. For the purpose of this study the switch identity is the Common Language Location Identifier (CLLI code);

• *Company Type.*   The type of company supplying telecommunications services: Regional Bell Operating Company and name of RBOC;

• *Average Fixed Costs.*   Proxy measure for the average fixed costs of a xDSL provider is calculated as fixed costs divided by the number of access lines at wire center. Average fixed cost is the fixed cost divided by the number of DSL subscribers. Since we do not have data for the latter value, we use lines to represent the potential market for the service.

• *Line Density.*   The number of access lines per square mile.

• *Demographics.*   Race, age, education, income, and residence in urbanized area.

• *Availability.*   Dummy equals one if residential DSL or cable modem service is available.

For a list of the variables in the final dataset, see table 11.1.

Basic Estimation Model

We are modeling the rollout of advanced telecommunications services. The decision to deploy advanced telecommunications services is effectively binary—either advanced services are or are not available. A few econometric techniques have been developed to deal with experiments in which there are just two possible outcomes. We have employed one of these specifications, logit. If we had used a different specification, say probit, our qualitative results would not have changed.

In this section we outline the logit specification. Readers who are most interested in the results of the analysis may want to jump ahead to the sections on results or policy implications of the study.

Let D_i = line density; R_i = dummy equals 1 if RBOC; U_i = percentage of households in urbanized area; M_i = median year housing structure was built; H_i = household income; and T_i = percentage of households without telephone, for the ith wire center, where $i = 1, 2, \ldots 286$. Further, let π_i = the conditional probability that DSL or cable modem service is

Table 11.1
Variable description

DENLINE1	Line density (total telephone lines per square mile)
RBOC	Telephone service provided by a Regional Bell Operating Companies
AM_SW_PB	RBOC dummy for Ameritech, Southwest, PacBell
NX_BA	RBOC dummy for NYNEX or Bell Atlantic
BS	RBOC dummy for Bell South
US	RBOC dummy for US West
PCTNPHOH	Percent households without telephone service
PCTURBHU	Percent housing units—in urbanized area
MEDYRBLT	Median year housing structure built
MEDHHINC	Median household income
PCTBLKH	Percent householders—Black
PCTAMIH	Percent householders—Amer Ind, Esk, Aleut
PCTASIH	Percent householders—Asian, Pacific Island
PCTNWHTH	Percent householders—Non-white
P_A13	Percent persons age 13 or younger
P_A1418	Percent persons age 14–18
P_A1924	Percent persons age 19–24
P_A2529	Percent persons age 25–29
P_A3034	Percent persons age 30–34
P_A3539	Percent persons age 35–39
P_A4049	Percent persons age 40–49
AVG_FC	Fixed costs divided by number of access lines
TOT_CHG	Estimated monthly charge for connection to the nearest Internet backbone
MISSTOT	Equals 1 for the 25 wire centers without information on connection charges
PCTLHSP	Percent of persons with less than high-school education
PCTHSP	Percent of persons with high-school education
PCTSCOLP	Percent of persons with some college education
PCTCOLP	Percent of persons with four-year college education
PCTCOLMP	Percent of persons with graduate-level education
PCTFORBP	Percent of persons who are foreign-born

available at wire center i, and $(1 - \pi_i)$ the conditional probability that they are not available, given D_i, R_i, U_i, M_i, H_i, and T_i. Then the logistic regression model for the log odds of service being available is

$$\log\left[\frac{\pi_i}{1 - \pi_i}\right] = \log Y_i = \alpha + \beta_1(D_i) + \beta_2(R_i) + \beta_3(U_i) + \beta_4(M_i) + \beta_5(H_i) + \beta_6(T_i),$$

where Y_i is simply the conditional odds of DSL or cable modem service being available, given the explanatory variables.

Results of different specifications of this model, including the addition of demographic and other variables, are presented in the "Results" section.

Testable Hypotheses

Given the basic model and the available data, the parameter estimates from the regression afford the opportunity to test the following hypotheses:

1. *Number of Access Lines or Average Fixed Costs.* The coefficient estimate can be used to test the significance of economies of scale in influencing availability.

2. *Line Density.* Defined as number of access lines per square mile. The coefficient estimate can be used to test the significance of the potential size of customer pool per square mile.

3. *Bell Operating Company.* The coefficient estimate can be used to test whether the line-of-business restrictions established by the 1996 Telecommunications Act are promoting or hindering the development of broadband services.[36]

4. *Percentage of Households without Telephones.* The coefficient estimate can be used to test whether or not having a telephone decreases the likelihood that DSL service is available to a household.

5. *Median Year Housing Structure Built.* This variable can be considered a proxy for the age of the communications infrastructure. The coefficient estimate can be used to test whether it is more costly to provide advanced services where infrastructures are relatively old, hence decreasing the likelihood of these services being available.

6. *Percentage of Households/Residents in Rural or Metropolitan Area.* The coefficient estimate can be used to test if rural and urban areas of the United States have equal access to broadband services.

7. *Percentage of Black/Hispanic/Native American/Asian Households.* The coefficient estimate can be used to test if broadband access is less available to minority groups.

8. *Age of Residents.* The coefficient estimate can be used to test if availability is significantly different between different age groups.

9. *Median Household Income.* The coefficient estimate can be used to test if broadband access is less available to lower income groups.

10. *Educational Attainment.* The coefficient estimate can be used to test if availability is significantly different between groups with different educational attainment.

11. *Percentage of Foreign-Born Residents.* The coefficient estimate can be used to test if broadband access is less or more available to foreign-born residents.

Results

This section presents the results of the model. First we look at the availability of either cable modem or DSL service. We then focus on just the DSL market.

The logit regression results suggest that the availability of DSL or cable modem services in a wire center area increases in those areas with decreasing monthly costs of connecting to the Internet backbone and increasing line density, percent of population in an urbanized area, and median income. Model A (table 11.2) shows the results for the preferred model specification. The dependent variable is AVAIL, which takes on the value of 1 if either DSL or cable modem service is available in the wire center area. Variables such as race, education, and foreign-born population do not appear as explanatory variables in the regression. In determining whether certain variables should be included, we conducted likelihood ratio (LR) tests for each set of these variables. The LR test evaluates whether the maximized log-likelihood for the restricted model (LnL_R) is significantly less than that from the unrestricted model (LnL_{max}), the restriction being the exclusion of the variables tested.[37] That is, if ($LnL_R - LnL_{max}$) is significantly different from zero, it means that by including the variables being tested, the overall significance of the model increases, and those variables should be included in the model. The results of separate LR tests on education, race, and foreign-born population suggest that these variables should not be included in our regression. Stated differently, the statistical test suggests that after controlling for other factors, such as income and urban location, there is no discrimination in the provision of advanced services to minority households.

Table 11.2
Model A

Logit estimates		Number of obs = 287		
		chi2(7)	= 193.840	
		Prob > chi2	= 0.000	
Log likelihood = −39.215		Pseudo R2	= 0.712	

AVAIL	Coef.	Std. err.	z	P > |z|
DENLINE1	0.001	0.001	1.780	0.075
PCTURBHU*	1.941	1.313	1.478	0.139
MEDYRBLT	0.060	0.038	1.575	0.115
MEDHHINC	0.000	0.000	2.002	0.045
TOT_CHG	−0.012	0.004	−3.105	0.002
MISSTOT	0.010	0.003	3.155	0.002
P_A13	−33.932	17.704	−1.917	0.055
P_A1418	23.300	40.915	0.569	0.569
P_A1924	6.930	12.104	0.573	0.567
P_A2529	22.508	27.305	0.824	0.410
P_A3034	69.154	27.213	2.541	0.011
P_A3539	−62.002	37.476	−1.654	0.098
P_A4049	24.986	25.717	0.972	0.331
Constant	−122.515	74.381	−1.647	0.100

Variable	Marginal effect	Marginal effect on 100% scale	Mean of X
DENLINE1	0.000	0.001	516.196
PCTURBHU	0.019	1.906	0.235
MEDYRBLT	0.001	0.059	1959.493
MEDHHINC	0.000	0.000	26031.356
TOT_CHG	0.000	−0.012	514.403
MISSTOT	0.000	0.010	295.913
P_A13**	−0.333	−33.328	0.210
P_A1418	0.229	22.885	0.069
P_A1924	0.068	6.807	0.068
P_A2529	0.221	22.107	0.074
P_A3034	0.679	67.923	0.082
P_A3539	−0.609	−60.899	0.080
P_A4049	0.245	24.541	0.124
Constant	−1.203	−120.334	

Notes: * The value that the "percent urban" can take on is within the range 0.00 to 1.00. If PCTURBHU = 0.23, it means that 23% of the households in the wire center area live in an urbanized area.
** The value that the age variables can take on is within the range 0.00 to 1.00. If P_A3034 = 0.08, it means that 8% of the population in the wire center area belong to the age group.

One demographic factor that we included in the model is age. The coefficients suggest that the higher the percentage of persons in the 30–34 age group, the more likely that advanced services are available.

When the RBOC dummy is added to the regression, the coefficient is positive but insignificant. We also tried a specification with the set of dummies representing the individual RBOCs; the coefficients have different signs for the different RBOCs, but all are insignificant. As a last check, a LR test is done testing the joint significance of these dummies, and the results suggest that we should leave them out of the regression. These statistical tests suggest that residential customers in areas served by RBOCs, all else equal, are equally likely to have high-speed access to the Internet as customers served by independent telephone companies.

The percent of households without telephone service is not significant in any of our models. This is expected because there is not a lot of variation in this variable. For our sample of 287 wire centers, the mean value for this variable is 93%, suggesting that very few households are actually without telephone service. We did not include this variable in our preferred model. Line density is included instead of "number of access lines" because the two variables are highly correlated, and line density seems to be less correlated with other explanatory variables. For our preferred model, the pseudo R^2 is 0.712, a high value for cross-section analysis. This statistic suggests that approximately 71% of the variation in the dependent variable is being explained by our model specification. The model chi-square is 193.84, suggesting that our model is highly statistically significant.

Marginal effects evaluated at the mean are shown at the bottom of table 11.2. The age variables seem to have the largest effect on availability, but it is important to note that the value that the age variables can take on is within the range 0.00 to 1.00. If P_A3034 = 0.08, it means that 8% of the population in the wire center belong to the age group. Taking this into account by rescaling, the age coefficient on P_A3034 really suggests that, at the mean, a one-point increase in the percent of persons belonging to the 30–34 age range would increase AVAIL by 0.0067, which means that on a 100% scale, it increases the likelihood of service availability by 0.67 percentage point.

Similar rescaling needs to be done for the effect of "percent urban", which also ranges from 0.00 to 1.00. After rescaling, a one-point increase in the percent of persons in urbanized area would increase AVAIL by 0.00019, and on a 100% scale, it increases the likelihood of service availability by 0.019 percentage point.

The interpretation of the marginal effects of the other variables is more straightforward. A one-unit increase in the line density of the wire center increases the likelihood of service availability by 0.001 percentage point on a 100% scale. On a 100% scale, the marginal effect of a $1 increase in median household income on service availability seems insignificantly small. But if we change the scale and look at the effect of a $1,000 increase in median income on service availability, then the marginal effect needs to be multiplied by 1000. The result is that, at the mean, a $1,000 increase in median income increases the likelihood of service availability by 0.11 percentage point on a 100% scale. Similarly, a $10,000 increase in median income would increase the likelihood of service availability by 1.1 percentage points.

A $1 increase in the monthly cost of transport, the cost of connecting to an Internet backbone, would decrease the likelihood of service availability by 0.012 percentage point on a 100% scale. A $10 increase in this cost will decrease the likelihood of service availability by 0.12 percentage point on a 100% scale, and a $100 increase in this cost will decrease the likelihood of service availability by 1.2 percentage points on a 100% scale.

Table 11.3 shows the results for Model B, where the dependent variable is DSL, which takes on the value of 1 if DSL service is available in the wire center area and 0 otherwise. This contrasts with Model A whose dependent variable is AVAIL. AVAIL includes both DSL and cable modem service availability. Results for Model B are not much different from Model A, except for the coefficients on income and the age variables. The coefficient on median income is positive but *not* significant. Also, the marginal effects on the age variables are much smaller than those in Model A. A LR test is done for the age variables and the results suggest that for this model, we should exclude the age variables.

In table 11.4, the results of Model C are shown. The age variables are excluded, and the income coefficient becomes significant again. Comparing Model C to Model A, the results are similar, but the marginal effects for all the variables are smaller in Model C than in Model A. In other words, at the mean, the effects of these factors on DSL availability are less than on DSL and cable modem availability.

Table 11.3
Model B

Logit estimates		Number of obs = 287		
		chi2(7)	= 188.030	
		Prob > chi2	= 0.000	
Log likelihood = −29.811		Pseudo R2	= 0.759	

DSL	Coef.	Std. err.	z	P > |z|
DENLINE1	0.001	0.000	1.728	0.084
PCTURBHU*	2.872	1.548	1.856	0.063
MEDYRBLT	0.035	0.041	0.856	0.392
MEDHHINC	0.000	0.000	1.220	0.223
TOT_CHG	−0.009	0.004	−2.231	0.026
MISSTOT	−0.006	0.008	−0.688	0.491
P_A13**	−2.097	17.854	−0.117	0.906
P_A1418	−45.476	54.010	−0.842	0.400
P_A1924	4.309	13.444	0.321	0.749
P_A2529	−23.272	31.198	−0.746	0.456
P_A3034	64.676	37.081	1.744	0.081
P_A3539	−28.439	42.284	−0.673	0.501
P_A4049	33.419	33.982	0.983	0.325
Constant	−76.256	81.364	−0.937	0.349

Variable	Marginal effect	Marginal effect on 100% scale	Mean of X
DENLINE1	0.000	0.000	516.196
PCTURBHU	0.001	0.092	0.235
MEDYRBLT	0.000	0.001	1959.493
MEDHHINC	0.000	0.000	26031.356
TOT_CHG	0.000	0.000	514.403
MISSTOT	0.000	0.000	295.913
P_A13	−0.001	−0.067	0.210
P_A1418	−0.015	−1.459	0.069
P_A1924	0.001	0.138	0.068
P_A2529	−0.007	−0.746	0.074
P_A3034	0.021	2.074	0.082
P_A3539	−0.009	−0.912	0.080
P_A4049	0.011	1.072	0.124
Constant	−0.024	−2.446	

Notes: * The value that the "percent urban" can take on is within the range 0.00 to 1.00. If PCTURBHU = 0.23, it means that 23% of the households in the wire center area live in an urbanized area.

** The value that the age variables can take on is within the range 0.00 to 1.00. If P_A3034 = 0.08, it means that 8% of the population in the wire center area belong to the age group.

Table 11.4
Model C

Logit estimates		Number of obs = 287			
		chi2(7)	= 182.860		
		Prob > chi2	= 0.000		
Log likelihood = −32.392		Pseudo R2	= 0.738		

DSLFIN	Coef.	Std. err.	z		P > |z|
DENLINE1	0.001	0.000	1.694		0.090
PCTURBHU*	2.683	1.155	2.323		0.020
MEDYRBLT	0.030	0.036	0.825		0.409
MEDHHINC	0.000	0.000	3.811		0.000
TOT_CHG	−0.008	0.004	−2.261		0.024
MISSTOT	−0.004	0.006	−0.626		0.531
Constant	−64.593	71.301	−0.906		0.365

Variable	Marginal effect	Marginal effect on 100% scale	Mean of X
DENLINE1	0.000	0.000	516.196
PCTURBHU	0.003	0.307	0.235
MEDYRBLT	0.000	0.003	1959.493
MEDHHINC	0.000	0.000	26031.356
TOT_CHG	0.000	−0.001	514.403
MISSTOT	0.000	0.000	295.913
Constant	−0.074	−7.382	

Notes: * The value that the "percent urban" can take on is within the range 0.00 to 1.00. If PCTURBHU = 0.23, it means that 23% of the households in the wire center area live in an urbanized area.

Policy Implications

The objective of Section 706 of the Telecommunications Act of 1996 is to encourage deployment of advanced telecommunications capabilities (ATCs)[38] "on a reasonable and timely basis ... to all Americans." Specifically, Section 706(a) states:

The Commission and each [s]tate commission with regulatory jurisdiction ... shall encourage the deployment on a reasonable and timely basis of advanced telecommunications capability to all Americans (including, in particular, elementary and secondary schools and classrooms) by utilizing, in a manner consistent with the public interest, convenience, and necessity, price cap regulation, regulatory forbearance, measures that promote competition ... [or] ... that remove barriers to infrastructure investment.[39]

The Section encourages the participation of both the Federal Communications Commission (FCC) and state public utility commissions (PUCs) to ensure that its pro-competitive and deregulatory strategy is appropriately implemented. Removing barriers to infrastructure investment is emphasized as a way to accelerate private sector deployment of advanced telecommunications capabilities. Underlying this deregulatory strategy is the basic assumption that competitive market forces will produce the most efficient economic outcome. However, as is common in most markets, the government still plays a role in correcting for market failures. In the case of advanced telecommunications services, our research suggests that at this early stage of the industry, we are far from achieving the goal of ubiquitous access for all Americans. Specifically, we found evidence that advanced telecommunications service is not being deployed in low-income and rural areas. Hence, government intervention may be necessary in order to achieve the goal of Section 706. If indeed the market has failed and government intervention is necessary, different approaches have been proposed to address the problem.

Tax Incentives

To promote advanced capabilities, tax incentives could be used to encourage technology deployment. Implementing such a program would require that the size of the tax incentive be appropriately estimated and assigned, that is, the tax incentive should be sufficient to encourage firms to serve underserved markets but not sufficiently large that more funding is provided than is needed. In order to determine this, a government agency would need to create a model that estimates the cost of providing advanced services, and proceedings similar to those held for the implementation of the universal service program will have to be initiated. The process of establishing the support mechanism for the universal service program took the FCC over three years to complete, and there need to be improvements on what was adopted in November 1999.[40] Creating a cost model suitable for advanced services will prove to be even more complicated than that for universal service. There are at least four ways by which advanced services are provided: xDSL, cable modems, satellite, and fixed wireless. It would be a more time-consuming process to create a model that captures all four technologies, which is necessary to ensure that only minimum support would be required in the future. Taking a long period of time is, however, not acceptable in an industry where technology is changing so rapidly. By the time the model is completed, the industry would likely be introducing new variations of the four types of technologies or using completely new types of technology.

Auctions

An alternative to the provision of tax incentives is an auction, whereby firms state the minimum amount of money that they would require in order to provide high-speed access to the Internet in low-income and rural areas. The auction winner would obtain the rights to provide services in a given geographic area and also receive support for providing those services. Although this approach ensures that the lowest-cost firm will get the contract, there are a few concerns about an auction when applied to the market for advanced telecommunications services.

The government may want to award the right to serve an area to only one supplier. If this were the case, less of a subsidy would be required because a monopoly can more easily recover its investments in the technology over time. This brings up the question of for how long the monopoly is to be granted. The monopoly cannot be a permanent one, because that would be contrary to Congress's goal of promoting competition. But putting a time limit on the monopoly contract would discourage firms from even participating in the auction because there is less assurance that their investments could be completely recovered.

It would be difficult to establish the geographical unit for the auction contract because the different technologies have different potential levels of coverage. For the satellite companies, it makes sense to hold one auction for the 48 contiguous states because their reach is nationwide. But the companies that use the other technologies have smaller footprints that are scattered across the country. Hence, a single auction for all 48 states would not work. This approach could be made feasible for the competitors of the satellite technologies if grand coalitions are allowed to be formed in order to have ubiquitous coverage. But the government would not want to encourage the industry players to form such horizontal coalitions, for they would be contrary to the pro-competitive goal of Congress. Therefore, it is unlikely that one auction could be held for the entire 48 states.

If a smaller geographical unit were to be used, then the cost to the satellite companies of participating in the auction could be raised significantly. Because their market is the entire country, they would incur the administrative costs of participating in auctions for multiple geographical areas. Even if the satellite companies are willing to bear these costs, there is still the question of how the service geographical areas should be defined. Should they be defined as the service territories of the wireless, cable, or the incumbent telephone companies? Choosing one of these would provide some advantage to one of the technologies. This violates the regulatory objective that the support mechanism should be technologically neutral.

Federal policy makers may find the auction approach unattractive for another reason. With auctions, regulators have no control over the outcome. The government officials do not determine the level of support that needs to be provided; rather, the bidding determines the value. The policy makers will probably be uncomfortable with a process where the auction determines the level of support but the policy makers have to create a tax that raises the revenues associated with the outcome of the auction. Also, with the FCC universal service fund, the federal government has a greater opportunity to pass on most of the taxation to the States. The federal government provides support for only 25% of the fund for voice services. For high-speed access to the Internet, a service that the FCC has deemed to be exclusively interstate, arguably the federal government would have to provide 100% of the support. The federal policy makers will likely be unwilling to take on the financial burden associated with the auctions.

Apart from these two proposed regulatory approaches, whether state or federal government is in a better position to address the needs of the country is an important issue. Arguably, the states know their needs for infrastructure investment better than the federal government. If this proposition is true, it is the states that should be determining the need for support, rather than the federal government. On the other hand, the federal government needs to be involved as a mediator that balances the interest of rural states and those states that have no or little need for the creation of such a fund.

Discussion of different regulatory approaches may seem contradictory to the pro-competitive, deregulatory strategy of the Telecommunications Act of 1996. Section 706 states that the government agencies should remove barriers to infrastructure investment in order to speed the deployment of advanced services. But it does not require the agencies to provide any kind of support for these services. There is, however, another section in the 1996 Act that does mention a support require- ment. Section 254 states that the government should provide support for those services that are subscribed to by a majority of telecommunications users. Reading these two sections in conjunction provides a more com- plete and more consistent picture of the 1996 Act.

At the current state of the development of these technologies, we rec- ommend that the government continue to monitor the issue of "ubiqui- tous access for all Americans" and not offer any prescriptive remedy. There is a lot of innovation taking place in this industry that may pro- vide a quick solution to the problem. Given the complications and costs associated with the proposed regulatory approaches, government should hold off providing tax incentives or any other type of support until there is clear evidence of market failure. At this early stage of the industry, it is not clear that there will be a market failure. It is possible that the market is in the process of achieving the goal of Section 706 on its own, with little government intervention, as new technologies become avail- able to make deployment less costly.

Although our research suggests that in the first quarter of 2000, rural and low-income households are less likely to have access to cable modem and xDSL service, this shows only that the technology is being deployed faster in urbanized, high-income areas. It does not, however, provide evi- dence that technology will not be deployed in other areas in the near future. To address this question, we will have to continue to collect data and create a database that will allow us to look at changes in technology deployment over time.

Appendix: Sample Selection—Stratified Sampling

There are 19,928 wire centers in the United States. We determined a sta- tistically valid sample size of 287 using the formula:

$$n = \left[\frac{z\sqrt{p(1-p)}}{e} \right]^2$$

where n = sample size, z = z-value for 95% level of confidence, p = probability that DSL service is available at a central office, and e = acceptable level of error (3%).

Dslreports.com posts a list containing the number of central offices by state and the number of those central offices with DSL. From this, we calculated p, the probability that DSL service is available at a central office in the United States. Based on our objectives of having a sample size where our margin of error was within three percentage points of the population mean ninety-five percent of the time, we determined that we needed a sample size of 286 addresses.

We then needed to select a random sample of this size from the wire centers. We decided that a stratified random sampling method is appropriate because about 75% of all wire centers have fewer than 7,500 access lines. In these small wire centers the fixed cost of providing xDSL service makes it less economical to provide service than in larger central offices. In these small wire centers, there is less of a likelihood that service will be available. Therefore, we divided wire centers into three strata: fewer than 7,500 lines, 7,501–45,000 lines, and more than 45,001 lines.

For the three strata, we selected random samples of 43, 122, and 122 wire centers respectively. These are 15.0%, 42.5%, and 42.5% of the total sample size. Whereas this sampling produces a sample that is not representative of the characteristics of the population of wire centers,[41] we make adjustments in our regression analysis by assigning appropriate weights to wire center in each strata.

The data were collected in February 2000.

Notes

1. We would like to thank StratSoft Inc. for providing in-kind research support for this research project. We would also like to thank Steven Burns and Zeng Yu Chen for their able research assistance.

2. National Telecommunications and Information Administration. *Falling through the Net: Toward Digital Inclusion*, Washington, DC: US Department of Commerce, Oct. 2000. ⟨http://search.ntia.doc.gov/pdf/fttn00.pdf⟩, p. xv.

3. In our study, high-speed, advanced services are available where a customer can obtain either xDSL or cable modem services.

4. For example, the FCC has stated that "[t]he ability of all Americans to access these high-speed, packet-switched networks will likely spur our growth and development as a nation" (Federal Communications Commission. "First Report and Order and Further Notice of Proposed Rulemaking; In the Matters of Deployment of Wireline Services Offering Advanced Telecommunications Capability." FCC 99-48, Washington, DC: Federal Communications Commission, adopted 18 Mar. 1999, released 31 Mar. 1999, p. 5).

5. For example, SBC Communications has announced a $6-billion overhaul of its network, called "Project Pronto," that will allow SBC to provide 80% of its customers broadband access via xDSL technology (Greene, Tim and Denise Pappalardo, "SBC Pushes Toward Converged Net", Network World Fusion News, 10/25/99, ⟨http://www.nwfusion.com/archive/1999/78877 10-25-1999.html⟩). AT&T, through its MediaOne acquisition, is busy rolling out cable modem hookup options to consumers throughout the country.

6. William E. Kennard, *Consumer Choice Through Competition*, Remarks Before the National Association of Telecommunications Officers and Advisors 19th Annual Conference (September 17, 1999). It should be noted that the Federal Communications Commission (FCC) defines broadband as the ability to support a data rate of at least 200K bit/sec, both upstream and downstream. (Johnston, Margret. "11 billion needed for rural broadband upgrade." IDG News Service, 21 June 2000, ⟨http://www.nwfusion.com/news/2000/0621eleven.html⟩.)

7. Federal Communications Commission. "Third Report and Order and Fourth Further Notice of Proposed Rulemaking in CC Docket No. 96-98." *FCC 99-238*, Washington, DC: Federal Communications Commission, released 15 Sept. 1999.

8. Note 2, *supra*, at 5.

9. Federal Communications Commission. "Notice of Proposed Rulemaking and Notice of Inquiry in WT Docket No. 99-217 and Third Further Notice of Proposed Rulemaking in CC Docket No. 96-98." *FCC 99-141*, Washington, DC: Federal Communications Commission, released 7 Jul. 1999.

10. U.S. Congress. Telecommunications Act of 1996 §706(a), 47 U.S.C. 706(a) (1996); see also S. Conf. Rep. No. 104–230, 104th Cong., 2d Sess. at 1 (1996).

11. Federal Communications Commission. "First Report and Order and Further Notice of Proposed Rulemaking; In the Matters of Deployment of Wireline Services Offering Advanced Telecommunications Capability." FCC 99-48, Washington, DC: Federal Communications Commission, adopted 18 Mar. 1999, released 31 Mar. 1999, p. 21.

12. *Id.*, at 17.

13. See, for example, Olbeter, Eric R., and Matt Robison. "Breaking the Backbone: The Impact of Regulation on Internet Infrastructure Deployment." *Iadvance Internet Facts*, 27 Jul. 1999, appendixes A and B.

14. Time-Warner Cable. "In Your Neighborhood." *Time–Warner Cable Website* assessed on 15 Sept. 2000, ⟨http://www.twcnyc.com/rr/maps/man base. html⟩.

15. National Telecommunications and Information Administration. *Falling through the Net: Defining the Digital Divide*. Washington, DC: US Department of Commerce, July 1999, p. 85.

16. National Telecommunications and Information Administration. *Falling through the Net: Toward Digital Inclusion*, Washington, DC: US Department of Commerce, Oct. 2000, p. xvi.

17. Ibid.

18. Ibid., p. xv.

19. Downes, Thomas A. and Shane M. Greenstein. "Do Commercial ISPs Provide Universal Access?" Working Paper for the Fall 1998 Telecommunications Policy and Research Conference, 2 Dec. 1998.

20. U.S. household telephone penetration rate as of December 1998 is estimated at 94.1% (National Telecommunications and Information Administration. *Falling through the Net: Defining the Digital Divide.* Washington, DC: US Department of Commerce, July 1999).

21. Load coils and bridge taps were used to enhance the quality of voice traffic over the copper but are incompatible with DSL, hence need to be removed before DSL can be deployed (Federal Communications Commission. "Deployment of Advanced Telecommunications Capability: Second Report," *CC Docket No. 98-146,* Washington, DC: Federal Communications Commission, August 2000, p. 23.)

22. Ibid., p. 22.

23. Ibid., pp. 19–21.

24. Ibid., pp. 19–20.

25. Approximately one-third of U.S. homes currently have access to at least one high-speed Internet access service (Doyle, Lee. "Broadband to the Home: A Revolution in Internet Access." IDC Opinion January 2000 ⟨http://www.idc.com:8080/EI/content/040600.stm⟩.)

26. National Telecommunications and Information Administration. *Falling through the Net: Toward Digital Inclusion,* Washington, DC: US Department of Commerce, Oct. 2000, p. 22. The term "broadband" is used in this study to include the two most common technologies, Digital Subscriber Line (DSL) and cable modems, as well as such technologies as Integrated Services Digital Network (ISDN). These technologies usually feature broadband capabilities, although some applications or connections may possess speeds lower than the 200 kilobits per second that the Federal Communications Commission defines as broadband (National Telecommunications and Information Administration. *Falling through the Net: Toward Digital Inclusion,* Washington, DC: US Department of Commerce, Oct. 2000, p. 23 footnote 9).

27. Ibid., pp. 24–25.

28. Federal Communications Commission. "FCC Issues Report on the Availability of High-Speed and Advanced Telecommunications Services." *CC Docket No. 98-146,* Washington, DC: Federal Communications Commission, 3 August 2000. Only the press release had been issued. Our data set does not include any information from U.S. territories.

29. National Telecommunications and Information Administration, and Rural Utilities Service. *Advanced Telecommunications in Rural America: The Challenge of Bringing Broadband Service to All Americans,* Washington, DC: National Telecommunications and Information Administration and Rural Utilities Service, Apr. 2000, p. ii.

High-speed access is also available to residential customers through satellites, but this technology only provides one-way broadband service. For example, DirectPC upstream communications is via standard telephone lines and therefore should not be characterized as two-way broadband service.

30. Kinetic Strategies. "Cable Modem Customer Count Reaches 2.7 Million in U.S. and Canada". *Kinetic Strategies Website*, accessed on July 17, 2000. ⟨http://www.kineticstrategies.com/cable count.html⟩.

At this point in time, there are fewer in-service xDSL modems. There were 754,770 DSL lines in service at the end of the first quarter of 2000 (xDSL.com Resources, "TeleChoice DSL Deployment Summary", updated 11/13/00).

31. Since we are modeling the decision to enter a market, it is appropriate to include economic and demographic data as variables that influence the decision to roll out the service in a community. Based on our conversations with network providers, the supplier is unable to observe the level of demand and instead relies on census information to estimate the interest in the service.

32. See, for example, National Telecommunications and Information Administration, and Rural Utilities Service. *Advanced Telecommunications in Rural America: The Challenge of Bringing Broadband Service to All Americans*, Washington, DC: National Telecommunications and Information Administration and Rural Utilities Service, Apr. 2000, p. 9.

33. U.S. Congress. Telecommunications Act of 1996, Pub. L. No. 104-104, 110 Stat. 56 (1996) (codified at scattered sections of 47 U.S.C.). See especially § 276.

34. In the Appendix we describe the method used to establish the sample size.

35. A wire center is the building in which one or more local switching systems are installed and where the outside lines leading to customer premises are connected to the switching equipment.

36. In subsequent research we will test to see if unregulated cable companies, relative to the regulated telecommunications industry, are more or less likely to provide broadband services.

37. Kennedy, Peter. *A Guide to Econometrics, Third Edition*, Cambridge, MA: The MIT Press, 1993, pp. 61–62.

38. U.S. Congress. Telecommunications Act of 1996, Pub. L. No. 104-104, section 706(c), 110 Stat. 153. ADVANCED TELECOMMUNICATIONS CAPABILITY.—The term "advanced telecommunications capability" is defined, without regard to any transmission media or technology, as high-speed, switched, broadband telecommunications capability that enables users to originate and receive high-quality voice, data, graphics, and video telecommunications using any technology.

39. U.S. Congress. Telecommunications Act of 1996, Pub. L. No. 104-104, section 706(a), 110 Stat. 153.

40. Federal Communications Commission. "Federal-State Joint Board On Universal Service To Convene An Open Meeting On Wednesday." *CC Docket No. 96-45*, Washington, DC: Federal Communications Commission, released 29 Jul. 1998.

41. The unit of the observation is the wire center because we are modeling the investment decisions of firms. Providers of xDSL service install the technology in wire centers and therefore this is the correct unit of observation for the modeling of xDSL technology. For cable modems, the unit used for investment decisions is not observable. As shown by the map of Manhattan, the geographical unit considered for investments is clearly not the city nor the borough. To the best of our knowledge, there is no publicly available data that identify at a finer level of detail the geographic area that cable companies consider when they decide whether to offer cable modem service. Nevertheless, the economic and demographic characteristics of a wire center should not be radically different from the similar characteristics of a cable company's service territory.

12

Re-Examining the Digital Divide

Benjamin M. Compaine

Disraeli observed that "as a general rule the most successful man in life is he who has the best information."[1] In an information-intensive economy, not having access to this information may be considered to be a handicap. According to some versions of the scenario, those who have access will further their distance from those who do not.

The "digital divide" popularly refers to the perceived gap between those who have access to the latest information technologies and those who do not. It has been applied to differences within a society, such as the United States.[2] It may also be applied to differences between developed and developing or underdeveloped countries.[3] Although there is some commonality between the two applications of the term, there are significant differences in policy responses and well as players and stakeholders. This paper refers to differences within the United States.

The topic of what should be public and private responses to the digital divide has taken precedence over what is or should be measured in determining a divide. But only by first addressing the latter can policy makers substantively debate whether there is indeed a chronic divide or simply a short-term gap that, like television or VCRs, will quickly disappear through natural forces.

The digital divide notion is a new label for a similar concept of the previous generation: information haves and have-nots. And this concept owes much to an even earlier construct that goes under the universal service rubric. The term "universal service" dates back at least to 1907 when Theodore Vail, then president of AT&T, used the phrase to refer to his desire to interconnect the highly fragmented local telephone companies into a single nationally interconnected system. The universal service provider would be AT&T.[4] The more modern concept of universal service was that of providing telephone service for everyone. That redefinition can be traced to the Communications Act of 1934, which directed the newly created Federal Communications Commission (FCC) to "make available, so far a possible, to all people of the United States, a rapid, efficient, nationwide and world-wide wire and radio communication service with adequate facilities and reasonable charges."[5] Notions of the federal government being responsible for providing digital access to all Americans are therefore derived as an extension of the "telephone gap" of the 1930s. It ultimately led to the phenomenon of nationwide averaging of telephone rates. That is, residential phone users paid roughly the same for a given level of local telephone service, regardless of the cost of providing that service. Thus, residential users in communities that were relatively inexpensive to serve, such as high-density urban areas where there may be hundreds or even thousands of subscribers in a square mile, were generally charged more by the phone companies—with the urging and blessing of the state regulators—than the cost of providing the service. This excessive "profit" helped subsidize subscribers in low-density areas, such as suburban and rural areas. Here there might be dozens or fewer subscribers in square mile.

What Are the Stakes in the Digital Divide?

Whether one buys in to the notion of a digital divide with substantial societal consequences is not of simply intellectual curiosity. It has very substantial economic and political implications from the taxes on telephone service that are targeted to fund remedies in rural areas and poor neighborhoods to the broader skills that will be available in the work force. When former President Clinton asked Congress for $50 million to provide computers and Internet access for poor families in his State of the Union address in 2000, that had political ramifications,[6] as did his proposal for $2 billion in tax incentives for digital-divide-inspired programs.[7] When the chairman of the Federal Communications Commission makes proposals to Congress and his fellow commissioners for legislation and rules, that is a political process.[8] Clearly the political players have raised the stakes.

This filters down to the costs. The specific costs are those taxes on telephone bills that are earmarked for digital divide subsidies. This includes the Universal Service Fund Fee, a charge to telephone companies that they typically pass on to their customers. As of April 2000, MCI, for example, was adding a 10% surcharge to the bills of its interexchange phone customers. In 2000, the FCC was requiring telecommunications carriers to contribute nearly 6% of their interstate and international calling revenues to subsidize schools and rural areas, an amount well in excess of $4 billion.[9] The economic stakes are considerable.

There are the human stakes. Access to the information available from networked devices may be critical in the education process—for both teachers and students. It could be useful in finding and improving jobs. It is already part of the routine of everyday life. But will the stakes be as high as some prognosticators proclaim? FCC chairman Kennard wrote "The high-skilled, well-paid jobs of tomorrow demand the ability to use computer and telecommunications."[10]

The Boundaries of the Digital Divide

The digital divide also has changing connotations. In the original iteration of the National Telecommunications and Information Agency (NTIA) survey[11] it meant primarily personal computer ownership. In follow-up surveys it has come to incorporate Internet access.[12] By 2000 it seemed to incorporate high-speed (broadband) access from slower dial-up modem access. In effect, it may be a moving target.

The term "digital divide" achieved mass media attention when it became part of the title of the second NTIA survey in 1998. Donna Hoffman and Thomas Novak credit Lloyd Morrisett, at the time president of the Markle Foundation, with coining the term.[13]

Although the goal of universal service was to make access to a dial tone affordable to all, it was never extended to incorporate subsidies for the actual *use* of the telephone. That is, long-distance calls were, until well after the breakup of AT&T in 1984, priced well above cost to further help subsidize local basic service. Information that could be accessed by phone—from time and weather to pay-per-call services such as 900-exchange calls—were not part of the universal service contract. But the digital divide debate has included some component of the cost of information that could be available online.

Thus there is the question of whether the cost of *information* should be part of the policy debate of the digital divide. If in fact there is a disadvantaged population on the short end of the divide, is providing hardware and access enough? Or should there be a provision to, in effect, subsidize the digital equivalent of newspapers, magazines and books? If so, where would one draw the line between information and entertainment? Much of what is available on cable and DBS, on newsstands and online, is reasonably characterized as content for entertainment. If public policy makers wanted to make content available to some disadvantaged groups, should they or could they differentiate between public affairs that might be useful to the body politic and the digital equivalent of "Beverly Hillbillies" reruns?

Evolution of the Issue

Before there was a "digital divide" issue there was the "information haves and the have-nots" issue. Commentators started making references to a need for access to personal computers almost as soon as the first school anywhere installed an Apple II in 1980. By 1983 a survey found that two-thirds of the schools in the wealthiest school districts had personal computers, compared to two-fifths in the poorest districts.[14]

The first high-profile survey by the federal government to address the have and have-not issue was initiated in 1994 by the NTIA within the U.S. Department of Commerce.[15] That was the year in which the World Wide Web got its first national attention, as Netscape commercialized an early graphical interface, the Mosaic browser. Although the Internet traces it origins to 1968 and the World Wide Web to 1991, they remained the relatively obscure preserve of academics and defense contractors until the graphical browsers made the Web user-friendly. Thus, it is not surprising that the NTIA I survey, "Falling through the Net," all but ignored Internet access. "Net" referred to the safety net, not the Internet. "Internet" was mentioned twice, once in an endnote to the first reference. The Web was mentioned only in that same endnote. The focus of the survey was on access to telephone service, personal computers, and modems. In 1994, PCs with modems were for the most part still used to connect to proprietary online services, such as CompuServe, Prodigy, and America Online.

NTIA I reported that the poorest households had the lowest telephone, computer, and modem penetration. But it further subdivided the poor by where they lived: rural, central city and urban, as well as by racial and ethnic group, age, and education. There were a few noteworthy twists for those willing to mine the data. One was that telephone penetration was higher among the rural poor than among the central-city poor. The paradox is that telephone rate cross subsidies have long been aimed at "overcharging" urban subscribers to subsidize rural subscribers, regardless of income.

Hoffman and Novak focused on the most recent Web users.[16] Among their findings was that there were few, if any, differences between whites and African Americans. They also noted that rates of cable and satellite dish penetration among African Americans was increasing dramatically, making that group better prospects than whites for high-speed Internet access.

The NTIA III report, "Falling through the Net: Defining the Digital Divide," found that although penetration rates for computers and Internet access had risen across all demographic groups and geographic areas, "penetration levels currently differ—often substantially—according to income, education level, race, household type, and geography, among other demographic characteristics."[17] Though not reported in the text, the data did suggest that the rates of computer and Internet access were increasing most rapidly among those groups that were most prominently on the negative side of the "divide" in its previous studies.

Neither the NTIA studies nor those of Hoffman and Novak used statistical measures to determine the significance of the differences in their findings among groups. They have not employed analysis of variance or similar measures that can help factor out the spurious from the valid factors (e.g., ethnicity, income, education, age, gender, etc.) that can help us know which factors really matter.

In 1999 about 6% of household did not have wired telephone service.[18] But the reason for not having basic service is not always purely economic. With various subsidies that make it possible to have phone service for as low as $4 or $5 monthly, one would reason that there is little excuse not to be at 100% penetration. Schement and Mueller interviewed households without telephone service in a low-income neighborhood of Camden, New Jersey.[19] They found that at least some proportion of these non-subscribers chose not to be connected. In some cases it was because they would prefer to spend their money on the high entertainment value of a more expensive cable subscription than a telephone connection. In other cases it was because they feared they would run up sizeable monthly long-distance bills if the phone were too convenient. They concluded that it was often the use of the telephone beyond basic local service that caused concern, not the cost of access itself. Thus, some gaps may be self-imposed.

In the debate over what should be included in the expanded concept of universal service, Compaine and Weinraub differentiate between access to an infrastructure and access to content.[20] For example, while cross subsidies helped make basic residential dial-tone service priced lower than real cost, they could find no serious proposals to subsidize 900 services that charge for horoscopes or sports scores. They noted that though public funds have made books available in libraries and for many decades subsidized postal rates for magazines, U.S. policy has not provided newspaper or magazine subscriptions nor book purchases for the less well off economically. So in the debate of online access, what, if anything, might be subject to some sort of need-based subsidy: the hardware needed for access (the ability to connect to the Internet) or the cost of services available online?

The Current Study

The sum of the historical context of the recent surveys documenting a digital divide is often unclear about what services or substance is involved in determining any "divide." Nor is it always clear what the fault line is for a divide: income, ethnicity or race, gender, all of these, any of these? Even the oft-cited NTIA reports include data that run counter to their basic conclusions in that the groups that had the largest gaps are catching up, based on the rate of change in Internet access.

Technologies in general and information technologies in particular are being developed and implemented at historically unprecedented levels. Those who are motivated to learn about the impact of information technology quickly discover the mantra: smaller, faster, cheaper, better. That is, anything touched by silicon—the raw material of computer chips—has been impacted by Moore's Law since the development of the microprocessor.

What much of the research data lacks in the attempted documentation of a digital divide is recognition of the consequences of the forces and trends shaping the information landscape, particularly the economics of the Internet and computers. The next part of this paper addresses this particular gap.

The Economics of Online Access: In Brief

The economics of online involve the consumer's capital cost—equipment and its upkeep—and the operating costs—subscription and connection fees. Sociocultural factors address the McLuhanesque nature of screens versus paper, keyboards or dictation versus pens and pencils. The two have some relationship: if wireless connections and paper-like reading devices are economical (we know they are technologically feasible), then some of the sociocultural nuances could be diminished.

This chapter highlights the economics of online to suggest where the technology could go next. For some discussion of the social and cultural nature of online, see Compaine's "The New Literacy" as well as the work of Sherry Turkle, among others.[21]

Consumer Costs

There is a cost to consumers even when the content is "free." Users must pay, in some form, for any information they access via the media. For broadcast television and radio, the direct cost is periodic investment in television and radio receivers, antenna, and occasional repairs.[22] Readers, listeners, and viewers must subscribe to newspapers and magazines, purchase books and records, subscribe to cable, rent videos or a pay-per-view showing. Table 12.1 identifies examples of the monthly costs of some of these media. Consumer spending on media was estimated to be an average of more than $49 per month per person in 1999, not including online access.[23]

The average household had 2.4 television sets and 5.6 radios in 1996.[24] More than 84% of households had videocassette players, four times the penetration of 10 years earlier.[25] Overall, consumers increased the

Table 12.1
Monthly and capital cost of traditional media, 1999–2000

Medium	Monthly Cost	Capital Cost
Daily newspaper subscription:		
Atlanta Journal & Constitution	$17	$0.00
Pottstown Mercury (PA)	14	
The Wall Street Journal	15	
USA Today	10	
Cable television, standard tier:	$31 (1998 national ave.)	$250 (per 27″ TV set)
Home Box Office	9.95	
Pay per view movie	3.95	
Pay per view special event	19.95 and up	
Direct broadcast satellite:	$29.99 (2000 DirecTV Total Choice)	$0–$99 for dish and one receiver
		$250 (per 27″ TV set)
Books:		
Bag of Bones, Stephen King	$28 list, $19.60 discount	$0.00
Technologies of Freedom, Pool	16.50 (paper)	
Silver Palate Cookbook	$25 list, $17.47 discount	
U.S. Statistical Abstract	$50 (paper)	
Babe—The Gallant Pig	$5 list, $4 discount	
Magazine subscription:		
PC Magazine	$2.90 (2 issues)	$0.00
Fortune	5.00 (2 issues)	
The Atlantic Monthly	1.25 (1 issue)	
Time	4.30 (4.3 issues)	
Consumer Reports	2.00 (1 issue)	
Avg. total per consumer spending on all media	$49.43	

Sources: Newspapers—From each newspaper's Web site, February 10, 1999, Cable—Seth Schiesel, "FCC Notes Lack of Cable TV Competition," *The New York Times Interactive*, January 14, 1998. Magazines—from Web sites, Feb 11, 1999. Books—from Amazon.com, February 10, 1999. DBS—from DirecTV price list at Web site, May 3, 2000, and *Parade* magazine ad for Dish Network, May 7, 2000; Hardware cost—from Best Buy advertisement, May 7, 2000. Total per consumer: See note 16.

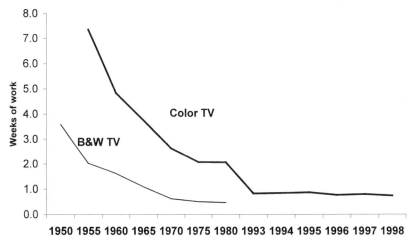

Figure 12.1
Cost of television sets, selected years, 1950–1998. Sources: Television set prices, 1950–1976: Christopher Sterling and Timothy Haight, *The Mass Media: Aspen Institute Guide to Communications Industry Trends*, New York: Praeger Publishers, 1978) pp. 360–362. 1979–83: *U.S. Statistical Abstract*, 1985, p. 777, from Merchandising, 62nd Annual Statistical and Marketing Report. 1993–1996: U.S. Bureau of the Census, *Current Industrial Reports, Manufacturing Profiles*, annual. Wages: U.S. Bureau of Labor Statistics, *Employment and Earnings*.

proportion of their personal consumption expenditures on media from 2.5% in 1980 to 2.9% in 1996.[26]

Just as consumers had to buy radios, phonographs, televisions and VCRs to make use of previous waves of new media technologies, to make use of online media they must have access to other devices. Initially these were personal computers but supplemented by less expensive options such as dedicated TV set-top boxes. One brand was WebTV, a Microsoft subsidiary that used the TV set as the display.[27] Another option is the Web appliances, Web browsing and e-mail devices that sold for about $499 from a variety of vendors such as Compaq and Gateway.[28] From home, consumers must have telecommunications access to the Internet, via a telephone line, cable wire, or wireless.

Figure 12.1 looks at the costs of television sets from 1950 to 1998. The measurement is in number of weeks of work at the average weekly pay for private-sector wage earners. In essence, it shows that the first television sets were expensive: equal to 3.6 weeks of earnings. By the late

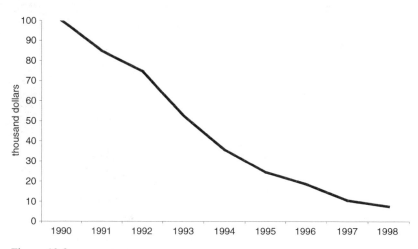

Figure 12.2
Cost of MIPS, 1990–1998. Source: Eva Freeman, "No More Gold-Plated MIPS: Mainframes and Distributed Systems Converge," *Datamation*, March 1998. Data from Hitachi Data Systems.

1990s, the cost had declined to under four days of work. Meanwhile, the quality improved as well. From 9″ black and white screens with high-maintenance tubes to 27″ and larger solid-state color and remote control, the cost by any measure fell continuously and substantially throughout the decades.

The cost of the hardware associated with online information has followed even a steeper declining curve. Figure 12.2 charts one of the measures of computer costs over the decade of the 1990s, the decline in computer processing costs. It is consistent with Moore's Law.[29] Moore's observation described a trend that has been maintained for at least 35 years. It is the basis for many planners' performance forecasts. In 26 years the number of transistors on a chip had increased more than 3,200 times, from 2,300 on the Intel 4004 in 1971 to 7.5 million on the Intel Pentium-II processor that was the standard in 1999.[30] Meanwhile, other components also decreased in cost while increasing in capacity: mass storage, modems, CD-ROMs drives, even monitors. Between 1996 and 1998 alone, the retail cost of personal computers fell nearly 23% annually.[31] This brought the retail price of Web-ready full-featured (for that date) personal computers to about $600, or about 1.4 weeks of average weekly earnings. This was a level not reached for color television sets until the mid-1980s. By 1999 multiple vendors offered Web-enabled PCs free. They were provided in return for recipients providing personal demographic information or willingness to be exposed to added advertising as they use the Web,[32] or are provided to consumers willing to sign a long-term contract with an Internet Service Provider.[33]

Table 12.2 shows examples of the costs associated with access to the Internet in 1999. Based on historical trends, the capital cost of hardware is likely to continue to decrease in both current and real dollar terms, as is the cost of access fees. The cost of information is likely to stay constant or decrease as the audience online expands.

Adoption of Technologies

Figure 12.3 compares the rate of Internet adoption to other popular technology-created goods and services, including the personal computer. It is based on the "invention" date of the graphical browser rather than the initial implementation of ARPANet, the predecessor of the Internet. The rate of adoption for the Internet and PCs is historically unprecedented compared to radio, television, VCRs, or microwave ovens. Of the 11 products in figure 12.3, two (electrification and telephone) relied on direct government programs to targeted populations to help with those on the margin.

Factors in Internet and PC Adoption Rate

The rate of adoption of personal computers and the Internet has been stimulated by at least five trends: rapidly declining costs and increasing power of the hardware; improving ease of use; increasing availability of points of presence (POPs) for local Internet Service provider access; decreasing cost of Internet access; and network externalities associated with e-mail and chat.

Rapidly Declining Costs and Increasing Power of the Hardware
Figure 12.2 best measures this phenomenon based on the cost of computer capabilities. The difficulty in directly graphing the decline in computer cost alone is that capabilities and features have been increasing while absolute prices have declined.

For example, an Apple II+ personal computer with an 8-bit central processing unit (CPU), running at 1 mHz, with 64 kb of memory, two floppy drives that each stored about 160,000 bits and a crude monochrome

Table 12.2
Capital and operational costs for consumer Internet access, 2000

Access device	Street cost
Personal computer*	$848
Dedicated Web device**	$129
Dedicated e-mail device***	$100

Internet Service Providers	Monthly cost
America Online	$21.95 unlimited use
	19.95 with annual contract
	4.95 for 3 hours + 2.50/hour
juno.com	$0, basic service
	8.95, premium service
MediaOne.Net—cable	29.95 unlimited for cable subscribers
	39.95 for non-cable subscribers
Telocity 640kps DSL	$49.95, free modem
Telephone charges	Varies depending on service level and location. None if using flat-rate (nonmeasured) service to local POP. May be one to two cents per minute for measured service or more for more distant POP.

Internet-accessed Content Providers	Monthly cost
The Atlanta Journal-Constitution online	$0.00
The Mercury (Pottstown, PA)	0.00
The Wall Street Journal Interactive	5.00
USA Today online	0.00
ZDNet (includes PC Magazine and others)	0.00
U.S. Statistical Abstract	0.00
Consumer Reports	2.00
Time, Fortune, Newsweek	0.00

Notes: * HP Brio 200, 64 mb with CDROM, 56K modem, 15″ monitor. *PC Connection* catalog, v. 221, April 2000.
** WebTV, with keyboard, www.rca.com. March 6, 2001.
*** Mailstation. Monthly access was $8.33 on annual contract. ⟨http://www.mailstation.com⟩, August 11, 2000.

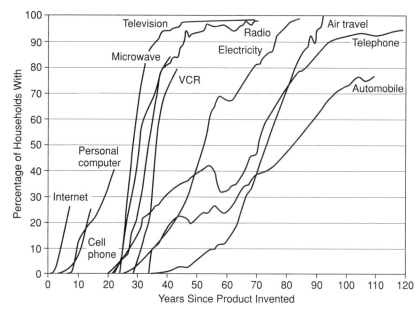

Figure 12.3
Rate of household adoption of selected products (years since invention). Source: W. Michael Cox and Richard Alm, *Myths of Rich and Poor* (New York: Basic Books, 1999), p. 162.

monitor, sold in 1981 for about $3000.[34] A 300-baud modem added later cost $300. Word processing and the VisiCalc spreadsheet were the two useful applications.

In 2000, $1700 bought a personal computer running a 32-bit Pentium-III CPU at 800 mHz, with 128 mb (that's 2000 times more memory), 13.6 gb of hard disk storage, a 17″ high-resolution color monitor, a 56 kps modem and a host of other features that did not even exist for PCs in 1981: sound and speakers, 100 mb removable mass storage, CD drive, and so on.[35]

This is the high end and far more than most households need. Dell Computer, for example, offered a quite capable PC system for $779 that included a year of Internet access as well as Microsoft word processing and spreadsheet software. As has been noted previously, various special-ized devices for Web only or dedicated e-mail use became available for as low as $99. There is every reason to expect the declining cost curve to continue in hardware.

Improved Ease of Use, via Apple Macintosh and Microsoft Windows
"Point-and-Click" Operating Systems
Before the graphical user interface (GUI), operating a PC took a certain
determination and level of learning that most casual users found to be on
the losing end of the cost-benefit equation. The breakthrough of point-
and-click, first developed by Xerox and then implemented in the Apple
Macintosh and later Microsoft Windows, greatly lowered the technical
barriers to entry. Similarly, the original Internet and first iteration of the
World Wide Web were character-based, meaning they required lots of
typing of commands to make things happen. It was not until the Mosaic
browser was popularized by Netscape in 1994 that the Web and with it
the Internet became transparent enough to interest a mass nontechnical
audience.

The next breakthrough in ease of use, just starting to fulfill a long-held
promise, is reliable voice recognition. In 1999 several programs became
available for under $100. Combined with ever more capable computers,
voice recognition will further lower the skill level required to access information, create documents and otherwise perform functions that have
heretofore required some modicum of skill in operating a keyboard and
mouse.

Increasing Availability of Points of Presence (POPs) for Local Internet
Service Provider Access
At the end on 1999 there were 5078 Internet Service Providers in the
United States, up 233 from a year earlier. These were the "on and off
ramps" for the Internet. Among these, 184 were considered "national"
ISPs by virtue having a presence in more than 25 area codes.[36] By the
spring of 1998, barely four years after Netscape introduced the Web to
the mass audience, 92% of the U.S. population had access by a local
phone call to seven or more ISPs. Fewer than 5% had no access by other
than a toll call.[37] As might be expected, the few areas that are underserved tended to be in lower-population—primarily rural—counties.

Decreasing Cost of Internet Access
Only 2.55% of the population lived in counties with three or fewer ISPs,
while more than 85% of the population lived in or adjacent to counties
with 21 or more competitors.[38] Greater competition is generally associated with lower prices and higher quality of services. Meanwhile, several
services have developed business models that offered no charge to con-

sumers. In 2000 these include Juno.com, NetZero.com and Bluelight.com. The latter claims that it offers local access to 96% of the U.S.[39]

In 1996 AT&T Worldnet introduced the first flat-rate unlimited-use consumer ISP service for $19.95 per month. Previously most services, such as America Online, charged about $9.95 for only five hours of use, then a per-hour rate, typically $2.50. After Worldnet, most services followed suit at similar prices. Popular services charged $20–22 per month in 2000, with some as low as $8.95, as well the advertiser-supported free services. Discounts of 10% or more were often available for yearly contracts.

Expanding Availability of Broadband Access
As Gabel and Kwan explain in chapter 11, concern is being expressed at the highest policy levels that access to the Internet means not simply dial-up access but high-speed access that allows the Internet to be used for quality audio, video, server-based applications, and real-time games played with remote users. Early evidence was that broadband access was initially being provided to higher-income communities. What Gabel and Kwan found in their statistical analysis was exactly what any economist would expect: initial investment did in fact go to high-income or commercial areas that were *also* high density. Thus, rural estate neighborhoods were not being wired at the expense of urban low-income communities; rather, the initial investment was in territories where it was cost-effective. The authors of that research found no racial or ethnic bias. High-income, low-density areas are not the first wired for the same reason as low-income communities: high-density economics. Based on their analysis and observations, they conclude, "It is possible that the market is in the process of achieving the goal" of the deployment of advanced services to all Americans on a reasonable and timely basis "as new technologies become available to make deployment less costly."

Network Externalities Associated with E-mail Utility
Network externalities refer to the increase in value to all users of a network as more users join the network. When only a few businesses and households had telephones, they were of limited value. The postal network, by contrast, was of great value because anyone could reach anyone else. In the early days of e-mail, systems were proprietary. That is, large companies had internal e-mail not connected to the outside world. Online services, such as Prodigy and America Online, had e-mail systems

that allowed exchange only with other members of that service. Thus, e-mail had not been an application that drove many people online.

Whereas in the early 1990s there were roughly 15 million e-mail accounts worldwide, by the end of 1999 there were 569 million.[40] In the United States there were about 333 e-mail boxes. Accounting for multiple accounts and home/household overlap, an estimated 110 million Americans were using e-mail, or 52% of Americans more than 14 years old. This compared to about 7% six or seven years earlier. As the Internet's reach accelerated, consumer demand and commercial practicality quickly forced—or encouraged—the various networks to open their systems to sending and receiving e-mail over the Internet, using standard protocols.

Internet Relay Chat (IRC) has undergone similar growth. IRC is the basis of chat rooms, which allow users to engage in real time text (and increasingly voice) conversation. Like e-mail, the early chat rooms were service-specific, but chat is now available across the Internet, using software that is available free.

Summary of Forces and Trends

Data presented here or in the research cited in this paper support the following conclusions:

• Compared to other technology innovations, there has been unprecedented rapid adoption of the Internet and e-mail between 1994 and 2000 among all strata of the population.
• Many other similar technology-inspired products achieved near-universal adoption without massive government or even private programs, radio, television sets, and VCRs among them.
• Prices for computers and similar devices have been falling constantly and substantially to levels equal to a decent color television set.
• Though services such as telephony and cable have tended to lag behind in adoption rates due to ongoing fees, free Internet access is available using a broadcast TV and radio model in areas that include most of the population.
• Rates of adoption for those groups variously included on the unwired side of the early divide are greater than for the population as a whole.
• Some gaps have already disappeared. For example, from 1994 to 1997 there was high visibility of the gender gap: initially more than two thirds of Internet users were male. By 2000 that gap all but disappeared, as

50.4% of Internet users were women.[41] The gap had simply reflected that early users came from computer science and engineering discipline that were more heavily male.

• Access points are available to nearly all households, often at low cost or no marginal cost (beyond a telephone line). Broadband access, while less pervasive, is being rolled out starting in high-density/high-income areas, with reasonable expectation that it will continue to expand to a broader universe.

• Among those who do have access to computers and the Internet, patterns of use are similar across income, gender, and ethnic lines.

From a policy perspective, there are other reasons the digital divide is less a crisis than a temporary and normal process. The following sections address some of the specific subsets of the digital divide concerns.

Concerns for Rural Users

Surveys such as those from NTIA and Vanderbilt implicitly link "poor" and "rural" together. For decades telephone service prices were adjusted so that rural dwellers paid roughly the same for service as urban dwellers, despite higher cost in servicing the former.

There remain assumptions that rural dwellers need help with networks because they live in low-density, more expensive-to-wire territories. There are, to be sure, poor rural families. But the subsidies in the past also went to middle-class farmers and wealthy ranchers who, when unable to get cable routinely, installed $15,000 satellite dishes. Meanwhile single working mothers in the cities and mom-and-pop store owners paid telephone rates that helped subsidize the rural subscribers.

Although most attention has focused on the higher cost of serving rural areas and the "burden" of charging full cost recovery in the pricing to rural users, policy makers seem to have overlooked factoring in the countervailing economics associated with rural living. These savings, when compared to urban and suburban dwellers, may be ripe for consideration when determining whether continued subsidies for telecommunications are justified and fair.

Phone Service versus Auto Insurance

It is beyond the scope of this paper to compare fully the cost of living in urban and rural areas. It highlights instead a single service that is almost as ubiquitous and of similar economic and cultural importance as

Table 12.3
Auto insurance in three communities, 2000

City/Town and ZIP	Lowest Rate*	Low to High Gap
Philadelphia, PA 19122	$3940	+$3323
Carlisle, PA 17013	1070	+2253
Atchison, KS 66002	617	—

Note: * For identical coverage on 1996 Ford Taurus GL, married male driver, age 50. Used lowest quote if more than one.
Source: ⟨http://www.insuremarket.com⟩, May 4, 2000

Internet access: automobile ownership, in particular the cost of automobile insurance. Assuming that there is general agreement that access to an automobile is at least as important as access to a computer and the Internet, it's meaningful to realize that there are huge real gaps in costs for auto insurance. Table 12.3 shows that a resident of a low-income neighborhood in Philadelphia might pay nearly four times what a resident of the suburban town of Carlisle, Pennsylvania, about 120 miles west of Philadelphia would pay, and more than six times as much as a resident in rural Atchison, Kansas.[42]

It could be rationalized in that the rural residents of Atchison pay less in insurance because there are fewer accidents and auto thefts—that is, the cost of service is lower than in an urban area. This calls into question policy responses for subsidizing Internet access in rural areas because there costs are higher there than in urban areas. Similar gaps may exist in other large-ticket and important items, such as the cost of urban housing compared to rural areas. As a percentage of total household budgets, telecommunications, including cable or DBS fees, would under any scenario be substantially less than items such as housing and auto insurance. Similar reasoning would apply to schools in rural versus urban communities. Expanding this type of analysis would seem appropriate for a more realistic context for deliberating the need—or even direction—for future cross subsidies across gaps.

The Case of Voluntary Nonusers

In the statistics on nonsubscribers to telephone, cable service, PC ownership or Internet connectivity there has been scant attention paid to voluntary nonusers—those who could afford it but choose not to. A study of Hispanic households found that the second most voiced reason for not owning a computer, nearly 40%, was "Don't need." Another 6% had similar reasons—"Too old" or "Not interested."[43] This is generally consistent with a survey conducted by National Public Radio, the Kaiser Foundation and Harvard's Kennedy School of Government. Of those characterizing themselves as being "left behind" in computers, barely 20% blamed cost.[44] A third were just not interested. Mueller and Schement, drawing from interviews with non-telephone subscribers, found households that were willing to pay $20 or more per month for cable but not $6 for a dial tone.[45]

Thus, among the fourth of households that did not subscribe to cable or DBS in 2000, it is reasonable that many, if not most, passed on the opportunity by choice. Some elderly are quite happy watching the existing over-the-air stations and see no need for 85 channel cable options. Other nonsubscribers opt out for many possible reasons: distain for programming, fear that their kids will watch too much, and so on.

There is both anecdotal evidence and increasing statistical verification that large numbers of individuals are voluntary nonparticipants, whom no manner of programs of financing will change until they see the personal value. Further research is needed to help determine an accurate number of those who *want* PCs and Internet access but don't have it because of cost. It is likely to be somewhat smaller than the absolute nonuser number.

Wiring Schools and Libraries

The policy of helping schools and libraries with their education and information missions in light of changing technologies is on more solid historical and policy footing than policies directed at individuals and households. Still, there remain caveats that seem to have been given little attention in the digital divide debate.

Foremost among them is the type of aid that should be given schools and the conditions, if any, that should be attached. Currently, the Universal Service Fund tax on telephone bills is providing billons of dollars earmarked for wiring institutions to the Internet and providing related equipment. With the money available, schools are spending sums for

Table 12.4
Computers and Internet access in school districts based on race and wealth

Measurement criteria:	None	Computers per student:			
		Under 5%*		Over 50%	
		1998	1999	1998	1999
Minority enrollment		5.3	5.0	7.1	6.5
Qualify for free lunch program	4.9			N.A.	6.2

	% Schools with Internet Access:			
	1997	1999	1997	1999
	6% < poverty level		> 29% poverty level	
Poverty-level students	78	94%	59	84

Note: * 0–10% for Internet access
Source: Technology in Education: A Comprehensive Report on the State of Technology in the K–12 Market, Market Data Retrieval, 1999, figs. 16, 17, 40

construction and hard wiring far in excess of what it might take to install an improving breed of wireless technologies.

A study by the Benton Foundation raises questions about how these "E-Rate" funds are being used. There is often not a clear sense of what they will do with their wired buildings. In Cleveland, for example, though the Educational Technology Office has programs to train teachers on computers, it is not coordinated with the Curriculum and Instruction Department, which would be responsible for bringing technology uses into the classroom.[46] And where there is the semblance of a plan, it is often in the absence of a sound pedagogical footing.

Having computers available in the schools is an unassailable necessity, just as is having a school library. That there are differences between the libraries in wealthier school districts and poorer ones has long been a reality as well. However, as seen in table 12.4, by 1999 those differences in Internet connectivity were small and narrowing, at least along minority and income lines. Schools with high minority enrollments (50% or greater) had one computer per 6.5 students, compared to one computer per 5.0 students in schools with under 5% minority enrollment. Results were slightly better when comparing poor students with wealthier ones.

In schools where over 50% of students qualified for the federal free lunch program, there was one computer per 6.2 students, compared to one per 4.9 students in schools with no such students. Thus, a "wealthy" school with 1000 students might have 204 PCs, while the poorest schools of similar size had 161 PCs. That would translate to a potential of about six hours of computer time per student per week available in the wealthiest schools and almost five hours per student in the very poorest.

Table 12.4 further shows that poorer schools were a minimal 10% lower in Internet access in 1999, with 84% of the schools with the poorest students having access compared to 94% of the wealthiest. As significant, the poorer schools are closing the gap rapidly. Between 1997 and 1999 the poorer schools had a 42% improvement in access, compared to half that rate for the wealthiest schools. Moreover, most if not all these improvements came prior to significant expenditures from the E-Rate programs of the Universal Service Fund, indicating they are the result of local budget commitments. There is also reason to conclude that the poorer schools, having been later to the game, are benefiting from lower costs for equipment and the improved performance of PCs compared to those that would have been purchased by the "cutting-edge" schools at higher prices a few years earlier.

Public libraries have long been the preferred societal mechanism for leveling the information access field. As with the schools, district-to-district discrepancies in resources are not a new issue. Acquiring browsing devices, printers, Internet access and subscriptions, online archives, and databases are part of the budgeting process. At some point—if not now—all libraries will have to realize that online access reduces the need for periodical subscriptions and many reference works that accounted for portions of their budgets. The digital library will have to take away allocations that heretofore went to the analog library.

Furthermore, libraries may take advantage of the virtual world by reducing the need for bricks and mortar. Although it may be decades before fiction and biographies become more practical in digital form than as printed books, the increased availability of reference material online should reduce the need for library expansions. Moreover, once digital, it makes no sense to require patrons to come to the library to use a terminal if the same data can be accessed from home connections. The library card of the future may be in the form of a password that gives holders access to the subscriptions the library has. The savings in real estate could thus become available for services for those users who do not have home access. Making these sorts of changes in priorities is not easy after centuries of buildings and books.

In many communities the cost of high-speed access will be covered by cable systems that have been obligated to provide access to libraries, school and other municipal facilities under the terms of their franchise agreements with their municipalities.

As a policy matter, there are or can be mechanisms in place to manage whatever discrepancies remain, primarily at the state level but in federal programs as well. Decisions of how much to spend on hardware, software and training are not new to budgeters. With the declining cost of hardware, increasingly it will be teacher training—and teacher enthusiasm—that can be the focus of the educational policy process as it applies to new learning and teaching approaches.

Policy Issue: Democracy or Entertainment?

Schement characterizes the digital divide debate as a "lively, dynamic and enlightening" process that is one of the joys of democracy.[47] Politicians in particular are prone to wrap their rhetoric on the digital divide in terms of furthering democracy. And in many respects this is a political issue as much as a social one. Typical is the FCC Chairman William Kennard: "Our society is not represented by a chat among a homogeneous few, but rather a democratic chorus of many different voices and divergent views."[48] However, it may be more tenuous to equate access to the Internet or to cable as one on which the republic depends.

Much of this is "déjà vu all over again." Television raised the expectations of many social theorists for education and the political process. The Kennedy–Nixon presidential debates of 1960 seemed to lend some hope for these expectations. But despite television's important roles in forming public opinion during the Vietnam War and creating shared experiences during events such as the O. J. Simpson trial in 1996, for most viewers most of the time it is a source of simple entertainment. Ratings for national network news shows, never high, have been moving steadily down. The all-news cable networks get ratings of 0.5% while special interest networks such as all-public-service all-the-time C-SPAN have even lower viewership. Home shopping shows have higher viewership than public affairs. The old commercial broadcast networks, though way down from their pre-cable peaks, still get 15% or so of households each during prime time. The issue for policy makers: Is it a national policy priority to keep basic cable rates low to provide Americans with "Rug Rats" (a popular children's show in 2000)?

The Internet is similarly a mixed bag. Undoubtedly being connected has its value. But surveys have found that services such as chat rooms (sex is popular), sports, and game-playing top the list of activities. It is wonderful having access to news and finance and diverse opinions from providers who would never have a world-wide audience pre-Internet. But as research repeatedly confirms, once digitally enabled, all groups— by income, ethnicity, gender, and education—fall into almost identical patterns of usage. News and public affairs is way down the list of uses. Connecting those not yet connected will likely result in a continuation of this pattern.

Conclusion

The overwhelming weight of the data, from the NTIA surveys to the Cheskin Research study, all points in a direction that is historically consistent and socially positive. New and expensive technologies have to start somewhere and almost variably that means with two groups: those who find it undeniably useful—often commercial entities—and those who can simply afford it. Similarly, where infrastructure must be built, the provider will start their buildouts aimed at audiences who are most likely to understand the value and be amenable to their service. Again, that typically means a focus on commercial ventures and wealthier residential areas.

The economic advantage of this market-driven self-interest is that it creates an invisible cross subsidy for those who follow. The early adopters pay higher per-unit costs that reflect lower production volumes of manufactured products (such as PCs) or start-up costs of services, such as Internet access via cable system. But as production builds, unit costs decline, product costs decline, and manufacturers are able to lower prices. In the case of personal computer devices, that process is compounded by advances in component technologies such as hard disk drives as "box" manufacturers increase their own output.

The builders of networks—traditional and new telephone, wireless, cable, and even electric distribution players—similarly know that the marginal cost of adding users to a network is low and thus highly profitable. Once the fixed cost of the network has been covered, not only do additional users cost them little to add, but network externalities actually make their service of greater value to current and new customers. Thus they have an incentive to lower price and increase utilization.

Does cost create a barrier? The simple answer is, of course. Any cost is a barrier. The real question is: is this a fatal or unfair barrier, given the standard of living (referring here to the United States, but applicable to societies of similar wealth)? It is, perhaps, a huge testimony to the overall prosperity and well-being of American society at this point in history that an issue such as the digital divide can marshal the attention and commitments it has.

The data are clear that there are households and institutions that are disadvantaged, in information access as in other arenas. It is endemic to the democratic capitalist system and to any other systems that have been tried. By the same token, programs and policies historically have taken the hardest edge off those gaps. But in the past, where goods or services are truly important to people there has been great success in minimizing differences among groups—automobiles, radio, television and cable are examples in this context.

Information access *is* important. But where does it sit among the schedule of other phenomena for which there has been little or no concern about gaps and few advocates who demand government programs to remove them? Having access to an automobile and having a license to operate one was certainly more critical to one's livelihood in the second half of the 20th century than having access to e-mail may be today. And undoubtedly there were gaps between those who could afford an automobile and its ongoing operating expenses and those who could not. Were there studies of income and ethnicity and gender to document the auto have and have-not gap? The policy question is not whether some group of citizens has more of something than another. It is abundantly obvious that that is true and will continue to be true.

The forces and trends summarized in this paper suggest that self-evident forces of declining cost, natural acculturation and growing availability are so far moving quickly in the direction of widespread adoption. At some point before the end of this decade, the declining cost curves and adoption curves will flatten. At that point it will be time to take stock of whether a true divide remains and who is on each side, and then determine what policies can best address the resolution.[49]

Notes

1. Benjamin Disraeli (Earl of Beaconsfield), *Endymion* (London: Longman, Green and Co., 1881), p. 155.

2. "Falling through the Net: Defining the Digital Divide," National Telecommunications and Information Administration, U.S. Department of Commerce, 1999.

3. Calvin Sims, "Group of 8 Pledges to Help Poor Countries," *The New York Times,* July 24, 2000 at ⟨http://www.nytimes.com/library/world/global/072400g8-meeting.html⟩.

4. Thomas G. Krattenmaker, *Telecommunications Law and Policy*, 2nd ed. (Durham, NC: Carolina Academic Press, 1998), p. 350.

5. 47 U.S.C. § 151 (1994).

6. Pamela Mendels, "Internet Access Spreads to More Classrooms, Survey Finds," *The New York Times*, December 1, 1999.

7. Marc Lacey, "Clinton Enlists Help for Plan to Increase Computer Use," *The New York Times*, February 3, 2000.

8. William E. Kennard, "Equality in the Information Age," *Federal Communications Law Journal*, 51: 3, May 1999, at ⟨http://www.law.indiana.edu/fclj/pubs/v51/no3/KenMac1.pdf⟩.

9. Proposed First Quarter 2000 Universal Service Contribution Factor, CC Docket No. 96-45, Public Notice, DA 99-2780 (⟨http://www.fcc.gov/Bureaus/Common_Carrier/Public_Notices/1999/da992780.doc⟩) and Separate Statement of Commissioner Furchtgott-Roth (⟨http://www.fcc.gov/Bureaus/Common_Carrier/Public_Notices/1999/d992780a.doc⟩).

10. Kennard, *op. cit.*, note 8.

11. "Falling through the Net: A Survey of the 'Have Nots' in Rural and Urban America," National Telecommunications and Information Administration, U.S. Dept of Commerce, July 1995, at ⟨http.//www.ntia.doc.gov/ntiahome/fallingthru.html⟩.

12. NTIA, "Falling through the Net," 1999.

13. Donna L. Hoffman and Thomas P. Novak, "The Evolution of the Digital Divide: Examining the Relartionship of Race to Internet Access and Usage Over Time," working paper, May 1999, at ⟨http://www2000.ogsm.vanderbilt.edu/digital.divide.html⟩.

14. "School Uses of Computers—Reports from a National Survey," No. 1, April 1983, The Johns Hopkins University Center for Social Organization of Schools, p. 3.

15. Found at ⟨http://www.ntia.doc.gov/ntiahome/fallingthru.html⟩.

16. D. L. Hoffman and T. P. Novak (1999), *op. cit.*, note 13.

17. "Falling through the Net: Defining the Digital Divide" (NTIA III), ⟨http://www.ntia.doc.gov/ntiahome/fttn99/part1.html⟩, Part I, Section A.

18. NTIA III 1999, Part I, Section B.

19. Milton Mueller and Jorge R. Schement, "Universal Service from the Bottom Up: A Profile of Telecommunications Access in Camden, New Jersey," *The Information Society* 12, 3 (1996), pp. 273–291.

20. Benjamin Compaine and Mitchell Weinraub, "Universal Access to Online Services: An Examination of the Issue," *Telecommunications Policy*, Vol. 21, No. 1 (1997), pp. 15–33.

21. Benjamin M. Compaine, "The New Literacy: or How I Stopped Worrying and Learned to Love Pac-Man," in Benjamin M. Compaine, ed., *Understanding New Media* (Cambridge, MA: Ballinger Publishing Co., 1984); Benjamin M. Compaine, "Information Technology and Cultural Change," in Benjamin M. Compaine, ed., *Issues in New Information Technology* (Norwood, NJ: Ablex Publishing Corporation, 1988). Sherry Turkle, *Life on the Screen: Identity in the Age of the Internet* (New York: Touchstone Books, 1997).

22. Even the programming that is apparently "free" has some cost in the form of marketing costs that are part of the prices we pay for goods and services that advertise. How much that cost really is and how much different prices would be if there were no advertising (and hence less competition and thus hypothetically perhaps *higher* prices for many goods and services) is left to another venue.

23. *Statistical Abstract of the United States, 1999*, p. 580, Table 920. Source of the table is *The Veronis, Suhler & Associates Communications Industry Report*, annual.

24. *Ibid.*, p. 581, Table 921.

25. *Ibid.*

26. Calculated by adding books, newspapers and magazines, video, audio and computer products, radio and TV repair, and motion picture theater admission to personal consumption expenditures. From U.S. Bureau of Economic Analysis data in *The U.S. Statistical Abstract, 1985* and *1998*.

27. John Markoff, "Microsoft Deal to Aid Blending of PCs and TVS," *The New York Times Interactive*, April 7, 1997, at ⟨http://www.nytimes.com/library/cyber/week/040797webtv.html⟩.

28. At ⟨http://www.cnet.com/news/0-1006-2000-5032190.html⟩, March 6, 2001.

29. As the story goes, in 1965 Gordon Moore, a founder of Intel, which has developed most of the central processing units (CPUs) used in personal computers, was preparing a speech. When he started to graph data about the growth in chip performance, he realized there was a striking trend: each new chip contained roughly twice as much capacity as its predecessor, and each chip was released within 18 to 24 months of the previous chip. If this trend continued, he reasoned, computing power would rise exponentially over relatively brief periods of time.

30. "What is Moore's Law?" Intel Corporation, ⟨http://www.intel.com/intel/museum/25anniv/hof/moore.htm⟩. Accessed Feb. 12, 1999.

31. James Padinha, "Taking PC Prices Out of the Equation," TheStreet.Com, February 3, 1999, at ⟨http://www.thestreet.com/comment/economics/713190.html⟩.

32. Don Clark, "Free_PC to Offer Free Computers in Exchange for Exposure to Ads," *The Wall Street Journal Interactive*, February 8, 1999 at ⟨http://interactive.wsj.com/articles/SB918431496866451000.htm⟩.

33. Margaret Kane, "ISP Offers Free PCs to Subscribers," *ZDNet*, February 17, 1999, ⟨http://www.zdnet.com/zdnn/stories/news/0,4586,2210090,00. html⟩.

34. Author's personal experience, from receipts.

35. Dell Web site, ⟨http://www.dell.com⟩, May 5, 2000.

36. *Directory of Internet Service Providers*, Boardwatch, 11th ed, 1999.

37. Thomas A. Downes and Shane M. Greenstein, "Do Commercial ISPs Provide Universal Access?" in Sharon Eisner Gillett and Ingo Vogelsang, eds., *Competition, Regulation and Convergence: Current Trends in Telecommunications Policy Research* (Mahwah, NJ: Lawrence Erlbaum, 1999), p. 195.

38. *Ibid.*, p. 204, Table 12.1.

39. Bluelight.com Web site, ⟨http://www.bluelight.com/freeinternet/⟩, accessed August 10, 2000.

40. "Year End 1999 Mailbox Report," *Messaging Online*, ⟨http://www.messagingonline.com/⟩, accessed May 5, 2000.

41. Laurie J. Flynn, "Internet Is More Than Just Fun for Women," *The New York Times*, August 14, 2000, accessed at ⟨http://www.nytimes.com/library/tech/00/08/biztech/articles/14gend.html⟩. The article cites a study by Jupiter Communications based on a survey of 55,000 households.

42. Personal observation also suggests that gasoline is considerably less expensive in northeastern Kansas than in Philadelphia.

43. "The Digital World of the U.S. Hispanic," Cheskin Research, April 2000, p. 5.

44. "National Survey of American Adults on Technology," National Public Radio/Kaiser Family Foundation/Kennedy School of Government, at ⟨http://www.kff.org/content/2000/20000228a/TechnologyToplines.pdf⟩, accessed August 10, 2000, p. 3.

45. Mueller and Schement, *op. cit.*, note 19.

46. Andy Carvin, ed., "The E-Rate in America: A Tale of Four Cities," Benton Foundation, February 2000, p. 22.

47. Jorge Reina Schement, "Of Gaps by Which Democracy We Measure," *Information Impacts Magazine*, Dec. 1999 at ⟨www.cisp.org/imp/december_99/1299schement.html⟩.

48. William E. Kennard, "Equality in the Information Age," *Federal Communications Law Journal* 51: 3, May 1999, p. 556.

49. In October 2000, after this paper was written and pressented, the U.S. Commerce Department released its followup to the 1999 "Falling through the Net" survey. The latest paper had a significantly updated spin in its title: "Falling through The Net: Toward Digital Inclusion." In summary, the report confirms that while differences among various groups remain, they are closing fast, with the most rapid growth in access and use among those that were feared to be the most behind. ⟨http://www.ecommerce.gov/PressRelease/fttn00.pdf⟩.

V

Information Policy and Commercial Internet Behavior

13

Sorting Out the Search Engine Market

Neil Gandal

1 Introduction[1]

Many observers believe that the emergence of the Internet has profoundly changed society. Perhaps the most important feature of the Internet is the tremendous amount of publicly accessible information. According to estimates by Lawrence and Giles (1998, 1999), the number of publicly indexable pages on the World Wide Web grew from 320 million in December 1997 to 800 million in February 1999.

Search engines hold the key to helping consumers access and sort the wealth of information on the web. Many search engines are consistently among the top 25 most visited Web sites. This suggests that Internet users spend a significant amount of time using search engines to find relevant information. Indeed, a recent study by Statistical Research Inc. (2000) estimates that 57 percent of Internet users search the Web every day, making searches the second most popular activity on the Web, after e-mail. Approximately 81 percent of users check e-mail each day.[2]

Despite the sophistication of the search engines, they are far from comprehensive. For example, search engines are more likely to index "popular" sites (i.e., those sites that have more links to them) and sites that are in the United States.[3] Lawrence and Giles remark that "search engines can be compared to a phone book which is updated irregularly, is biased toward listing more popular information, and has most of the pages ripped out"[4] (http://wwwmetrics.com/).

In this chapter I examine the evolution of and competition in the Internet search engine market. The goal of my analysis is to examine whether early entrants benefit in the long run from their first-mover position in Internet markets. Does first-mover advantage in Internet markets translate into market leadership in the long run? This paper will analyze the Internet search engine market in order to provide some answers to these important questions.

Despite the recent surge of research activity on e-commerce, to the best of my knowledge, Gallaugher and Downing (1999) is the only other paper that examines competition in the Internet search engine market. In their study, they restrict attention to four early firms (Yahoo, Lycos, Excite, and Infoseek) and focus on a very early period in the evolution of the industry. Using market reach data, where market reach is the percent of consumers conducting searches with a particular search engine in a given month, they find that the fixed (brand) effects explain most of the variation in market reach. Market reach is similar to market share; the difference is that (the sum of) market reach can exceed one if consumers use more than a single search engine during a given month.

Both market share and market reach are problematic variables because they do not capture the tremendous growth in demand for searches. Media Metrix data on market reach (available at www.searchengine. com) show that market reach for Yahoo, Lycos, Excite, and Infoseek varies only slightly during the March 1997–December 1998 period, the period examined by Gallaugher and Downing (1999). Yet the number of unique users of search engines grew from 43.1 million in August 1997 (the earliest date for which I have data) to 96.1 million in December 1998. Thus, it is not surprising that the fixed (brand) effects explain most of the variation in market reach. Their conclusion that pure brand effects are quite strong in this market is surprising and is probably due to the fact that they (1) analyze a very early period in evolution of the industry, (2) restrict attention to the four leading firms at the time, and (3) use market search as the dependent variable. Indeed, the trade press suggests that there is fierce competition in the search engine market. Barry Parr, director of Internet and e-commerce strategies at International Data Corp., believes that "search is pretty much a commodity service."[4] According to industry analysts, most users "can't even differentiate between the major search engines."[5]

My analysis differs from that of Gallaugher and Downing (1999) in several important ways. I use the number of unique visitors to search engines to measure demand and include all of the competitors in the search engine market in my analysis. In addition, I estimate models that are typically employed in the analysis of oligopoly markets. I find that while early entrants (Yahoo, Lycos, Excite, Infoseek, and Altavista) still have an advantage, the pure "brand name" advantage has been declining over time. The success of a recent wave of new entrants in the Internet search engine market suggests that entry barriers are still quite low. This makes sense, given that consumers pay no fee for the use of search engines and there are few (if any) consumer switching costs.

In section 2, I briefly describe the search engine industry. Section 3 describes the data I employ; the empirical analysis and discussion of the results are in section 4. Section 5 provides a brief followup to the formal analysis, while section 6 concludes.

2   The Search Engine Industry

Search engine competition began in 1994 with the entry of Yahoo and Lycos. By 1995, three additional search engines were competing in the market: Excite, Infoseek, and Altavista. Until mid-1998, these five firms dominated the market and Yahoo was the industry leader. In August 1997, Yahoo had 14.8 million unique users, while Infoseek and Excite respectively had 7.9 million and 7.6 million unique visitors during the month; Lycos and Altavista followed with 4.9 and 4.7 million unique users during the same period. Webcrawler, an early entrant that quickly lost significant market share, had approximately 3.2 million unique users in August 1997. No other search engine had more than 1.7 million unique users. Ignoring a small competitive fringe, there were approximately 43.1 million unique visitors to search engines in August 1997.

As the market for searches grew, market structure began to change. The concentrated oligopoly market broke down in the middle of 1998 when several "late" entrants obtained a fairly significant share of the market by offering high-quality products. Table 13.1 shows that by August 1999, five late entrants had each obtained market shares in the 5–6 percent range, nearly as much as the 7 percent share held by Altavista at that time.

Table 13.1 shows that the number of unique users of search engines increased by more than 100 percent during the August 1997–August

Table 13.1
The search engine market, August 1997–August 1999

Product	Entry date	Unique users in millions		
		August 1997	August 1998	August 1999
Yahoo	1994	14.8	26.0	33.0
Infoseek/Go	1995	7.9	12.5	18.5
Lycos	1994	4.9	12.0	14.9
Excite	1995	7.6	14.5	14.1
Altavista	1995	4.7	9.5	9.2
Webcrawler	1995	3.2		
About	1996		*	8.6
Looksmart	1996		3.2	8.5
Snap	1997		4.0	8.3
Hotbot	1996		5.5	7.2
GoTo	1998		2.6	7.1
Askjeeves	1997		0.4	4.0
Total # of unique users of search engines (millions)		43.1	90.2	133.7
Total # of Web users (millions)		44.7	55.5	63.1

Notes: * Data on unique visitors are not available for About for the August 1998 period. In November 1998, About had approximately 4.2 million unique visitors.

1998 period and by nearly 50 percent during the August 1998–August 1999 period. Consequently, despite the fact that Yahoo's number of unique users increased by 125 percent during the August 1997–August 1999 period, its market share fell from 34 to 25 percent during same period.

Table 13.1 also shows that in August 1997, the number of unique visitors to search engines divided by the number of Web users was approximately 1.0. This ratio rose steadily from 1997 to 1999, stood at 1.6 in August 1998, and reached 2.1 in August 1999. Since nearly all Web users visit at least one search engine per month, the data suggest that in 1997 each user employed a single search engine; by August 1999, consumers were on average using multiple search engines.

Why was there such an increase in the average number of search engines used by each consumer? Lawrence and Giles (1998) estimate that several search engines covered more than 20 percent of the indexable Web in December 1997; Lawrence and Giles (1999) estimate that no search engine covered more than 16 percent of the indexable Web in February 1999.[6]

Similarly, Notess has consistently found that there is very little overlap among search engines' results. In an analysis he undertook in September 1999, he found that five "very small" searches run on thirteen search engines yielded 140 unique pages. Sixty-six of the 140 pages were found by a single search engine, while 30 were found by only two engines (see ⟨http://www.searchengineshowdown.com/stats/9909overlap.shtml⟩ for details). Another interesting finding is that there is little overlap among the Inktomi-based databases, which include Snap, HotBot, and Yahoo from my data.

An additional reason for the increase in the use of search engines is due to the relative ease with which additional searches can be conducted. Several search engines now routinely offer a "second opinion" at the end of the search; that is, a click of the mouse yields additional results for the search by another search engine.

3   Data Description

The goal is to determine empirically to what extent (i) being a "first mover" in this industry was enough to establish a long-run leadership position, and (ii) inherent quality matters. This question was addressed by using Five months of data from the August 1998–August 1999 period, using equally spaced intervals: August 1998, November 1998, February 1999, May 1999, and August 1999. (Unfortunately, in the early part of 2000, Media Metrix, the Internet's oldest rating service and the source of my data, made a major change in the way it collects data. Rather than reporting data by Web site as well as Web property (which includes many Web sites), Media Metrix now only reports data on Web properties. Hence, it is not possible to extend the data series employed in my analysis.)

One data point per quarter is used because the monthly changes are relatively small. Data prior to August 1998 are not used because (with the exception of August 1997 data) only market reach data are publicly available for the earlier period. As discussed above, such data do not capture the growth in the number of unique visitors to each search engine over time.

Included are all search engines that had more than 3.6 million searches (or 2 percent of the market) in August 1999. Media Metrix does not publicly report the data for firms with a smaller market share. Hence, there are 11 firms in my data set. Following *PC Magazine* and Media Metrix, excluded are America Online, Netscape, and Microsoft in the "search engine" category. While these firms provide search services, their Web sites have significant traffic not associated with searching capabilities.

All of the firms are in the data set for the full period.[7] No firm exited during this period. The only significant firm to fall below the cutoff during the 1997–1999 period was Webcrawler, and its market size was already well below the cutoff in August 1998. Descriptive statistics on the variables in the study are in table 13.2. I now describe the variables in some detail.

Table 13.2
Descriptive statistics

VARIABLE	N	Mean	Std. deviation	Minimum	Maximum
LOG(SEARCHES)	54	2.06	0.87	−0.86	3.51
LOG(SEARCHES/ [POPULATION- UNIVERSE])	54	−3.30	0.87	−6.22	−1.83
EARLY	54	0.46	0.50	0.00	1.00
AGE	54	3.28	1.23	1.00	5.00
UNIVERSE	54	59.05	2.82	55.50	63.16
RELEVANTHITS	54	1.91	0.68	1.00	3.00
ELIMDEAD	54	1.56	0.50	1.00	2.00
ELIMDUPL	54	1.46	0.50	1.00	2.00
ANTICIPATES	54	1.65	0.48	1.00	2.00
CUSTOMIZES	54	1.81	0.59	1.00	3.00
PERWEB	35	9.40	4.63	2.50	15.50
PERDEAD	35	5.26	3.95	2.20	14.00
MEDAGE	35	75.57	44.56	33.00	174.00

3.1   Variables Used in the Analysis

1. Monthly data on unique visitors to each search engine comes from Media Metrix, the leader in the provision of such data (see http://www.mediametrix.com). The variable denoted SEARCHES measures (in millions) the number of unique visitors to each search engine. Media Metrix data are attractive because (during the period I employ) they measure Web traffic by individual Web sites rather than by Web properties.[8] LSEARCHES is the natural logarithm of this variable.

2. The variable UNIVERSE is the number of people (in millions) who use the Web. This variable is likely a function of the quality-adjusted price of Internet access. As the price of Internet access fell and the quality of Internet access increased, more consumers obtained access to the Web. Table 13.1 shows that the number of Internet users increased by 38 percent from August 1998 to August 1999. The variable LUNIVERSE is the natural log of UNIVERSE.

3. The variable AGE denotes the number of years that a search engine has been in the market. This variable is defined as 1999 less "the year that the firm entered the market." There are no qualitative changes in the results if I define the variable so that I measure age in quarterly intervals.

4. The dummy variable EARLY takes on the value 1 if the firm was among the five firms that dominated the market in its early years.

5. Data on characteristics of search engines comes from two sources: *PC Magazine* and Lawrence and Giles (1999). *PC Magazine* analyses all of the 11 search engines in the data set, while Lawrence and Giles (1999) examine seven search engines in my data set. Both the PC Magazine and Lawrence and Giles analyses were conducted during the period I use in the analysis.

The *PC Magazine* data, available at ⟨http://www.zdnet.com/pcmag/stories/reviews/0,6755,2330316,00.html⟩, contain ratings on five characteristics listed below. The ratings are poor (assigned a value of zero), fair (one), good (two), and excellent (three). *PC Magazine* sent 50 different requests to all of the search engines on various topics, first using the basic search and then using refined searching methods. They report results in the following five areas:

• "RHelevant Hits from the Initial Search," denoted RELEVANTHITS, where the top ten hits from each query are evaluated for relevance by examining the content in the pages.

• "Eliminates Dead Links," denoted ELIMDEAD, counts the number of "dead" links in the top 10 hits from each query and then assigns a rating.

• "Eliminates Duplicate Links," denoted ELIMDUPL, counts the number of duplicate links in the top 10 hits and then assigns a rating.

• "Customizes Search Effectively," denoted CUSTOMIZES, examines the tools and options that a search engine has available in order to refine a search. These tools are then rated by examining the quality of the hits from these advanced searches.

• "Effective Anticipatory Results," denoted ANTICIPATES, measures how well a search engine anticipates the goal of the search, and whether this leads to more relevant results.

Two of these characteristics (ELIMDEAD, ELIMDUPL) are purely quantitative, while RELEVANT HITS is also essentially quantitative, since it is easy to design fairly objective tests. The other two characteristics are clearly subjective; I discuss this issue further below.

The Lawrence and Giles (1999) article contains the following quantitative data on the performance of seven search engines (Yahoo, Go/Infoseek, Excite, Lycos, Altavista, Hotbot, and Snap) in my data set:

• "Percentage of Invalid Links," denoted PERDEAD, estimates the percentage of dead links using 1050 queries.

• "Coverage with Respect to Web Size," PERWEB, which measures the percentage of the Web covered by each search engine. As mentioned above, no search engine in the data set covered more than 16 percent of the Web in 1999.

• "Median Age of Matching Documents," MEDAGE, which measures the (median) time between when new documents were added to the search engines and when these documents were last modified. This variable may be problematic, since not all Web pages list the date of the last update.

The one overlapping variable between the PC Magazine and Lawrence and Giles (1999) data relates to dead links. It is reassuring to know that there is a negative correlation (-0.48) between PERDEAD and ELIMDEAD for the seven search engines in my data set that were examined by *PC Magazine* and Lawrence and Giles (1999).

4   Analysis of the Data

Here I employ two models that have been used to examine competition in oligopoly markets. In section 4.1, I employ a variant of a growth model. Growth models are often employed to examine industry dynamics. In section 4.2, I employ a model based on recent advances in estimating discrete-choice models of product differentiation.

4.1 A Simple Growth Model

Although the Internet server industry is still in its infancy, it is possible to estimate a simple growth model of the form

$$\log(\text{SEARCHES}_{j,t}) = \beta_0 + \beta_1 \log(\text{SEARCHES}_{j,t-1}) + \varepsilon_{j,t}, \tag{13.1}$$

where the subscript j refers to the product and the subscript t refers to time; $\varepsilon_{j,t}$ is an i.i.d. error term with mean zero and constant variance. This model has a "partial adjustment" towards an optimal size interpretation, i.e.,

$$S_{j,t} = (1 - \lambda)S_{j,t-1} + \lambda S_{j,t}^*, \tag{13.2}$$

where $S_{j,t}$ is the size of the firm at time t, $S_{j,t}^*$ is the optimal size at that time, and $0 < \lambda < 1$. Equation 13.2 means that the size of the firm at time t is a weighted average of the actual size of the firm at time $t - 1$ and the optimal size at time t. See Geroski et al. (1997) and Sutton (1997).

Since I have characteristic data on each product in the sample, the simple growth model can be enriched. With a single characteristic that does not change over time (x_j), the enriched growth model can be written

$$\log(\text{SEARCHES}_{j,t}) = \beta_0 + \beta_1 \log(\text{SEARCHES}_{j,t-1}) + \beta_2 x_j + \varepsilon_{j,t}, \tag{13.3}$$

Hence in the long run, $\log(\text{SEARCHES}_{j,t}) = (\beta_0 + \beta_1 x_j)/(1 - \beta_1)$, that is, differences in the product characteristics drive the long-run differences in market share among the products.

In the estimation, of course, I employ more than one characteristic, and some of these characteristics are industry-specific (i.e., UNIVERSE) while other characteristics are product-specific. The above discussion helps interpret the estimated parameters of the product characteristics (such as ELIMDEAD) that do not change over time.[9]

The results using the enriched growth model in equation 13.3 with product and industry characteristics are shown in table 13.3. The positive coefficient on EARLY and the negative coefficient on AGE show that, other things being equal, the early entrants still have an advantage, but that this advantage has been declining over time. (The coefficient of EARLY is statistically significant, while the coefficient on AGE is not statistically significant.) The coefficient on LUNIVERSE measures the

Table 13.3
Enriched growth model: dependent variable: log(SEARCHES)

| | Enriched growth model | |
	Coefficient	T-statistic
CONSTANT	−2.28	−0.76
Log(SEARCHES.₁)	0.72	9.20
EARLY	0.34	1.79
AGE	−0.051	−1.15
LUNIVERSE	0.69	0.93
RELEVANTHITS	0.21	2.17
ELIMDEAD	0.073	0.94
ELIMDUPL	−0.10	−1.21
ANTICIPATES	0.071	0.88
CUSTOMIZES	−0.17	−2.31
Durbin–Watson (DW) statistic	2.08	
Number of observations	43	
Adjusted R-squared	0.95	

elasticity of searches with respect to the size of the Internet universe. The positive sign on LUNIVERSE suggests that an increase in Internet users has led to an increase in the number of searches. Although its effect on the number of searches is not statistically significant, this estimated elasticity (0.69) is fairly large in an economic sense.

Table 13.3 shows that providing relevant hits (RELEVANTHITS) is the characteristic that consumers value most; the coefficient on RELEVANTHITS is statistically significant. The coefficients on eliminating dead links (ELIMDEAD) and ANTICIPATES are also positive, but not statistically significant. The coefficient on eliminating duplicate links is negative and insignificant. The effect of CUSTOMIZES is negative and significant. Since CUSTOMIZES is a very subjective characteristic, the results suggest that the tastes of the reviewers may differ from the preferences of consumers. The results are virtually unchanged if the three data points of the GoNetwork are excluded.

Adding a dummy variable for Yahoo in the estimation of the enriched growth model (equation 13.3) yields an associated coefficient of 0.26, with a *t*-statistic of 0.22. In other words, controlling for quality, the

Yahoo brand name only adds marginal value to the product. Hence, the results suggest that the brand name Yahoo is much less important to consumers than the fact that the search engine provides relevant hits and does a good job in eliminating dead links.

4.2   A Discrete-Choice Model of Product Differentiation

In order to examine the robustness of the results using the growth model, I now employ a model based on recent advances in estimating discrete-choice models of product differentiation. These techniques, developed by Berry (1994) and Berry, Levinsohn, and Pakes (BLP) (1995), enable structural estimation of the demand side of a differentiated product markets. (This literature began with Bresnahan (1987).)

The utility of product j to consumer i, denoted $u_{i,j}$, depends on both product and consumer characteristics. Following Berry (1994), I employ a random utility model of the form

$$u_{i,j} = x_j\beta - \alpha p_j + \xi_j + \varepsilon_{i,j}, \tag{13.4}$$

where the first two terms are the mean valuations of product j's observed characteristics, x_j is a vector of observable product characteristics, and p_j is the price. The parameters α and β represent the mean valuations of the observable characteristics. ξ_j represents the average value of product j's unobserved characteristics, while $\varepsilon_{i,j}$ is the deviation of buyer preferences around this mean.

The error term $\varepsilon_{i,j}$ introduces heterogeneity and determines the substitution patterns among products. The multinomial logit model assumes that the $\varepsilon_{i,j}$ are identically and independently distributed across consumers and choices with the extreme value (Weibull) distribution function. Given the discrete choice set, under this assumption it can be shown that the probability of choosing product j (the market share of product j) is

$$s_j = e^{\delta_j} / \sum_k (e^{\delta_k}), \tag{13.5}$$

where

$$\delta_j = x_j\beta - \alpha p_j + \xi_j \tag{13.6}$$

is the mean utility level from product j. Since there is little or no vertical differentiation among products and since income plays no role in consumer choice in the search engine market, the logit model seems quite appropriate.[10] By inverting the market share equation 13.5, one obtains

$$\log(s_j/s_0) = x_j\beta_0 - \alpha p_j + \xi_j, \tag{13.7}$$

where s_0 is the proportion of consumers who do not use search engines. I assume that all Internet users access a search engine in a given month. Hence, s_0 is the percent of the U.S. population in millions (denoted POPULATION) without Internet access. Hence, $\log(s_j/s_0)$ is log(SEARCHES/[POPULATION-UNIVERSE]).[11]

Once consumers have Internet access, there is no cost to consumers of using a search engine. This is because most consumers in the U.S. pay a monthly Internet access fee that allows unlimited use and local phone service in the U.S. is typically not metered. Further, there is no charge to consumers for the use of search engines. Hence the price term drops out of equation 13.7. Since the product characteristics are exogenous in the short run, consistent estimates of the β parameters can be obtained by an OLS regression on equation 13.7.

Since the percentage change in the numerator of searches is much larger than the percentage change in [POPULATION-UNIVERSE] over the 12-month period of the analysis, the left-hand side of the modified growth model (equation 13.3) and the left-hand side of the discrete-choice model of product differentiation (equation 13.7) essentially differ by a constant factor. The main difference between the two is that (13.3) captures the dynamics more explicitly than (13.7). Hence it is not surprising that the results from the first discrete-choice model of product differentiation (model I) in table 13.4 are qualitatively similar to the results from the growth model in table 13.3. The main empirical difference is that the t-statistics are smaller for the parameters in the growth model. This is because the variable $\log(\text{searches}_{-1})$ explains quite a bit of the variation in (3).

Table 13.4 presents the results from estimating the demand functions in equation 13.7. Similar to the growth model, the positive and significant coefficient on EARLY and the negative and significant coefficient on AGE in table 13.4 show that the early entrants still have an advantage, but that this advantage has been declining over time. The positive and significant (elasticity) coefficient on LUNIVERSE suggests that an increase in the number of Internet users has led to an increase in the number of searches.[12]

Table 13.4
Discrete choice models of product differentiation: dependent variable LOG (SEARCHES/[POPULATION-UNIVERSE])

Independent Variable	Model I: *PC Magazine* data		Model II: Lawrence and Giles data	
	Coefficient	*T*-statistic	Coefficient	*T*-statistic
CONSTANT	−22.14	−6.52	−14.51	−6.53
EARLY	3.40	9.93	2.05	5.43
AGE	−1.13	−6.54	−0.24	−1.43
LUNIVERSE	4.84	5.88	2.19	4.08
RELEVANTHITS	1.61	9.42	0.66	3.48
ELIMDEAD	0.17	1.71		
ELIMDUPL	−0.14	−1.23		
ANTICIPATES	−0.93	−4.67		
CUSTOMIZES	−0.21	−2.06		
PERWEB			0.051	3.57
PERDEAD			−0.043	−1.48
MEDAGE			0.0064	4.45
Durbin–Watson (DW)	1.51		1.95	
Number of observations	54		35	
Adjusted R-squared	0.89		0.92	

Similar to the growth model, relevant hits (RELEVANTHITS) and eliminating dead links (ELIMDEAD) are the characteristics that consumers value most. The estimated coefficients for these characteristics are positive and statistically significant in this case, while only relevant hits was statistically significant in the case of the growth model. Again the estimated coefficient on ELIMDUPL is insignificant, suggesting that duplication of results is not that bothersome to consumers.

The coefficients on ANTICIPATES and CUSTOMIZES are negative and significant; one possible explanation may be that consumers do not care about these advanced features. As noted earlier, these two characteristics are very subjective.[13]

Model II in table 13.4, estimates equation 13.7 using the Lawrence and Giles data. They examined only seven search engines in the data set;

hence there are just 35 observations. Since "relevant hits" appears to be a key characteristic, this variable is also included from the *PC Magazine* ratings. The results using the Lawrence and Giles data are fairly similar to the results from model I in table 13.4. The estimated coefficient for EARLY is positive and significant, while the estimated coefficient for AGE is negative although not quite statistically significant; the coefficient on LUNIVERSE is positive and statistically significant.

The coefficient on RELEVANTHITS is again positive and significant. The positive and significant coefficient on the percentage of the Web covered (PERWEB) suggests that consumers do care about coverage, at least up to a certain point. (Recall that no search engine covered more than 16 percent of the Web.) The coefficient estimate for PERDEAD is negative as expected, but not quite statistically significant. The one surprise here is that the coefficient on median age (MEDAGE) is positive and significant. This may be because of the selection problem associated with this variable. (Recall that many Web pages do not report the last date the page was modified.) The discrete-choice model of product differentiation provides evidence that the results using the enriched growth model are quite robust.

5   Updates and Trends: Where Is Google?

As noted earlier, Media Metrix made a major change in the way it collects data that means it is not possible to extend the data series employed in the formal statistical analysis. Nevertheless, it is possible to discuss recent trends in the industry. Perhaps the most important event was Google's entry into the search engine market in late 1999. Google has topped the NPD New Media Services survey on user satisfaction with search engines the last three quarters. It recently achieved a 97 percent satisfaction rate, where satisfaction is defined to be users who respond either "most of the time" or "every time" to the question "How often do you find what you are looking for?" Google's success has not gone unnoticed in the industry. Yahoo recently switched from Inktomi to Google. According to Media Metrix, Google had 6.5 million unique users in October 2000. (Google is one of the few firms for which Media Metrix still reports data by Web site. This is because Google does not have any other associated Web properties.)

6 Conclusion

This paper examined the evolution of and competition in the emerging Internet search engine market. Both a growth model and a discrete-choice model of product differentiation suggest that the pure first-mover advantage of early entrants (Yahoo, Lycos, Excite, Infoseek, and Altavista) has declined over time. This suggests that the search engine market has relatively low barriers to entry and that competition is fierce. Google's recent success adds supporting evidence to the statistical finding that the entry barriers are not very high in the search engine market.

The results also suggest that consumers are primarily interested in search engines that provide relevant hits and, to a lesser extent, search engines that eliminate dead links. This makes sense, since these two characteristics essentially measure how up-to-date the search engine is. The coverage that Notess' site gives to the issue of dead links provides independent support for the importance of this characteristic.

This analysis suggests that, in Internet markets with low switching costs and no obvious signs of network externalities, early entrants will benefit from their first-mover position in the long run only to the extent that they continue to innovate and stay ahead in the quality dimensions. Pure brand rents in these markets will likely be short-lived.

Notes

1. This paper draws extensively on Gandal (2001). I am grateful to Paul Geroski, Shane Greenstein, and Jose Mata for many helpful suggestions and comments.

2. See ⟨http://www.sriresearch.com/press/pr20000217.htm⟩ and ⟨http://www.searchenginewatch.com/reports/seindex.html⟩. The third most popular activity is checking product information. 46 percent of users perform this activity daily.

3. For further discussion, see two outstanding Web sites: Daniel Sullivan's Web site at ⟨http://www.searchenginewatch.com⟩, and Greg Notess' Web site at ⟨http://www.notess.com/search/⟩.

4. Most Internet search engines do not in general permit advertisers to pay to improve their position in search engine results. The exceptions are GoTo and Lycos. See ⟨http://www.searchenginewatch.com⟩ for more information.

5. See Weisul, Kimberly, "Search Engines Chase Profit," *Interactive Online*, May 10, 1999, at ⟨http://www.zdnet.com/intweek/stories/news/0,4164,2255145,00.html⟩.

6. Ibid.

7. The decline in coverage is due, in part, to the fact that the number of publicly indexable pages on the World Wide Web grew from 320 million in December 1997 to 800 million in February 1999.

8. Data on unique visitors is not available for About for the August 1998 period. Hence there is one missing observation. Miningco changed its name to About in the spring of 1999. For ease of presentation, in the paper, I refer just to About.

9. The only exception regarding search engine data is in the case of the Go Network. In January 1999, Infoseek was acquired by Disney and Media Metrix lumped together three Web sites, disney.go.com, infoseek.go.com, and espn.go.com, into the go.com data. Hence the increase in Infoseek/Go Network's market share in 1999 is due to the aggregation of the data.

10. Greg Notess' search-engine comparison site issues "Dead Link Reports" once every two to three months. The problem with these data is that they do not include all of the search engines in my sample. If these reports had included all of the search engines in the sample, this characteristic would have changed over time. Nevertheless, this addition probably would not affect the analysis, since Notess's reports show that firm performances are highly correlated over time. In other words, the relative ratings are quite similar over time.

11. In order to employ this model, it is necessary to assume the same demand function over time, but this seems reasonable since the data set is for a single year: August 1998–August 1999.

12. Since some consumers use more than one search engine in a month, this model can be thought of as an approximation to the true choice model. Nevo (1999) similarly uses a discrete-choice model of product differentiation to model demand in the market for breakfast cereals.

13. Note that the dependent variable is a (very nonlinear) function of LUNIVERSE. Given the low correlation of 0.25 between LUNIVERSE and the dependent variable, this does not pose a serious problem.

14. Again, the results are also virtually unchanged if the three data points of the GoNetwork are excluded. In the case of the discrete choice model with an additional (dummy) variable for Yahoo, the coefficient on the Yahoo dummy variable is slightly larger than in the enriched growth model, yet not quite statistically significant (0.55, $t = 1.48$). Again, this suggests that inherent quality is more important than brand name in this market.

References

Berry, S., 1994, "Estimating Discrete-Choice Models of Product Differentiation," *Rand Journal of Economics*, 25: 334–347.

Berry, S., J. Levinsohn, and A. Pakes, 1995, "Automobile Prices in Market Equilibrium," *Econometrica*, 63: 841–890.

Bresnahan, T., 1987, "Competition and Collusion in the American Auto Industry: The 1955 Price War," *Journal of Industrial Economics*, 35: 457–482.

Gallaugher, J., and C. Downing, 1999, "Market Leadership and the Web Portal Industry: An Empirical Investigation," mimeo.

Gandal, N., forthcoming 2001, "The Dynamics of Competition in the Internet Search Engine Market," *International Journal of Industrial Organization.*

Geroski, P., S. Machin, and C. Walters, 1997 "Corporate Growth and Profitability," *Journal of Industrial Economics*, 45: 171–89.

Lawrence, S., and L. Giles, 1998, "Searching the World Wide Web," *Science*, 280: 98–100, ⟨http://www.neci.nj.nec.com/~lawrence/science98.html⟩.

Lawrence, S., and L. Giles, 1999, "Accessibility of Information on the Web," *Nature*, 400: 107–109.

Nevo, A., 1999, "Measuring Market Power in the Ready-To-Eat Cereal Industry," U.C. Berkeley, mimeo.

Sutton, J., 1997, "Gibrat's Legacy," *Journal of Economic Literature*, 35: 40–59.

14

Copyright in the Age of Distributed Applications

Seth D. Greenstein

This chapter explores the pressures exerted on traditional principles of copyright liability and enforcement when networking software applications that are specifically designed to exchange copyrighted works—thus inherently having both infringing and noninfringing uses—become widely disseminated and virally popularized.

Existing copyright case law imposes liability on third parties for the infringing acts of others, based on the third party's ability to exercise effective supervision over those acts or knowledge that certain devices or facilities could not be used for substantial purposes other than for infringement. New technology, and the complex and uncertain task of discerning what constitutes a noninfringing or fair use of such technology, challenge these principles from the perspectives of both copyright owners and the public interest. One response has been to enact noncopyright legislation to address, through imperfect balances, the economic consequences of unauthorized access to and copying of copyrighted works.

Recently, technologies have been developed that obsolete traditional concepts underlying the standards for imposing third-party liability for infringement. Software applications such as Napster and Gnutella create a virtual telecommunications network by which a community of thousands of simultaneous users exchange copyrighted works (in both infringing and noninfringing acts), without the ability to monitor or control, in advance, user conduct. For such distributed network technologies, infringing activity becomes efficient and widespread: legal enforcement against each individual infringer is impractical, if not impossible; and there is no central authority (other than the creator of the software) to seek to hold liable for infringing user activity.

The paper explores how traditional legal analysis might adapt to these technologies while maintaining the traditional balance between the rights of copyright owners and the privileges of copyright users, and giving due regard for the intellectual property rights of technology companies and the progress of technology. Specifically, the paper suggests additional factors that should inform any decision on third-party liability, including the evaluation of:

· The nature of each potential noninfringing use;
· The likelihood that any consumer would acquire and use the product for these noninfringing purposes;
· The role of the technology in facilitating the infringing uses;
· The role of the technology in facilitating the noninfringing uses;
· The likelihood that, if the technology is or is not deemed to be infringing, that noninfringing uses will proliferate; and,
· The impact that a finding of infringement would have upon the technology and technological progress.

Distributed Network or "Peer-to-Peer" Applications

The Internet generally operates as a system of service providers providing access for subscriber clients that access data from host servers. This model spawned its own set of daunting legal issues for companies that provided the backbone of the telecommunications infrastructure, such as AT&T, Sprint, and MCI; Internet service providers, such as Netcom, UUNet and Concentric Networks; online service providers, such as America Online and Compuserve; "post your own" personal website hosts such as Geocities; and information location tools, such as Yahoo!. District court decisions suggested that in certain factual circumstances such providers could, as a matter of law, be held liable for the infringing acts of their subscribers.[1] In response, Congress enacted a "safe harbor" immunity for these providers against claims of vicarious liability and contributory infringement arising from the actions of their subscribers and customers.[2]

Even after 1998 passage of the Digital Millennium Copyright Act (DMCA), copyright owners threatened legal action against search engines tailored to the location of copyrighted material, including search engines that facilitated searching for music files encoded in the MP3 format.[3] Settlements between copyright owners and the sites reportedly followed the DMCA Title II model whereby the site promised to disable links to files identified by the copyright owner as unauthorized and infringing.[4] The recording industry also pursued schools and individuals who hosted large numbers of music files, prosecuting one student under the so-called "No Electronic Theft" Act of 1997.[5]

In mid-1999, a new technology now known as "peer-to-peer" file sharing emerged under the name "Napster." This software altered the typical "end-to-end" Internet topology by permitting searching, identification, and direct exchange between individual users of music files in the MP3 format. This topology is shown generically in figure 14.1.

The Napster software essentially provides a client browser interface to a host-server search engine for the network of users of its software, which enables the users to search for and share music files with other Napster users online at that particular time. In figure 14.1, the server in the middle represents the server owned by Napster, Inc.; around the

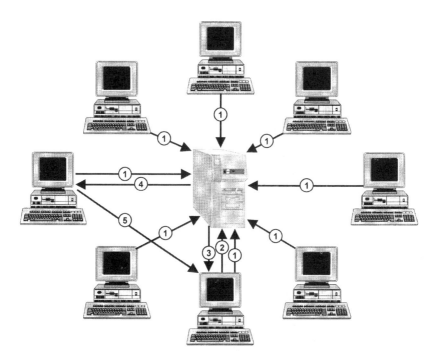

Figure 14.1
Topology of a centralized server in a distributed networking application.

perimeter are PCs currently running the Napster client browser. When a user starts the Napster program, the program communicates to a Napster server the names of all MP3 files that the user offers to share with other users. (This communication is illustrated in figure 14.1 in the lines numbered 1.) These file names (which are created by the user) are entered into Napster's database of files then available online from persons then using the Napster software. The database changes dynamically each time a user starts or exits the Napster program.

Using the Napster browser, a Napster user can place a search request by artist name or song title, shown in figure 14.1 as line 2. The Napster server searches its central database of file names, and returns a list of files from any Napster users then online who have on their hard disk drives files responsive to the search request, illustrated as line 3. The Napster software displays the search request results with the names and attributes of those files, including file size, bit rate and transmission speed. If the user selects a file for downloading, the Napster server instigates transmission of the file via file transfer protocol from the other user's computer, as shown in line 4, to the requesting user's computer, as shown in line 5. Napster's servers neither store any music files nor copy any of the music files being transferred between computers.

Essentially, the Napster server acts as a traffic cop allowing communication among Napster users and, with respect to the search and download functionality, makes the users' computers the equivalent of individual servers that the Napster server networks together. The Napster software verifies that the files are using the MP3 data file format. However, nothing inherent in the MP3 data allows Napster to determine whether the file contains music or other sound, whether the data constitutes copyrighted material, whether such material has been authorized for transmission or file-sharing, or whether the music contained in that file is, in fact, the song identified in the name of the file.

Without any advertising (other than the flood of press articles generated by copyright controversies),[6] and without generating any revenue, Napster reportedly has attracted approximately 40 million users worldwide. Other technologies, such as Macster (for Apple users), Scour-Exchange, and CuteMX, follow this same topographical model.

In March 2000, two America Online programmers who had previously created the popular Winamp program for playing MP3 files

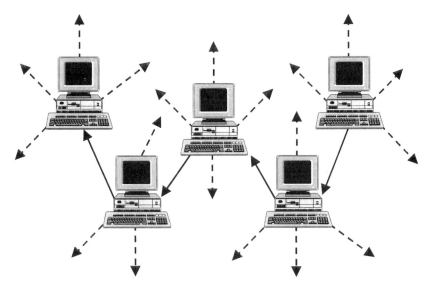

Figure 14.2
Decentralized distributed application network topology.

released a more decentralized file-sharing technology. The program, known as Gnutella, was notable in at least three key respects. First, Gnutella enabled searching and sharing of all file types, including music, motion pictures, images, and text. Second, Gnutella was an "open-source" program, meaning that the program code was published for copying, implementation, and enhancement, without any assertion of either copyright or commercial rights. Third and most relevant to this analysis, Gnutella does not require a central server to connect users. The topology of this decentralized distributed network application is shown as figure 14.2.

Each Gnutella user must know the Internet Protocol address of at least one other Gnutella user then online. Once connected, each Gnutella user becomes a server connected to any and every computer along the network, as shown by the dotted arrows in figure 14.2. Every search request by a Gnutella user can generate results directly from all other online Gnutella users, in a search path shown in figure 14.2 by the solid arrows.[7]

Most recently, a programmer in the United Kingdom created a peer-to-peer networking program known as "Freenet" that operates along the same general topological model as Gnutella. Freenet reportedly is designed with a more efficient method of searching for material by mirroring popular content across the network to speed transactions. Freenet protects user and publisher anonymity so that not even the host computer may know what data it stores for access via the Freenet network. As such, Freenet's author has articulated its mission as less to locate media files than to promote democratic values, thwart efforts to censor the Internet, and secure the free exchange of ideas against potential intervention by governmental and other policing authorities.[8]

Rights Implicated by Distributed Network Applications

Under the Copyright Act, copyright owners are granted five discrete exclusive rights, including (as most relevant to this paper) the rights to reproduce the work in copies and to distribute copies of the work.[9] Certain copyrighted works may consist of more than one copyrightable work. Copyrights in a downloaded music file can subsist separately in both the underlying musical works (the composition as written) and the sound recordings (the performance of that composition). Motion pictures are copyrightable in the whole, but may also include copyrightable material in the screenplay (and the book or story on which it may be based) and musical works included in the soundtrack. The five rights to each of these works may be held by distinct copyright owners and administered separately by different entities or collecting societies.

The exercise of any of these rights, unless authorized by the copyright owner or by an exemption or defense established by statute or case precedent, constitutes copyright infringement.[10] Direct copyright infringement occurs when the defendant itself exercises any of the rights without authorization of the copyright owner or the law. The defendant's intent/knowledge is *not* an element of direct infringement, inasmuch as even innocent infringers deprive copyright owners of their rights and infringers could easily claim a lack of knowledge of the infringement as a defense.[11]

The use of distributed network applications could implicate the following rights (without consideration of whether the particular use constitutes infringement):

Distribution Right
• By launching the program, the user authorizes the distribution of files containing copyrighted works.
• By permitting downloading, the user distributes a copy of files containing copyrighted works.

Reproduction Right
• Copying the works to a computer hard drive in order to make such files available for distribution.
• Recording downloaded files to a hard drive or other storage medium.

Traditional Standards for Imposing Third-Party Liability

Historically, copyright owners have refrained from suing individuals for personal, noncommercial infringing conduct. Copyright owners from time to time have pursued particularly egregious offenders, hoping to establish valuable legal precedents and instill *in terrorem* respect for copyright. Users of distributed network applications could be subject to liability to copyright owners for any direct infringements. However, these systems can obscure or protect individual user identities, and the magnitude of users makes litigation for direct infringement an impracticable if not impossible method of enforcement. Moreover, individual infringers are generally unable to adequately compensate copyright owners through statutory or actual damages, or to reimburse litigation costs through awards of attorney fees.

The more logical approach has been to hold responsible a third party in situations where, by having a "deeper pocket," there is a greater potential reward for the litigation efforts; or where, by virtue of being higher up in the chain of infringement, the imposition of liability will deter or enjoin a substantial number of infringing acts. Third-party liability traditionally has been imposed under one of two legal theories, vicarious liability or contributory infringement, as described below.

Vicarious Liability
Vicarious liability focuses on the relationship of the third party with the direct infringer.[12] Courts impose vicarious liability for the actions of the direct infringer where the defendant has both (1) the right and ability to control the infringer's actions, *and* (2) received a direct financial benefit

from the infringement.[13] Liability may be found even though the defendant neither knows of nor encourages the infringing activity.[14]

The early cases addressing indirect liability under the copyright law arose primarily in two contexts. In the "landlord-tenant cases,"[15] a landlord leases property to a tenant who engages in copyright infringement on the leased premises. In such cases, the courts generally found the degree of control and the relationship between rental payments and the infringement too tenuous to impose liability. However, in the so-called "dance-hall cases,"[16] a dance hall owner or manager hires a performer who performs copyrighted material without the permission of the copyright holder. Generally, courts find the degree of control and the relationship between the remuneration and infringement sufficient to impose liability. Some examples of cases finding vicarious liability:

• In *Shapiro Bernstein & Co. v. H.L. Green Co.*, Green, the owner of a chain of department stores, licensed Jalen to run its record department in 23 stores. Plaintiffs, copyright holders of popular musical compositions, alleged that Jalen directly infringed their copyrights by manufacturing bootleg recordings containing copyrighted works without obtaining a license. The court held Green vicariously liable for selling the bootlegged recordings because it had both the power to exercise control over the infringing activity and a "direct financial interest in the exploitation of copyrighted materials—even in the absence of actual knowledge that the copyright monopoly is being impaired."[17]

• In *RCA/Ariola International Inc. v. Thomas & Grayston Co.*,[18] owners of retail stores that allowed customers to use for a fee audio-cassette duplicating machines were held liable for direct infringement where their employees actively participated in the infringing duplication of copyrighted prerecorded cassettes. Metacom, the manufacturer of the cassette duplicating machines, and the manufacturer's president were found liable as vicarious infringers because they retained ownership and control over the machines.

• In *Fonovisa Inc. v. Cherry Auction*, the court allowed the plaintiff to proceed against the owner of a swap meet for renting space to record bootleggers, where the defendant had the right and ability to control the activities of vendors and derived a financial benefit from admission and parking fees and concessions.[19]

Contributory Infringement

Contributory infringement occurs when one person knowingly induces another to directly infringe the copyright or materially contributes the direct infringing activities of another.[20] In *Gershwin*, for example, ASCAP brought an infringement action against an organization ("CAMI") that managed concert artists and promoted their concerts. The court held CAMI liable as a contributory infringer on the basis that CAMI knew that its artists included copyrighted compositions in their performances without securing licenses from the copyright holders; and in providing the audience and promoting the concert, CAMI had the requisite level of participation to be found liable. In the *Netcom* case, the court held that although the service providers were not direct infringers, they could be liable for contributory infringement. The court found that notice from the copyright owner was sufficient to raise a question of fact as to whether Netcom and the BBS owner knew or should have known of the infringement; and that providing services that distributed the infringing material constituted substantial participation in the infringing activity.[21] However, the court stated that a mere unsupported allegation of infringement by a copyright owner may not automatically provide an ISP with notice of an infringing activity, and so the court did not impose on either Netcom or the BBS operator an obligation to independently investigate infringement absent notice.[22]

Contributory infringement liability also may be found where the defendant provides the instrumentality used to commit a direct infringement by another. For example, a court issued a preliminary injunction against a BBS operator who sold copiers used to reproduce copyrighted video games.[23] Similarly, contributory liability was imposed upon a seller of cable descrambling chips used in the infringing activity of consumers.[24] In each of these two cases, however, the particular devices at issue were not capable of substantial noninfringing uses. Because the devices lacked such noninfringing uses, the court reasonably could find that the manufacturer had knowledge of the infringement sufficient to impose liability as a contributory infringer.

The "Sony" Standard

In 1984, the Supreme Court enunciated a standard for analyzing when the manufacturer of a device might be held liable for contributory infringement. Where the device at issue is a "staple article of commerce" that can be used for multiple purposes, the Court held that it is not enough that a manufacturer knows that the equipment *might* be used for infringing purposes. The defendant will be deemed a contributory infringer only if the items are not capable of "substantial" or "commercially significant" noninfringing uses.[25] In addressing the contributory liability of the Sony Betamax Video Cassette Recorder, the Court held that the sale of copying equipment does not constitute contributory infringement if that product is "widely used for legitimate, unobjectionable purposes"; and that, "indeed, it need merely be capable of substantial noninfringing uses."[26] Applying this standard, the Court found that the manufacturer of a videocassette recorder could not be held liable for the infringing acts of home consumers—even though Sony knew consumers were using the VCRs to infringe copyright—because the VCR could also be used for noninfringing "fair-use" purposes such as to "time-shift" broadcast programming that consumers were invited to watch without charge, and to record programming where the copyright owner did not object.

Not every possible noninfringing use of a product may be considered "commercially significant." For example, the manufacturer of certain imported ROMless motherboards was held as a contributory copyright infringer where there was no evidence showing actual use of the motherboards with legitimate Apple ROM chips (rather than infringing ROM chip imports).[27] In *Vault Corp. v. Quaid Software Ltd.*, the court of appeals affirmed that the producer of a software program designed to defeat Vault's anticopying computer software program had not infringed Vault's copyright and was not contributorily liable for infringing use of its product by some customers, in light of the commercially significant noninfringing use of making permissible backup and archival copies of the protected software. However, the court discounted the significance of other potential uses of the software that the defendant conceded had no commercial value.[28] Synthesizing these case principles, "commercial significance" or "substantiality" may be established if a consumer reasonably would acquire or use the product for the noninfringing purposes.

When evaluating noninfringing uses, courts will only look to noninfringing uses of those aspects of the products alleged to be put to infringing uses. For example, in *Sony*, the Supreme Court did not take into account the use of the VCR for playback purposes and, instead, evaluated only the noninfringing uses of the recording function of the product. Similarly, in *Oak Industries, Inc. v. Zenith Electronics Corp.*,[29] a court imposed contributory patent infringement liability where there were noninfringing uses for some elements of the accused product, but not for the particular aspects of the device that were alleged to infringe. The court distinguished this from the situation, such as in *Sony*, in which a device to perform one function necessarily but incidentally is capable of infringement.

Using Technology to Police Infringements

One mantra of content owners over the last decade is that "the answer to the problem of the machine lies in the machine." Technologies that regulate copying and redistribution can protect content through technological enforcement of individual compliance within the scope of behavior authorized by the copyright owner. In effect, technology can move the otherwise impossible task of enforcement against individuals one step higher in the chain, so as to place the burden upon the developers and manufacturers of recording and distribution technologies. Tasking technology companies and manufacturers with prevention of infringement therefore becomes an attractive option for an overall enforcement strategy.

However, the modest purpose of technological protection systems, to "keep honest people honest," acknowledges that even the most robust systems at some point will be defeated. Consequently, recent legislation mandates use of particular technologies and/or proscribes devices and actions that circumvent them. While intended to protect copyrighted works, such legislation regulates commerce rather than copyright. The result is a higher degree of protection for copyright owners, but less protection for the public interests that copyright was intended to serve, inasmuch as the explicit limitations and exemptions of copyright law, including fair use, do not apply to general commercial legislation.

The trend began with the Audio Home Recording Act (AHRA) of 1992, which required implementation in certain products of a simple system to prevent further digital copying of digital copies.[30] The Serial Copy Management System specifies two bits: one that signifies whether copy protection is being invoked over the content, and another that indicates whether the data is "original" or a "first-generation" copy. The law imposes requirements in two technical areas:

• Devices that transmit and carry the content ("digital audio interface devices") must accurately carry or transcode the SCMS data, and not strip it.

• Recorders covered by the AHRA must read and respond to these codes. If the bits indicate that the incoming data has protection asserted and is "original," the recorder permits the making of a copy and marks it as a "first-generation" copy. If the bits indicate that the incoming data has protection asserted and is already a first-generation copy, the recorder prevents the making of a second-generation or "serial" copy. Unlimited copies can be made from content where protection has not been asserted.

The AHRA has no exemption for fair use. It balances the technological protections for copyright owners with protections for consumers by "encoding rules" that ensure consumers the ability to make first-generation copies from unencrypted compact discs and, in the future, digital radio broadcasts.[31] These compromise protections are a proxy for, rather than an implementation of, fair use, and thus imperfectly reflect through a binary "copy/no-copy" choice some subset of the copying that might otherwise be sanctioned through a case-by-case weighing of multiple factors.

The battle resumed in 1995, with the issuance of the Report on Intellectual Property and the National Information Infrastructure, consummating with the 1998 passage of the DMCA. The DMCA presses copyright protection obligations upon technology companies in three ways:

• First, the DMCA proscribes services and technologies that circumvent access control systems such as encryption and authentication.[32] Provisions clarify that this proscription applies to "self-enforcing" technologies such as would only be circumvented through intentional conduct, and does not mandate that device manufacturers affirmatively respond to these systems;[33] except that mandatory response is required to current analog video protection systems, balanced by encoding rules that impose limits on the types of content to which copy protection can be applied.[34]

• Second, the DMCA requires preservation of "copyright management information" (such as identifying watermarks) against intentional removal.[35]

• Third, Title II of the DMCA sets forth obligations that can be voluntarily adopted by an Internet service provider, online service provider or information location site; and, in return, obtain a "safe harbor" limitation of monetary and injunctive liability against allegations of contributory infringement.[36]

Like the AHRA, the DMCA has no exemption for fair use.[37] The few exemptions to these DMCA provisions, intended primarily to benefit research, archives, and education, permit less personal copying and use than the AHRA.

As a result, digital media increasingly are being released in encrypted formats. CSS, the "Content Scrambling System" for DVD video, was the first step in a copy protection chain. Data from a DVD or other digital video source will be encrypted for transmission between devices along a home network; recording devices will, again, encrypt the recorded data in other formats. DVD audio and other media will soon follow the same pattern of encrypted delivery, transmission, and recording.

Watermarks also will assume a higher-profile role in this new paradigm. The recording industry established late in 1998 the "Secure Digital Music Initiative" (SDMI), which relies on watermarks initially to screen content so as to determine whether the content may be securely shared with devices that will respect the usage rules set by the content owner. In the video context, motion picture companies advocate use of watermarks for the dual purposes of "record control"—limiting or preventing the recording of watermarked content—and "playback control"—refusing to play back watermarked media that, but for the inevitable hacking of other protection mechanisms previously applied to the content, should not have been recorded. However, unlike the encryption and authentication systems protected under the DMCA, watermarks are not "self-enforcing." The requirement to read and respond to watermarks most efficiently can be imposed by legislation or licenses to other necessary technologies.[38]

The Dilemma for Distributed Applications

Although users of distributed network applications may engage in direct infringement, the technology itself inherently remains neutral. Both the centralized and decentralized topologies operate in exactly the same way regardless of whether all files being exchanged are authorized or unauthorized. At either extreme (all lawful/all unlawful), applying existing copyright law would be simple. The cases for distributed applications arise at points along a spectrum between the extremes, and therein lies the dilemma.

The Dilemma of Imposing Vicarious Liability upon Automatic Processes

With respect to vicarious liability, the dilemma is compounded by the different topologies described above for centralized and decentralized applications. For the decentralized "Gnutella" model, each participant along the network is both host and client. The right and ability to control user conduct resides only with the users themselves. As a result, vicarious liability for the acts of those who download is effectively inseparable from the direct act of authorizing the file for distribution. Enforcement for decentralized network applications therefore is identical to, and equally as problematic as, suing for direct infringement against each individual infringer. Hence, the concept of vicarious liability for decentralized distributed network applications has become irrelevant, if not entirely obsolete.

Centralized peer-to-peer systems, such as the "Napster" model, further test the vitality and extensibility of existing case law concerning vicarious liability. Some courts have suggested the possibility of vicarious liability where the technology could feasibly examine the exchanged data for indicia of permission.[39] However, in many cases the server responds to incoming requests in an automatic process, and has no actual ability to discern lawful from infringing conduct.

For the typical vicarious liability cases cited above, the law developed around fact patterns in which physical contact and human intervention enabled the defendant to identify and remedy infringing conduct, whether it be supervising a store employee copying tapes or overseeing the goods sold at a flea market. In each case, the imposition of liability followed from the actual physical capacity for supervision by more than just an "absentee landlord."

For centralized systems, the server does perform an ongoing function in operating the system, and hence the temptation exists to view service providers as more like the dance-hall or swap-meet operator. Yet the server's ability to exercise control may be limited and ineffective. If "control" translates as "the burden of screening all files," depending upon the nature and magnitude of the service, this could be infeasible; or it could so engulf processing capacity as to degrade the system to an unacceptable level of performance. In this connection, in enacting "safe harbors" for service providers under the DMCA, Congress recognized that the impracticality or impossibility of screening data files justified limiting service provider liability for contributory or vicarious infringement allegations. While courts should be wary of creating new exemptions that Congress has declined to enact, the policies underlying the "safe harbor" provisions of the DMCA caution that the concept of "technological control" by automated systems may be more oxymoron than axiom.[40]

In any event, screening would likely be ineffective or futile for content that lacks indicia differentiating between authorized and infringing uses. MP3 files cannot be screened for copyright infringement, since the MP3 format lacks any "flags" or bits indicating whether copyright is being asserted over the material, or whether the copyright owner permits or objects to the exchange and reproduction of the sound recording. Moreover, any user can disguise the content by assigning an alternative name to the file. Hence, efforts to screen infringements using file names will be both overbroad and underinclusive. Such screening will miss works whose names have intentionally been changed to hide infringing popular music, but conversely will exclude files whose names have been intentionally changed to the names of popular songs or artists so as to induce downloads of unknown artists. Further, screening by file name could eliminate access to different versions of the same song or different songs with the same name, even though some of the affected copyright owners might not object to such access.

Therefore, in cases where the capacity to supervise is technologically infeasible or ineffective in sifting infringing from noninfringing acts, it seems unrealistic to ascribe to automated centralized servers the "right and ability to exercise control" over users, particularly where the data lacks copyright management information or other indicia of protection. It is more likely that, with the trend toward technological protection mechanisms, vicarious liability will become a less potent weapon, and the norm for enforcement will be anticircumvention legislation.[41]

A Quantitative Approach to Contributory Infringement

With respect to contributory infringement claims, where products have both noninfringing and infringing uses, the courts must decide at which point the right to prevent unlawful activity outweighs the right to engage in legitimate conduct. The Supreme Court in the *Sony* decision enunciated a standard without drawing bright lines—indeed, specifically declining to declare how much use is "commercially significant"—effectively leaving quantification for future case-by-case analysis (464 U.S. at 442).

Notwithstanding, at least two aspects of the *Sony* decision suggest that a quantitatively small usage can defeat a claim for contributory infringement. First, the Court drew its standard from its cases interpreting the patent statute providing for contributory infringement,[42] noting that imposing liability upon staple articles of commerce effectively extends the patent monopoly beyond the statutory grant, and that there is a public interest in access to products that can be used for noninfringing purposes (464 U.S. at 440–441). The patent cases cited by the Court suggest that *any* commercial noninfringing use would be sufficient defense against liability.[43]

Second, in applying the "capable of substantial noninfringing use" standard, the *Sony* Court found two independent and sufficient grounds for affirmance: (a) consumers could record programming that either was not copyrighted or whose owners did not object to the recording; and, (b) unauthorized time-shift recording for subsequent viewing was fair use. As to the first ground, the Court cited the district court finding that only some 7.3% of programming recorded by consumers fell into this category (*id.* at 424); yet the Court held that imposing contributory liability would unfairly stifle the interests of those who welcomed time-shifting as a means to expand their audience (*id.* at 446).[44]

Toward a New Mode of Analysis

Ultimately, "substantiality" or "commercial significance" should not be addressed solely as a quantitative inquiry. Quantitative analysis implicitly measures past or current usage. Moreover, a pure quantitative analysis ignores the public interests underlying copyright law, and in affording the public access to the means of engaging in noninfringing conduct.

The Supreme Court *Sony* standard, that a product need merely be "capable" of substantial noninfringing uses, suggests a more expansive assessment: current uses; the prospects for those current uses extrapolated into the future; and the potential emergence of new noninfringing uses. Thus, even a small but socially valuable noninfringing use should be considered both for its current intrinsic importance and its potential impact should such use become widespread.

To address the capability of future noninfringing uses, therefore, the analysis also should encompass a qualitative examination of both the current and potential noninfringing uses. Such a qualitative inquiry more fully comports with the public and private interests implicated by intellectual property. As an example, the most fundamental public interest fostered by the grant of copyright is promoting the dissemination of copyrighted works. With reference to the above discussion of *Sony*, that public interest is fostered by file-sharing among interested consumers, but is outweighed by the impact of infringement to which all copyright owners object. Notwithstanding, as *Sony* suggests, this policy gains significance where copyright owners approve of or do not object to the dissemination.[45]

The public interest further extends to the progress and exploitation of new technology. From the printing press to the PC, technology is the means of bringing copyright works to the public. Inasmuch as one technological development may serve as building block for the next, a decision that bans new technologies—especially ones as innovative as peer-to-peer networking software systems—could have effects that reach much further than the case under consideration. Similarly, a proper analysis must also consider the impact of a decision upon the copyrights and patent rights of the manufacturers of products and software, since their independent rights to exploit their intellectual property could be negated by improvidently imposing contributory liability.

The following pages suggest a method for a evaluating third-party liability for the manufacture and dissemination of new technologies that have both infringing and noninfringing uses that takes into account both current analysis and these additional policies. These factors are not intended to be exclusive, nor the examples comprehensive. Rather, they illustrate the types of policies at issue when examining the existence and significance of noninfringing uses.

1. What Is the Nature of Each Potential Noninfringing Use?

In evaluating the claims of infringement, courts describe the acts of infringement, their current impact upon copyright owners, and the potential impact of these acts should the infringing acts continue unabated. In ruling on third-party liability claims, a court similarly should examine the character and value of the noninfringing uses of those particular aspects of the product used to commit the allegedly infringing acts. In this regard, this inquiry echoes the first factor of the fair use analysis. As such, it is not a "test," but a first step in identifying the uses that will be evaluated in several of the factors below.

This examination should consider the intrinsic value of the uses to both the individual users (i.e., what benefit does the user derive from the use?) and the owners of the material that is being used (e.g., what benefit is derived by copyright owners that do not object to the distribution or reproduction of their works?). A court also should consider whether the uses have any ancillary beneficial effects, such as whether the uses implement legitimate facilities provided for by law (e.g., the backup copying of software at issue in *Vault v. Quaid*), or create socially valuable structures (e.g., communication among admirers of particular art forms or artists, or among advocates of particular sociopolitical points of view). However, courts should resist giving weight to only the types of journalistic, educational, or scientific purposes enumerated in the fair use statute,[46] inasmuch as the *Sony* decision finds that even copying of entertainment programming in its entirety can be deemed a fair and protected use.

Importantly, the *Sony* standard—being "capable" of substantial noninfringing uses—requires courts to focus beyond the current extent of existing uses. The inquiry encompasses both the potential extent of existing uses in the future, and new potential uses as well. In this latter connection, courts should attempt to extrapolate new potential uses based on current uses of the technology and on analogous acts accomplished by other means. For example, if lending or exchange of physical objects today is commonplace, a court safely could presume that these practices would also become commonplace for digitized files.

Such analysis requires reasoned foresight, and admittedly it is easy for subjective preconceptions to cloud objective judgments. Yet today's products often become popular for surprising and initially unintended purposes. Few among us could accurately have predicted the pervasive role in daily life of facsimile machines, cell phones, laptop and palm-top computers, personal music players and recorders, or the World Wide Web.

The inevitable myopia of the present day counsels caution in how we envision our cohabitation with technology even two or five years hence.

Applying this factor, then, implies that the greater the potential intrinsic value of a noninfringing use, the greater the care that must be taken not to stifle or preclude that use by banning the technology.

2. What Is the Likelihood That Any Consumer Would Acquire and Use the Product for These Noninfringing Purposes?

As noted, current case law deems a use "insubstantial" if it is unlikely that the public actually would employ the accused technology for that purpose. Thus, noninfringing uses may be "substantial" as a matter of law if a significant number of persons would engage in those uses at least some of the time.

A lawsuit would not be brought if all persons used the product for noninfringing purposes all the time, and might not be seriously contested if all persons used the product for infringing purposes all the time. Thus, the purpose of this factor is to assess where the evidence lies along a spectrum of how many users engage in noninfringing conduct for what percentage of the time.

As discussed under factor 1 above, quantification of existing uses is but one element of this analysis. Evidence suggesting quantification of potential uses also should be considered (e.g., by reference to sales and penetration rates for analogous technologies and services). Moreover, a court should attempt to qualitatively evaluate these existing and potential uses, so as to assure that intrinsically valuable uses will receive due consideration.

Under this factor, if the evidence suggests a number of existing or potential noninfringing uses whose uses are not insubstantial, or the existence of intrinsically valuable noninfringing uses that would be fostered by the technology, then this factor should weigh against a finding of third-party liability.

3. What Is the Role of the Technology in Facilitating the Infringing Uses?

This factor addresses whether the technology facilitates previously unknown means of infringement, or whether alternative means have been available to commit the same acts of infringement. The court should consider whether there is a genuine difference in the magnitude of infringement using the various means, or whether the difference lies in the efficiency of infringement. For example, the mere existence of other means of infringement should not justify the existence of another or more efficient means. Notwithstanding, an increase in infringement or efficiency might be outweighed by other factors.

4. What Is the Role of the Technology in Facilitating the Noninfringing Uses?

The *Sony* decision was founded explicitly upon the public interests implicated in the availability of noninfringing uses of the technology. Thus, in reviewing claims for third-party liability, a court also must consider how the technology facilitates such uses. Does the technology enhance the means by which the public accesses or uses copyrighted works for noninfringing purposes? Does the availability of such technology induce more copyright owners to make their works available for such licensed or unobjectionable uses? Does the technology otherwise increase the efficiency of disseminating copyrighted works for such noninfringing uses? For example, does the accused technology facilitate provide an easier interface; improve file compression size, performance characteristics, or transmission speeds; or expand the database of works available for noninfringing uses?

Under this factor, a manufacturer should be able to establish a need for the technology if there are no alternate or equivalent access to noninfringing uses, or if the technology meaningfully increases public access to noninfringing uses. A showing of need, coupled with intrinsically valuable noninfringing uses, would support a finding of no contributory infringement.

5. What Is the Likelihood That, If the Technology Is or Is Not Deemed to Be Infringing, Noninfringing Uses Will Proliferate?

Fair-use analysis considers the potential harm to the copyright owner should the alleged infringement become widespread. The factor suggested here essentially inverts that fair-use factor to assess the impact of the technology in facilitating future noninfringing uses. It is based upon the same premise underlying factor 4, i.e., that a technology that may substantially expand noninfringing uses has greater entitlement to a favorable judgment than a technology that has no perceptible impact on noninfringing use.

Courts therefore should consider the extent to which the technology makes possible the noninfringing uses, and whether previous means to achieve the noninfringing uses are equally efficient and equally accessible to the public as the technology at issue. Similarly, a court should consider whether a finding of infringement would compel the technology owner to eliminate certain product capabilities and, as a result, reduce the capacity for certain noninfringing uses. In such cases, a court should consider the impact on noninfringing uses if the technology were altered so as to accommodate the interests of aggrieved copyright owners. For example, if a music sharing program would be required to be redesigned so as to accept only encrypted content, a court could evaluate the potential harm to any new and established artists who wished to disseminate their music in unprotected formats.

6. What Impact Would a Finding of Infringement Have upon the Technology and Technological Progress?

This factor evaluates the public interest in the availability of the technology. Consideration should be given to whether hindering current uses of this technology might also impede development and use of the technology for other purposes. For example, a court might assess whether or how a finding of infringement with respect to the sharing and copying of music might deter development of similar technology for other unprotected media, such as photographs or text, or for protected media. In balancing these factors, a court should hesitate to impose liability where such a finding might impede the use of the technology for other noninfringing purposes.

Conclusion

Copyright ultimately serves a public purpose. When public and private interests collide, the public interests emerge as paramount.[47] For that reason, this paper suggests factors that reflect the public policies underlying copyright and third-party liability, and the public interests in securing access both to noninfringing uses of copyrighted works and to technologies that facilitate these and future noninfringing uses.

Courts face a difficult task in balancing public and private interests, and we cannot expect omniscience in their decision making. Nevertheless, the interests of all parties can only be protected with careful analysis and reasoned foresight. Particularly when evaluating evolutionary technologies such as peer-to-peer network applications, the risks facing copyright owners, technology companies, and the public at large are genuine and complex. Copyright owners bear tremendous financial risk from widespread infringement that may be facilitated by such technologies, and restraining technology can provide more direct, effective and efficient enforcement than the courts. Yet imposing constraints on technology can kill the goose that lays the golden egg. The same technology that facilitates infringement often creates new markets for copyright owners and socially beneficial opportunities for consumers.[48]

It bears repeating that the VCR navigated a tortuous path through the courts to remain on the retail shelf. In 1976, the movie studios sued Sony Corporation for contributory copyright infringement. A district court first found for Sony, but the court of appeals then reversed, in favor of the plaintiff movie studios. More than seven years after suit was filed, the Supreme Court found for Sony—after two oral arguments, and by only a single vote.[49] How different our world would be today without the VCR and the technologies it spawned—such as digital audio tape recorders and digital video cassette recorders (which use the same helical-scan recording head technology), and DVD and DVD recorders (built upon the existing consumer appetite for home video). How different will our world be tomorrow if the courts deal Internet technologies, like distributed network applications, a different fate?

Notes

1. *See Religious Tech. Center v. Netcom On-Line Communication Serv., Inc.,* 907 F. Supp. 1361 (N.D. Cal. 1995).

2. Title II of the DMCA, 17 U.S.C. § 512.

3. MP3 is a voluntary audio file format standard adopted by the Motion Picture Experts Group in the late 1980s as the audio layer 3 of the MPEG-1 audiovisual format. Based on technology from the Fraunhofer Institute, MP3 has become the Internet music format of choice because it reproduces quality sound in a file com-

pressed more than 10 times smaller than the CD Red Book audio format. Unlike other formats such as CD audio or DAT, MP3 lacks any "flag" bits that indicate whether the file may be copied, or other technological protections that might inhibit copying and distribution.

4. See ⟨http://www.riaa.com/News_Story.cfm?id = 69⟩.

5. Public Law 105–147, 111 Stat. 2678. See ⟨http://news.cnet.com/news/ 0-1005-200-346316.html⟩.

6. On December 6, 1999, 18 recording companies filed suit against Napster based on contributory infringement and vicarious liability. On July 26, 2000, Judge Marilyn Hall Patel entered a preliminary injunction against Napster, finding that plaintiffs had established a likelihood of success on the merits of both claims. The injunction was stayed two days later by the Ninth Circuit Court of Appeals. On August 11, 2000, Judge Patel issued her written opinion addressing the preliminary injunction motion, ⟨http://www.cand.uscourts.gov/cand/ tentrule.nsf/4f9d4c4a03b0cf70882567980073b2e4/74bf2867dde99f0f8825693 8007a1205/$FILE/NapsterF%26C2.pdf⟩ (hereinafter referred to as "*Napster II*").

7. See ⟨http:/www.gnutella.wego.com/⟩.

8. See ⟨http://freenet.sourceforge.net/⟩. A separate company named Uprizer has been formed to commercialize and exploit the Freenet technology. ⟨http://www. uprizer.com⟩.

9. Section 106 provides: Subject to sections 107 through 120, the owner of copyright under this title has the exclusive rights to do and to authorize any of the following:

a. to reproduce the copyrighted work in copies or phonorecords;

b. to prepare derivative works based upon the copyrighted work;

c. to distribute copies or phonorecords of the copyrighted work to the public by sale or other transfer of ownership, or by rental, lease, or lending;

d. in the case of literary, musical, dramatic, and choreographic works, pan-tomimes, and motion pictures and other audiovisual works, to perform the copy-righted work publicly;

e. in the case of literary, musical, dramatic, and choreographic works, pan-tomimes, and pictorial, graphic, or sculptural works, including the individual images of a motion picture or other audiovisual work, to display the copyrighted work publicly; and

f. in the case of sound recordings, to perform the copyrighted work publicly by means of a digital audio transmission.

10. *Sony Corp. of America v. Universal City Studios*, 464 U.S. at 417, 432–33, 104 S. Ct. 774, 784, 78 L. Ed.2d 574 (1984).

11. *See Playboy Enter., Inc. v. Frena*, 839 F. Supp. 1552, 1559 (M.D. Fla. 1993).

12. *Religious Tech. Center v. Netcom On-Line Communication Serv., Inc.*, 907 F. Supp. at 1375.

13. *Fonovisa Inc. v. Cherry Auction, Inc.*, 76 F.3d 259, 264 (9th Cir. 1996).

14. *Shapiro Bernstein & Co., v. H.L. Green Co.,* 316 F.2d 304, 307 (2d Cir. 1963).

15. *Deutsch v. Arnold,* 98 F.2d 686 (2d Cir. 1938); *Fromont v. Aeolian Co.,* 254 F. 592 (S.D.N.Y. 1918).

16. *Buck v. Jewell-LaSalle Reality Co.,* 283 U.S. 191, 198–99 (1931); *Dreamland Ball Room, Inc. v. Shapiro, Bernstein & Co.,* 36 F.2d 354 (7th Cir. 1929); *M. Witmark & Sons v. Tremont Soc. & Athletic Club,* 188 F. Supp. 787 (D. Mass. 1960); *Renmick Music Corp. v. Interstate Hotel Co.,* 58 F. Supp. 523 (D. Neb. 1944), *aff'd,* 157 F.2d 744 (8th Cir. 1946).

17. 316 F.2d at 308.

18. 845 F.2d 773 (8th Cir. 1988).

19. 76 F.3d 259 (9th Cir. 1996).

20. *Netcom,* 907 F. Supp at 1374–75, 1382.

21. *Netcom,* 907 F. Supp at 1374–75, 1382.

22. *Id.,* 907 F. Supp. at 1374.

23. *Sega Enters. Ltd. v. MAPHIA,* 857 F. Supp. 679 (N.D. Cal. 1994).

24. *Cable/Home Communication Corp. v. Network Prods., Inc.,* 902 F.2d 829, 845–47 (11th Cir. 1990).

25. *Sony Corp. of America v. Universal City Studios, Inc.,* 464 U.S. at 421, 435 n. 17, 439. *See also A&M Records, Inc. v. Abdallah,* 948 F. Supp. 1449, 1456 (C.D. Cal. 1996), noting that *Sony* applies to cases involving "staple articles or commodities of commerce," such as VCRs, photocopiers, and blank, standard-length cassettes tapes. Contrast this with the finding in *Napster II* that it was sufficient that Napster knew that infringement was occurring, even though it was incapable of determining whether any particular file transfer constituted infringement. Opinion at 26–27.

26. *Sony Corp. of America v. Universal City Studios, Inc.,* 464 U.S. at 439.

27. *In re Certain Personal Computers and Components Thereof,* Inv. No. 337-TA-140, 6 ITRD 1140, 1150 (1984).

28. 847 F.2d 255, 263–64 and n. 16 (5th Cir. 1988).

29. 697 F. Supp. 988 (N.D. Ill. 1988).

30. 17 U.S.C. §1001, *et seq.*

31. 17 U.S.C. §1002(a) requires use of serial copy protections; §1002(c) prohibits circumvention of the systems; and §1002(d) proscribes intentional misencoding of original works so as to prevent copying.

32. 17 U.S.C. §1201(a) and (b). *See also* 17 U.S.C. §114(d)(2)(C)(v)–(vii), imposing limited technological protection obligations on entities newly eligible for the statutory license to perform sound recordings.

33. 17 U.S.C. §1201(c)(3).

34. 17 U.S.C. §1201(k).

35. 17 U.S.C. §1202.

36. 17 U.S.C. §512.

37. It is clear that 17 U.S.C. § 1201(c)(1) means that the DMCA does not diminish the fair use defense in cases alleging copyright infringement, not that fair use is a defense under § 1201(a) or (b) for users and manufacturers of circumvention devices. See *Universal City Studios, Inc. v. Reimerdes*, 00 Civ. 0277 (LAK) (S.D.N.Y.), Opinion, August 17, 2000 at 40–45 (stating that neither fair use nor the *Sony* standard applied to a case under Section 1201 of the DMCA involving the dissemination of unlicensed software to decrypt scrambled DVD movies). See also *RealNetworks, Inc. v. Streambox, Inc.*, 000 U.S. Dist. LEXIS 1889 pars. 15–16 (W.D. Wa. Jan. 18, 2000) (noting that devices that could be used for fair use, and thus be immune from liability under the *Sony* doctrine, are nevertheless liable under Section 1201 of the DMCA); and Statement of Marybeth Peters, Register of Copyrights, before the House Subcommittee on Courts and Intellectual Property, on H.R. 2281, 105th Congress, 1st Session, September 16, 1997, at ⟨http://lcweb.loc.gov//copyright/docs/2180_stat.html⟩.

38. On June 7, 2000, Disney Chairman and CEO Michael Eisner made this point in an address to the Joint Economic Committee of Congress:

On offense, we ask you to begin to explore with us legislation that would assure the efficacy of technology solutions to copyright security. As we seek to develop measures such as watermarking, we need the assurance that the people who manufacture computers and the people who operate ISPs will cooperate by incorporating the technology to look for and respond to the watermarks. This same mandate could be part of the solution to a host of other Internet security issues as well. (⟨http://www.senate.gov/~jec/eisner.htm⟩).

39. See, e.g., *Religious Tech. Center v. Netcom On-Line Communication Serv., Inc.*, in which the court declined summary judgment on a claim of vicarious infringement lodged against an Internet service provider, where the system users uploaded alleging material to the system using automatic and indiscriminate processes that operated without human intervention. The court found that the plaintiff had raised a question of fact whether Netcom could have exercised control by identifying and removing infringing postings to Usenet. 907 F. Supp. at 1375–76.

40. The court in *Napster II* acknowledged Napster's argument that it is "technologically difficult, and perhaps infeasible to distinguish legal and illegal conduct." Opinion at 30. But, apparently referring to Napster's "blackballing" of more than 330,000 directly infringing users identified by the band Metallica, the court concluded that Napster had the right and ability to supervise user conduct based on its ability to block individual users from access to the system. Opinion at 30. This seems erroneous in that it equates Napster's ability to respond after the fact with the ability to control in advance the individual uses. Only the latter should be relevant for purposes of finding the ability or right to control, otherwise defendants would always incur liability without the capacity to prevent it. Moreover, it would seem contrary to public policy to punish the centralized server for providing incomplete assistance to copyright owners where complete control is not possible. Under such circumstances, imposing liability might drive adoption of the decentralized model that cannot help copyright owners.

41. One such technological measure was recently announced by an online distributor of music in digitally downloaded form, Emusic.com. The technology analyzes objective data concerning a music file, including a cryptographic "hash"

value of the file and an audio "fingerprint" of a portion of the music, to determine whether a file offered for distribution by a Napster user originated from the Emusic.com service. The user then receives a notice from Emusic requesting that the user cease distribution of the files. If the user fails to comply within 24 hours, Emusic will request Napster to block the user's account. *See* "EMUSIC TARGETS NAPSTER WITH EFFORT TO HALT ILLEGAL DISTRIBUTION OF EMUSIC MP3s," November 21, 2000, ⟨http://www.emusic.com/about/pr/pr138.html⟩.

42. "Whoever sells a component of a patented machine, manufacture, combination or composition, or a material or apparatus for use in practicing a patented process, constituting a material part of the invention, knowing the same to be especially made or especially adapted for use in an infringement of such patent, and not a staple article or commodity of commerce suitable for substantial non-infringing use, shall be liable as a contributory infringer," 35 U.S.C. § 271(c).

43. "These cases deny the patentee any right to control the distribution of unpatented articles unless they are 'unsuited for any commercial noninfringing use.' *Dawson Chemical Co. v. Rohm & Haas Co.,* 448 U.S. 176, 198 (1980). Unless a commodity 'has no use except through practice of the patented method,' *id.*, at 199, the patentee has no right to claim that its distribution constitutes contributory infringement.... '[A] sale of an article which though adapted to an infringing use is also adapted to other and lawful uses, is not enough to make the seller a contributory infringer. Such a rule would block the wheels of commerce.' *Henry v. A. B. Dick Co.,* 224 U.S. 1, 48 (1912), overruled on other grounds, *Motion Picture Patents Co. v. Universal Film Mfg. Co.,* 243 U.S. 502, 517 (1917)."

44. If there are millions of owners of VTR's who make copies of televised sports events, religious broadcasts, and educational programs such as Mister Rogers' Neighborhood, and if the proprietors of those programs welcome the practice, the business of supplying the equipment that makes such copying feasible should not be stifled simply because the equipment is used by some individuals to make unauthorized reproductions of respondents' works. The respondents do not represent a class composed of all copyright holders. Yet a finding of contributory infringement would inevitably frustrate the interests of broadcasters in reaching the portion of their audience that is available only through time-shifting.

Of course, the fact that other copyright holders may welcome the practice of time-shifting does not mean that respondents should be deemed to have granted a license to copy their programs. Third-party conduct would be wholly irrelevant in an action for direct infringement of respondents' copyrights. But in an action for contributory infringement against the seller of copying equipment, the copyright holder may not prevail unless the relief that he seeks affects only his programs, or unless he speaks for virtually all copyright holders with an interest in the outcome. In this case, the record makes it perfectly clear that there are many important producers of national and local television programs who find nothing objectionable about the enlargement in the size of the television audience that results from the practice of time-shifting for private home use. The seller of the equipment that expands those producers' audiences cannot be a contributory infringer if, as is true in this case, it has had no direct involvement with any infringing activity. (*Id.*, 464 U.S. at 446–447; footnote omitted).

45. One puzzling aspect of *Napster II*, then, is the court's failure to take cognizance of numerous copyright owners, including several gold- and multiplatinum-

selling artists such as rapper Chuck D and the band The Offspring, who submitted affidavits indicating that they supported and did not object to the sharing of their works through Napster.

46. 17 U.S.C. §107.

47. "The immediate effect of our copyright law is to secure a fair return for an author's creative labor. But the ultimate aim is, by this incentive, to stimulate artistic creativity for the general public good. 'The sole interest of the United States and the primary object in conferring the monopoly,' this Court has said, 'lie in the general benefits derived by the public from the labors of authors.'" *Twentieth Century Music Corp. v. Aiken*, 422 U.S. 151, 156 (1975); citations and footnotes omitted.

48. In apparent recognition of the potential value of peer-to-peer technologies, on October 31, 2000, Napster announced that it had concluded an agreement with one of the five major recording companies, Bertelsmann AG, whereby Napster would create a membership-based service that would allow file-sharing activities and provide compensation to rightholders. The announced intention was to continue to offer Napster users access to all content, not just sound recordings owned by Bertelsmann. Once the service is in place, Bertelsmann agreed to drop its lawsuit against Napster. ⟨http://www.napster.com/pressroom/pr/001031. html⟩.

49. *See* "Betamax: The Inside Story," ⟨http://www.hrrc.org/html/inside_betamax.html⟩.

15

Should Congress Establish a Compulsory License for Internet Video Providers to Retransmit Over-the-Air TV Station Programming via the Internet?

Michael Wirth and Larry Collette

Introduction

The rollout of broadband systems, new video-streaming technology and improvements in the back-office capabilities of Internet Service Providers (ISPs) will someday combine to make wide-scale video delivery to consumers via the Internet both technologically possible and economically feasible (Potter, 2000; Tedesco, 1999). The movement toward increased delivery of video entertainment programming via the Internet raises a number of significant intellectual property issues (Hardy, 1999; Rosenoer, 1997; Grebb, 2000).

This public policy concern was highlighted by a January 2000 complaint filed in U.S. District Court by 10 motion picture and three broadcast companies against iCraveTV, a Canadian-based Internet company that retransmitted broadcast content, without permission, from a number of U.S. over-the-air (OTA) television stations (*Twentieth Century Fox Film Corporation v. iCraveTV*, 2000). The complaint alleged that iCrave TV was responsible for "one of the largest and most brazen thefts of intellectual property ever committed in the United States." The company was charged with seizing copyrighted materials (TV programs and motion pictures) and allowing public performance of them without authorization (Townley, 2000).

In November 1999, Congress passed the Satellite Home Viewers Improvement Act of 1999 (SHVIA) (1999). Copyright holders wanted Congress to outlaw the retransmission of OTA TV stations via the Internet in the absence of copyright holder retransmission consent (Peters, 2000). Several ISPs (including AOL) wanted Congress to allow ISPs to retransmit OTA TV stations utilizing program carriage copyright models previously established for direct broadcast satellite (DBS) and cable television entrepreneurs (Fusco, 1999). Ultimately, Congress decided not to include any Internet video-retransmission provisions in the SHVIA (Peters, 2000).

Congress will eventually have to grapple with the copyright issues presented by the retransmission of OTA TV stations via the Internet. In particular, Congress may decide to establish a model allowing Internet video providers to retransmit OTA TV station programming through the establishment of a compulsory license similar to the compulsory license established for cable and DBS. Alternatively, Congress may decide that Internet video providers must obtain retransmission consent from copyright owners in order to carry OTA TV stations.

Mitch Kapor's admonition that information on the Internet "wants to be free" refers to movement and access, not to the costs associated with it. Creators and copyright owners will demand to be paid just as they have for content delivered by other means. Yet the Internet's unique qualities defy the routine use of existing copyright licensing schemes. For example, the centralized control of distribution, which has made it fairly easy for license holders to control how and where their product is utilized, is generally absent in the Internet world (Cohen, 1996, 428). Likewise, the notions of geographic space that are often associated with fundamental property rights do not exist in cyberspace (Barlow, 1996).

This study examines the copyright issues associated with retransmission of OTA TV station programming via the Internet. The study's central research question is: Should Congress establish a compulsory license for Internet video providers to retransmit OTA TV station programming similar to the compulsory licenses established for cable and DBS?

We first provide a brief background on compulsory licensing for cable and satellite entrepreneurs. We then provide the arguments for and against establishing a compulsory license for Internet video providers. Next, we state and defend our policy objective, followed by a discussion of the key issues involved in deciding whether to establish a compulsory license. The study's final section contains our policy recommendations and conclusions.

Cable and Satellite Compulsory Licensing

In general, the owners of copyrighted works have the exclusive right to exploit their works in order to promote the production of creative works (17 U.S.C. Sec. 106). "Compulsory licenses are abrogations of one or more of these exclusive rights and permit certain parties to use the copyrighted work without the consent of the copyright owner" (Peters, 2000). Congress can statutorily grant compulsory licenses if it believes such a grant is in the public interest (Rooks, 1995, 275). In the case of the cable and satellite industry, Congress has established a compulsory license (17 U.S.C. Sec. 111 for cable; 17 U.S.C. Secs. 119 and 122 for satellites)

which allows cable operators and satellite carriers to retransmit (and consequently perform) the programming contained on television broadcast stations. Cable operators and satellite carriers are guaranteed access to broadcast programming; the copyright owners of these television programs cannot say no, nor can they bargain the price and terms of a license agreement. (Peters, 2000)

Utilization of the compulsory license requires cable and satellite entrepreneurs: to refrain from altering imported OTA TV signals in any manner (including stripping the retransmitted signal of advertising and substituting new ads), to refrain from importing OTA signals from other countries (with limited localized exceptions for Canadian and Mexican stations), and to simultaneously retransmit imported signals (although cable operators "may transmit a recording of an imported signal once") (Cates, 1990, 204). The highly regulated nature of the cable and satellite industry also played (and continues to play) a role here. Cable and satellite entrepreneurs are subject to such regulations as must-carry, syndicated and sports exclusivity, network nonduplication, and public interest requirements (U.S. Copyright Office, 1997, 96). These rules are designed to protect and preserve the local broadcast system and the rights of copyright owners and to require that cable and satellite entrepreneurs serve the public interest.[1]

Although many groups have argued that the compulsory licenses granted to cable and satellite entrepreneurs should be eliminated (see for example U.S. Copyright Office, 1997; Cates, 1990), they continue to exist. In fact, Congress recently extended the compulsory license for satellite carrier importation of distant signals for another five years and granted satellite carriers a permanent compulsory license for carriage of local TV signals (Satellite Home Viewers Improvement Act of 1999; The dish on satellite TV reform: redux, 1999).

Arguments in Favor of a Compulsory License for Internet Rebroadcasts

A number of industry groups, individuals, and academics favor establishment of a compulsory license (similar to the one provided for cable and satellite entrepreneurs) to allow Internet webcasters to retransmit the signals of distant signal and local OTA television stations. Parties favoring establishment of a compulsory license include: Peggy Miles, Chairman of the International Webcasting Association and President of Intervox Communication; Ian McCallum, Vice President of Corporate Sales and Development for TVRadioNow, Corporation (which operates iCraveTV.com); Jonathan Potter, Executive Director of the Digital Media Association (DiMA); Audio Net (now Broadcast.com); and Baoding Hsieh Fan, J.D. Arguments favoring establishment of a compulsory license are as follows.

Minimization of Transaction Costs
Granting Internet Webcasters a compulsory license to retransmit OTA television stations is economically efficient because it will minimize the transaction costs related to obtaining the rights to retransmit OTA television stations. It would be "impractical and unduly burdensome" to require every Internet webcaster to negotiate with every copyright owner whose work was retransmitted by an Internet webcaster (Miles, 2000; Fan, 2000, 634, 641; Cohen, 1996, 425; U.S. Copyright Office, 1997, 93).

Reducing Barriers to Entering the MVPD Marketplace for Internet Webcasters
A compulsory license will reduce barriers to entering the multichannel video program distribution (MVPD) marketplace. The increased competition for incumbent MVPD providers (i.e., cable and DBS) that results will clearly benefit consumers and serve the public interest (Miles, 2000; Potter, 2000; Fan, 634, 641; U.S. Copyright Office, 1997, 94).

Increased Consumer Welfare from Expanded Internet Video Offerings

If Internet webcasters receive a compulsory license it will positively impact the diversity of programming available to U.S. consumers. The First Amendment offers clear support to public policy that expands and enhances the marketplace of ideas (Miles, 2000; Potter, 2000; Fan, 2000, 635; U.S. Copyright Office, 1997, 94).

Serves a Different Audience

For the foreseeable future, Internet video webcasters will serve a different audience from OTA TV broadcasters, cable systems and satellite carriers (i.e., those who do not have access to a television set). Therefore, granting Internet webcasters a compulsory license will not impact the economic viability of incumbent MVPD systems nor harm the economic value of the copyrighted works they carry (McCallum, 2000).

No Impact on Retransmitted Advertisements

A compulsory license will not harm OTA TV stations' advertising base. Just as for cable and satellite providers, regulation can guarantee that OTA stations are retransmitted without alteration (Potter, 2000).

Economic Value of Increased Audiences for Local TV Stations

Granting Internet webcasters a compulsory license will increase the audiences generated by local TV stations. This in turn will allow local television stations to increase their advertising revenue by selling the additional audience generated to advertisers (Potter, 2000).

Minimizing Illegitimate Video Streaming

The problems related to illegitimate video streaming on the Internet will be minimized by a compulsory license. Creation of a legal method for compensating copyright owners of OTA-TV-station-delivered video content reduces the likelihood that illegitimate video-streaming sites will develop and that they will be tolerated when they do come into existence (Potter, 2000).

Convergence

Allowing webcasters to obtain a compulsory license clearly recognizes that convergence has rendered technology-based distinctions between video delivery platforms arbitrary and meaningless. Failure to create technology-neutral regulations (i.e., level the playing field) will significantly reduce the consumer welfare resulting from convergence (Potter, 2000).

Competition among Internet Webcasters

Creating a compulsory license will reduce the likelihood that a few large ISPs and copyright holders (e.g., AOL–Time Warner, Paramount, etc.) will dominate Internet webcasting. Minimization of the transaction costs of obtaining the right to retransmit OTA TV stations will potentially allow for the coexistence of small and large Internet webcasters (Fan, 2000, 633; Cohen, 1996, 426).

Catalyst for Broadband Deployment

A compulsory license will increase the speed of advanced telecommunication system deployment and penetration. Policies designed to speed broadband deployment are consistent with Section 706 of the Telecommunications Act of 1996, which requires the FCC to "encourage the deployment on a reasonable and timely basis of advanced telecommunications capability to all Americans" (U.S. Congress, 1996).

Arguments against a Compulsory License for Internet Rebroadcasts

A number of industry groups, individuals, and academics *are not* in favor of establishing a compulsory license to allow Internet webcasters to retransmit the signals of distant and local OTA television stations. Parties arguing against establishment of a compulsory license include: Marybeth Peters, Register of Copyrights of the U.S. Copyright Office; Jack Valenti, President and CEO of the Motion Picture Association of America; Thomas J. Ostertag, General Counsel in the Office of the Commissioner of Baseball; Edward O. Fritts, President and CEO of the National Association of Broadcasters; Dean Kay, President and CEO of Lichelle Music and Board Member of the American Society of Composers, Authors and Publishers; the Recording Industry Association of America; Broadcast Music Incorporated; the NCAA; the NBA; the NHL; ABC; Time Warner; NBC; Cox Communications; NPR; the Information Infrastructure Task Force's Working Group on Intellectual Property

Rights; and Trotter Hardy, J.D. Arguments against establishment of a compulsory license are as follows.

Inability to Limit Internet Retransmissions Geographically
A compulsory license should not be established for Internet webcasters because it is impossible to limit Internet retransmissions of OTA TV station signals geographically. Absent the discovery of a foolproof system for limiting retransmitted OTA TV station signals to local markets (similar to cable), OTA TV station signals, retransmitted under a compulsory license, will instantly become available worldwide with no control or compensation for the copyright owner (Peters, 2000; Fritts, 2000; Ostertag, 2000; U.S. Copyright Office, 1997, 97; Cohen, 1996, 428).

Perfect Digital Copies
There is currently no foolproof technological method of copy-protecting retransmitted OTA TV signals. In the absence of foolproof copy-protection technology, perfect digital copies of retransmitted OTA TV signals will be downloaded by recipients and "redisseminated without limit online" (Torpoco, 1997, 24). This situation is exacerbated by the fact that many consumers believe that information obtained on the Internet is free for their "taking, exploitation and unlimited distribution without payment to the copyright owner" (Peters, 2000; Ostertag, 2000; Torpoco, 1997, 22–3).

Detecting Unauthorized Reception of Copyrighted Material
Detecting unauthorized reception of copyrighted material on the Internet is very difficult (Cohen, 1996, 427–8; Torpoco, 1997, 24–5). Detection problems are exacerbated by the worldwide nature of the Internet and the intent of a significant number of Internet webcasters to retransmit to the widest audience possible (Peters, 2000; U.S. Copyright Office, 1997, 97). This will render "any sort of compulsory copyright license … untenable and unenforceable" (Fritts, 2000).

The Unregulated Nature of the Internet
At this point in time, the FCC and Congress have left the Internet largely free from regulation (Peters, 1999; U.S. Copyright Office, 1997, 96). Abandonment of a free-market approach to determining copyright fees

runs counter to the open-market, unregulated nature of the Internet (Fritts, 2000; Ostertag, 2000, Peters, 2000; U.S. Copyright Office, 1997, 95; Information Infrastructure Task Force, 1995, 199).

Survival of the Local Broadcasting System

A compulsory license could ultimately lead to the destruction of the OTA local system of broadcasting (Fritts, 2000; U.S. Copyright Office, 1997, 96). In the absence of adequate and enforceable regulatory restrictions (e.g., network nonduplication, syndicated program exclusivity, etc.) and foolproof technological solutions to implement these restrictions, the economic viability of local television stations could be severely impacted by establishment of a compulsory license for Internet webcasters (Fritts, 2000; U.S. Copyright Office, 1997, 96).

Program Migration

A compulsory license should not be established for Internet webcasters because it will lead copyright owners to migrate valuable programs from "free over-the-air television stations to services not covered by the compulsory license." This would harm consumers and result in a reduction of consumer welfare (Ostertag, 2000; Cate, 1990, 228).

Copyright Owners as Internet Distributors

Video copyright owners do not need third-party packagers to distribute their product via the Internet; they can do it themselves (U.S. Copyright Office, 1997, 95). This is because the delivery platform is already in place (i.e., the Internet), minimizing the up-front investment required to become a program distributor (Peters, 2000; Ostertag, 2000). Many copyright owners may still choose to use a third-party packager. However, given the security risks inherent in distributing one's video product via the Internet, copyright owners should not be forced, via a compulsory license, to make their product available to third-party Internet distributors (Peters, 2000).

Market vs. Government-Set Price Controls

Copyright owners will not receive fair market value for their works if a compulsory license is created (Peters, 2000; Ostertag, 2000; U.S. Copyright Office, 1997, 95). If government-set compulsory license royalties are too low, it will have a negative impact on investment and allocation efficiency within the program production industry because authors will "create less than they might have and the public is worse off as a result" (Hardy, 698, 702–3).

Shift of Transaction Costs from Retransmitters to Copyright Owners

A compulsory license will simply shift the transaction costs from Internet webcasters to copyright owners (Ostertag, 2000). In order to obtain the copyright fees collected annually under the compulsory license for cable operators and satellite carriers, copyright owners must negotiate/compete with each other to determine their share of the collected copyright royalties. This is typically a very time-consuming and expensive process (Ostertag, 2000).

Compliance with the Berne Convention

A compulsory license should not be established because, "[g]iven the present state of the technology, it appears unlikely that we could implement a Berne-compatible compulsory licensing regime that permits unencrypted retransmissions of television signals over the Internet" (Peters, 2000). According to the U.S. Copyright Office, reception of retransmitted OTA TV signals under a compulsory license must be restricted to within the United States to comply with the Berne Convention's territorial limitation on compulsory licenses (Peters, 2000).

Abrogation of the Reproduction Right

Unlike the compulsory license for cable and satellite carriers, which only involves the performance right, creation of such a license for Internet webcasters will result in the abrogation of two exclusive 17 U.S.C. Sec. 106 rights—the performance right and the reproduction right (Peters, 2000; U.S. Copyright Office, 1997, 98). This occurs because "Internet transmissions require the making of temporary copies within the computer systems delivering the retransmission [to] allow the audio or video programming to appear to be played in real time to the end user" (Peters, 2000; Torpoco, 1997, 38).

Statement of Policy Objective

Now that the arguments for and against adoption of a compulsory license for Internet webcasters, as put forth by the parties of interest, have been summarized, we turn to the statement of our policy objective. Our policy objective, which frames the remainder of our discussion, is as follows: To insure that the rights of video copyright owners are protected on the Internet while encouraging the timely development of the Internet as a viable video distribution system.

Defense of Policy Objective

The right of copyright owners to be compensated for uses of their works on the Internet is unquestioned. As a result, it is of primary importance that a system be created to adequately protect creative video works and to adequately compensate the creators of those works on the Internet. Failure to develop such a system will significantly inhibit the development of the Internet as a system for distributing traditional video product. With billions of dollars at stake, video copyright owners can ill afford to allow their works to be freely distributed on the Internet (Torpoco, 1997, 67; Cohen, 1996, 405–6). However, the decentralized and global nature of the Internet, coupled with the current limitations of technology capable of limiting geographic distribution and of providing copy protection, makes it very difficult to protect the rights of video copyright owners once their works are performed on the Internet (Peters, 2000).

Another reason for viewing the protection of video copyright owners rights as of primary importance here is the free-market nature of the Internet. Up to this point in time, regulators have taken a largely "hands-off" approach to the Internet. Such an approach appears to be working. The World Wide Web continues to expand its content geometrically under this laissez-faire regime. Likewise, the number of people online continues to grow at an astounding pace. The impetus to "get connected" is a social and cultural phenomenon that is not currently driven to any great extent by the desire to receive video entertainment. Although it is highly desirable to see the Internet develop into a viable delivery system for video entertainment/information programming, the establishment of policies designed to enhance the viability of Internet webcasters is of secondary importance if such policies have significant negative implications for video copyright owners. In the absence of strong evidence that government intervention is required here, the free market, with all its benefits and complexities, should be allowed to operate.

Discussion

The major issues involved in considering whether a compulsory license should be established here include: transaction costs, lack of market failure, reducing barriers to MVPD market entry, geographic limitations on Internet retransmissions, copy protection/security, the free-market nature of the Internet, local broadcasting system survival, copyright owners as Internet distributors, and obtaining fair market value.

Transaction Costs

There is no doubt that granting Internet webcasters a compulsory license to retransmit OTA television stations will minimize the transaction costs of obtaining the rights to retransmit OTA TV stations. However, this is hardly a compelling argument. As Hardy indicates, a compulsory license is a form of price fixing.

Other things being equal, price fixing always lowers transaction costs because it avoids the need for bargaining. If that were a suitable justification in general, then Congress ought to establish prices for every transaction in every market, copyright or otherwise. That Congress has never systematically attempted to fix the prices of all goods and services in the United States marketplace suggests that the transaction cost rationale alone must not in fact be a helpful explanation for the existence of compulsory licenses. (Hardy, 1999, 700–01)

Additionally, there can be no doubt that adoption of a compulsory license system here would, at least to some extent, shift the transaction costs from Internet webcasters to copyright owners. This is because copyright owners would have to expend significant resources annually to obtain the copyright fees collected under a compulsory license. Finally, the magnitude of transaction costs involved is probably not as high as suggested by compulsory license proponents. As Cate indicates:

... broadcasters have been negotiating for licenses for copyrighted programs without a legislative scheme for more than two decades.... [U]nder the compulsory license scheme, the lion's share of the royalties have been taken by only two distinct groups: MPAA and the sports program producers.... [And] the problems caused by ad hoc negotiation costs have been remedied in the past in the music field by the creation of private schemes—like ASCAP and BMI—which are more responsive to market pressures than any legislative scheme. (Cate, 1990, 222)

The use of a market-based blanket licensing scheme, rather than a compulsory license, could be further enhanced by technology, which allows "two parties to negotiate through a computer-based system containing a catalogue of copyrighted works and corresponding royalty charges" (Rooks, 1995, 270).

Lack of Market Failure

At this stage, precious little experience and little empirical evidence suggest that a direct negotiation scheme for retransmitted video programs over the Internet is unworkable. Internet Webcasters have not offered a list of failed negotiations as evidence that the market has failed and that a governmentally imposed compulsory license is needed here. In the absence of such evidence, establishing a compulsory license would make little sense. Public policy based on presumed outcomes is often built on shaky ground. This is particularly true in view of the potential availability of technology-based solutions as suggested by Rooks (1995) above.

Reducing Barriers to MVPD Market Entry

Establishing a compulsory license for Internet webcasters to retransmit OTA "free" television stations can be expected to lower the cost of entry into the MVPD market. The FCC has long decried the slow pace at which real competition has emerged in multichannel television in most markets (Federal Communications Commission, 2000). Consumer choice among MVPD providers in most markets is limited to either the local cable provider, DirecTV, and/or EchoStar. Alternative terrestrially based competition for local cable providers (i.e., cable overbuilds) exists in only a small number of markets. Although the number of market overbuilds appears to be expanding, the economics of such overbuilds continue to be difficult. Likewise, the large-scale entry into video services by telephone companies envisioned by the Telecommunications Act of 1996 (U.S. Congress, 1996) has yet to materialize. As a result, the MVPD marketplace is still highly concentrated.

As firms operating in a closely related business, Internet service providers might be good candidates for competitive MVPD market entry (Porter, 1988). The lack of a compulsory license for Internet Webcasters to retransmit OTA TV signals may represent a substantial barrier to entering the MVPD marketplace. However, reducing the barriers to entry at the expense of copyright owners, via a government-imposed price fixing scheme (i.e., the compulsory license), is problematic. This is particularly true in view of the nascent state of the Internet video market and the lack of any evidence that market-based solutions have failed to work here.

Geographic Limitations

The worldwide reach of the Internet provides a very strong argument against granting a compulsory license to Webcasters. This reach makes it difficult if not impossible to eliminate the potential for infringing on the rights of broadcasters and copyright owners in other markets/countries (Cohen, 1996, 428). As Peters suggests:

Our principal concern is the extent to which Internet retransmissions of broadcast signals can be controlled geographically. The Internet is a worldwide system with the capability of transmitting, or retransmitting, copyrighted works to hundreds of millions of viewers within seconds. If a compulsory license were created for retransmission of local broadcast signals, it is unclear how the retransmission of those signals could be limited to their local markets. (Peters, 2000)

The Internet by its very nature encourages distribution to the widest possible audience. In the absence of foolproof technology capable of limiting the retransmissions of OTA TV stations via the Internet to geographic areas corresponding to individual local television markets, establishment of a compulsory license for retransmission of OTA TV station signals will result in the potential for worldwide distribution of this content without compensation for copyright owners.

Copy Protection/Security

The inability to limit OTA TV station retransmissions via the Internet to their local markets (see above) is exacerbated by the seemingly endless ability of computer hackers to break copy protection/security schemes. Once the copy protection has been defeated, hackers would be able to download and redistribute perfect digital copies throughout the world.

Although Internet transmissions of television broadcast signals presumably would be "streamed" using technology intended to prevent the making of copies of broadcast programs,... it is all too easy for recipients of such transmissions to find ways to circumvent those measures and download perfect digital copies, which then could be redisseminated without limit online. The resulting harm to copyright owners in a global market could be irreparable. (Peters, 2000)

Free-Market Nature of Internet

The Internet continues to be largely free of regulation. By comparison, the cable and satellite industries face a heavily regulated environment.

This difference offers strong support for not extending the compulsory license to Internet Webcasters.

[Cable's] section 111 [compulsory] license ... was tailored to a heavily regulated industry subject to requirements such as must-carry, programming exclusivity, and signal quota rules—issues that have also arisen in the context of the satellite compulsory license. Congress has properly concluded that the Internet should be largely free of regulation, but the lack of such regulation makes the Internet a poor candidate for a compulsory license that depends so heavily on such restrictions (Peters, 1999).

If a compulsory license for Internet webcasters is established, will they be required to abide by such rules as Must Carry, Syndicated Exclusivity, Network Nonduplication, etc.? And, if they are required to abide by these rules, will they be able to actually do so? AudioNet (now Broadcast.com) was not optimistic about its ability to operate like a cable system:

Although it might be possible for AudioNet to operate like a cable system and enforce to some extent must-carry or other requirements or limitations on free carriage of signals, AudioNet takes the position that Internet broadcasters should be exempt from the must-carry rules. Rather, AudioNet claims to promote "localism" by the very act of distributing many local signals to a nationwide or worldwide audience. Regarding the must-carry responsibilities that must be shouldered by traditional cable systems and that are factored into the compulsory licensing equation,... AudioNet states that it "would likely be physically and economically impossible for any Internet broadcaster to carry all local channels in every market in which Internet access was available." (U.S. Copyright Office, 1997, 94)

Ultimately, Internet Webcasters would have to abide by the same (or very similar) requirements faced by cable and satellite distributors in this area if they hope to obtain a compulsory license. Inability to do so is likely to severely impede attempts to persuade Congress to establish a compulsory license.

Local Broadcast System Survival

If the integrity of local television station markets cannot be adequately protected by Internet webcasters, granting them a compulsory license could have a devastating impact on the long-term economic viability of local television stations.

If local viewers are able to watch network programs on distant stations imported by Internet companies, the basic economics of network affiliates are put in grave jeopardy ... [Likewise] Internet company importation of distant stations, which failed to protect local station syndicated program exclusivity would have severe negative consequences for long term local station viability and for local stations' ability to fulfill their local public service obligations. This is because TV stations carrying the same programming in distant cities [as local TV stations] would be available to every viewer in a local market with an Internet connection. (Fritts, 2000)

Thus, the establishment of a compulsory license for Internet webcasters could undermine the economic foundations of the broadcast industry along with related public-policy and public-interest initiatives such as localism.[2]

Copyright Owners as Internet Distributors

Video copyright owners face a much different distribution landscape on the Internet than for cable and satellite delivery. Since no one owns the Internet, anyone who wishes to use the Web for delivering creative works can do so. This means that video copyright owners can distribute their product on the Internet without the need of a third-party distributor (as in cable and satellite delivery). In such a marketplace, establishing a compulsory license to prevent video copyright owners from controlling the distribution of their product borders on a Fifth Amendment taking:

Parties that wish to make use of the Internet to retransmit broadcast programming do not have to build the delivery platform; it already exists. The technology is readily available and is not particularly expensive. Copyright owners of broadcast programming do not need to turn to someone else to place their content on the Internet; they can do it themselves. In fact, certain television broadcasters have already begun to place portions of their signals on the Internet, demonstrating that there is no need for a third-party packager to do it for them. (Peters, 2000)

Clearly, video copyright owners will not ignore the Internet as a distribution platform. The beauty of the Internet environment is the ease with which copyright owners, from Paramount Studios to Jerry's Famous Wedding Productions, can distribute their properties via the Internet. Likewise, some copyright owners will undoubtedly choose to contract with third-party Internet webcasters to distribute their video product. However, copyright owners should not be forced to do so via a compulsory license.

Obtaining Fair Market Value

The negotiation process itself is instrumental in establishing the market value of information products. A compulsory license undermines the "rigors of the marketplace" in assessing the value of a given work. The true market value of the content can never be determined under a compulsory license. The artificial price fixing that takes place as part of a compulsory license does not produce a true market price.

A compulsory license is a form of price fixing: Congress or an agency sets the price for a broad class of bargains—those that deal with the buying and selling of certain copyright licenses; the parties have little or no room to change the price term. As such, a compulsory license has whatever drawbacks price controls have. Absent significant market failures, a compulsory license makes for a wasteful allocation of social resources. (Hardy, 1999, 699–700)

In fact, a compulsory license may advantage the distributor over the copyright owner whose products are being pursued under the compulsory license. Thus, the artificial pricing may limit producer incentives by placing a "ceiling" on earnings for performance of a creative work. Given the risks of producing video or filmed entertainment, this could eventually have significant adverse consequences for the availability of content. The realization of profits, or even wide-eyed speculation about them, in a freely functioning marketplace is what often drives entrepreneurs to risk producing these creative works in the first place.

Policy Recommendations and Conclusions

The emergence of the digital world and the Internet has greatly complicated issues of copyright and copyright protection. As bandwidth capabilities continue to expand, wide-scale video distribution via the Internet is becoming increasingly viable. This has led Internet video webcasters to begin to push for establishment of a compulsory license that would allow them to pay a governmentally established fee to retransmit the signals of OTA television stations without obtaining either retransmission consent from television broadcasters or permission from the copyright owners of the individual programs broadcast by these stations.

The policy question on which this paper has focused is: Should Congress establish a compulsory license for Internet video providers to retransmit OTA TV station programming similar to the compulsory licenses established for cable and DBS? Our recommendations are as follows:

• Congress should not pass legislation establishing a compulsory license for Internet video providers.

• Congress should pass legislation that clearly establishes full copyright liability for any retransmitted OTA television signals carried by Internet video providers.

• Congress should encourage video copyright owners to develop a market-based blanket licensing scheme that takes full advantage of interactive computer technology, to minimize the transaction costs related to negotiations between video copyright owners and Internet video webcasters.

Economic reality dictates that producers be compensated for the fruits of their labor. This creates the incentives required for further development of creative works and ensures an environment in which continued output will be rewarded. The assertion that Internet video webcasters, as new, emerging distributors, are entitled to a compulsory license for retransmission of broadcast video is not supportable.[3]

At a time when the Internet as an industry seeks to be free from government regulation in order to permit the free market to maximize its potential development, it would seem unfair to the providers of the content that will ultimately be disseminated via the Internet not to afford them the same opportunities to maximize their potential over the powerful Internet medium. (U.S. Copyright Office, 1997, 99)

Additional factors favoring establishment of full copyright liability (and against establishment of a compulsory license) for retransmissions of OTA TV station signals on the Internet include: the inability to limit Internet retransmissions geographically; the lack of a foolproof technological method of copy protecting retransmitted OTA TV signals; the difficulty of detecting unauthorized reception of copyrighted material on the Internet; the potential impact on the long-term economic viability of local television stations; the fact that video copyright owners do not need third-party packagers to distribute their products via the Internet— they can do it themselves; and that compulsory licenses typically prevent copyright owners from receiving fair market value for their works. Finally, the potential existence of market-based solutions such as blanket licensing through "video licensing societies," and the fact that a compulsory license simply shifts the transaction costs from Internet webcasters to copyright owners, reduces the significance of any potential transaction cost savings that might be realized via a compulsory license.

Notes

1. Congress's decision, to allow local television stations to opt for either must-carry or retransmission consent with respect to cable and DBS carriage within a broadcaster's local market of operation, has greatly reduced the importance of the compulsory license for carriage of local television signals by cable and DBS multichannel program video distributors. The compulsory license remains unchanged, however, with respect to cable and DBS importation of distant market television signals.

2. At some point local television broadcasters are likely to embrace the Internet as a distribution platform for their existing video signals. If broadcasters wish to simulcast their over-the-air signals to extend their audience reach via the Internet, they will need to negotiate separate, exclusive Internet distribution licenses with copyright holders. However, until Internet retransmissions of television stations can be limited to the local television market served by these stations, copyright holders may be reluctant to sell Internet distribution rights to local broadcasters.

3. Given the nascent stage of Internet video webcasting, some believe that a compulsory license should be established for a limited period of time (i.e., a compulsory license with a sunset) in order to facilitate the development of a new industry. Unfortunately, it is very difficult to eliminate a compulsory license once it has been established. This is because elimination of the compulsory license necessarily disenfranchises consumers who have come to rely on the information distribution made possible by the compulsory license (the compulsory license for cable and DBS are examples of this). As a result, we oppose the establishment of a temporary compulsory license here.

References

Barlow, John P. (1996). Selling Wine without Bottles, *Wired: The Economy of Mind on the Global* Net. As found in Torpoco, 1997, 24–5 (see below).

Cate, Fred H. (1990). Cable Television and the Compulsory Copyright License. *Federal Communications Law Journal*, 42, 191–238.

Cohen, Barbara. (1996). A Proposed Regime for Copyright Protection on the Internet. *Brooklyn Journal of International Law*, 22, 401–35.

Copyright Revision Act of 1976. (1976). 17 U.S.C. Secs. 101–810.

Cote, Darlene A. (1994). Chipping Away at the Copyright Owner's Rights: Congress' Continued Reliance on the Compulsory License. *Journal of Intellectual Property Law*, 2, 219–43.

Fan, Baoding Hsieh. (2000). When Channel Surfers Flip to the Web: Copyright Liability for Internet Broadcasting. *Federal Communications Law Journal*, 52, 619–46.

Federal Communications Commission. (2000, January 14). *Annual Assessment of the Status of Competition in Markets for the Delivery of Video Programming.* Sixth Annual Report, CS Docket No. 99-230.

Fritts, Edward O. (2000, June 15). Testimony at *Oversight Hearing on Copy-righted Webcast Programming on the Internet*. Hearings before the Subcommittee on Courts and Intellectual Property Committee on the Judiciary, of the House Ways and Means Committee, 106th Cong., 2d Sess. ⟨http://www.lexis.com⟩ (visited July 20, 2000).

Fusco, Patricia. (1999, November 10). AOL Lobbies for License to Carry Local TV Stations. *InternetNews.com* (visited March 17, 2000). ⟨http://www.internetnews.com/isp-news/article/0,,8_236121,00.html⟩.

Grebb, Michael. (2000, May 8). Video Streaming: the Copyright Question. *Cablevision*, 98–9.

Hardy, I. Trotter. (1999). The Internet and the Law: Copyright and "New-Use" Technologies. *Nova Law Review*, 23, 657–705.

House of Representatives Report No. 1476. (1976). 94th Cong., 2d Sess. 89. Information Infrastructure Task Force. (1995, September). Intellectual Property and the National Information Infrastructure: The Report of the Working Group on Intellectual Property Rights.

Kay, Dean. (2000, June 15). Testimony at *Oversight Hearing on Copyrighted Webcast Programming on the Internet*. Hearings Before the Subcommittee on Courts and Intellectual Property Committee on the Judiciary, of the House Ways and Means Committee, 106th Cong., 2d Sess. ⟨http://www.lexis.com⟩ (visited July 20, 2000).

McCallum, Ian. (2000, June 15). Testimony at *Oversight Hearing on Copy-righted Webcast Programming on the Internet*. Hearings before the Subcommittee on Courts and Intellectual Property Committee on the Judiciary, of the House Ways and Means Committee, 106th Cong., 2d Sess. ⟨http://www.lexis.com⟩ (visited July 20, 2000).

Miles, Peggy. (2000, June 15). Testimony at *Oversight Hearing on Copyrighted Webcast Programming on the Internet*. Hearings Before the Subcommittee on Courts and Intellectual Property Committee on the Judiciary, of the House Ways and Means Committee, 106th Cong., 2d Sess. ⟨http://www.lexis.com⟩ (visited July 20, 2000).

Ostertag, Thomas J. (2000, June 15). Testimony at *Oversight Hearing on Copy-righted Webcast Programming on the Internet*. Hearings Before the Subcommittee on Courts and Intellectual Property Committee on the Judiciary, of the House Ways and Means Committee, 106th Cong., 2d Sess. ⟨http://www.lexis.com⟩ (visited July 20, 2000).

Peters, Marybeth. (1999, November 10). Letter to the Honorable Howard Coble, U.S. House of Representatives.

Peters, Marybeth. (2000, June 15). Testimony at *Oversight Hearing on Copy-righted Webcast Programming on the Internet*. Hearings Before the Subcommittee on Courts and Intellectual Property Committee on the Judiciary, of the House Ways and Means Committee, 106th Cong., 2d Sess. ⟨http://www.lexis.com⟩ (visited July 20, 2000).

Porter, Michael. (1998). *Competitive Strategy: Techniques for Analyzing Industries and Competitors*. New York: Free Press.

Potter, Jonathan. (2000, June 15). Testimony at *Oversight Hearing on Copyrighted Webcast Programming on the Internet*. Hearings Before the Subcommittee on Courts and Intellectual Property Committee on the Judiciary, of the House Ways and Means Committee, 106th Cong., 2d Sess. ⟨http://www.lexis.com⟩ (visited July 20, 2000).

Rosenoer, J. (1997). *Cyberlaw: The Law and the Internet*. New York: Springer Verlag.

Rooks, Jason S. (1995). Constitutionality of Judicially-Imposed Compulsory Licenses in Copyright Infringement Cases. *Journal of Intellectual Property Law*, 3, 255–76.

Satellite Home Viewers Act of 1988. (1988). 17 U.S.C. Sec. 119.

Satellite Home Viewers Improvement Act of 1999. (1999). Pub. L. No. 106-113, 113 Stat. 1501, 1536.

Tedesco, Richard. (1999, March 8). Who'll Control the Video Streams? *Broadcasting*, 20–4.

The Dish on Satellite TV Reform: Redux. (1999, November 22). *Broadcasting*, 18.

Torpoco, Mark S. (1997). Mickey and the Mouse: The Motion Picture and Television Industry's Copyright Concerns on the Internet. *UCLA Entertainment Law Review*, 5, 1–70.

Townley, John. (2000, January 21). Movie, Broadcasting Companies Sue iCraveTV. *InternetNews.com* (visited March 17, 2000) ⟨http://www.internetnews.com/intl-news/article/0,,6_291131,00.html⟩.

Twentieth Century Fox Film Corp. v. iCraveTV, 2000 U.S. Dist. LEXIS 1013 (W.D. Penn. January 28, 2000).

U.S. Congress, House of Representatives, Conference Committee. (1996, January 31). *Telecommunications Act of 1996*. House Report 104-458. Washington, DC: U.S. Government Printing Office.

U.S. Copyright Office. (1997, August 1). A Review of the Copyright Licensing Regimes Covering Retransmission of Broadcast Signals.

Valenti, Jack. (2000, June 15). Testimony at *Oversight Hearing on Copyrighted Webcast Programming on the Internet*. Hearings before the Subcommittee on Courts and Intellectual Property Committee on the Judiciary, of the House Ways and Means Committee, 106th Cong., 2d Sess. ⟨http://www.lexis.com⟩ (visited July 20, 2000).

Index